Art by Motoi Fuyukawa
Story by Kazuma Kamachi
Character Design by Kiyotaka Haimura

Scientific Railgun

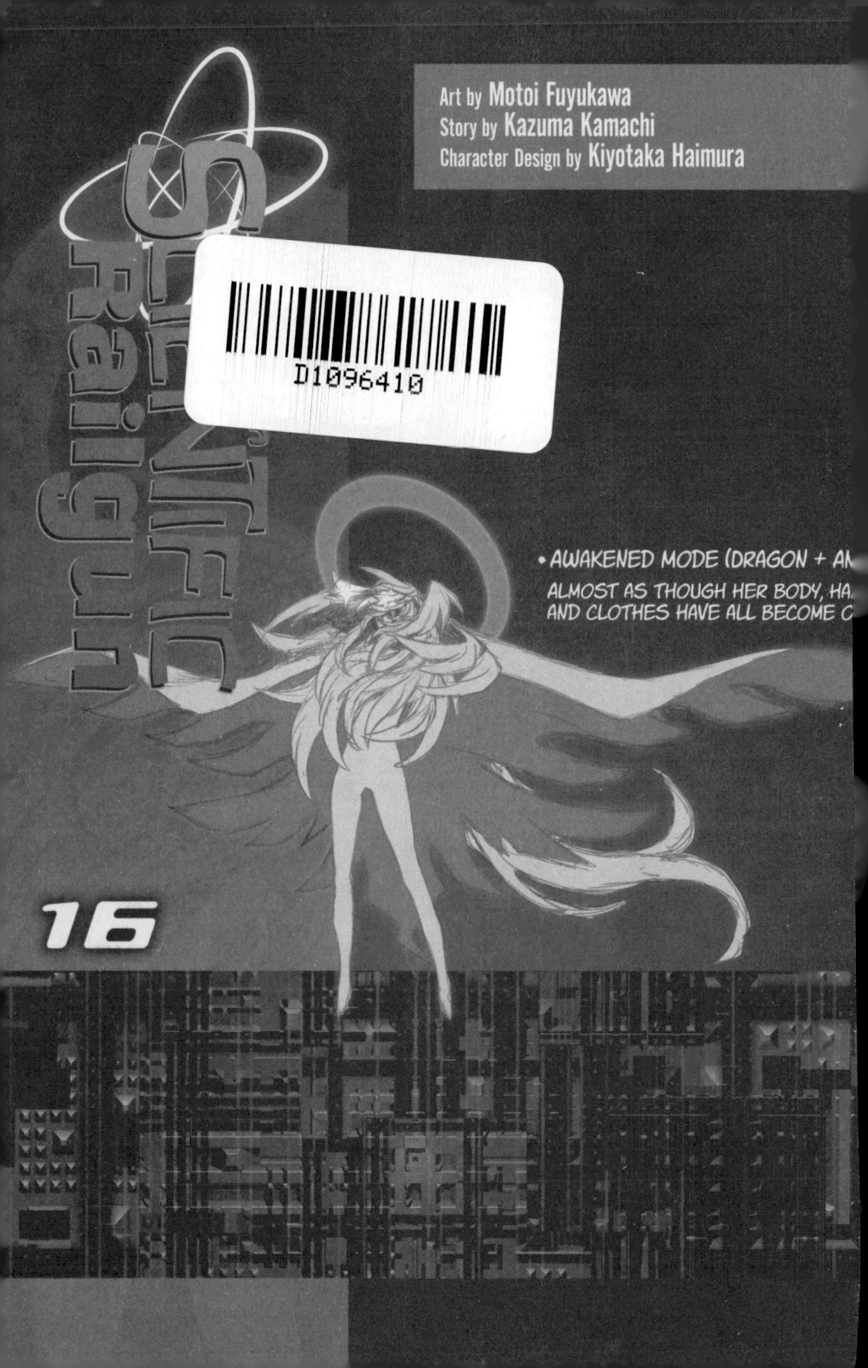
• AWAKENED MODE (DRAGON + AN
ALMOST AS THOUGH HER BODY, HA
AND CLOTHES HAVE ALL BECOME C

16

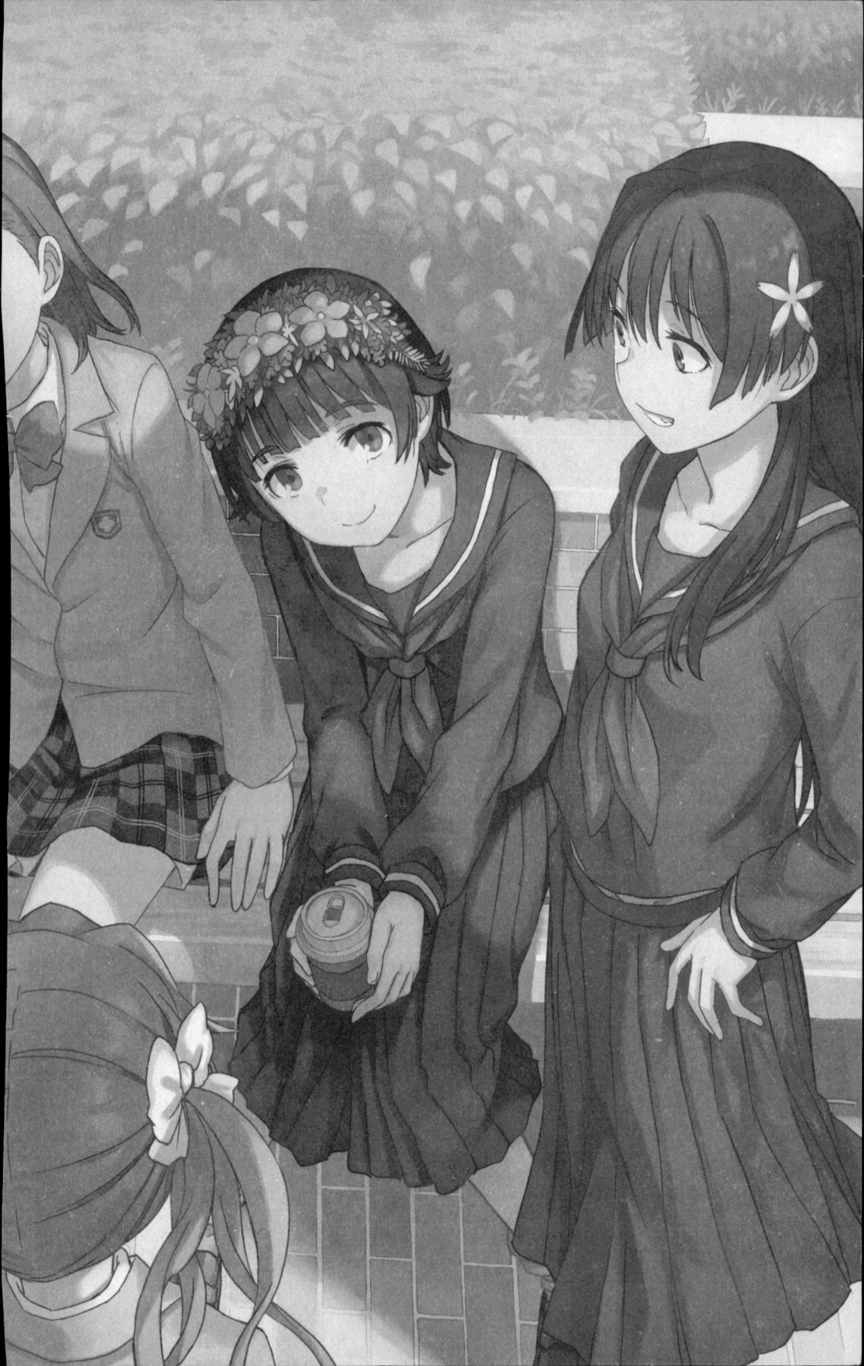

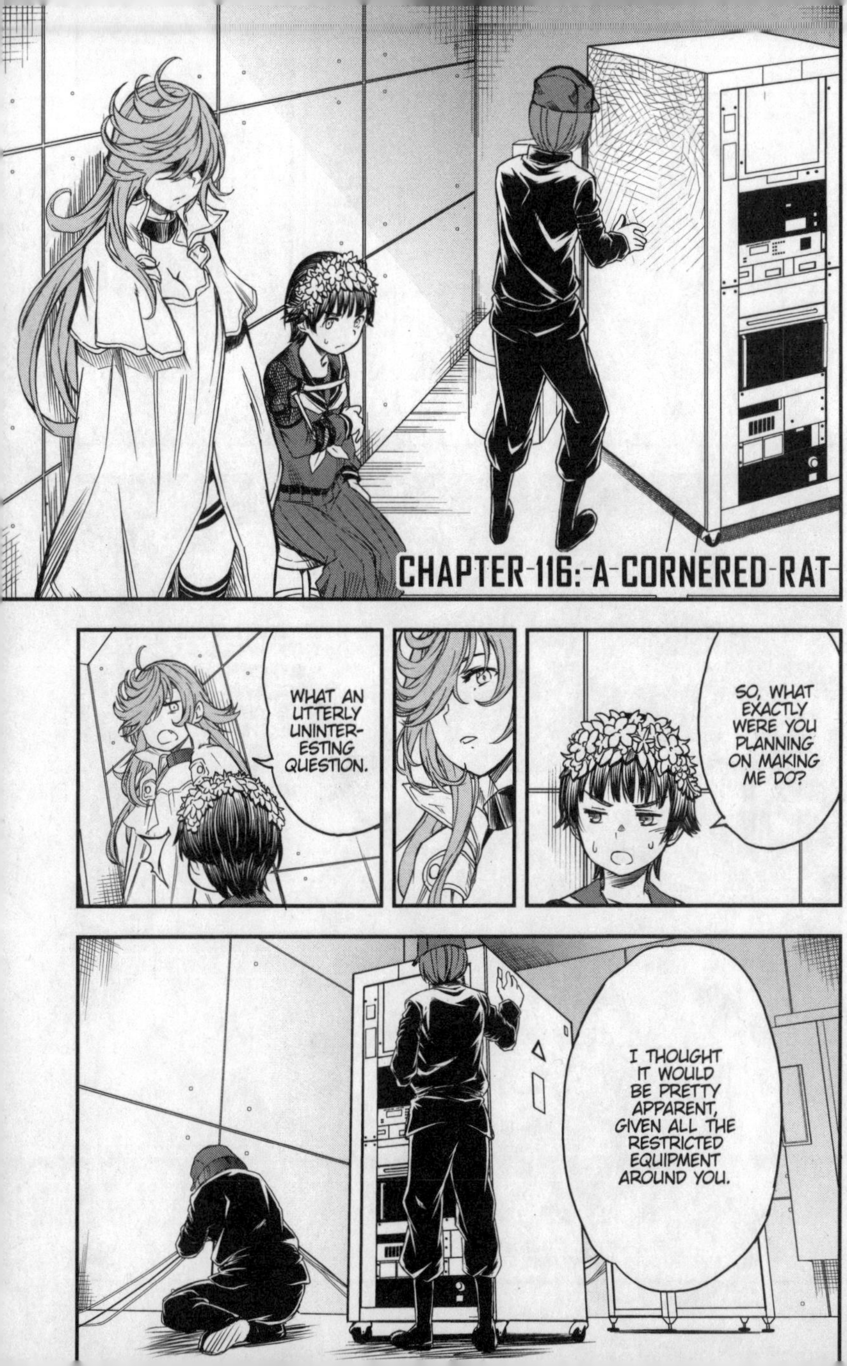
CHAPTER 116: A CORNERED RAT
SO, WHAT EXACTLY WERE YOU PLANNING ON MAKING ME DO?
WHAT AN UTTERLY UNINTER-ESTING QUESTION.
I THOUGHT IT WOULD BE PRETTY APPARENT, GIVEN ALL THE RESTRICTED EQUIPMENT AROUND YOU.

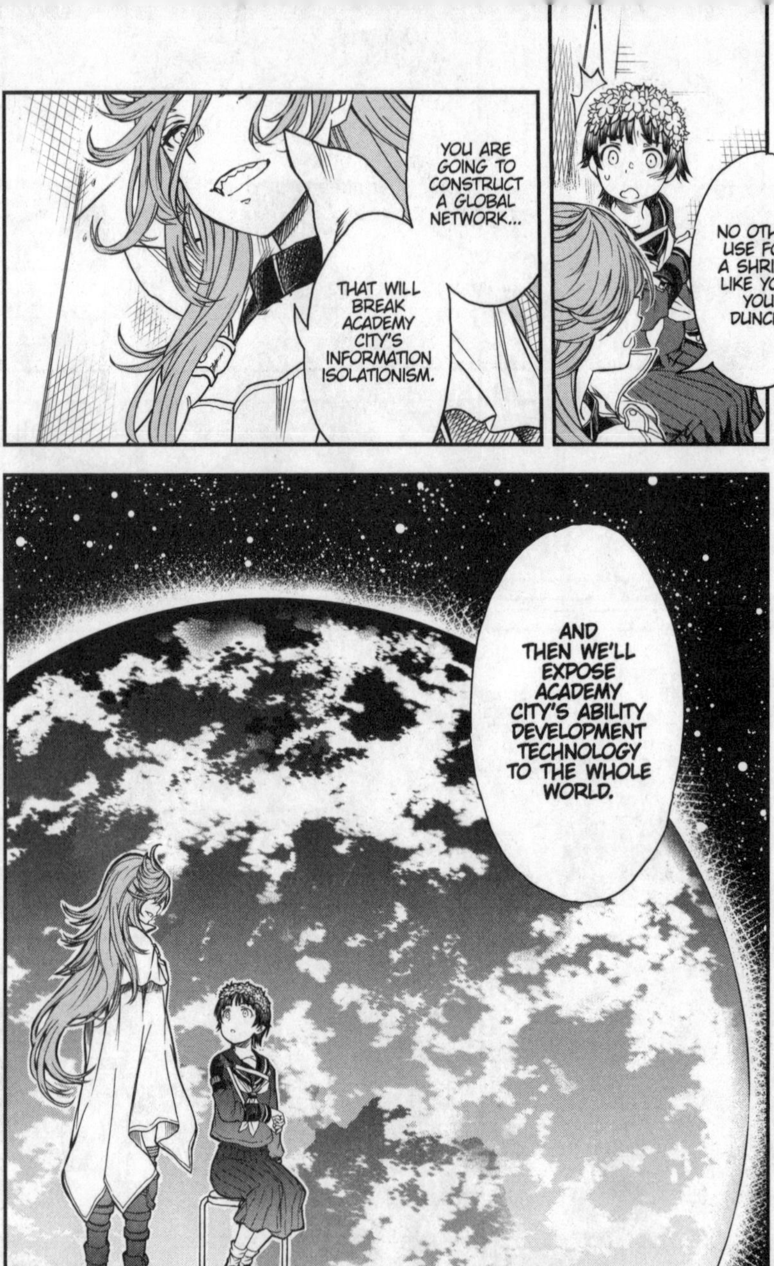
NO OTHER USE FOR A SHRIMP LIKE YOU, YOU DUNCE.
YOU ARE GOING TO CONSTRUCT A GLOBAL NETWORK...
THAT WILL BREAK ACADEMY CITY'S INFORMATION ISOLATIONISM.
AND THEN WE'LL EXPOSE ACADEMY CITY'S ABILITY DEVELOPMENT TECHNOLOGY TO THE WHOLE WORLD.

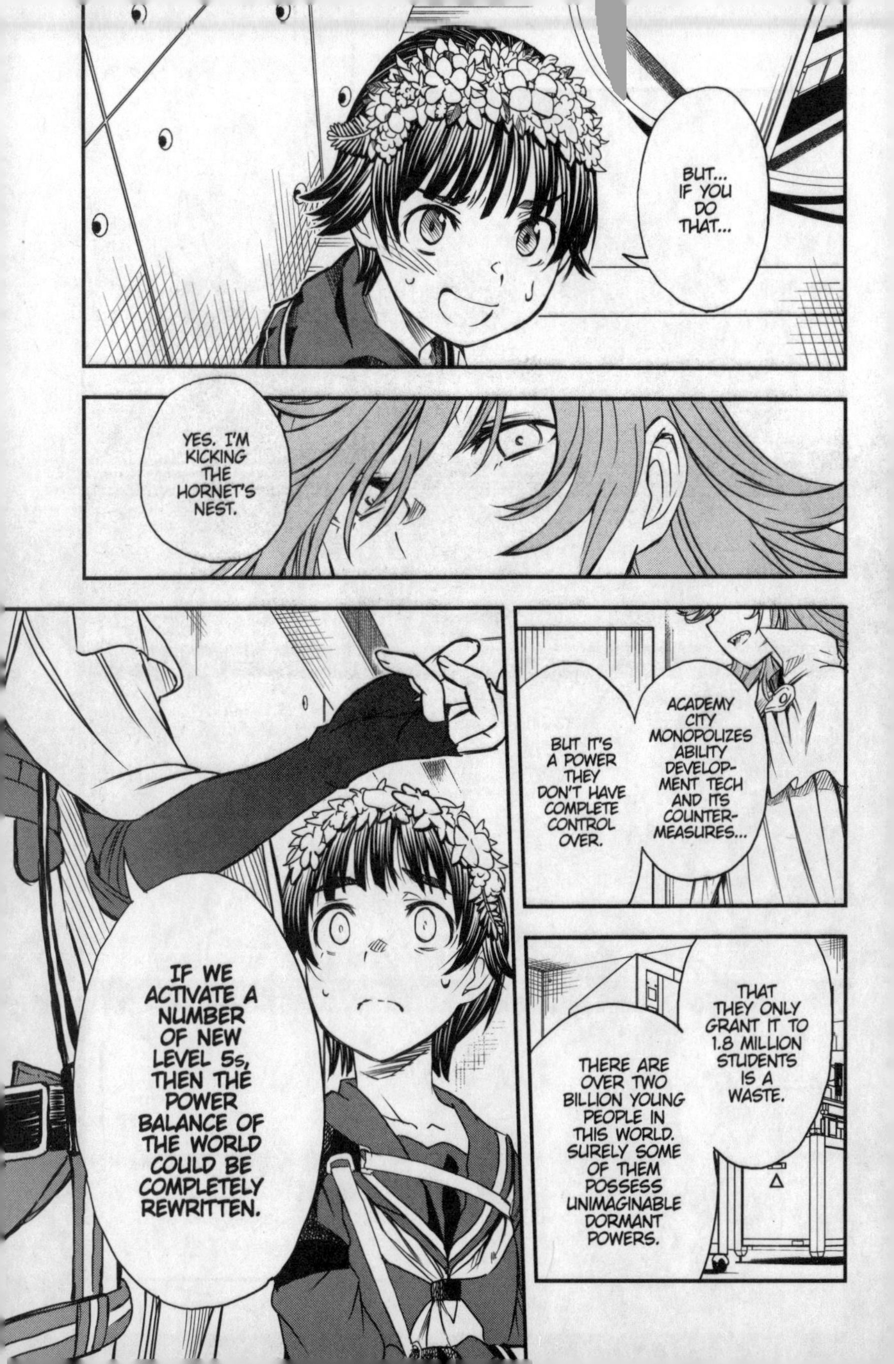
BUT... IF YOU DO THAT...
YES. I'M KICKING THE HORNET'S NEST.
ACADEMY CITY MONOPOLIZES ABILITY DEVELOPMENT TECH AND ITS COUNTER-MEASURES...
BUT IT'S A POWER THEY DON'T HAVE COMPLETE CONTROL OVER.
THAT THEY ONLY GRANT IT TO 1.8 MILLION STUDENTS IS A WASTE.
THERE ARE OVER TWO BILLION YOUNG PEOPLE IN THIS WORLD. SURELY SOME OF THEM POSSESS UNIMAGINABLE DORMANT POWERS.
IF WE ACTIVATE A NUMBER OF NEW LEVEL 5s, THEN THE POWER BALANCE OF THE WORLD COULD BE COMPLETELY REWRITTEN.

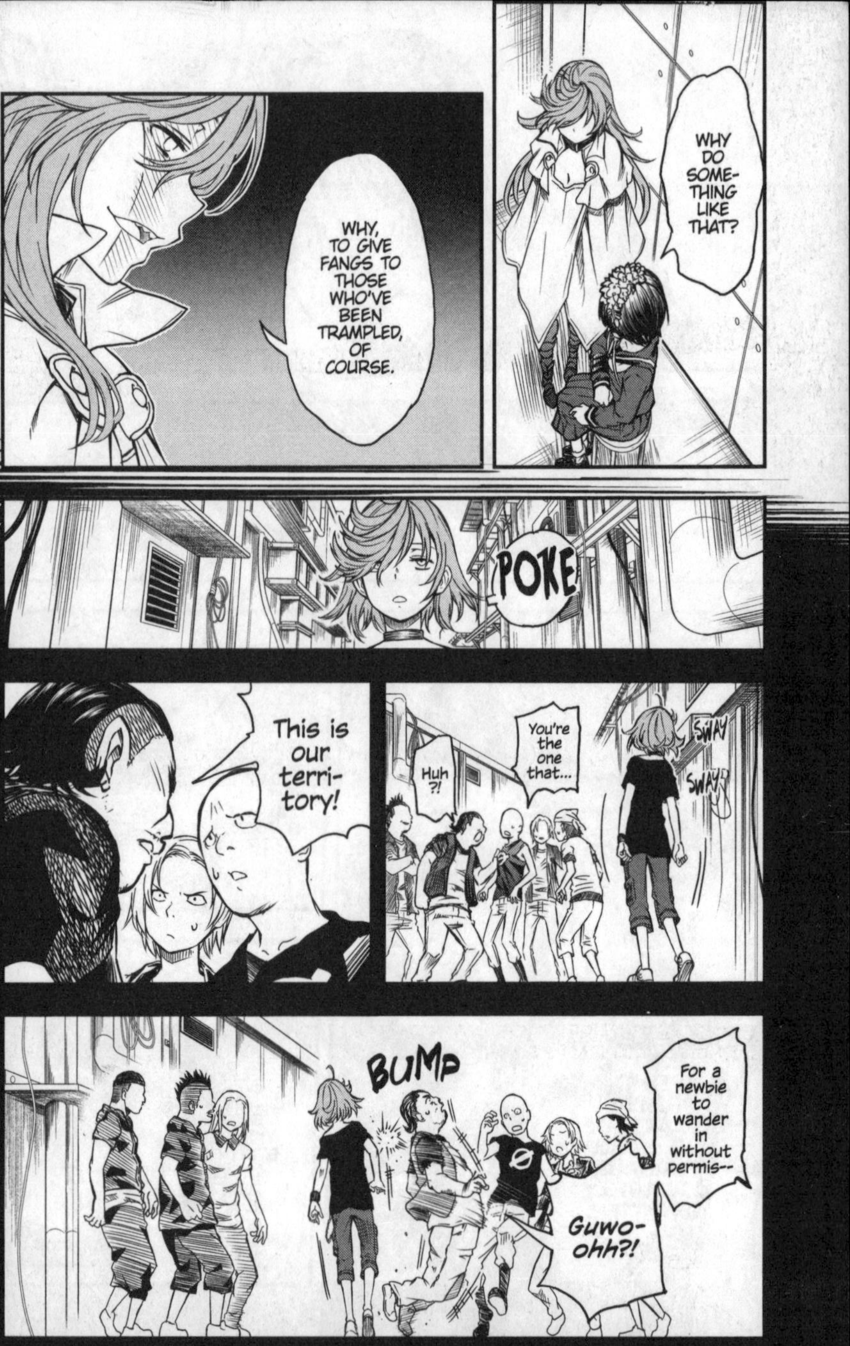
WHY DO SOMETHING LIKE THAT?
WHY, TO GIVE FANGS TO THOSE WHO'VE BEEN TRAMPLED, OF COURSE.
POKE
SWAY SWAY
You're the one that...
Huh?!
This is our terri-tory!
For a newbie to wander in without permis--
BUMP
Guwo-ohh?!

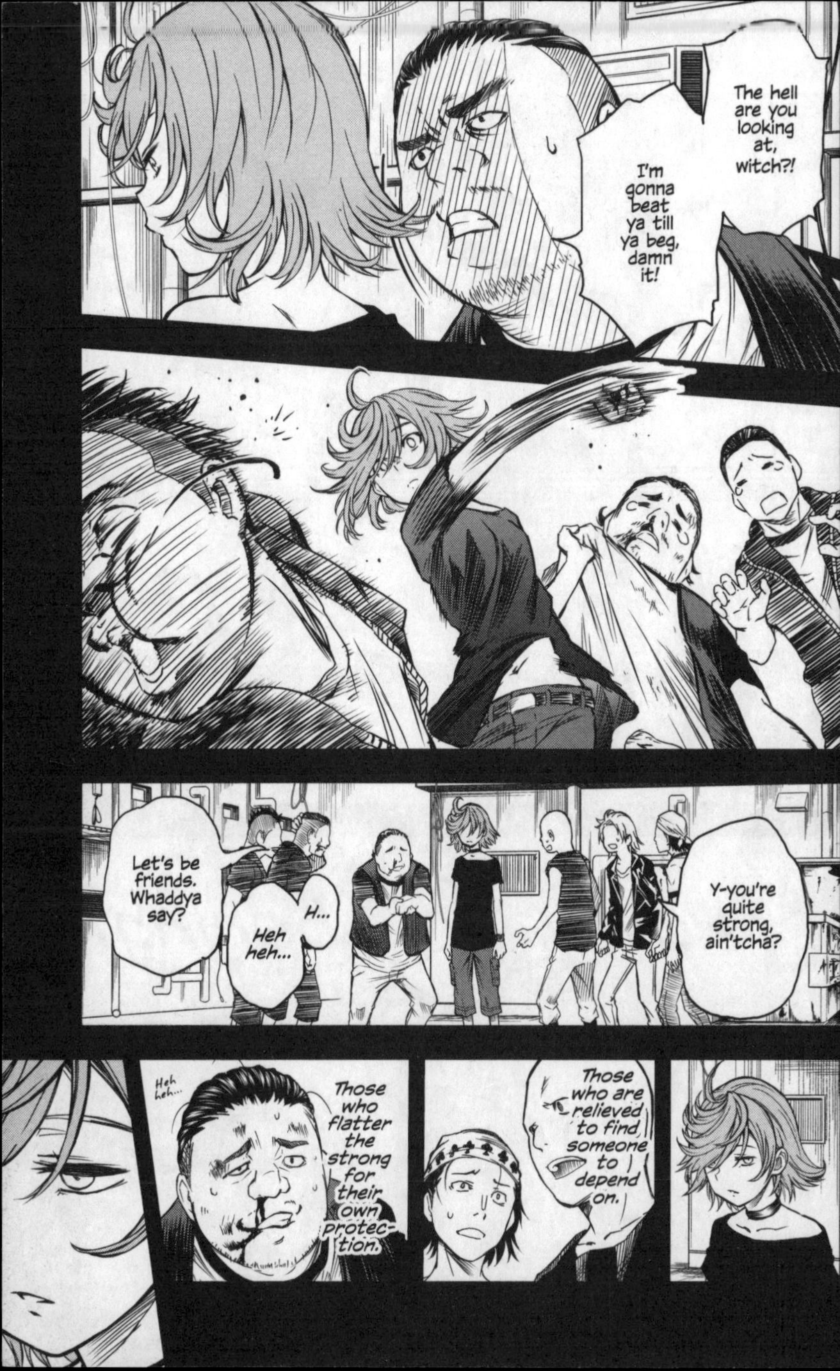

The hell are you looking at, witch?!
I'm gonna beat ya till ya beg, damn it!
Y-you're quite strong, ain'tcha?
H... Heh heh...
Let's be friends. Whaddya say?
Those who are relieved to find someone to depend on.
Those who flatter the strong for their own protection.
Heh heh...

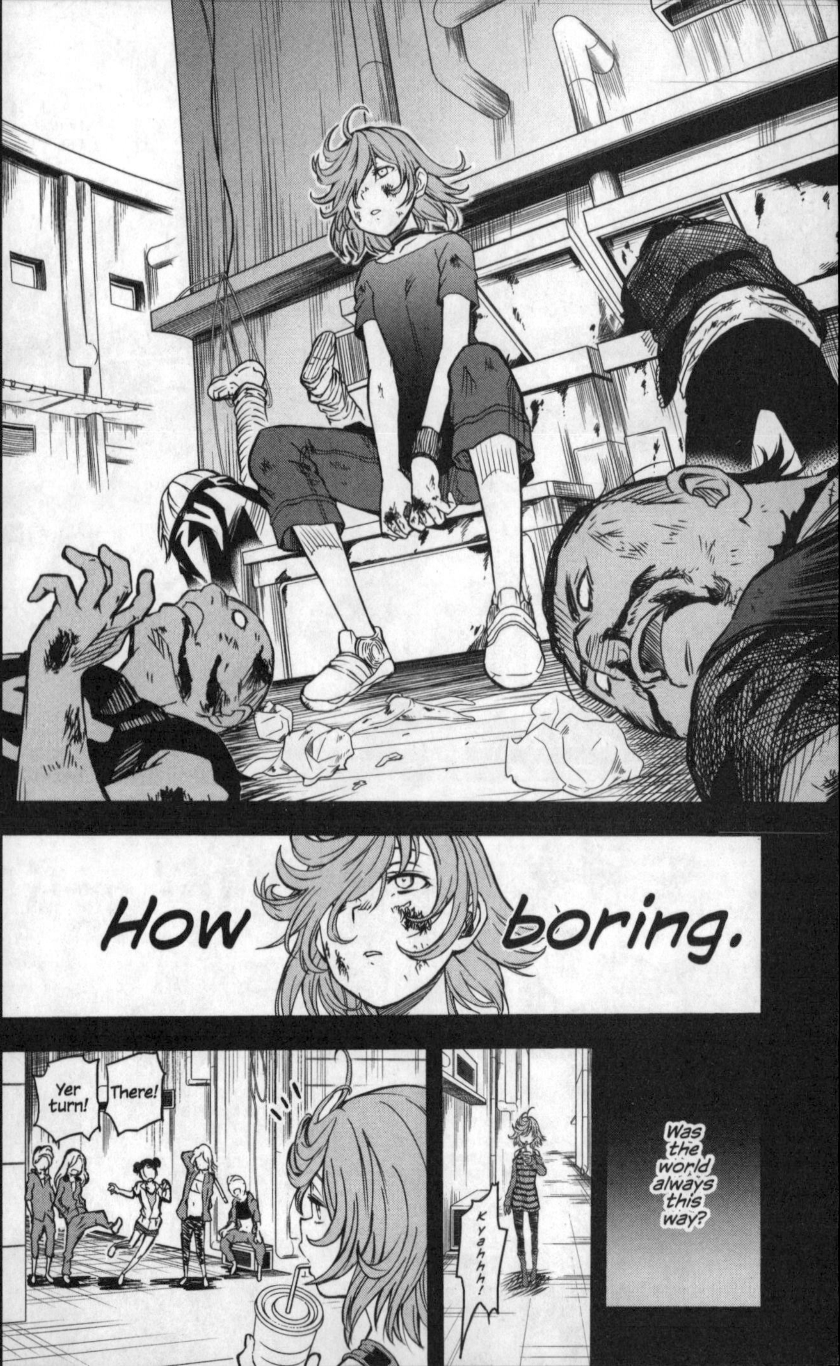
How boring.
Was the world always this way?
Kyahhh!
There!
Yer turn!

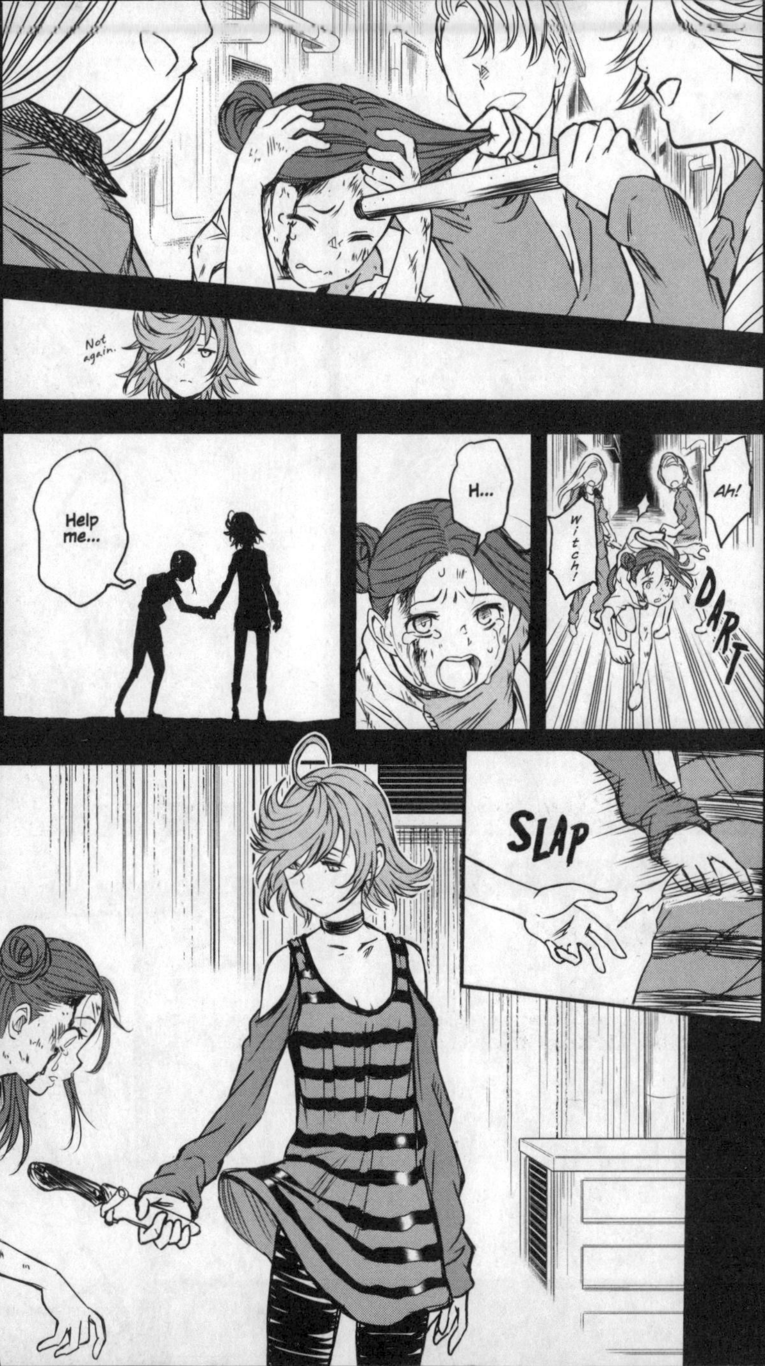
Not again.
Ah!
witch!
DART
H...
Help me...
SLAP

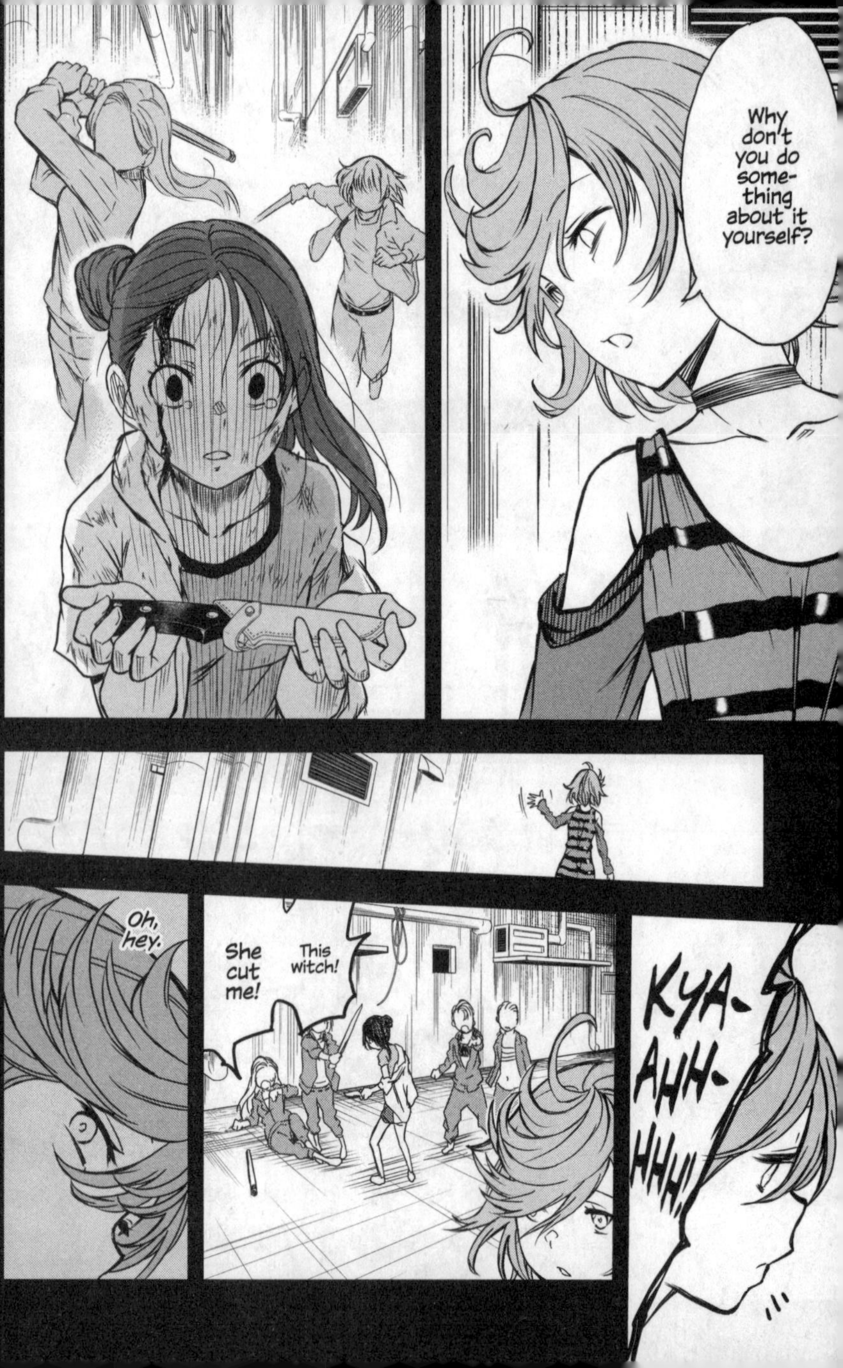
Why don't you do some-thing about it yourself?
KYA-AHH-HHH!
This witch!
She cut me!
Oh, hey.

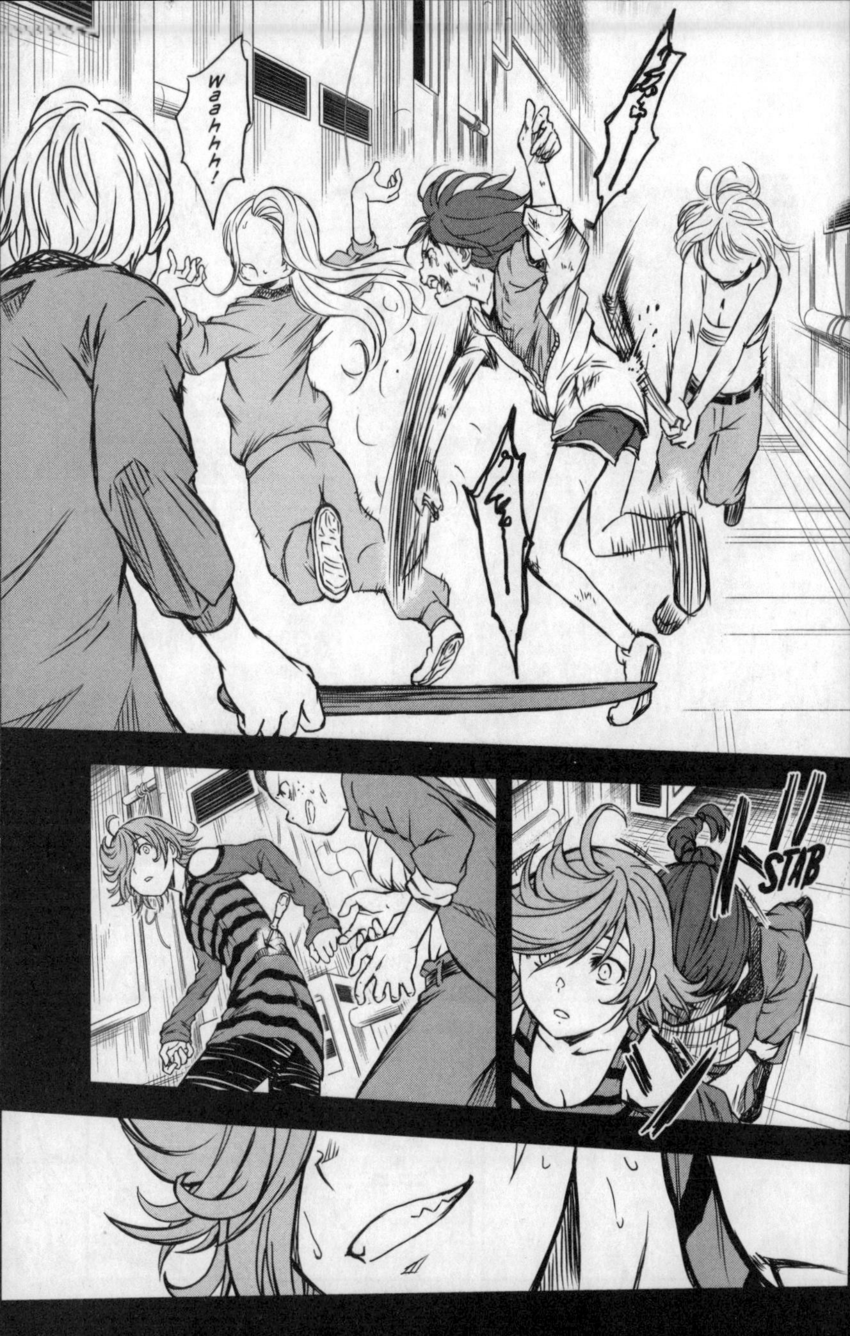
Waahhhh!
STAB

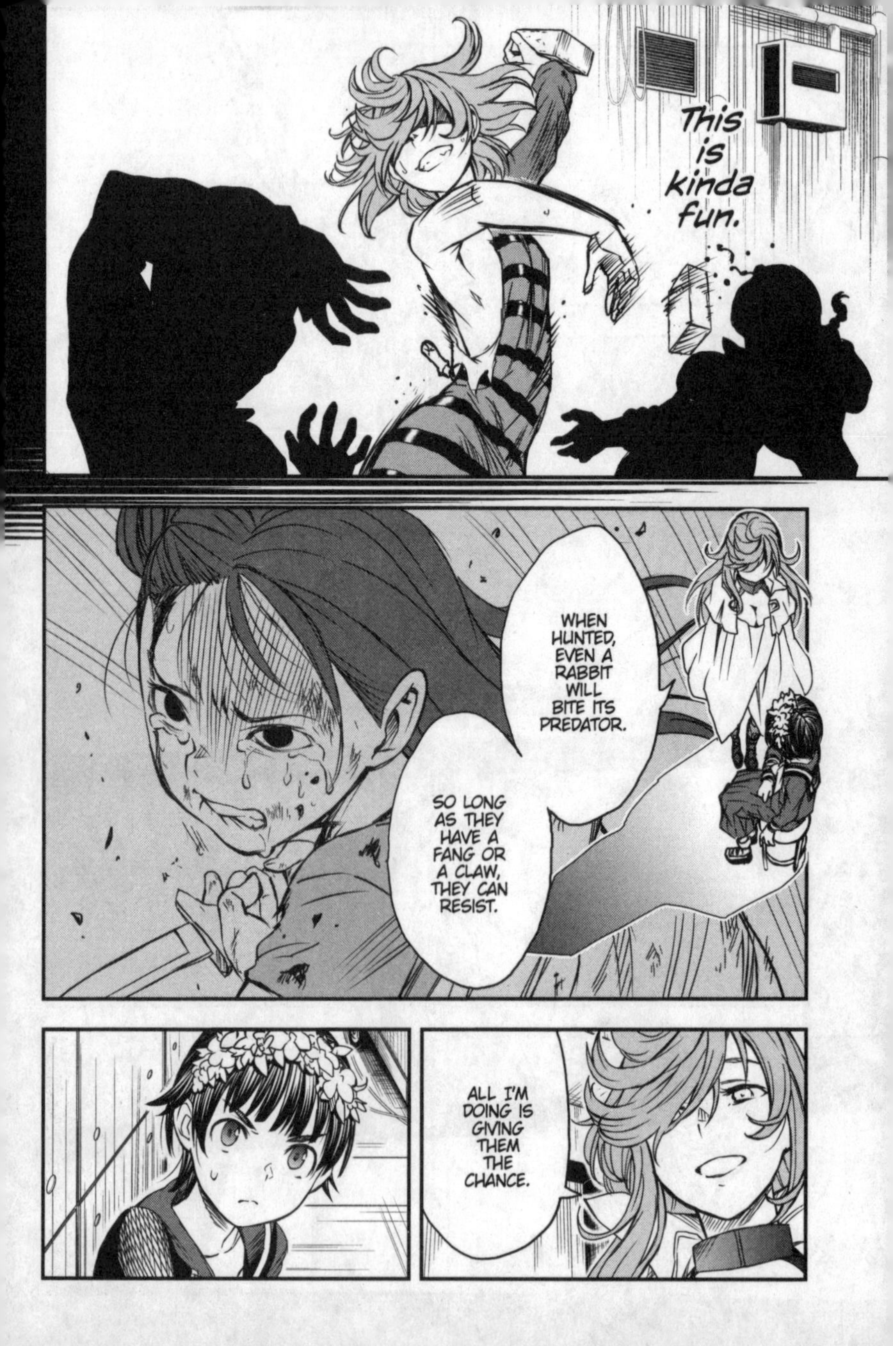
This is kinda fun.
WHEN HUNTED, EVEN A RABBIT WILL BITE ITS PREDATOR.
SO LONG AS THEY HAVE A FANG OR A CLAW, THEY CAN RESIST.
ALL I'M DOING IS GIVING THEM THE CHANCE.

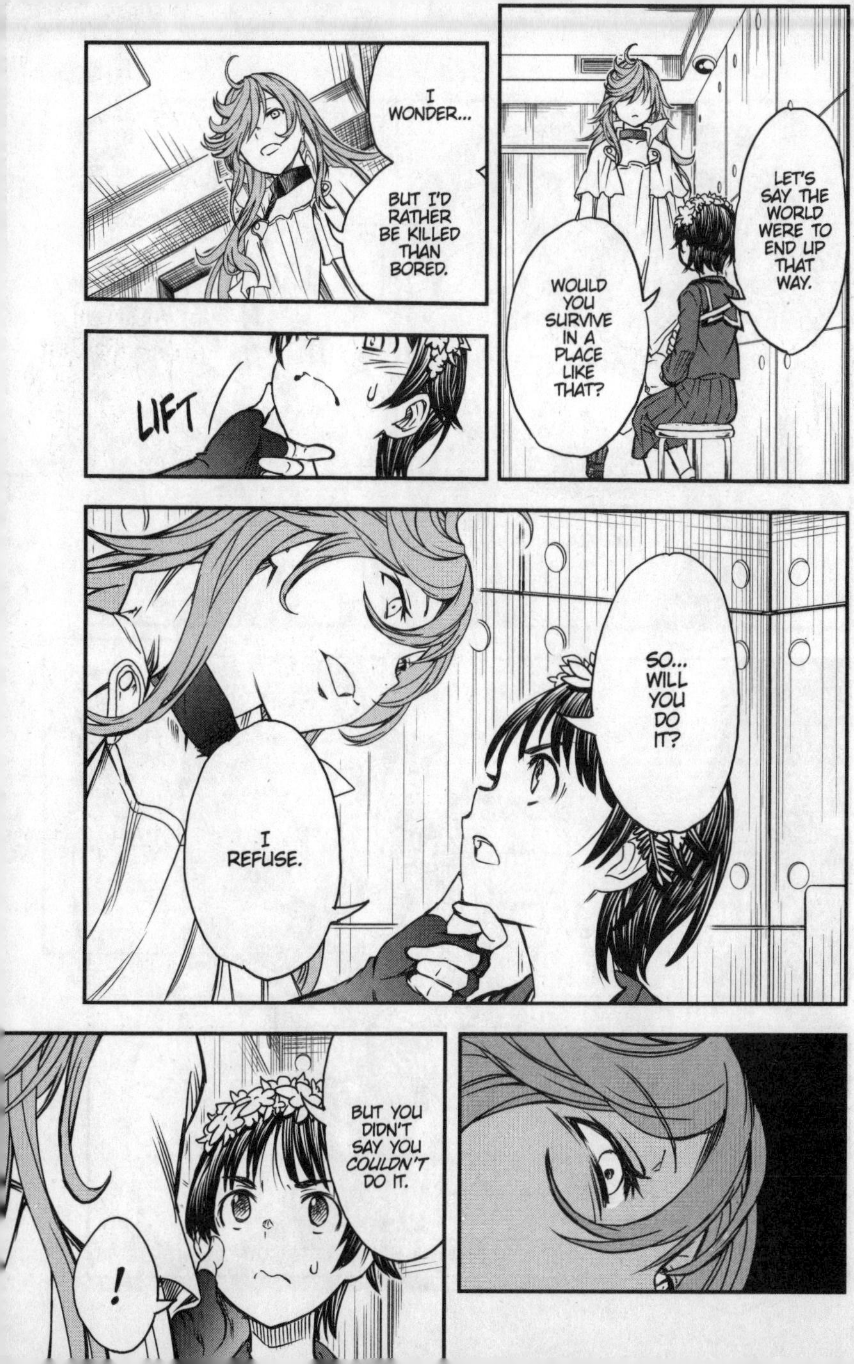
LET'S SAY THE WORLD WERE TO END UP THAT WAY.
WOULD YOU SURVIVE IN A PLACE LIKE THAT?
I WONDER...
BUT I'D RATHER BE KILLED THAN BORED.
LIFT
SO... WILL YOU DO IT?
I REFUSE.
BUT YOU DIDN'T SAY YOU *COULDN'T* DO IT.
!

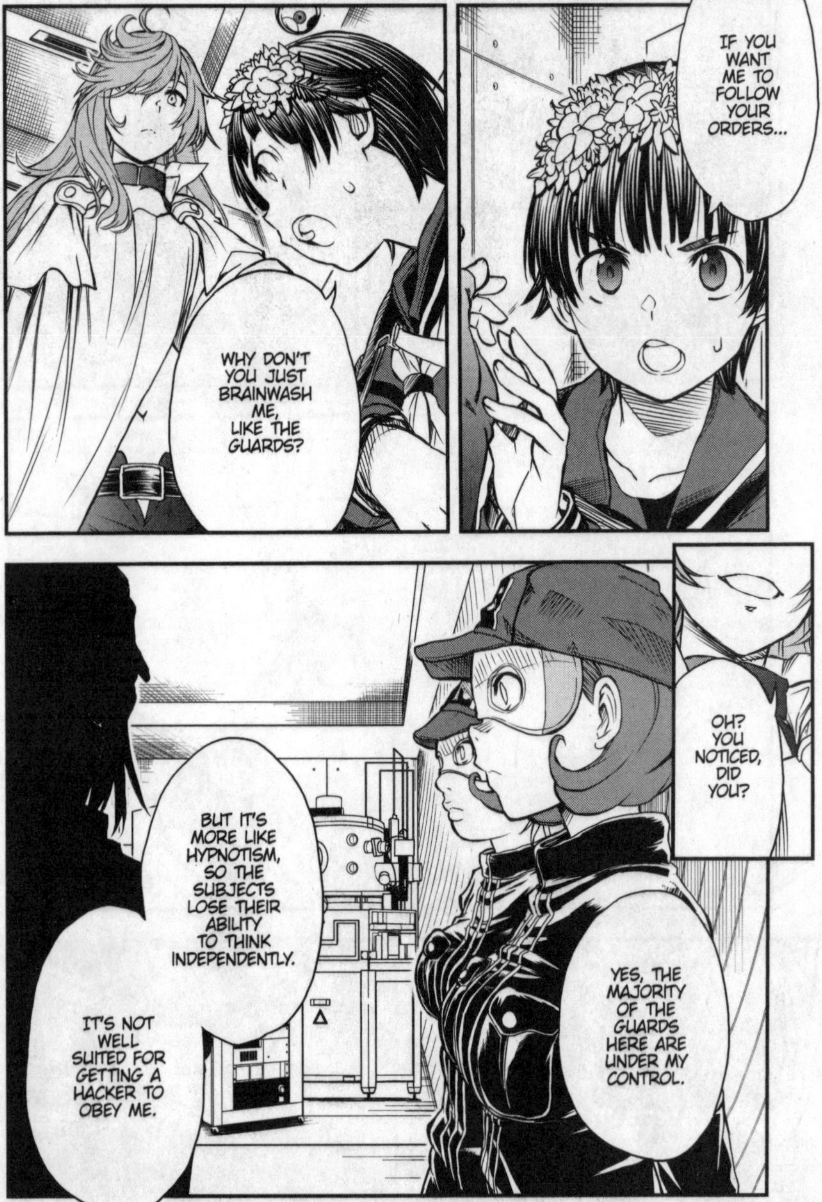

IF YOU WANT ME TO FOLLOW YOUR ORDERS...
WHY DON'T YOU JUST BRAINWASH ME, LIKE THE GUARDS?
OH? YOU NOTICED, DID YOU?
YES, THE MAJORITY OF THE GUARDS HERE ARE UNDER MY CONTROL.
BUT IT'S MORE LIKE HYPNOTISM, SO THE SUBJECTS LOSE THEIR ABILITY TO THINK INDEPENDENTLY.
IT'S NOT WELL SUITED FOR GETTING A HACKER TO OBEY ME.

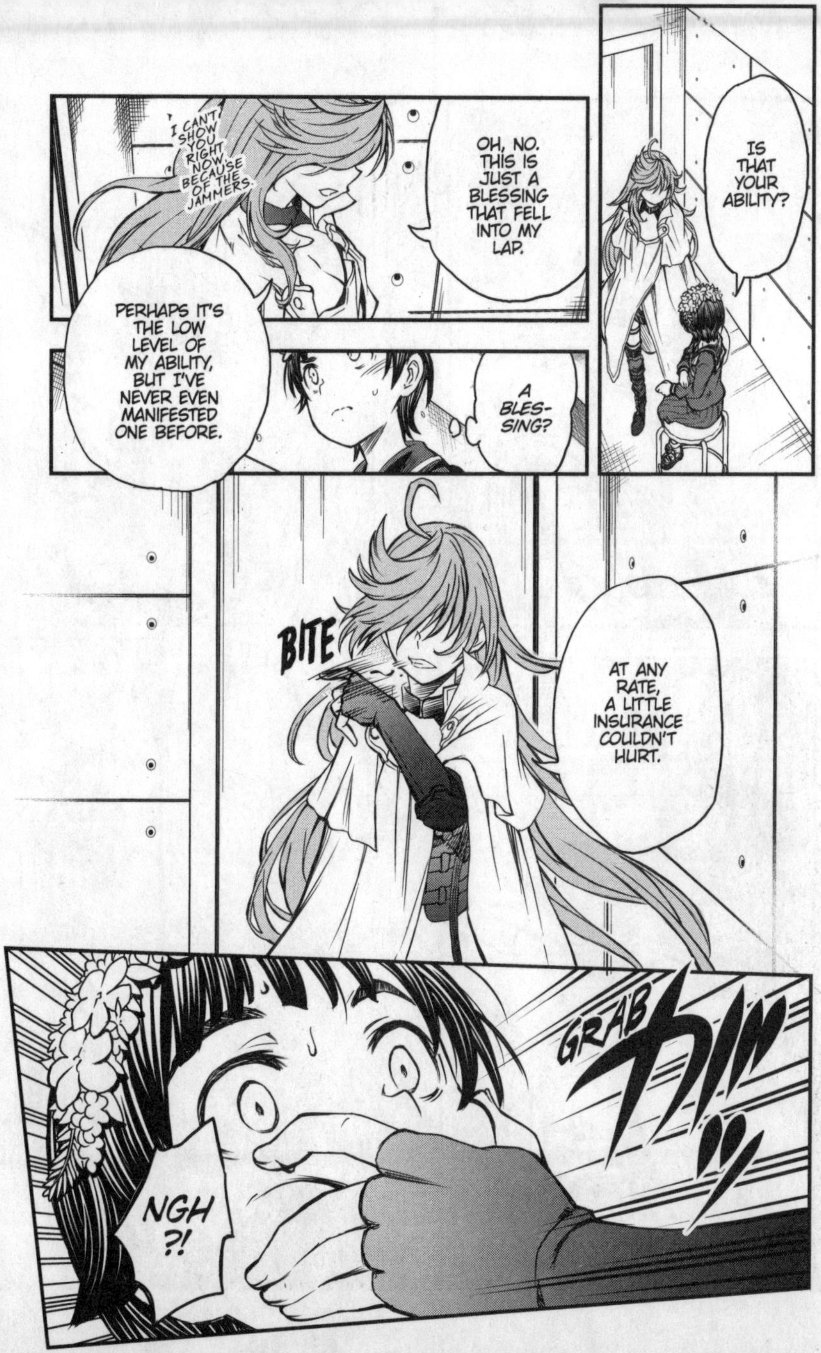
IS THAT YOUR ABILITY?
OH, NO. THIS IS JUST A BLESSING THAT FELL INTO MY LAP.
I CAN'T SHOW YOU RIGHT NOW, BECAUSE OF THE JAMMERS.
A BLES-SING?
PERHAPS IT'S THE LOW LEVEL OF MY ABILITY, BUT I'VE NEVER EVEN MANIFESTED ONE BEFORE.
AT ANY RATE, A LITTLE INSURANCE COULDN'T HURT.
BITE
GRAB
NGH ?!

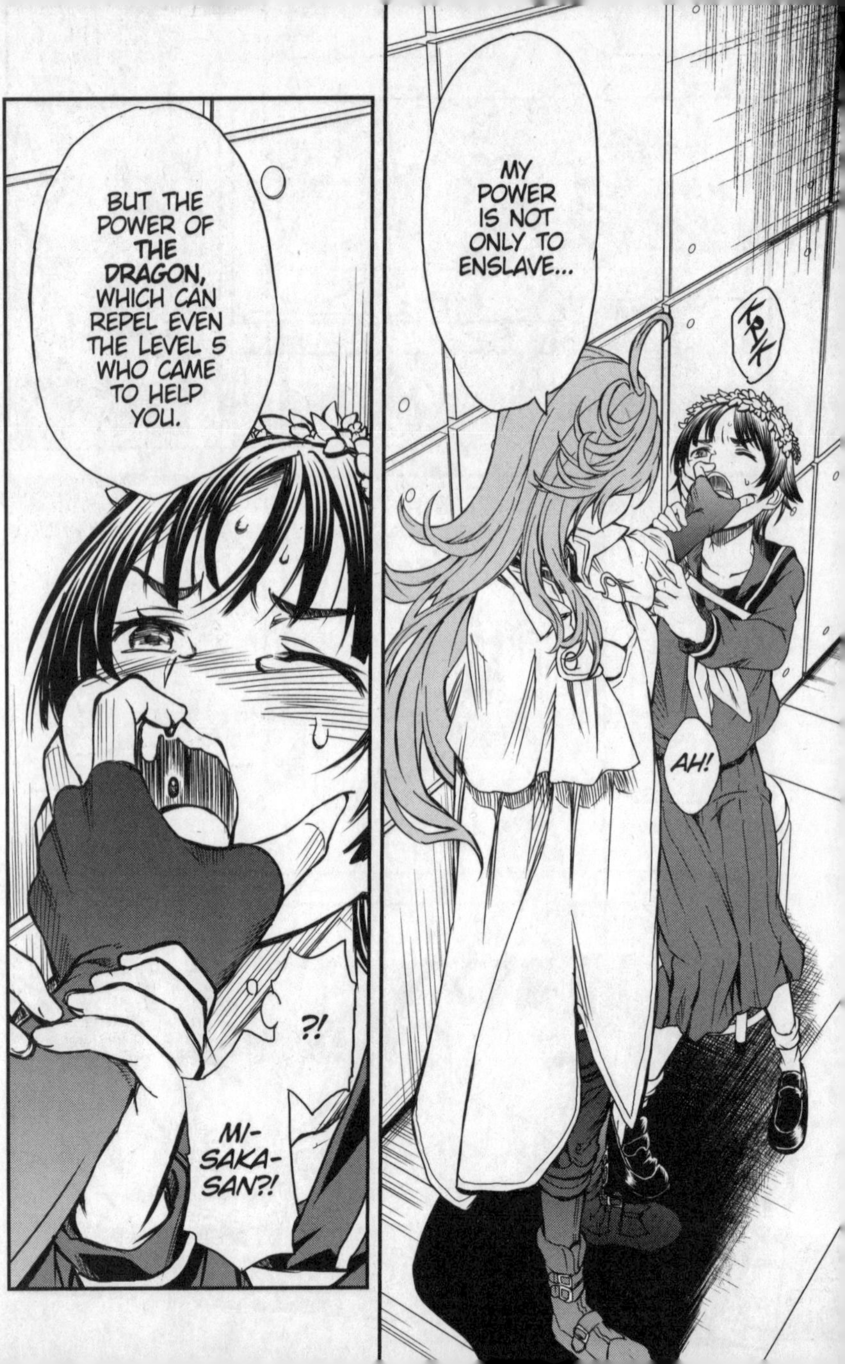

MY POWER IS NOT ONLY TO ENSLAVE...
KRIK
AH!
BUT THE POWER OF THE DRAGON, WHICH CAN REPEL EVEN THE LEVEL 5 WHO CAME TO HELP YOU.
?!
MI-SAKA-SAN?!

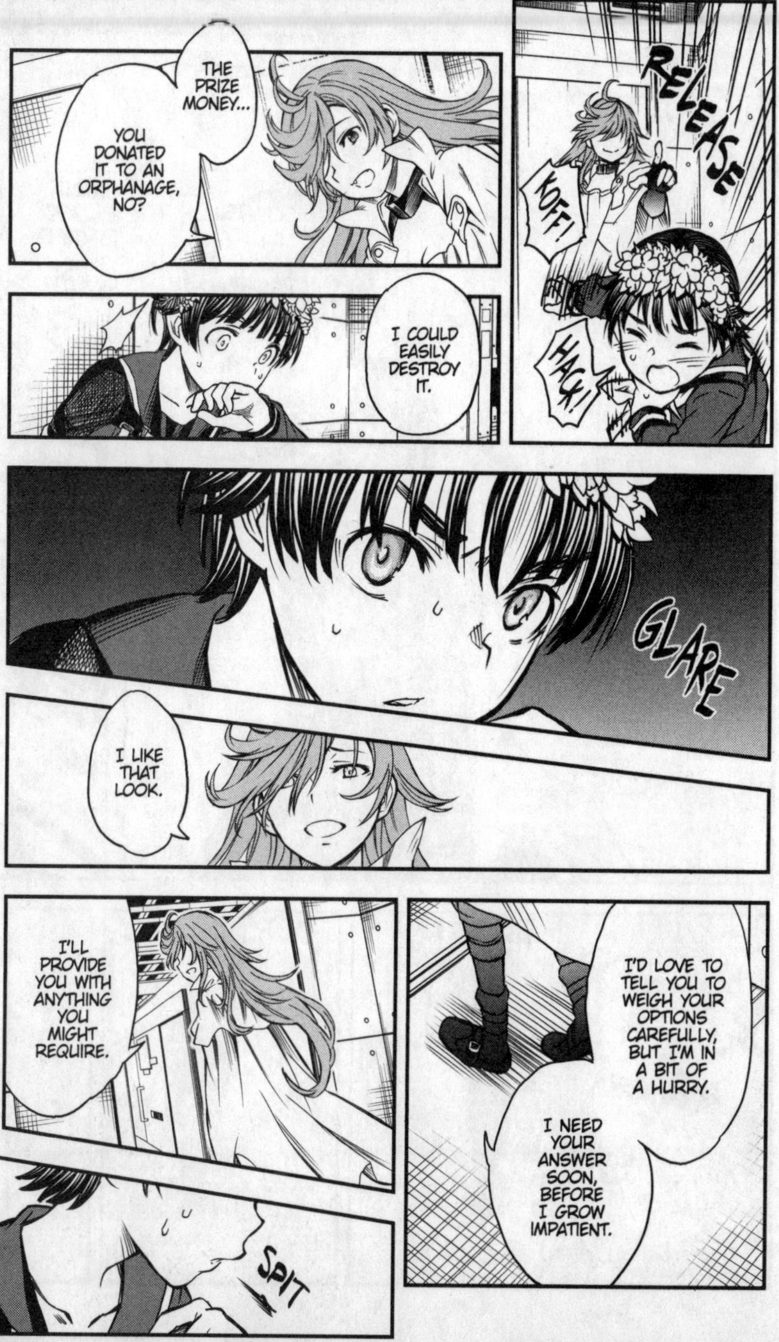
RELEASE
KOFF!
HACK!
THE PRIZE MONEY...
YOU DONATED IT TO AN ORPHANAGE, NO?
I COULD EASILY DESTROY IT.
GLARE
I LIKE THAT LOOK.
I'D LOVE TO TELL YOU TO WEIGH YOUR OPTIONS CAREFULLY, BUT I'M IN A BIT OF A HURRY.
I NEED YOUR ANSWER SOON, BEFORE I GROW IMPATIENT.
I'LL PROVIDE YOU WITH ANYTHING YOU MIGHT REQUIRE.
SPIT

YOUR BLOOD DIRTIED MY MOUTH.

SO I'LL *REQUIRE* AN ICED TEA WITH A TON OF SYRUP IN IT TO REMOVE THE BAD TASTE!

SUZU-NEE.

KIMI!

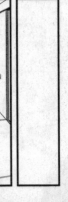

A Certain SCIENTIFIC Railgun

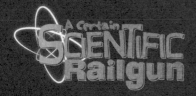

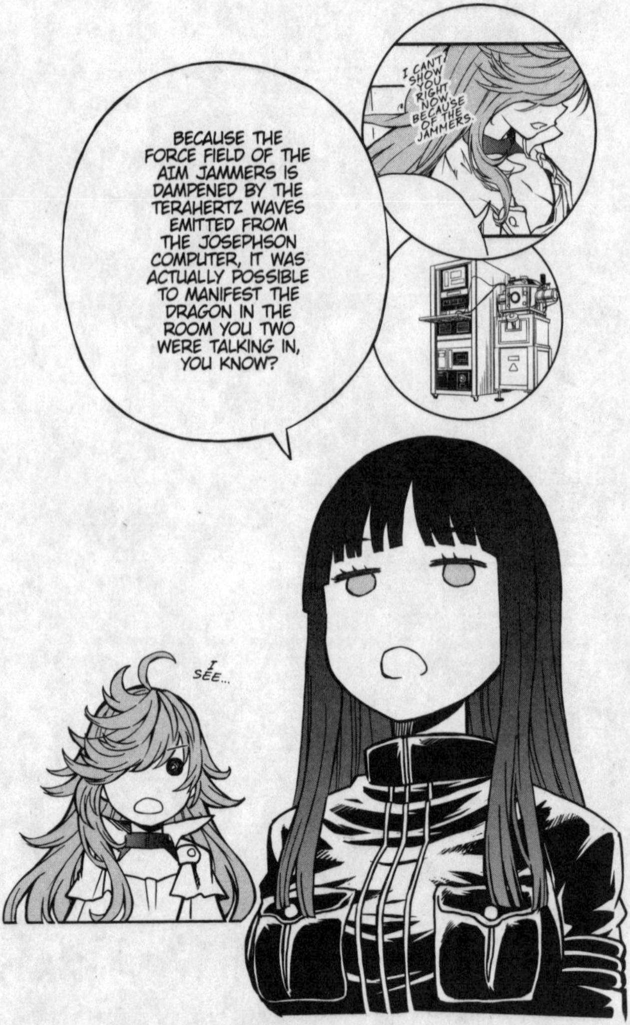
I CAN'T SHOW YOU RIGHT NOW, BECAUSE OF THE JAMMERS.
BECAUSE THE FORCE FIELD OF THE AIM JAMMERS IS DAMPENED BY THE TERAHERTZ WAVES EMITTED FROM THE JOSEPHSON COMPUTER, IT WAS ACTUALLY POSSIBLE TO MANIFEST THE DRAGON IN THE ROOM YOU TWO WERE TALKING IN, YOU KNOW?
I SEE...

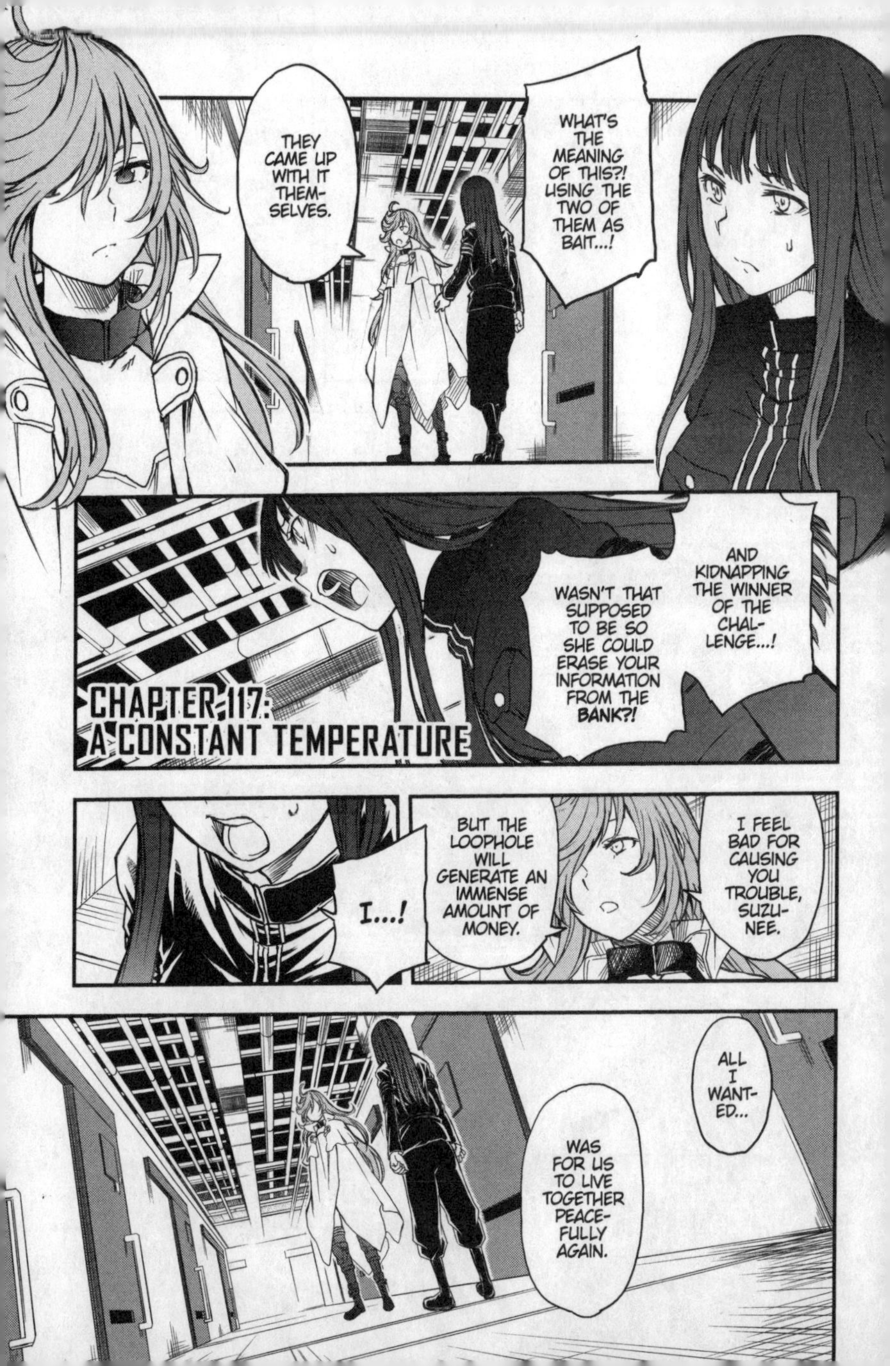
WHAT'S THE MEANING OF THIS?! USING THE TWO OF THEM AS BAIT...!
THEY CAME UP WITH IT THEMSELVES.
AND KIDNAPPING THE WINNER OF THE CHALLENGE...!
WASN'T THAT SUPPOSED TO BE SO SHE COULD ERASE YOUR INFORMATION FROM THE BANK?!
CHAPTER 117: A CONSTANT TEMPERATURE
I FEEL BAD FOR CAUSING YOU TROUBLE, SUZU-NEE.
BUT THE LOOPHOLE WILL GENERATE AN IMMENSE AMOUNT OF MONEY.
I...!
ALL I WANTED...
WAS FOR US TO LIVE TOGETHER PEACEFULLY AGAIN.

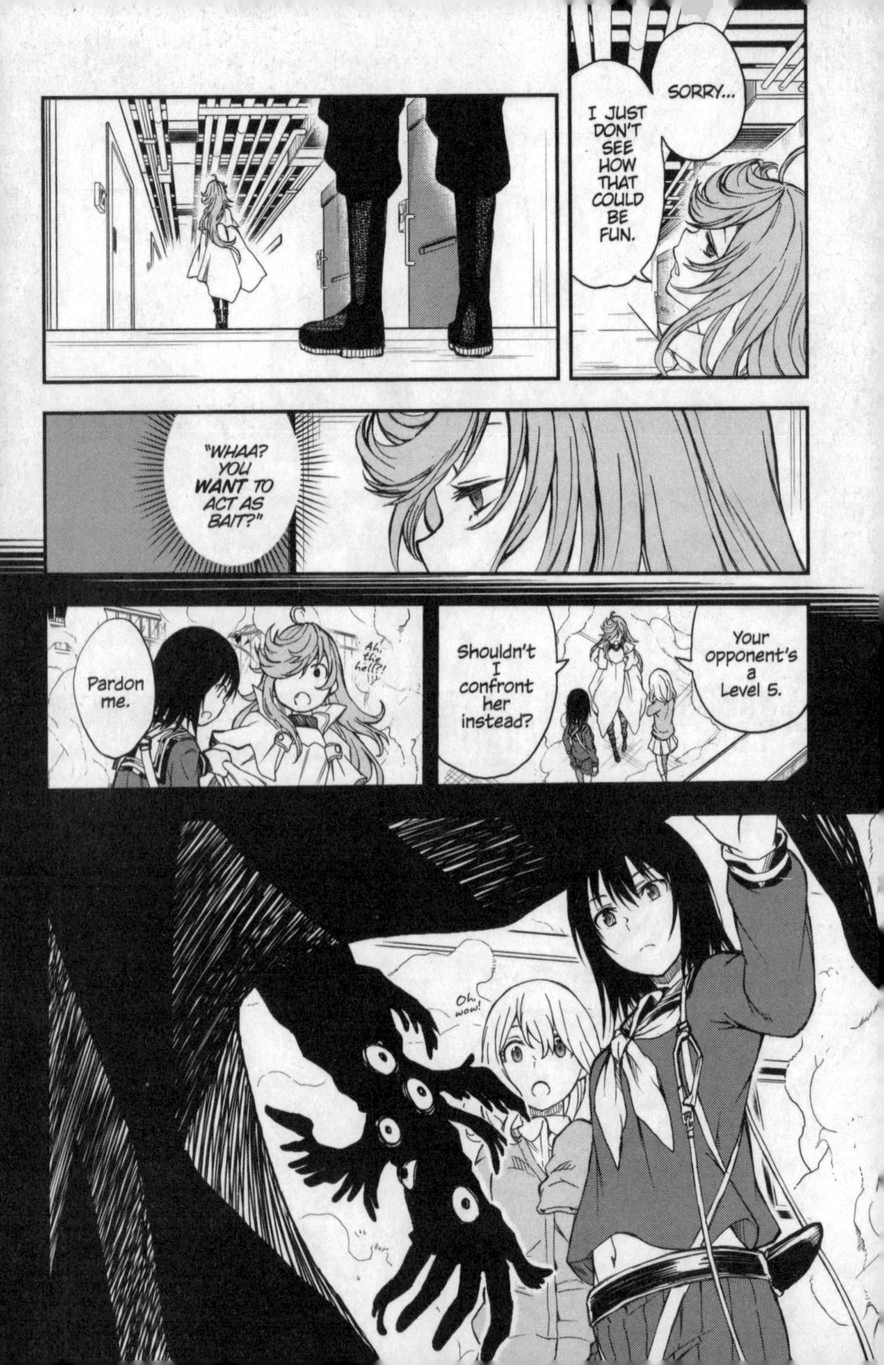
SORRY... I JUST DON'T SEE HOW THAT COULD BE FUN.
"WHAA? YOU WANT TO ACT AS BAIT?"
Your opponent's a Level 5.
Shouldn't I confront her instead?
Ah, the hell?!
Pardon me.
Oh wow!

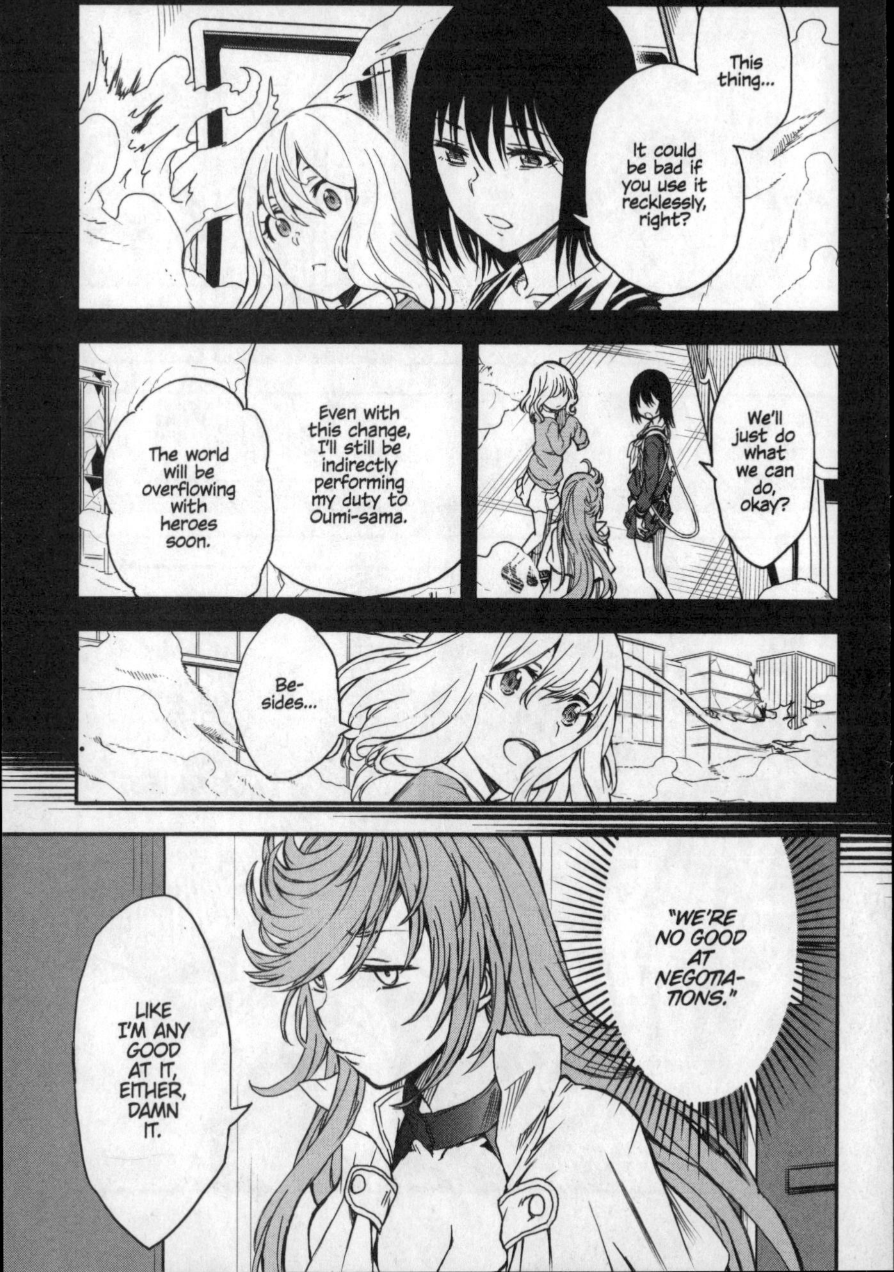
This thing...
It could be bad if you use it recklessly, right?
We'll just do what we can do, okay?
Even with this change, I'll still be indirectly performing my duty to Oumi-sama.
The world will be overflowing with heroes soon.
Be-sides...
"WE'RE NO GOOD AT NEGOTIA-TIONS."
LIKE I'M ANY GOOD AT IT, EITHER, DAMN IT.

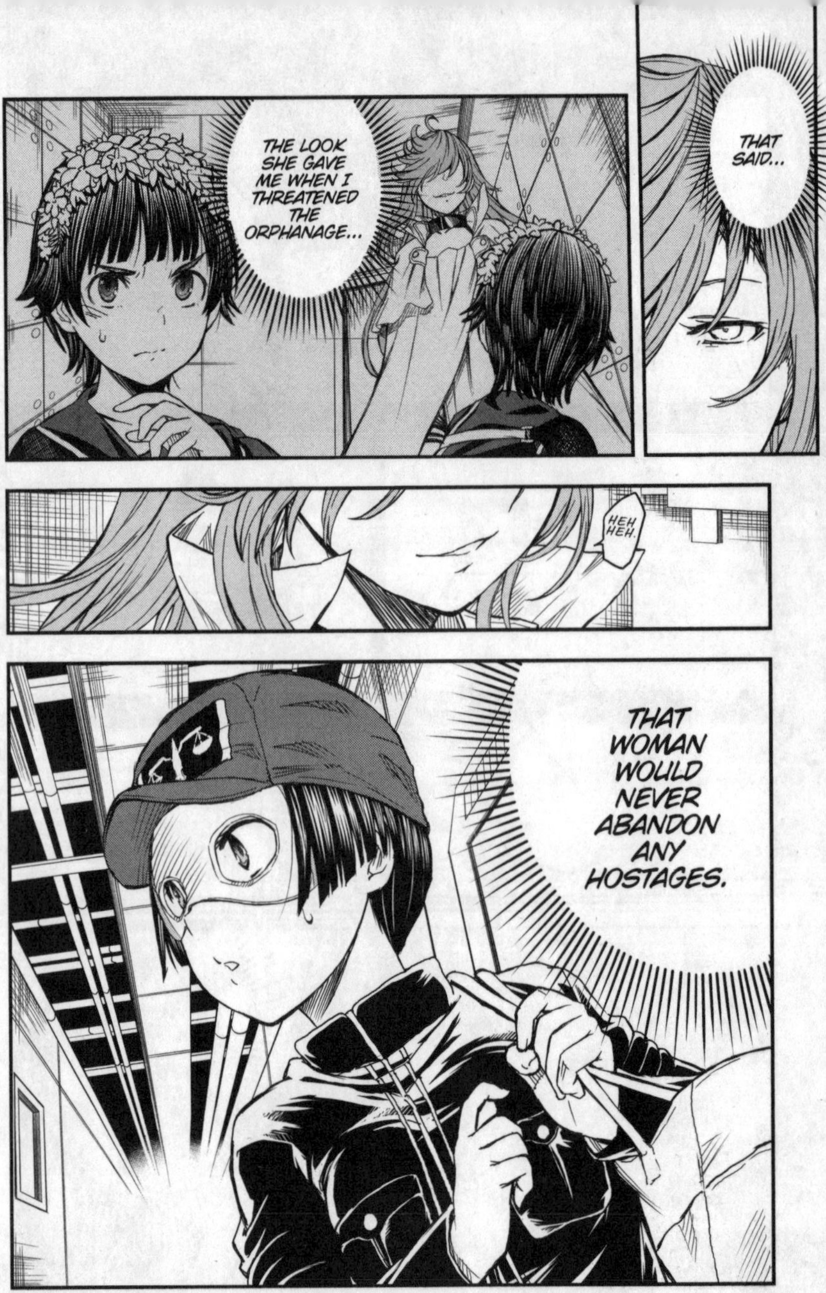
THAT SAID...
THE LOOK SHE GAVE ME WHEN I THREATENED THE ORPHANAGE...
HEH HEH.
THAT WOMAN WOULD NEVER ABANDON ANY HOSTAGES.

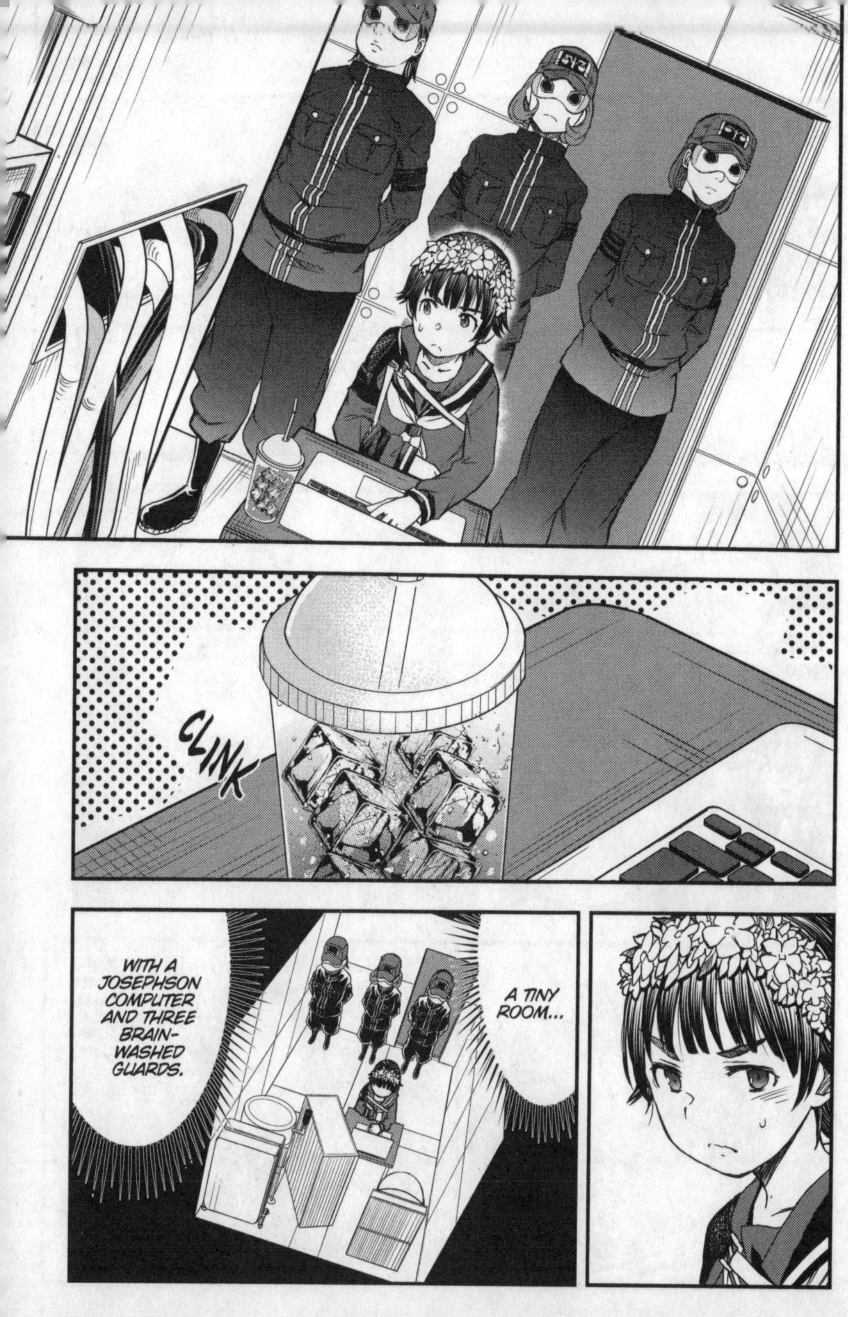
CLINK
A TINY ROOM...
WITH A JOSEPHSON COMPUTER AND THREE BRAIN-WASHED GUARDS.

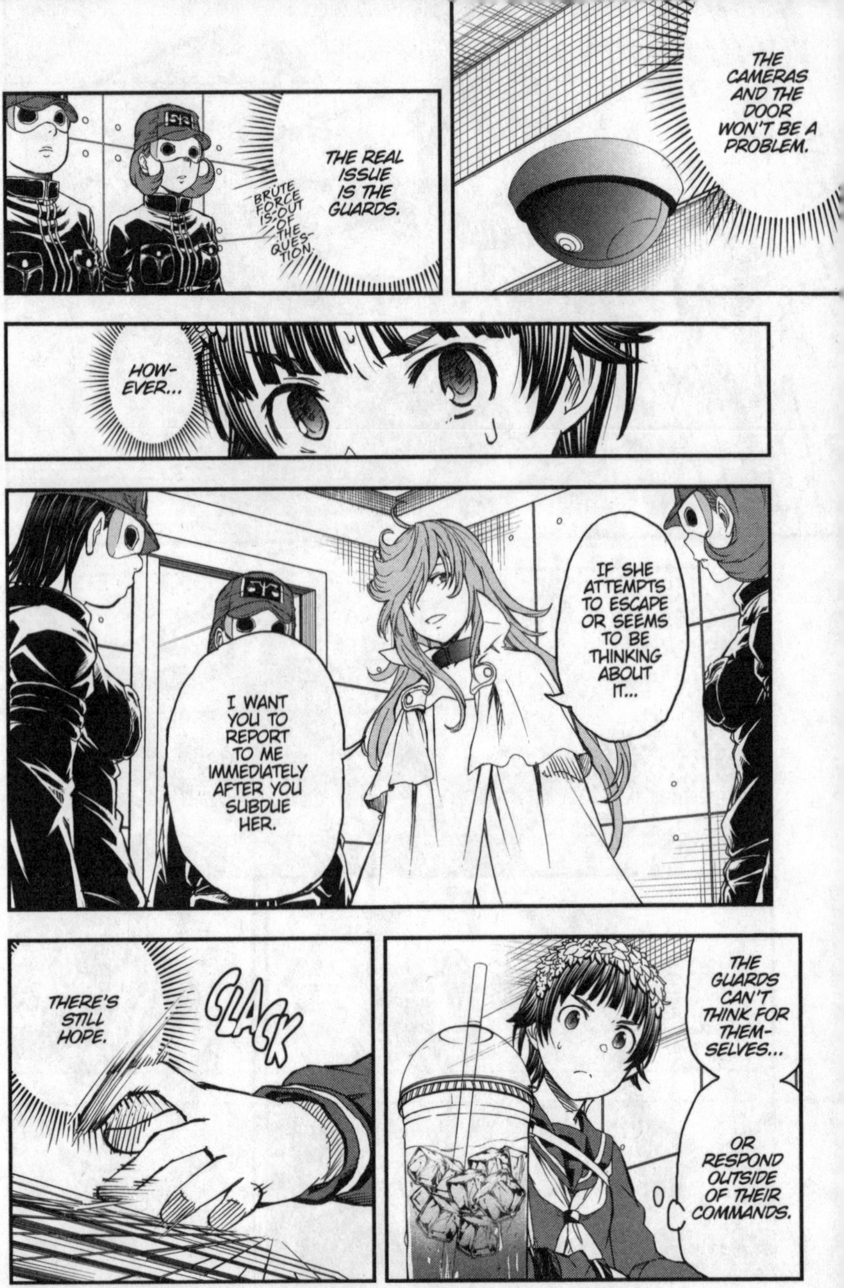
THE CAMERAS AND THE DOOR WON'T BE A PROBLEM.
THE REAL ISSUE IS THE GUARDS.
BRÜTE FORCE IS OUT OF THE QUES-TION.
HOW-EVER...
IF SHE ATTEMPTS TO ESCAPE OR SEEMS TO BE THINKING ABOUT IT...
I WANT YOU TO REPORT TO ME IMMEDIATELY AFTER YOU SUBDUE HER.
THE GUARDS CAN'T THINK FOR THEM-SELVES...
OR RESPOND OUTSIDE OF THEIR COMMANDS.
THERE'S STILL HOPE.
CLACK

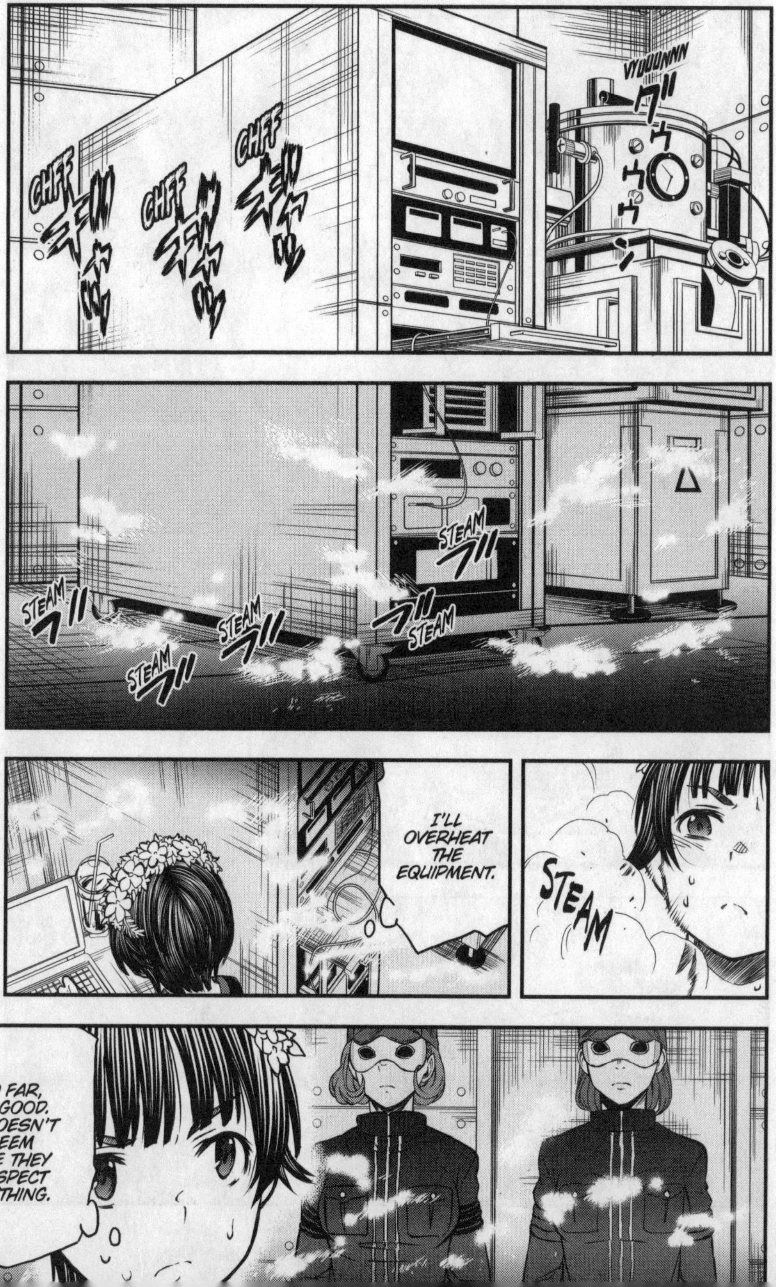
VVOOONNN
CHFF
CHFF
CHFF
STEAM
STEAM
STEAM
STEAM
STEAM
STEAM
I'LL OVERHEAT THE EQUIPMENT.
SO FAR, SO GOOD. IT DOESN'T SEEM LIKE THEY SUSPECT ANYTHING.

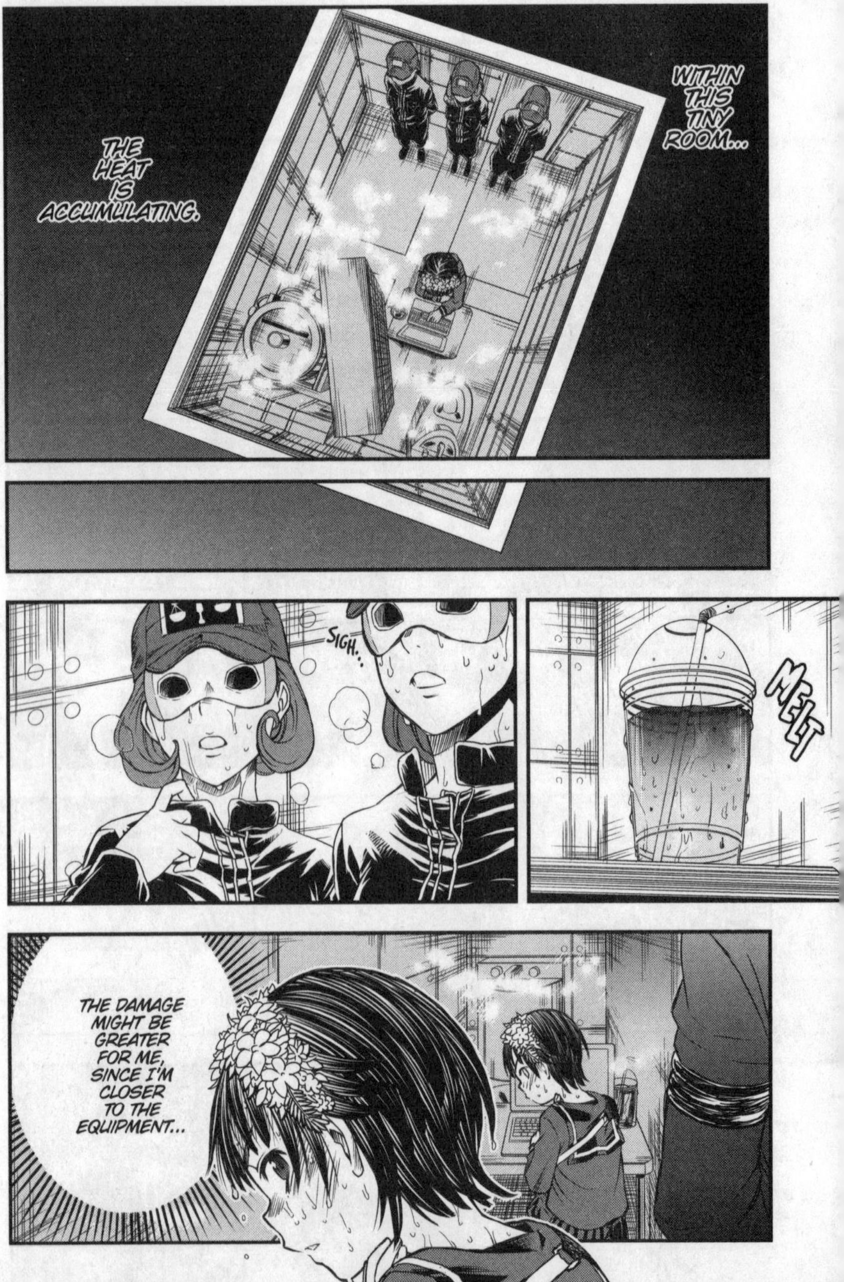
WITHIN THIS TINY ROOM...
THE HEAT IS ACCUMULATING.
MELT
SIGH...
THE DAMAGE MIGHT BE GREATER FOR ME, SINCE I'M CLOSER TO THE EQUIPMENT...

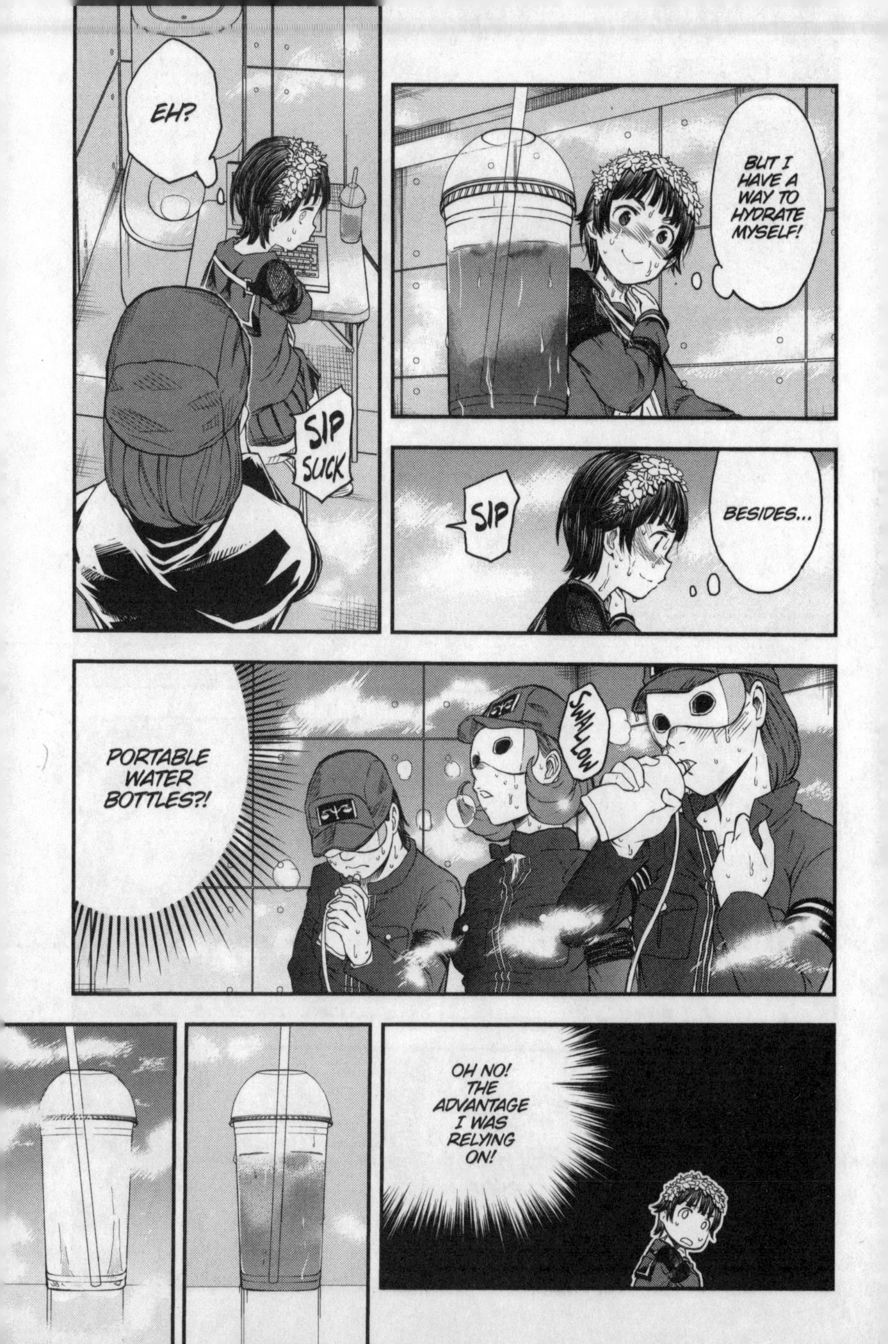
BUT I HAVE A WAY TO HYDRATE MYSELF!
BESIDES...
SIP
EH?
SIP SUCK
SWALLOW
PORTABLE WATER BOTTLES?!
OH NO! THE ADVANTAGE I WAS RELYING ON!

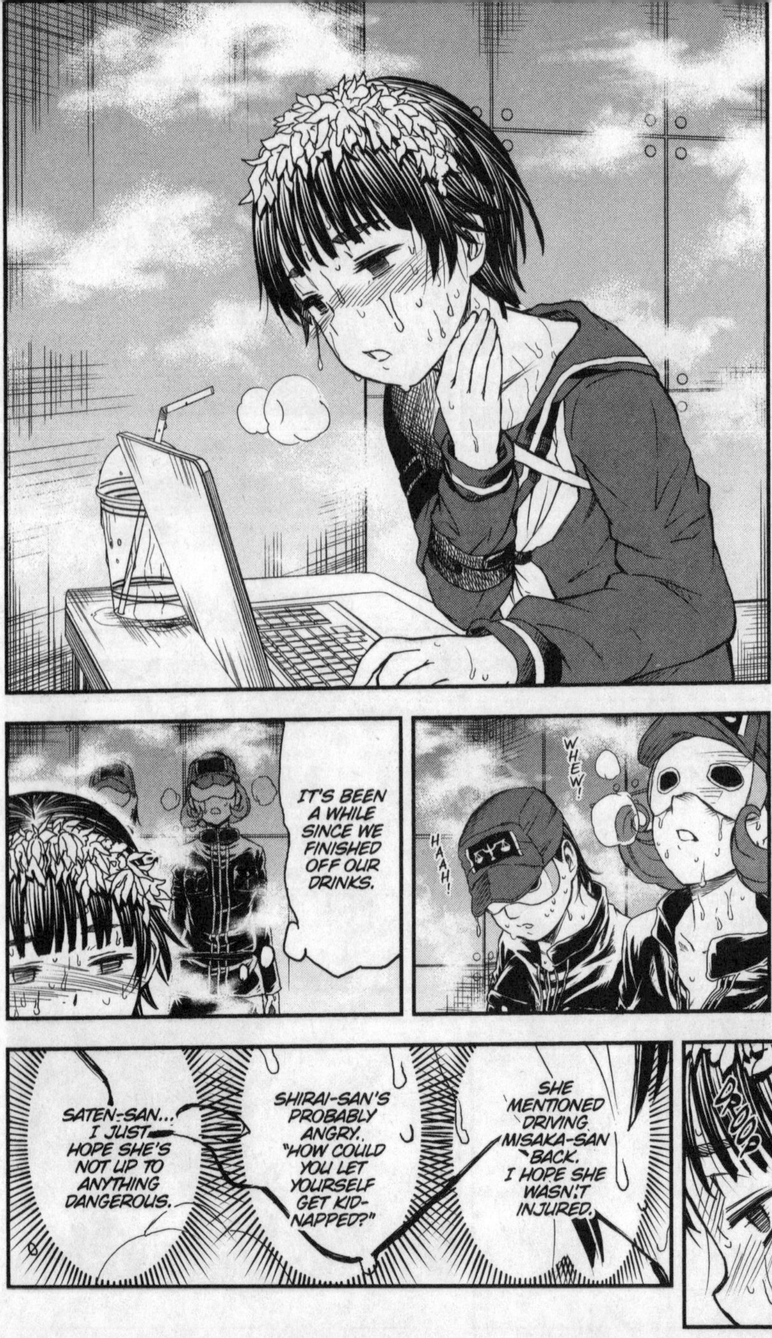
WHEW!
HAAH!
IT'S BEEN A WHILE SINCE WE FINISHED OFF OUR DRINKS.
DROOP
SHE MENTIONED DRIVING MISAKA-SAN BACK. I HOPE SHE WASN'T INJURED.
SHIRAI-SAN'S PROBABLY ANGRY. "HOW COULD YOU LET YOURSELF GET KID-NAPPED?"
SATEN-SAN... I JUST HOPE SHE'S NOT UP TO ANYTHING DANGEROUS.

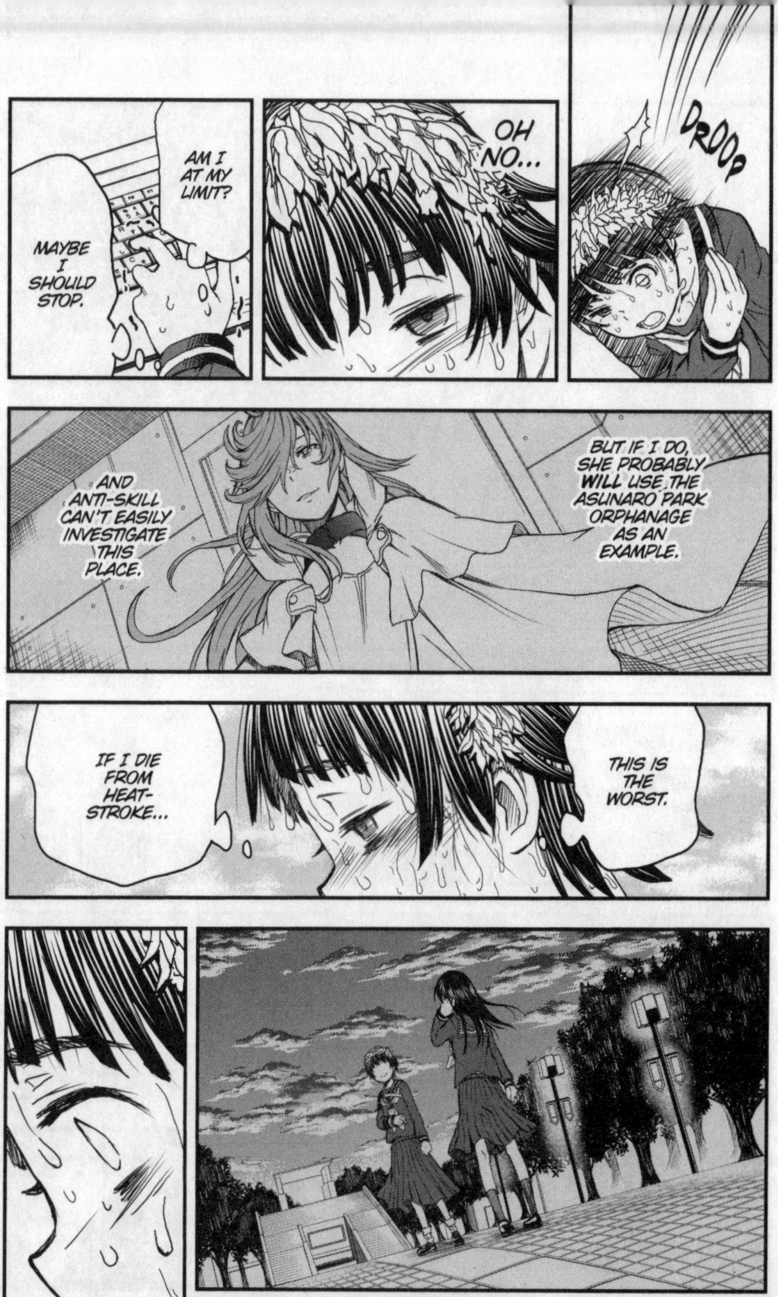
DROOP
OH NO...
AM I AT MY LIMIT?
MAYBE I SHOULD STOP.
BUT IF I DO, SHE PROBABLY **WILL** USE THE ASUNARO PARK ORPHANAGE AS AN EXAMPLE.
AND ANTI-SKILL CAN'T EASILY INVESTIGATE THIS PLACE.
THIS IS THE WORST.
IF I DIE FROM HEAT-STROKE...

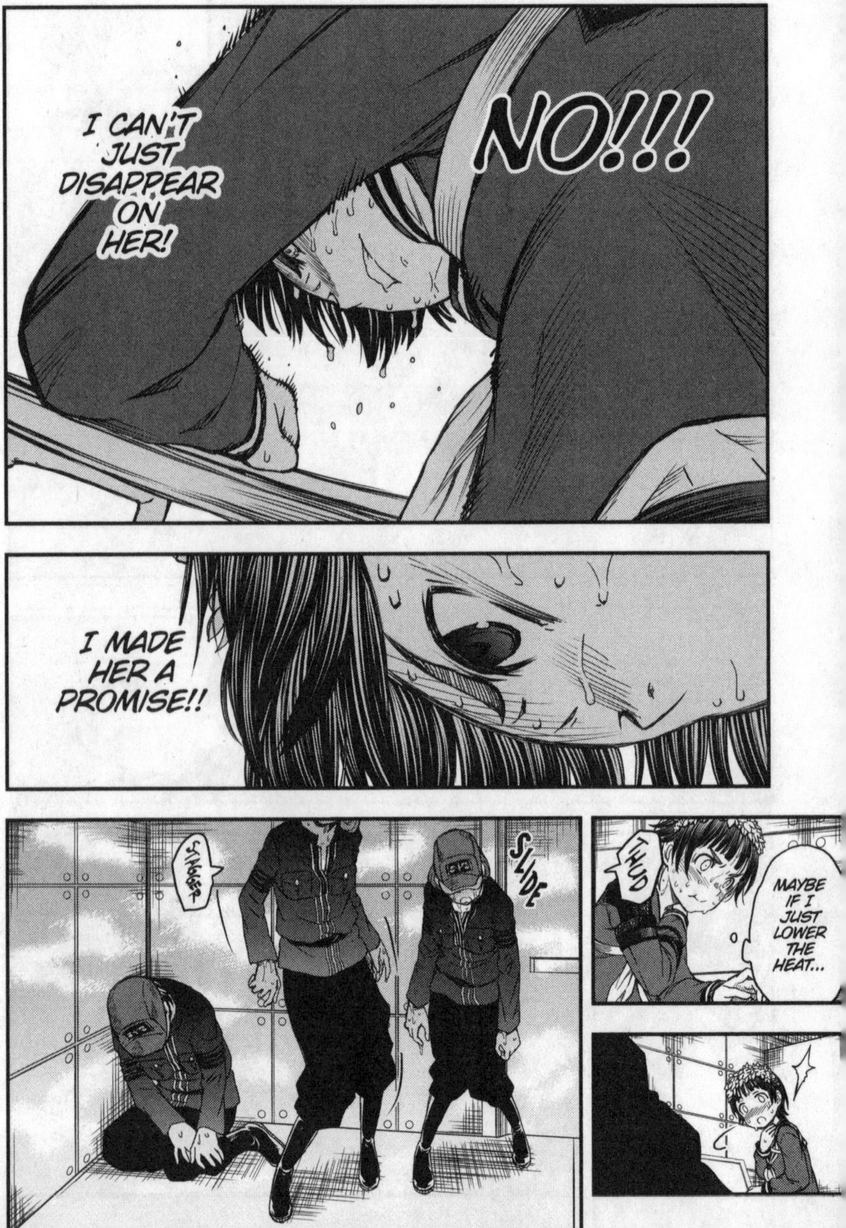
NO!!!
I CAN'T JUST DISAPPEAR ON HER!
I MADE HER A PROMISE!!
MAYBE IF I JUST LOWER THE HEAT...
THUD
SLIDE
STAGGER

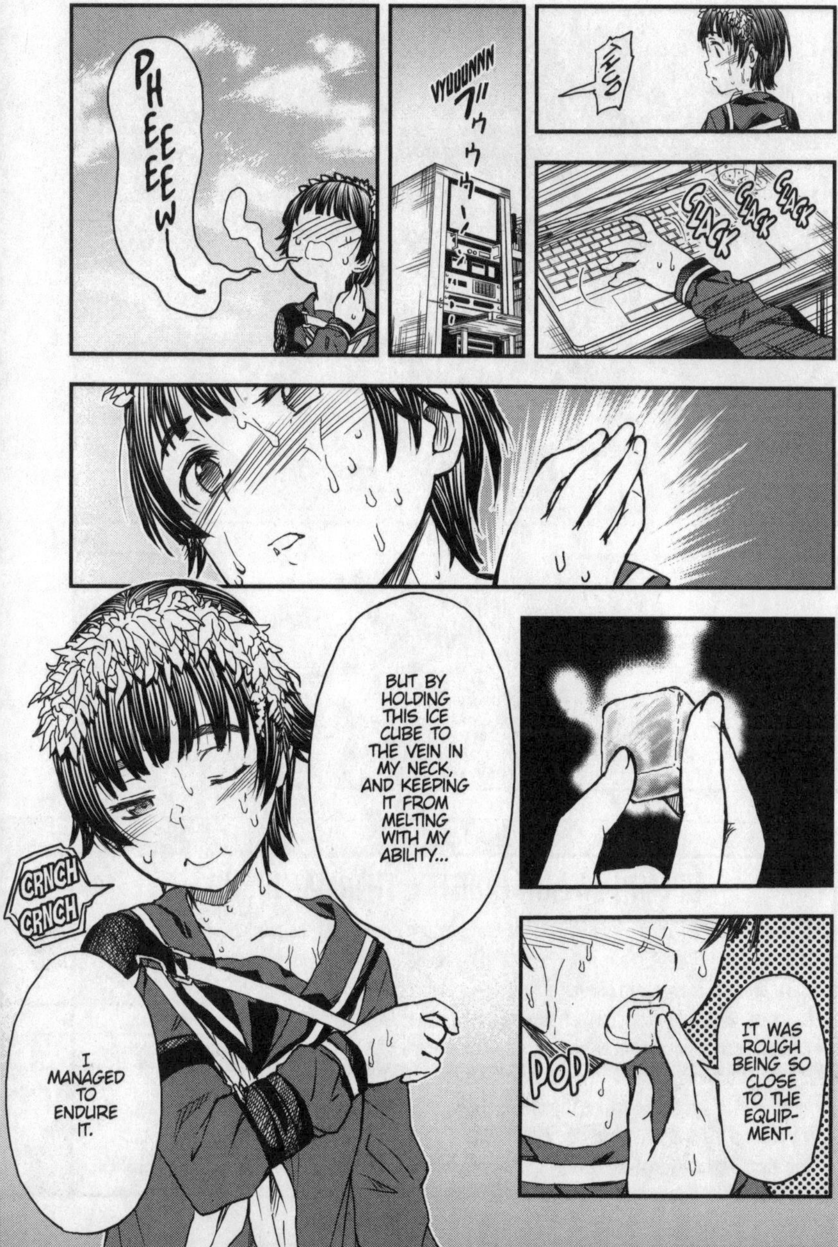
THUD
CLACK
CLACK
CLACK
VYUUUNNN
ブゥゥゥーン
PHEEEEW
POP
IT WAS ROUGH BEING SO CLOSE TO THE EQUIP-MENT.
BUT BY HOLDING THIS ICE CUBE TO THE VEIN IN MY NECK, AND KEEPING IT FROM MELTING WITH MY ABILITY...
CRNCH CRNCH
I MANAGED TO ENDURE IT.

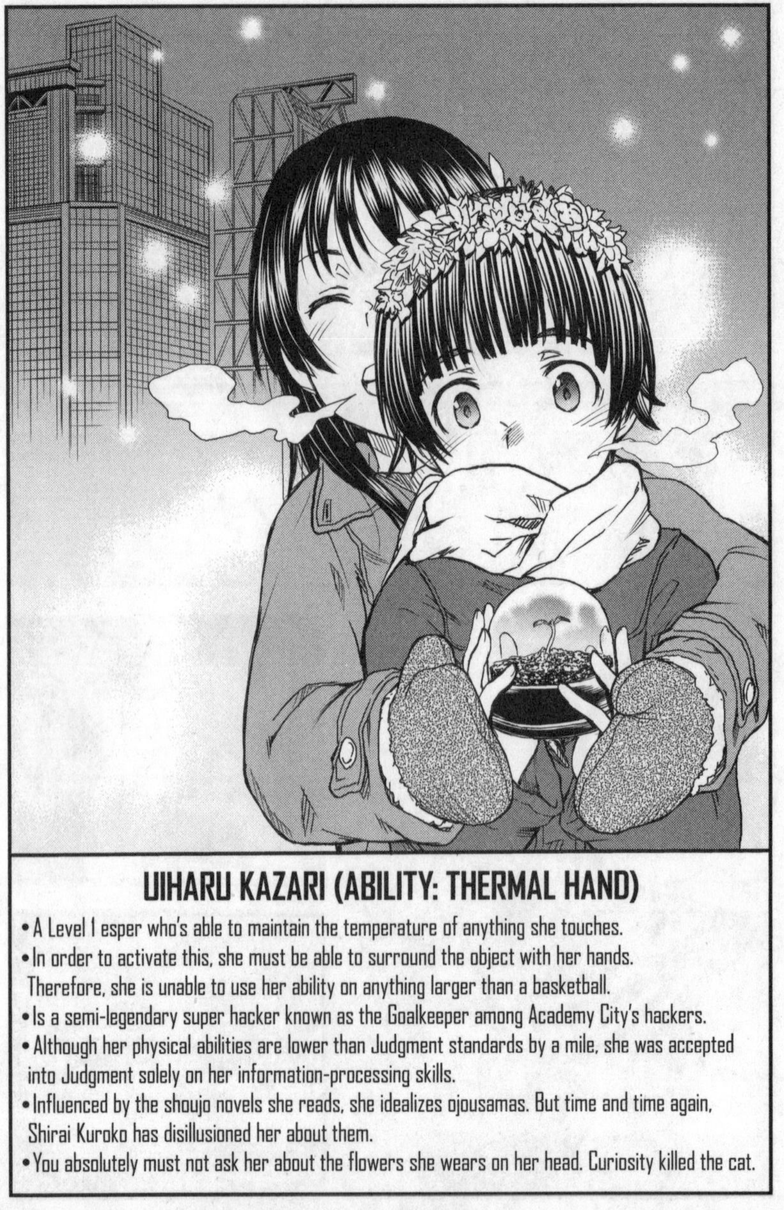

UIHARU KAZARI (ABILITY: THERMAL HAND)

- A Level 1 esper who's able to maintain the temperature of anything she touches.
- In order to activate this, she must be able to surround the object with her hands. Therefore, she is unable to use her ability on anything larger than a basketball.
- Is a semi-legendary super hacker known as the Goalkeeper among Academy City's hackers.
- Although her physical abilities are lower than Judgment standards by a mile, she was accepted into Judgment solely on her information-processing skills.
- Influenced by the shoujo novels she reads, she idealizes ojousamas. But time and time again, Shirai Kuroko has disillusioned her about them.
- You absolutely must not ask her about the flowers she wears on her head. Curiosity killed the cat.

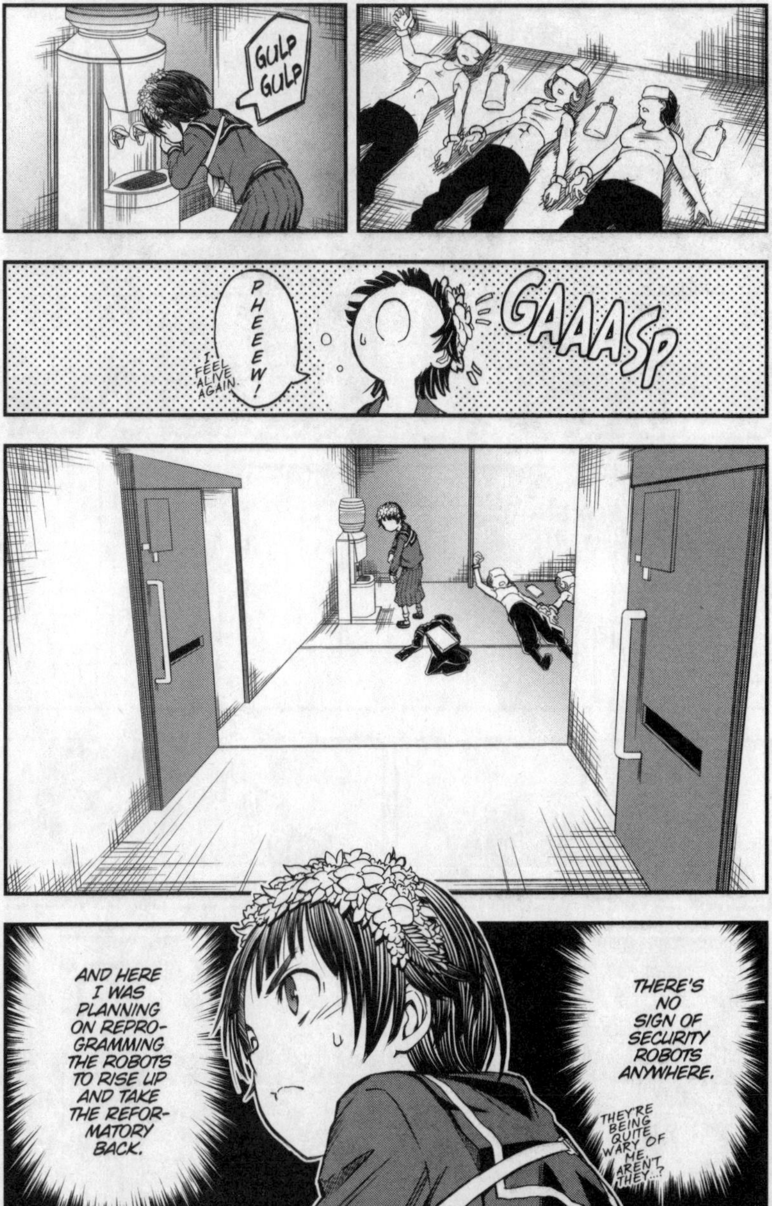
GULP GULP
GAAASP
PHEEEW!
I FEEL ALIVE AGAIN.
THERE'S NO SIGN OF SECURITY ROBOTS ANYWHERE.
THEY'RE BEING QUITE WARY OF ME, AREN'T THEY...?
AND HERE I WAS PLANNING ON REPROGRAMMING THE ROBOTS TO RISE UP AND TAKE THE REFORMATORY BACK.

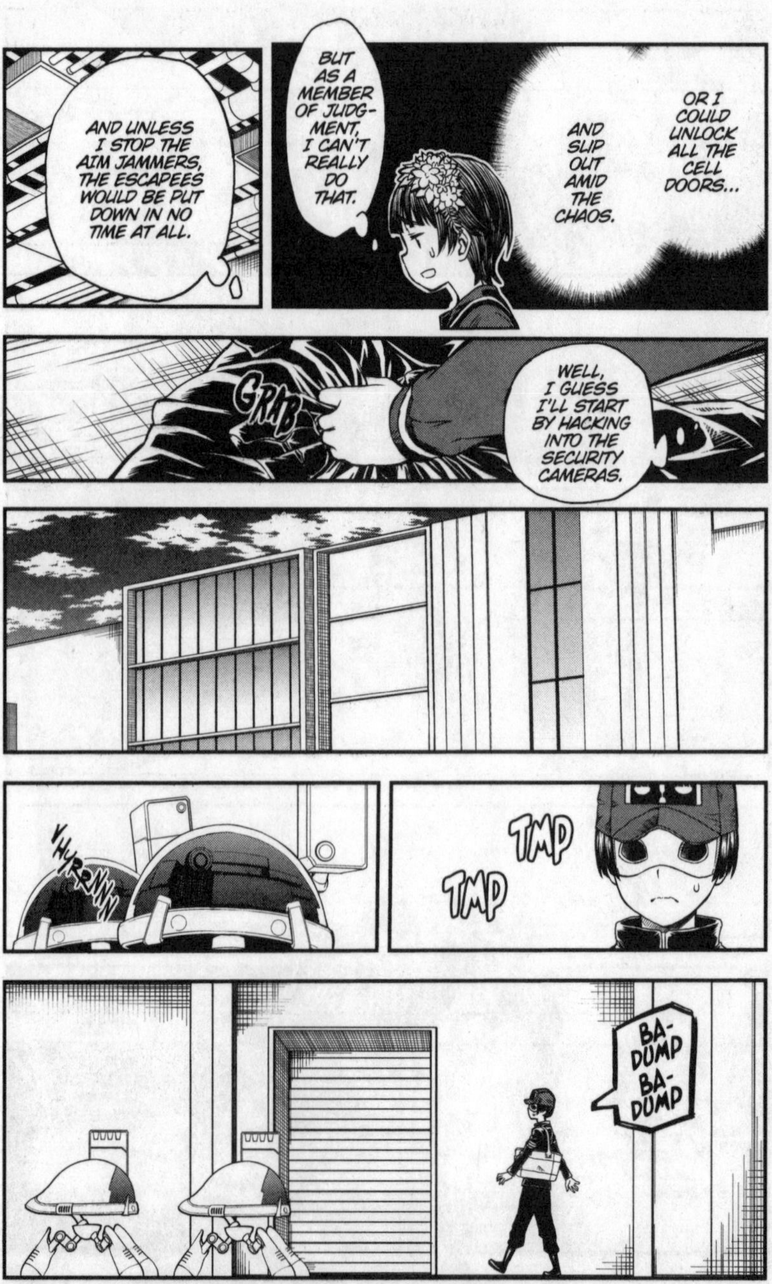
OR I COULD UNLOCK ALL THE CELL DOORS...
AND SLIP OUT AMID THE CHAOS.
BUT AS A MEMBER OF JUDGMENT, I CAN'T REALLY DO THAT.
AND UNLESS I STOP THE AIM JAMMERS, THE ESCAPEES WOULD BE PUT DOWN IN NO TIME AT ALL.
WELL, I GUESS I'LL START BY HACKING INTO THE SECURITY CAMERAS.
GRAB
TMP
TMP
VHYRRNNN
BA-DUMP BA-DUMP

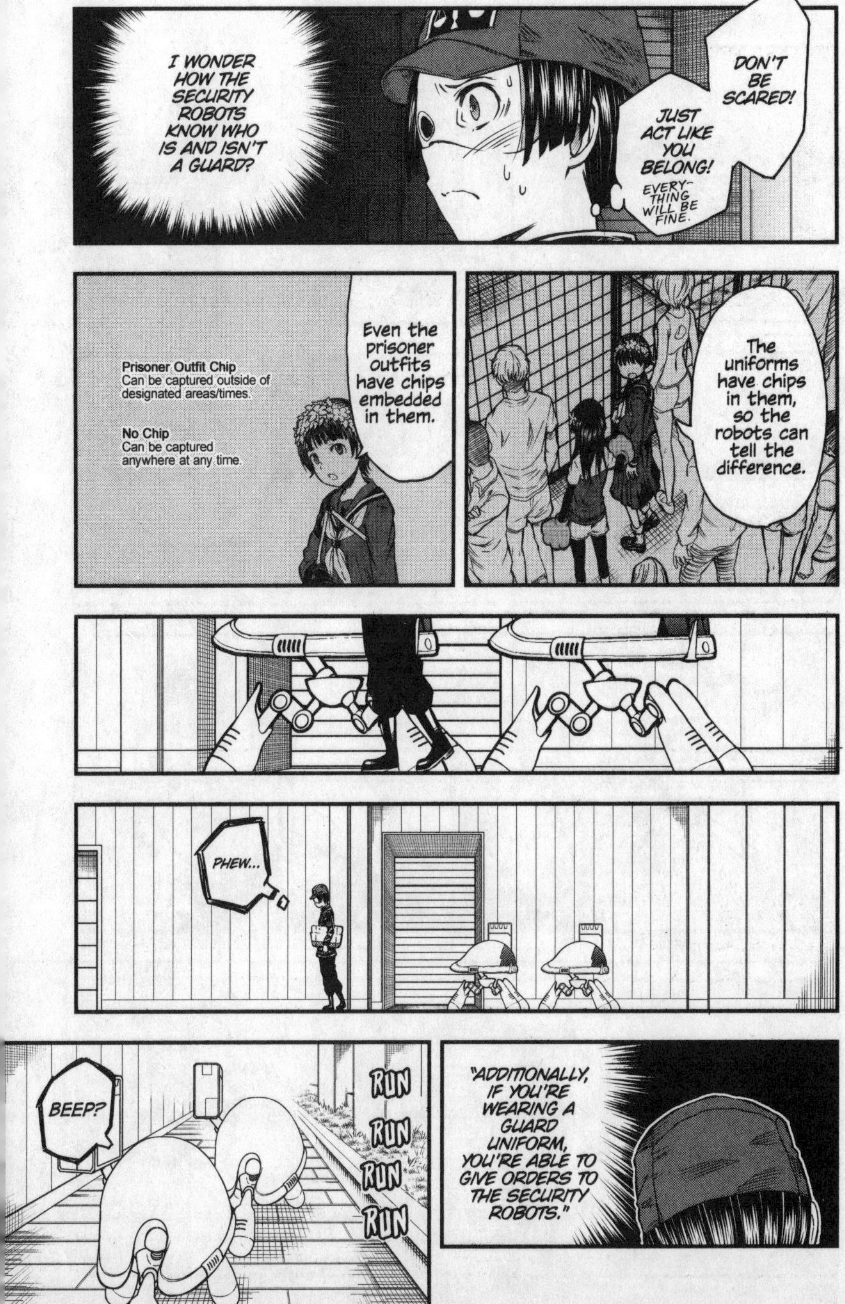
DON'T BE SCARED!
JUST ACT LIKE YOU BELONG!
EVERY-THING WILL BE FINE.
I WONDER HOW THE SECURITY ROBOTS KNOW WHO IS AND ISN'T A GUARD?
The uniforms have chips in them, so the robots can tell the difference.
Even the prisoner outfits have chips embedded in them.
Prisoner Outfit Chip
Can be captured outside of designated areas/times.
No Chip
Can be captured anywhere at any time.
PHEW...
"ADDITIONALLY, IF YOU'RE WEARING A GUARD UNIFORM, YOU'RE ABLE TO GIVE ORDERS TO THE SECURITY ROBOTS."
RUN
RUN
RUN
RUN
BEEP?

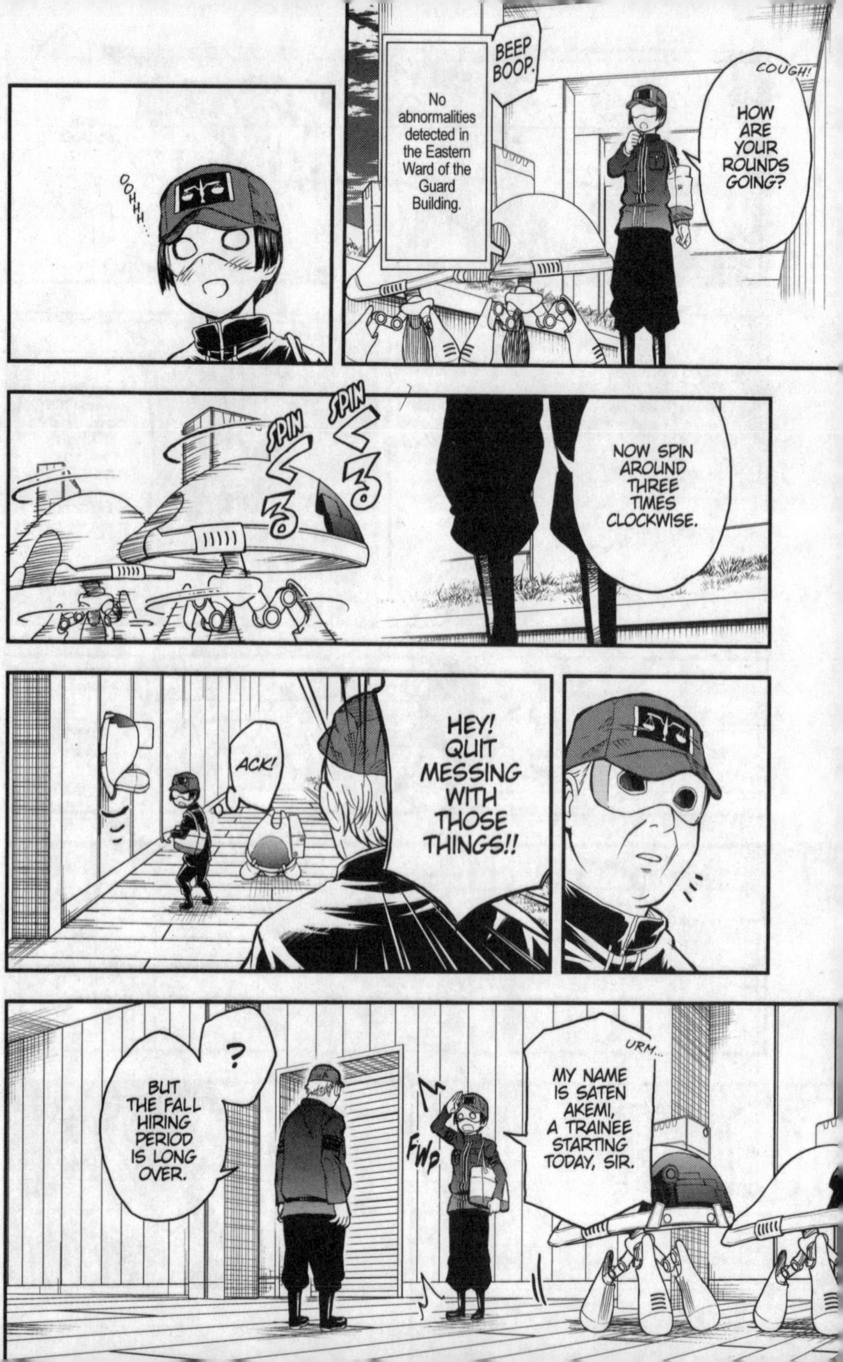
COUGH!
HOW ARE YOUR ROUNDS GOING?
BEEP BOOP.
No abnormalities detected in the Eastern Ward of the Guard Building.
OOHHH...
NOW SPIN AROUND THREE TIMES CLOCKWISE.
SPIN
SPIN
HEY! QUIT MESSING WITH THOSE THINGS!!
ACK!
URM...
MY NAME IS SATEN AKEMI, A TRAINEE STARTING TODAY, SIR.
FWP
?
BUT THE FALL HIRING PERIOD IS LONG OVER.

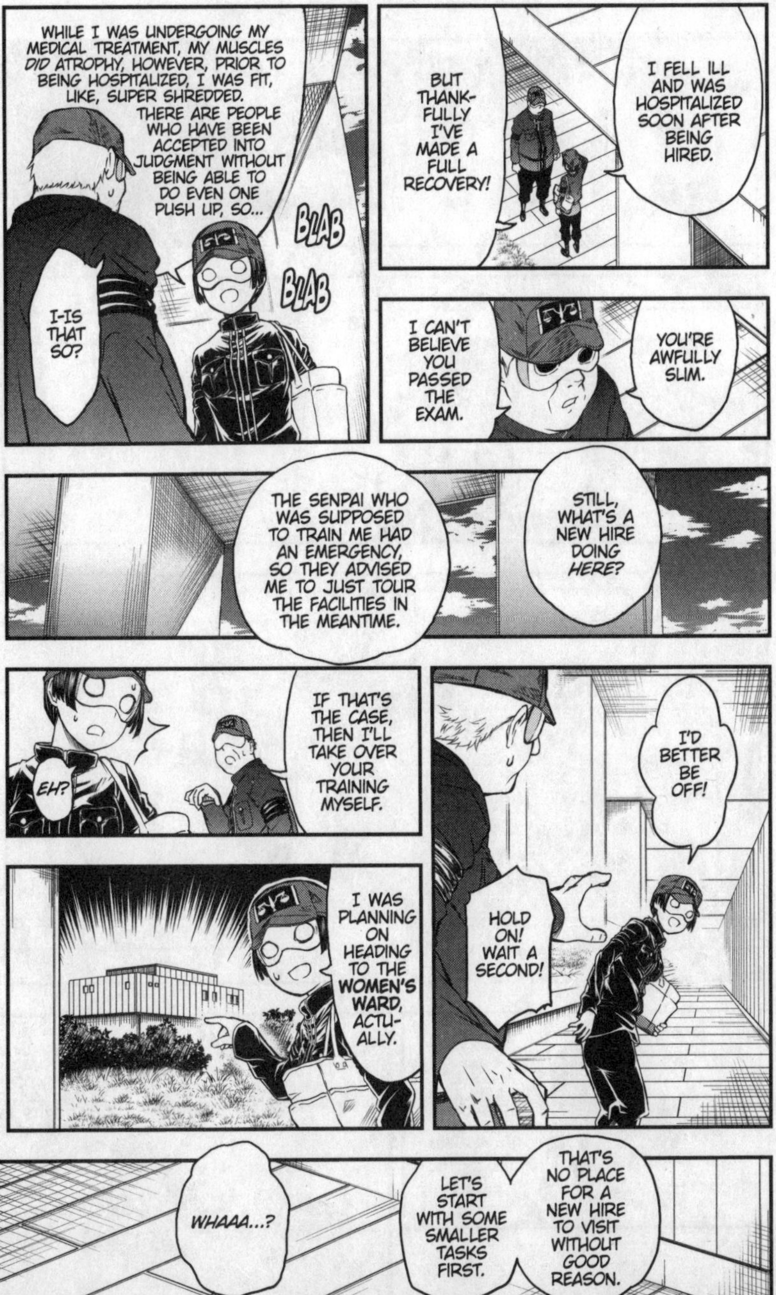
I FELL ILL AND WAS HOSPITALIZED SOON AFTER BEING HIRED.
BUT THANKFULLY I'VE MADE A FULL RECOVERY!
YOU'RE AWFULLY SLIM.
I CAN'T BELIEVE YOU PASSED THE EXAM.
WHILE I WAS UNDERGOING MY MEDICAL TREATMENT, MY MUSCLES *DID* ATROPHY, HOWEVER, PRIOR TO BEING HOSPITALIZED, I WAS FIT, LIKE, SUPER SHREDDED. THERE ARE PEOPLE WHO HAVE BEEN ACCEPTED INTO JUDGMENT WITHOUT BEING ABLE TO DO EVEN ONE PUSH UP, SO...
BLAB
BLAB
I-IS THAT SO?
STILL, WHAT'S A NEW HIRE DOING *HERE?*
THE SENPAI WHO WAS SUPPOSED TO TRAIN ME HAD AN EMERGENCY, SO THEY ADVISED ME TO JUST TOUR THE FACILITIES IN THE MEANTIME.
I'D BETTER BE OFF!
HOLD ON! WAIT A SECOND!
IF THAT'S THE CASE, THEN I'LL TAKE OVER YOUR TRAINING MYSELF.
EH?
I WAS PLANNING ON HEADING TO THE **WOMEN'S WARD,** ACTUALLY.
THAT'S NO PLACE FOR A NEW HIRE TO VISIT WITHOUT GOOD REASON.
LET'S START WITH SOME SMALLER TASKS FIRST.
WHAAA...?

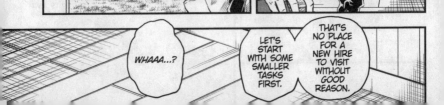

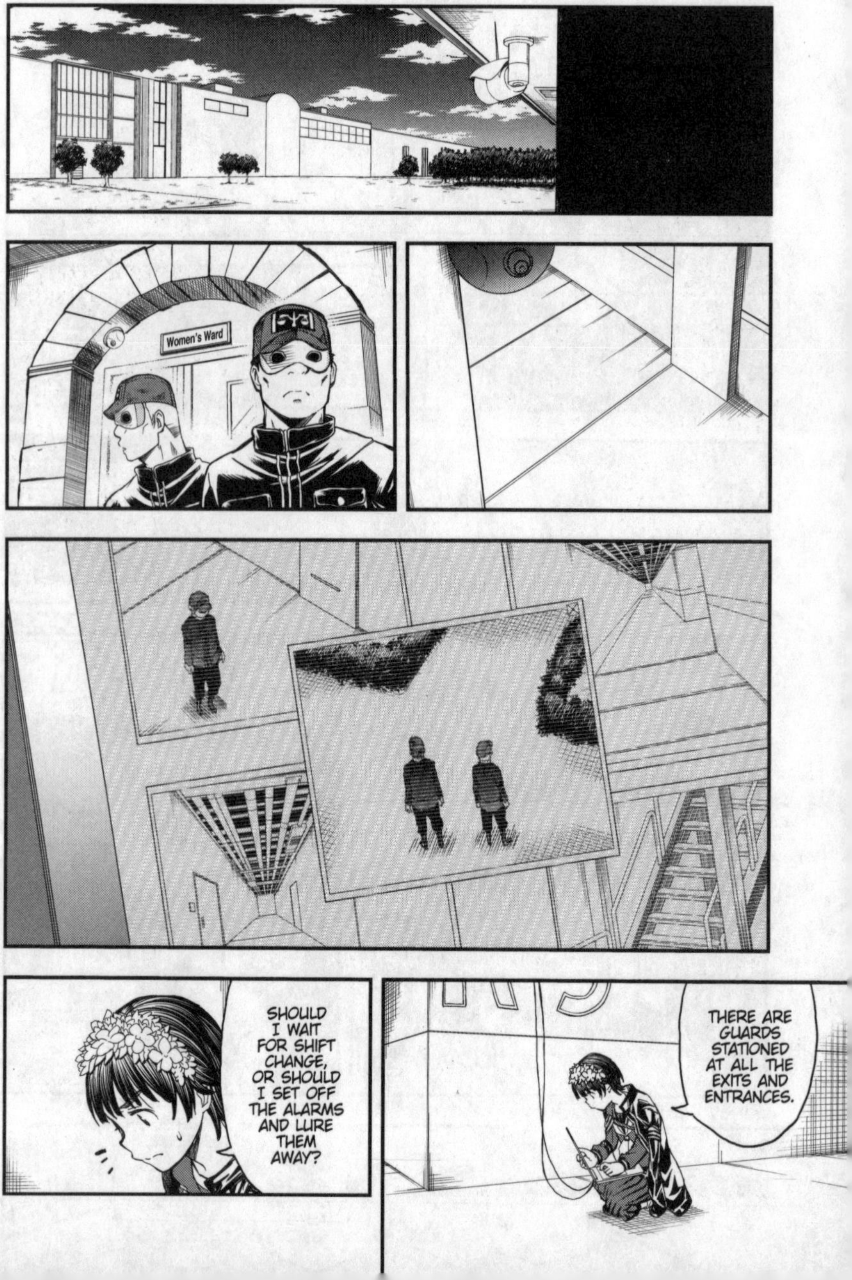
Women's Ward
THERE ARE GUARDS STATIONED AT ALL THE EXITS AND ENTRANCES.
SHOULD I WAIT FOR SHIFT CHANGE, OR SHOULD I SET OFF THE ALARMS AND LURE THEM AWAY?

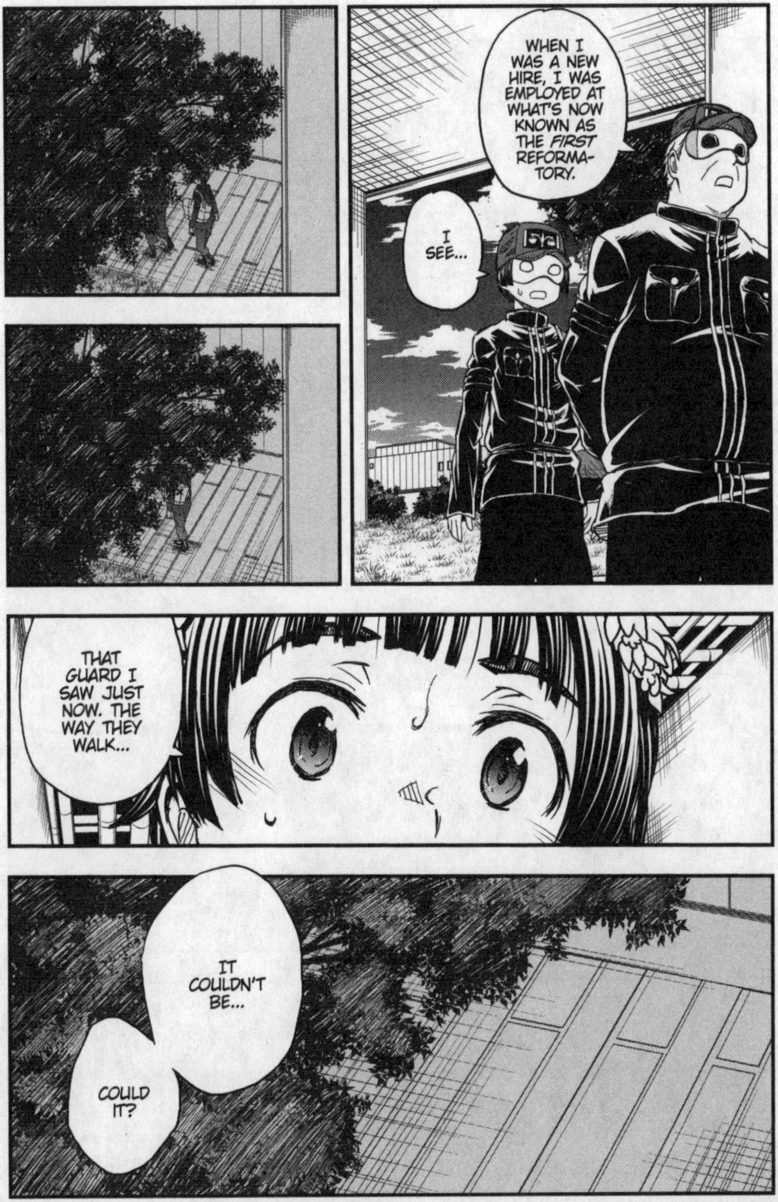
WHEN I WAS A NEW HIRE, I WAS EMPLOYED AT WHAT'S NOW KNOWN AS THE *FIRST* REFORMATORY.
I SEE...
THAT GUARD I SAW JUST NOW. THE WAY THEY WALK...
IT COULDN'T BE...
COULD IT?

A Certain
SCIENTIFIC
Railgun

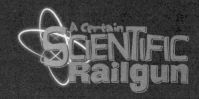

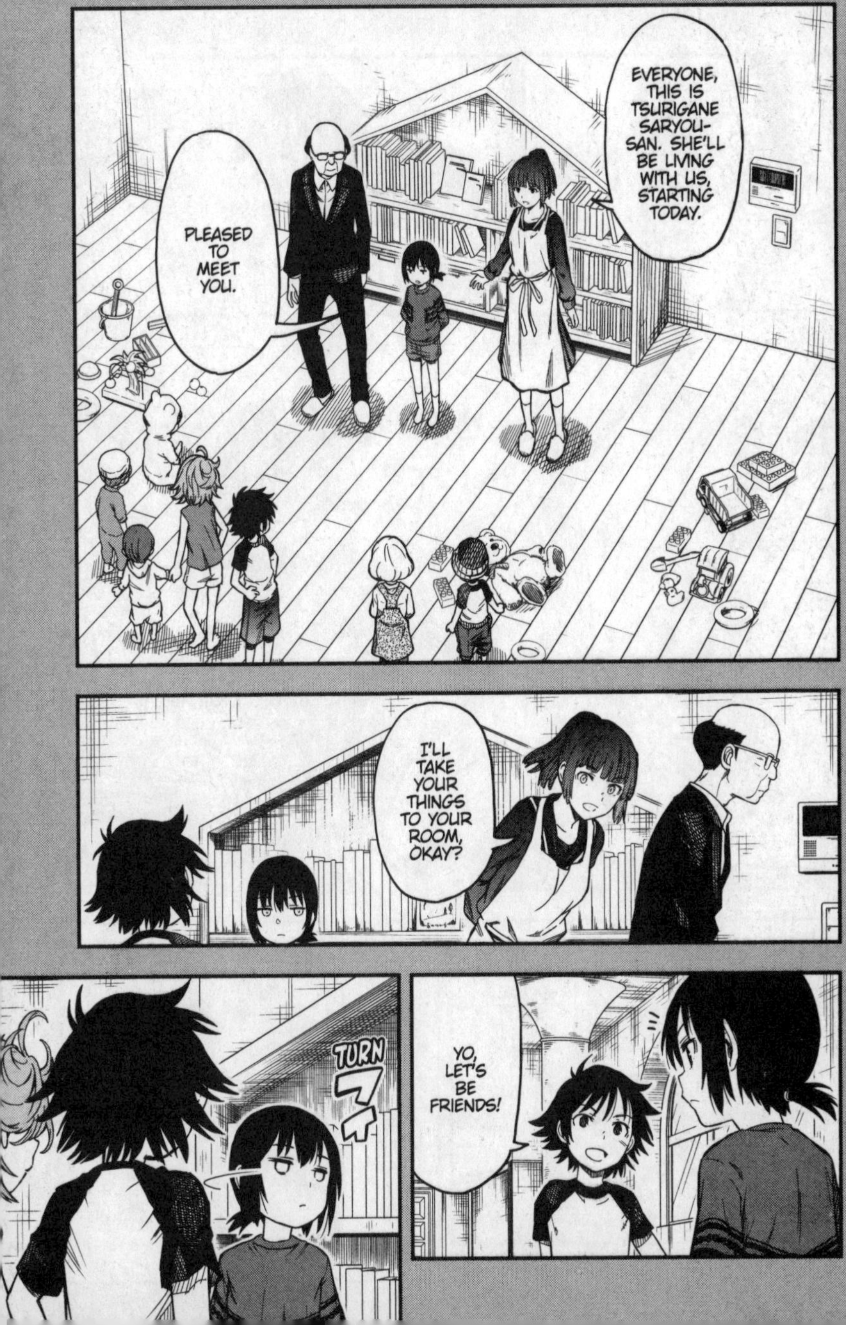
EVERYONE, THIS IS TSURIGANE SARYOU-SAN. SHE'LL BE LIVING WITH US, STARTING TODAY.
PLEASED TO MEET YOU.
I'LL TAKE YOUR THINGS TO YOUR ROOM, OKAY?
YO, LET'S BE FRIENDS!
TURN

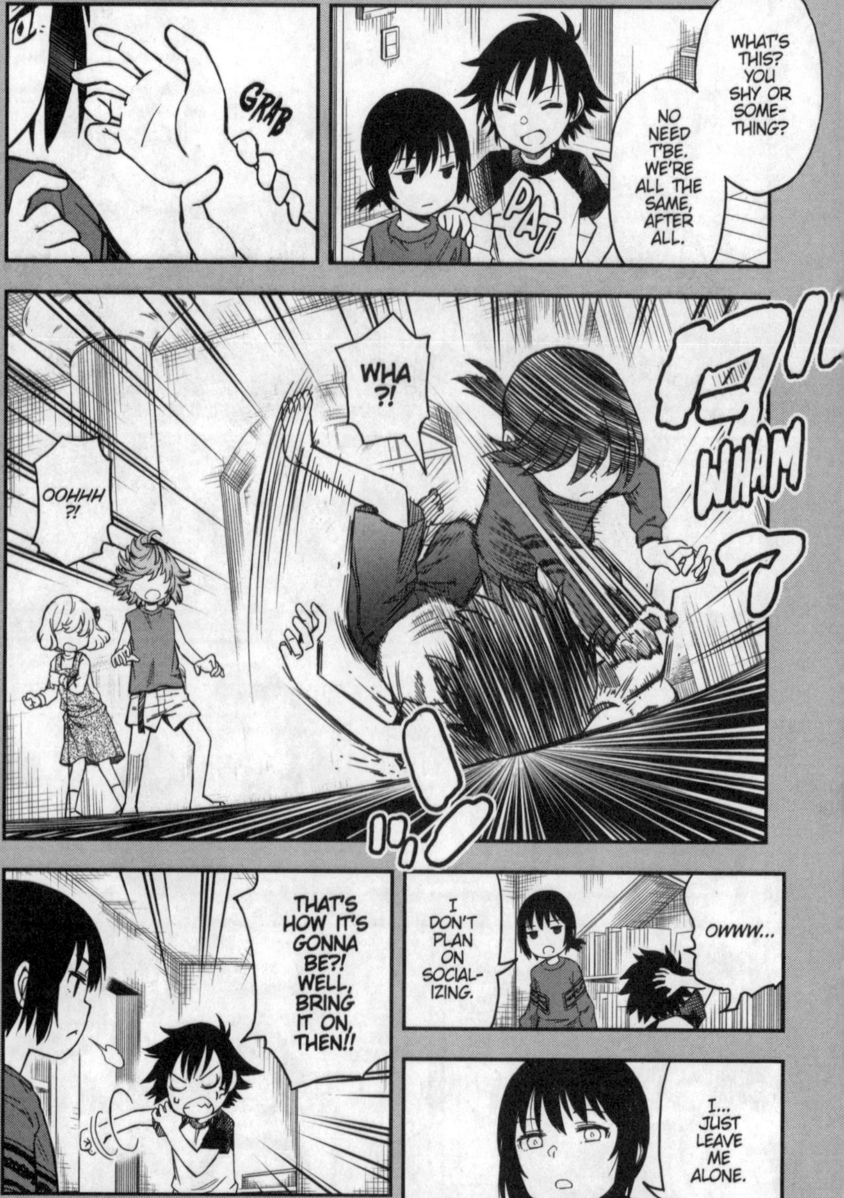
WHAT'S THIS? YOU SHY OR SOME-THING?
NO NEED T'BE. WE'RE ALL THE SAME, AFTER ALL.
PAT
GRAB
WHAM
WHA ?!
OOHHH ?!
OWWW...
I DON'T PLAN ON SOCIAL-IZING.
I... JUST LEAVE ME ALONE.
THAT'S HOW IT'S GONNA BE?! WELL, BRING IT ON, THEN!!

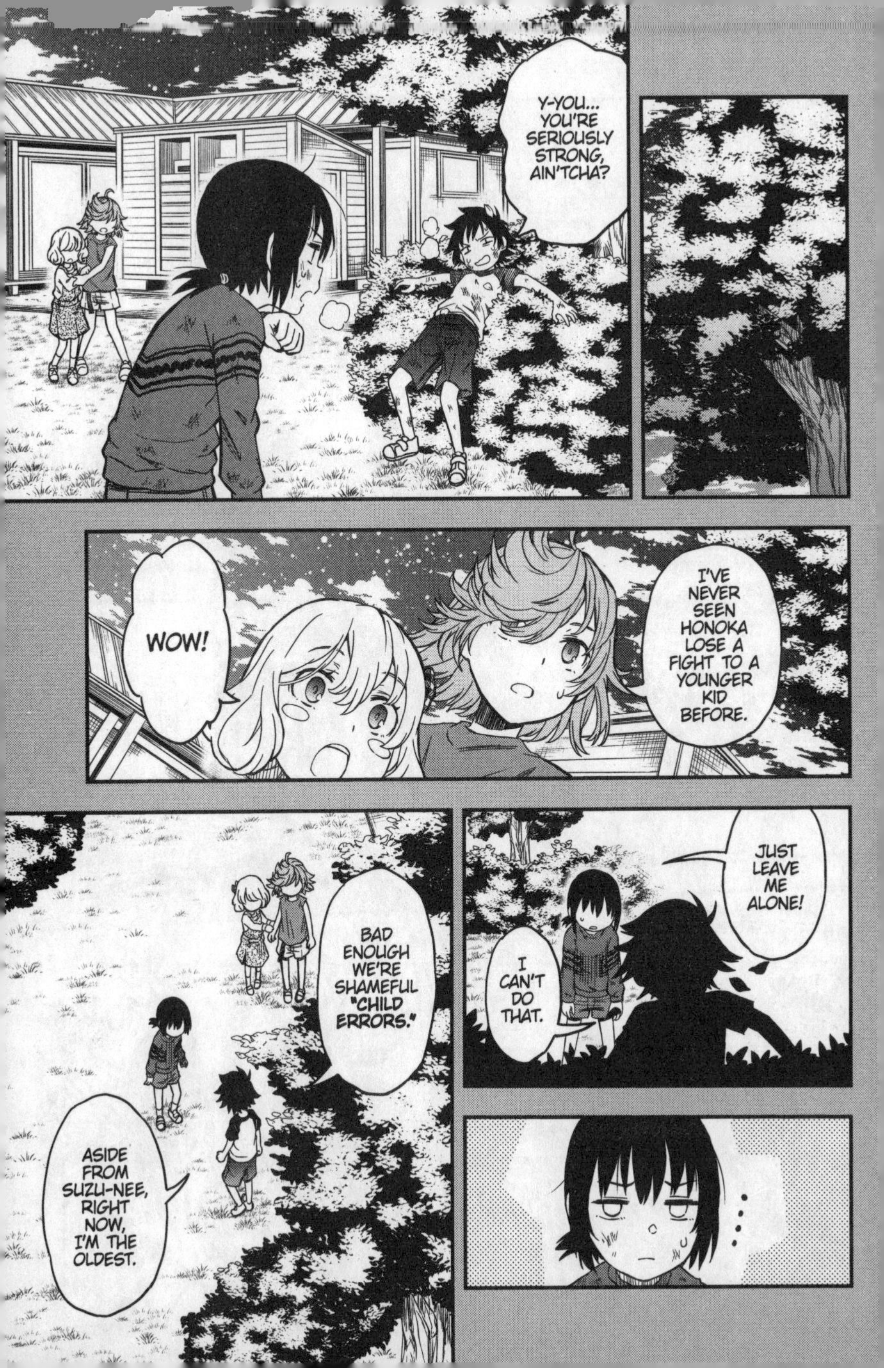
Y-YOU... YOU'RE SERIOUSLY STRONG, AIN'TCHA?
I'VE NEVER SEEN HONOKA LOSE A FIGHT TO A YOUNGER KID BEFORE.
WOW!
JUST LEAVE ME ALONE!
I CAN'T DO THAT.
...
BAD ENOUGH WE'RE SHAMEFUL "CHILD ERRORS."
ASIDE FROM SUZU-NEE, RIGHT NOW, I'M THE OLDEST.

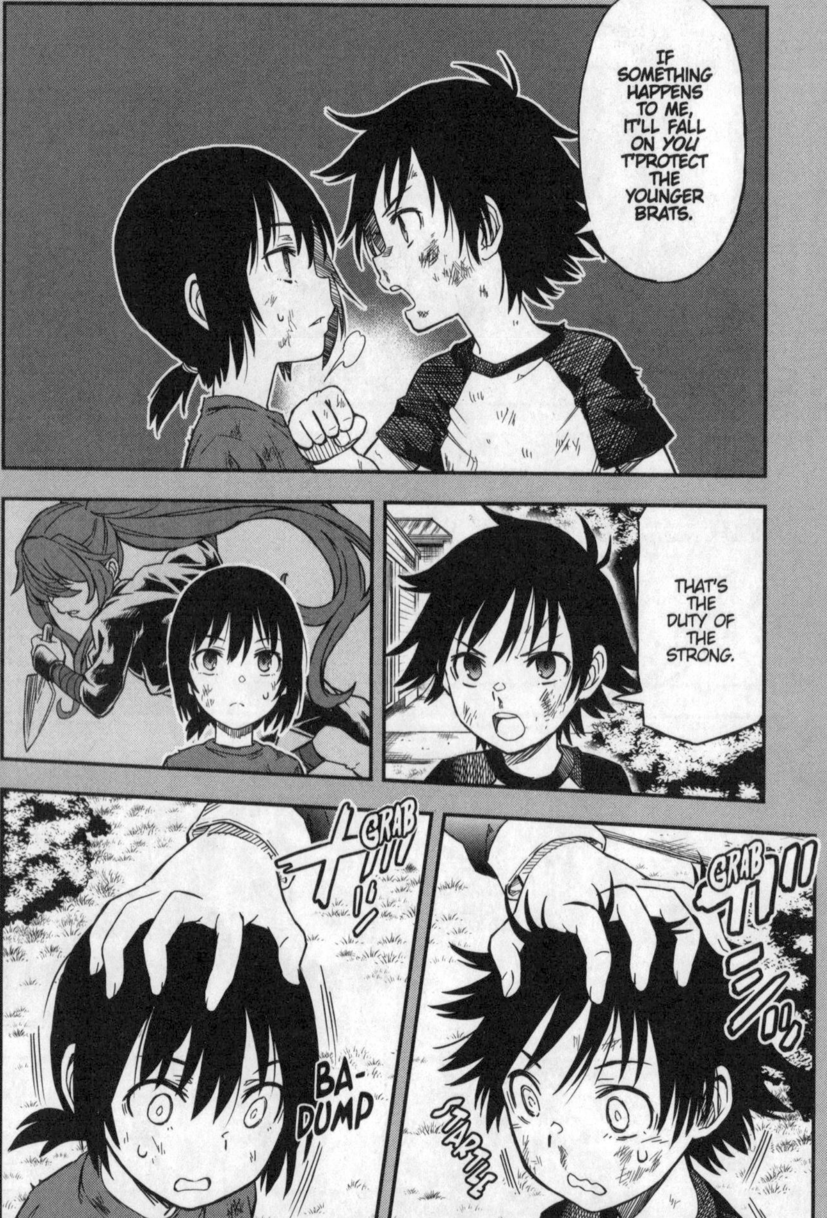
IF SOMETHING HAPPENS TO ME, IT'LL FALL ON *YOU* T'PROTECT THE YOUNGER BRATS.
THAT'S THE DUTY OF THE STRONG.
GRAB
STARTLE
GRAB
BA-DUMP

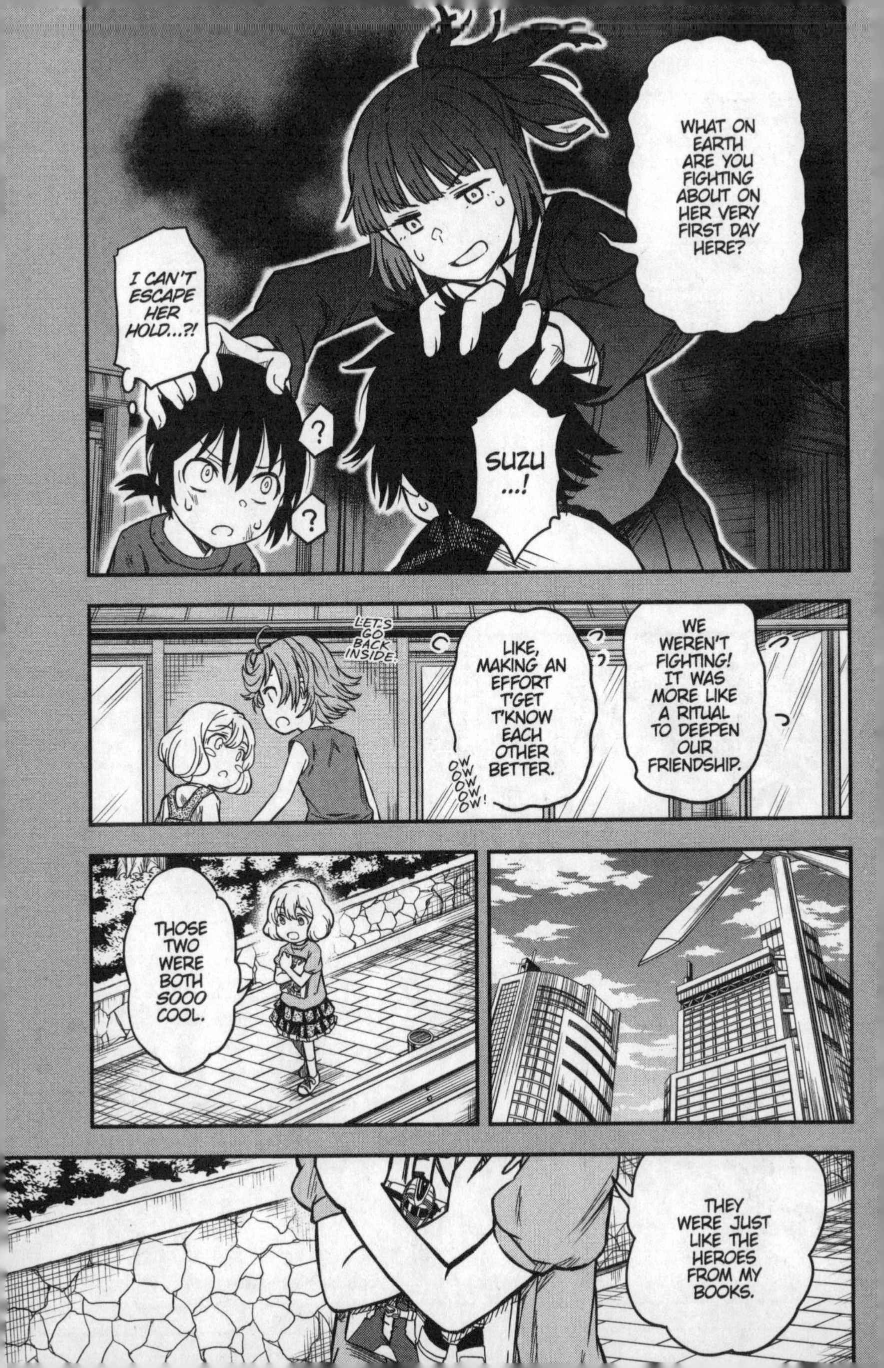
WHAT ON EARTH ARE YOU FIGHTING ABOUT ON HER VERY FIRST DAY HERE?
SUZU ...!
I CAN'T ESCAPE HER HOLD...?!
WE WEREN'T FIGHTING! IT WAS MORE LIKE A RITUAL TO DEEPEN OUR FRIENDSHIP.
LIKE, MAKING AN EFFORT T'GET T'KNOW EACH OTHER BETTER.
OW OW OW OW OW!
LET'S GO BACK INSIDE.
THOSE TWO WERE BOTH SOOO COOL.
THEY WERE JUST LIKE THE HEROES FROM MY BOOKS.

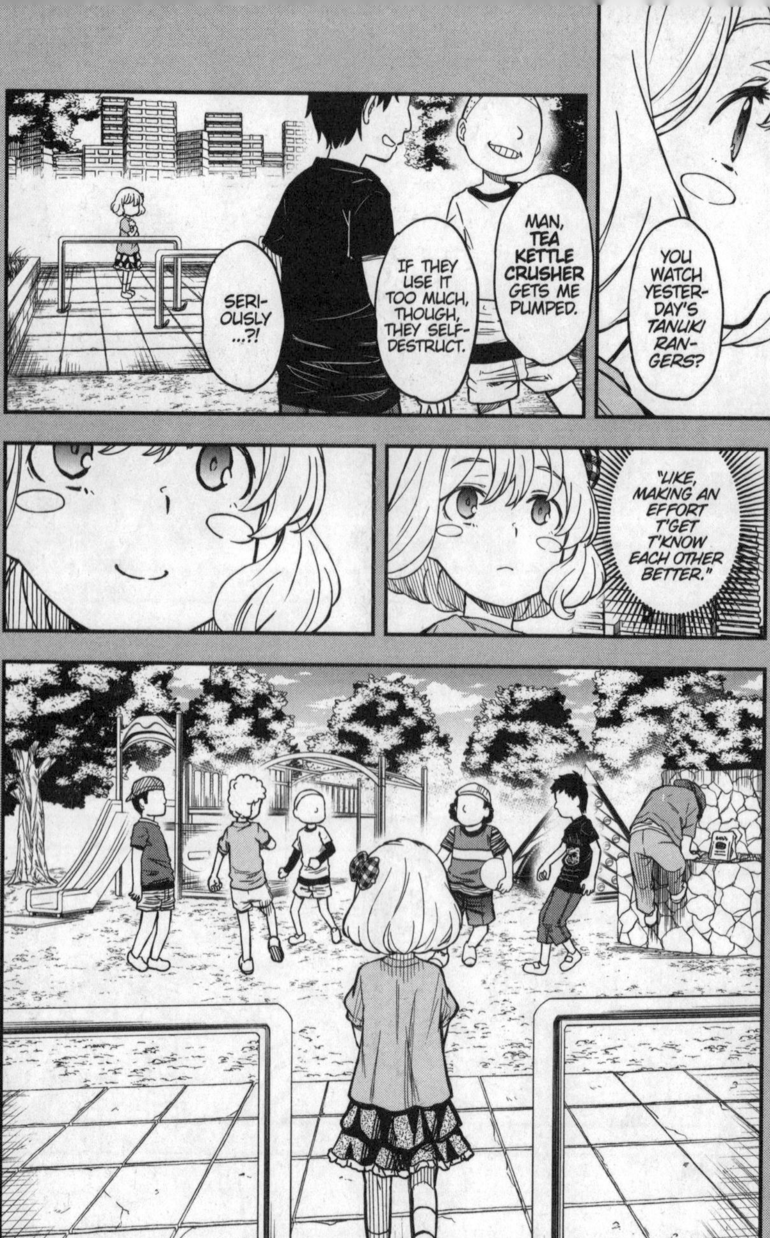
YOU WATCH YESTER-DAY'S TANUKI RAN-GERS?
MAN, TEA KETTLE CRUSHER GETS ME PUMPED.
IF THEY USE IT TOO MUCH, THOUGH, THEY SELF-DESTRUCT.
SERI-OUSLY ...?!
"LIKE, MAKING AN EFFORT T'GET T'KNOW EACH OTHER BETTER."

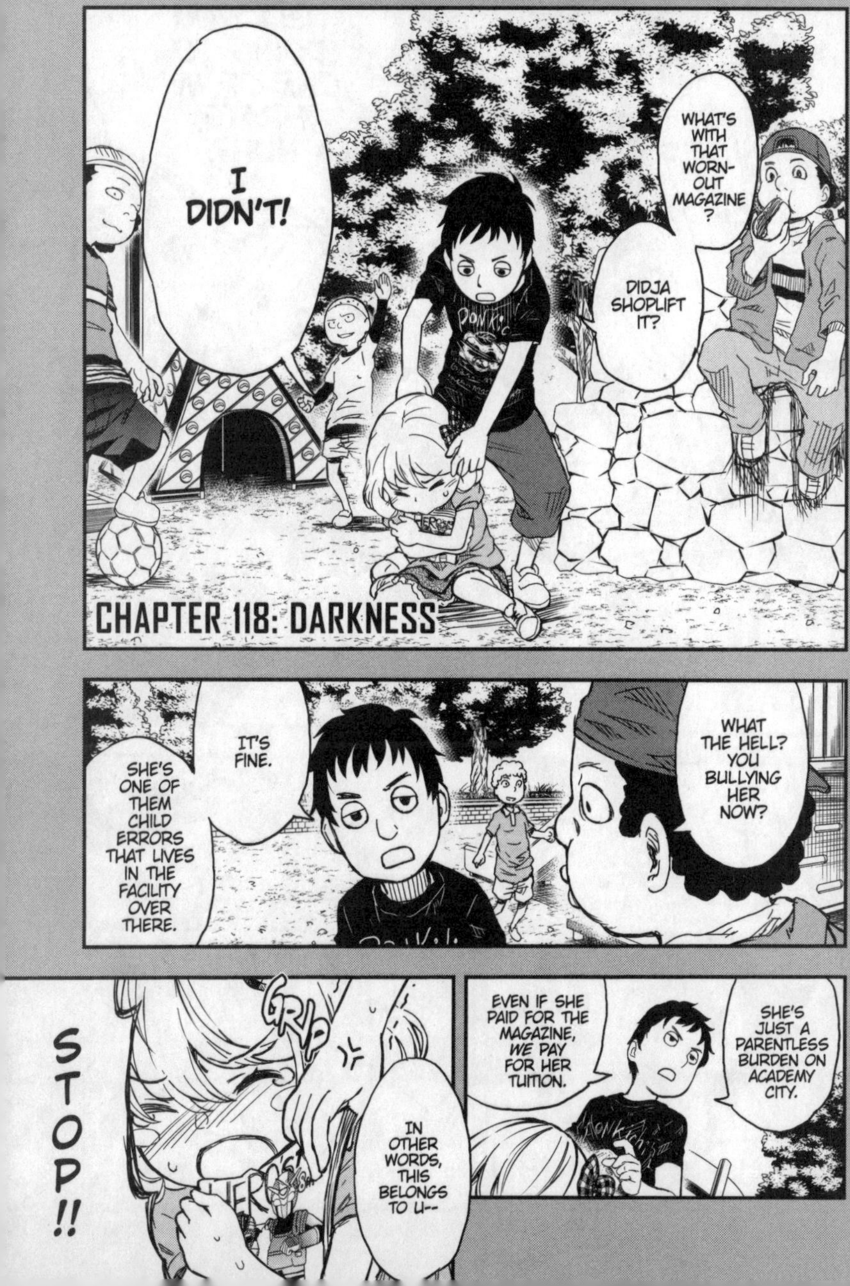
WHAT'S WITH THAT WORN-OUT MAGAZINE?
DIDJA SHOPLIFT IT?
I DIDN'T!
CHAPTER 118: DARKNESS
WHAT THE HELL? YOU BULLYING HER NOW?
IT'S FINE.
SHE'S ONE OF THEM CHILD ERRORS THAT LIVES IN THE FACILITY OVER THERE.
SHE'S JUST A PARENTLESS BURDEN ON ACADEMY CITY.
EVEN IF SHE PAID FOR THE MAGAZINE, WE PAY FOR HER TUITION.
IN OTHER WORDS, THIS BELONGS TO U--
GRIP
STOP!!

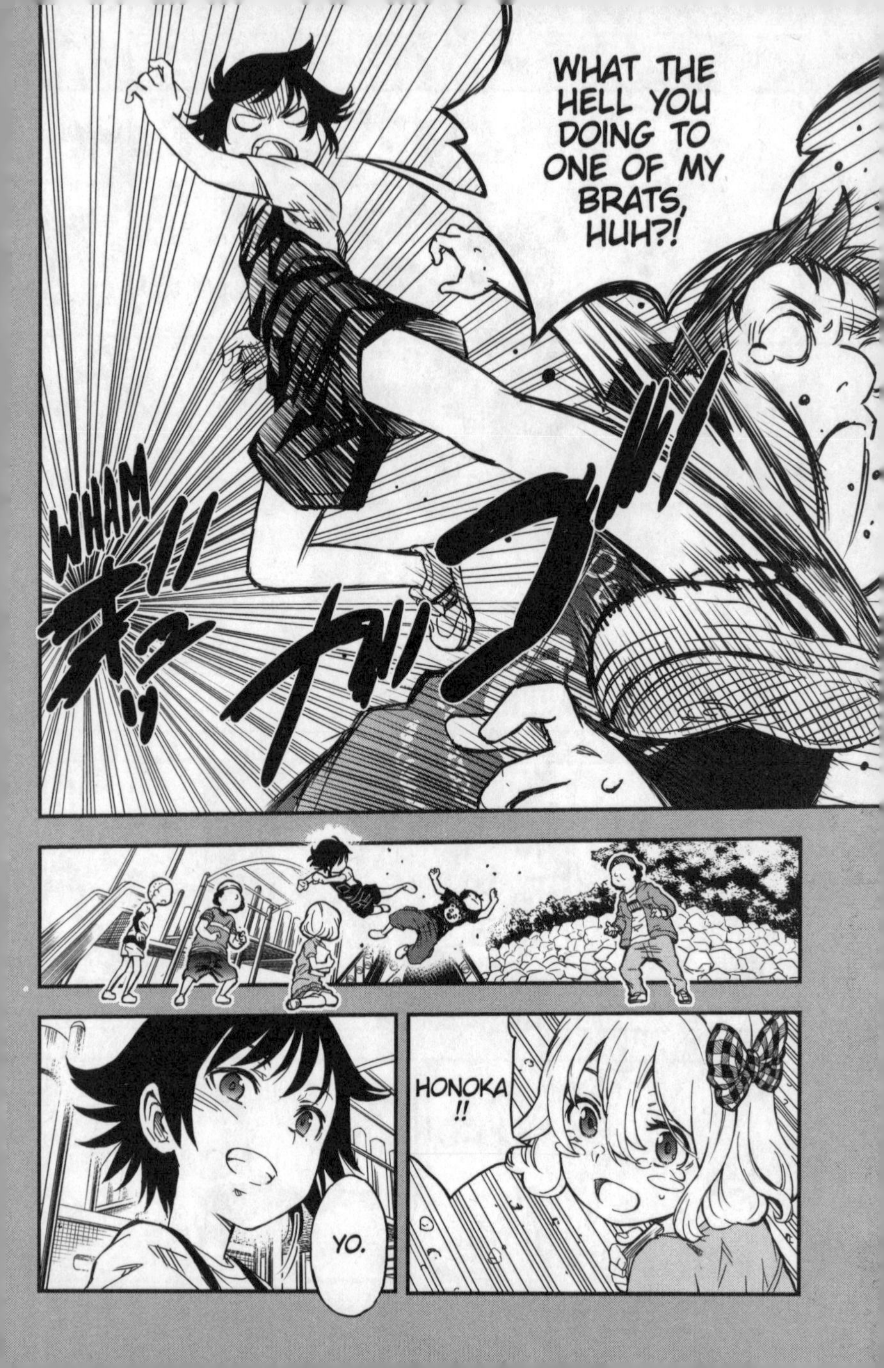
WHAT THE HELL YOU DOING TO ONE OF MY BRATS, HUH?!
WHAM
HONOKA !!
YO.

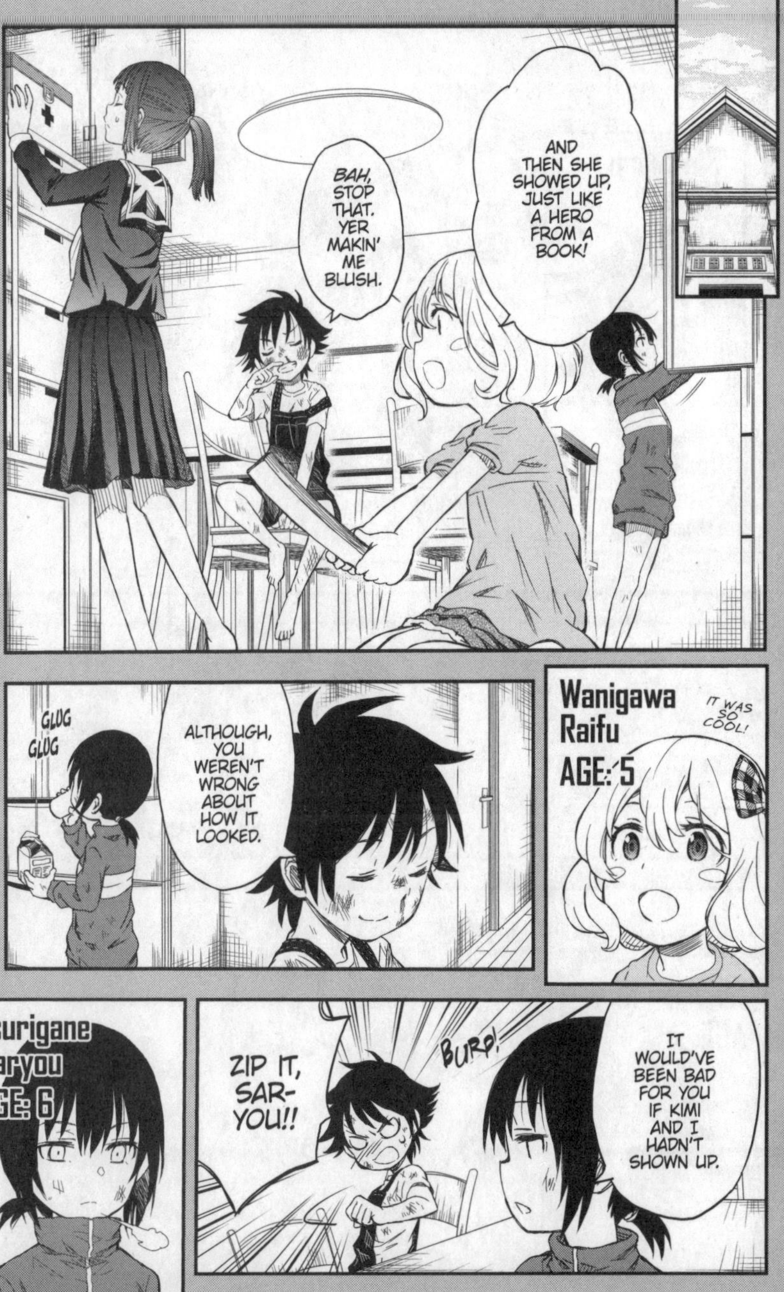
AND THEN SHE SHOWED UP, JUST LIKE A HERO FROM A BOOK!
BAH, STOP THAT. YER MAKIN' ME BLUSH.
Wanigawa Raifu
AGE: 5
IT WAS SO COOL!
ALTHOUGH, YOU WEREN'T WRONG ABOUT HOW IT LOOKED.
GLUG GLUG
IT WOULD'VE BEEN BAD FOR YOU IF KIMI AND I HADN'T SHOWN UP.
BURP!
ZIP IT, SAR-YOU!!
Tsurigane Saryou
AGE: 6

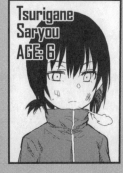

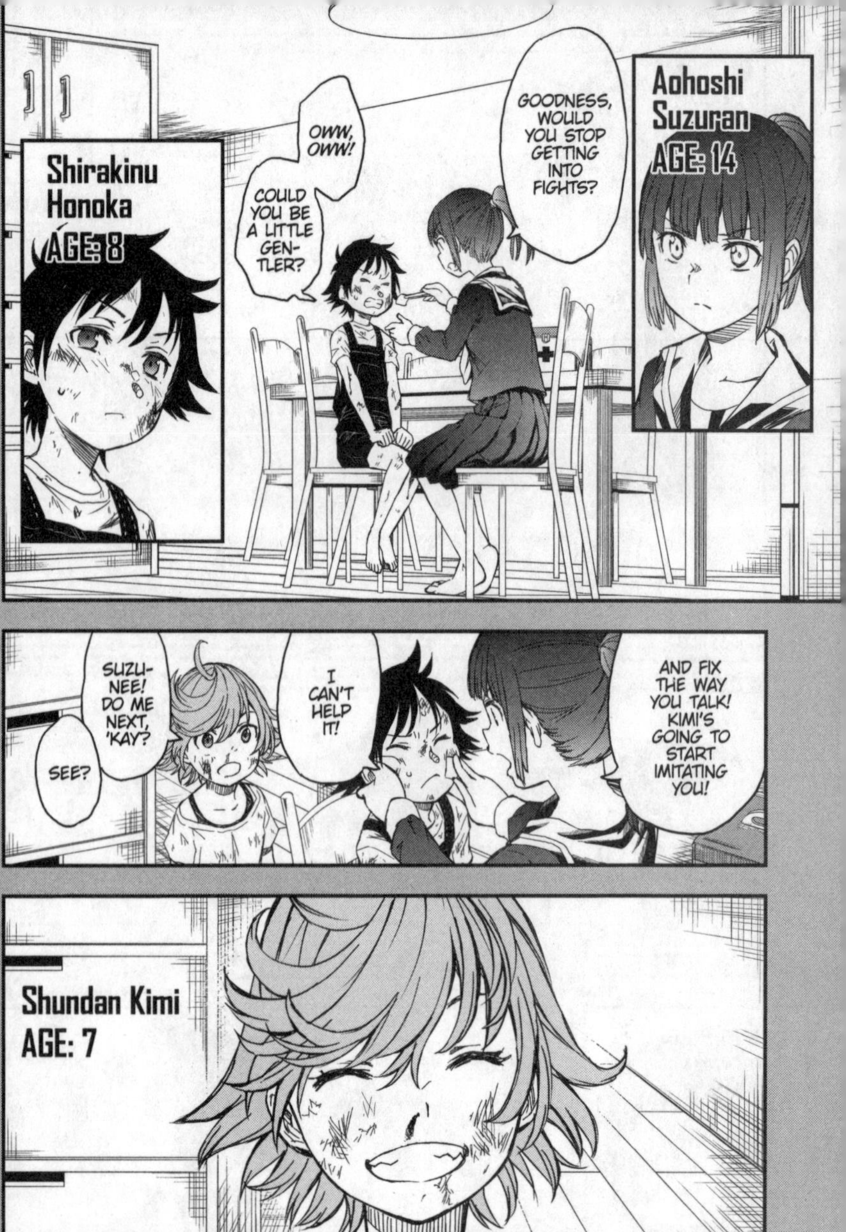
Aohoshi Suzuran
AGE: 14
GOODNESS, WOULD YOU STOP GETTING INTO FIGHTS?
OWW, OWW!
COULD YOU BE A LITTLE GEN-TLER?
Shirakinu Honoka
AGE: 8
AND FIX THE WAY YOU TALK! KIMI'S GOING TO START IMITATING YOU!
I CAN'T HELP IT!
SUZU-NEE! DO ME NEXT, 'KAY?
SEE?
Shundan Kimi
AGE: 7

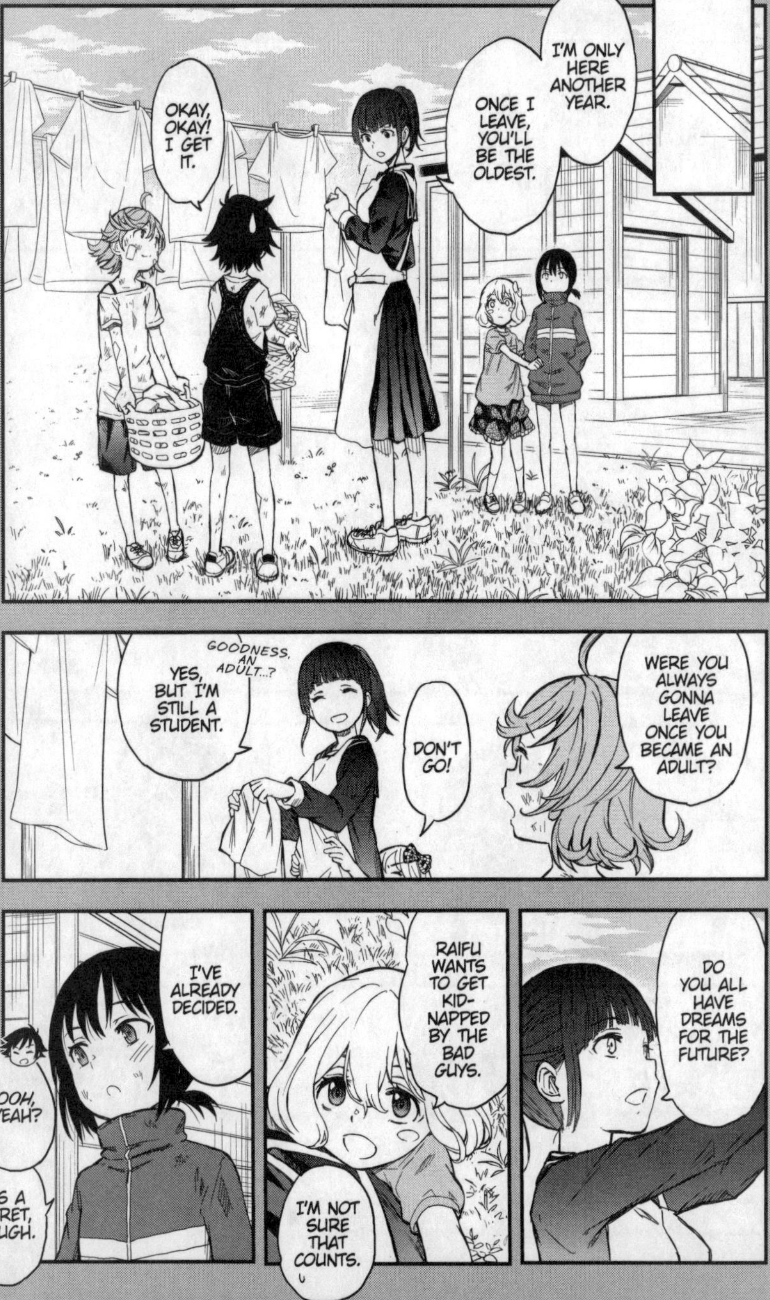
I'M ONLY HERE ANOTHER YEAR.
ONCE I LEAVE, YOU'LL BE THE OLDEST.
OKAY, OKAY! I GET IT.
WERE YOU ALWAYS GONNA LEAVE ONCE YOU BECAME AN ADULT?
GOODNESS, AN ADULT...?
YES, BUT I'M STILL A STUDENT.
DON'T GO!
DO YOU ALL HAVE DREAMS FOR THE FUTURE?
RAIFU WANTS TO GET KID-NAPPED BY THE BAD GUYS.
I'M NOT SURE THAT COUNTS.
I'VE ALREADY DECIDED.
OOH, YEAH?
IT'S A SECRET, THOUGH.

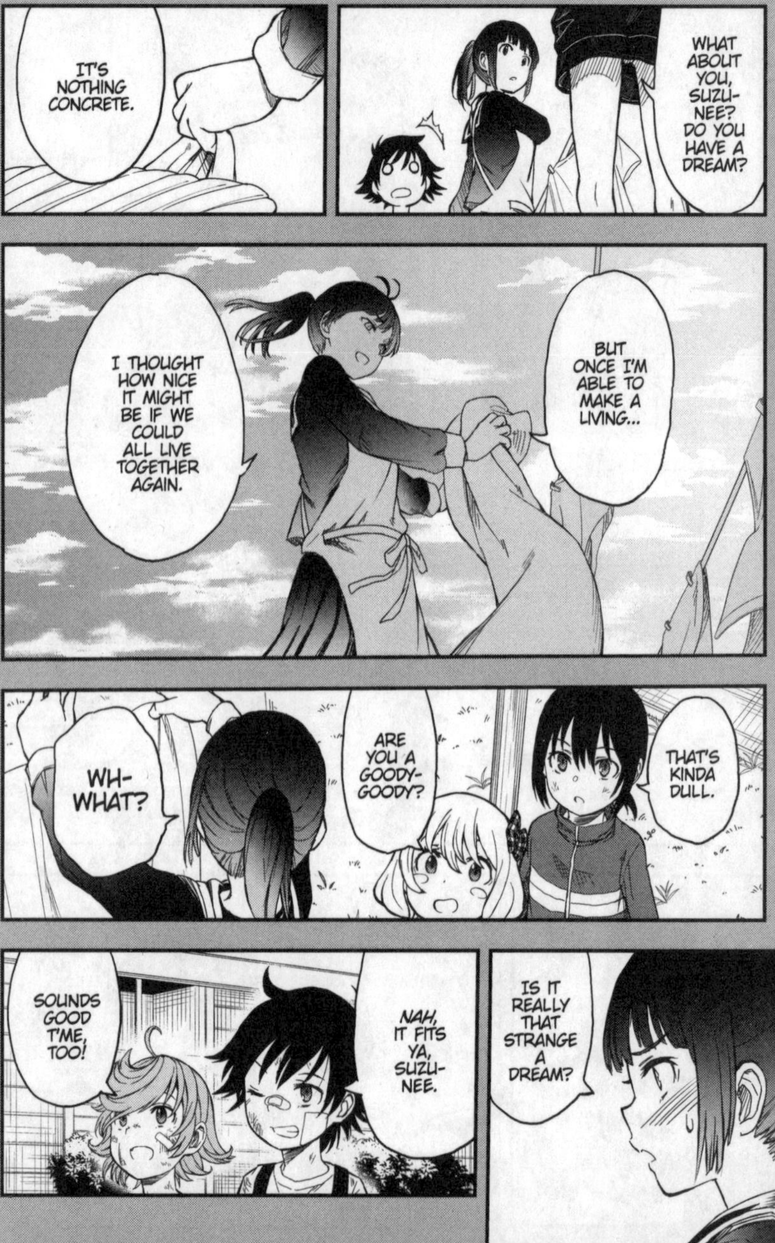
WHAT ABOUT YOU, SUZU-NEE? DO YOU HAVE A DREAM?
IT'S NOTHING CONCRETE.
BUT ONCE I'M ABLE TO MAKE A LIVING...
I THOUGHT HOW NICE IT MIGHT BE IF WE COULD ALL LIVE TOGETHER AGAIN.
THAT'S KINDA DULL.
ARE YOU A GOODY-GOODY?
WH-WHAT?
IS IT REALLY THAT STRANGE A DREAM?
NAH, IT FITS YA, SUZU-NEE.
SOUNDS GOOD T'ME, TOO!

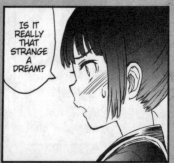

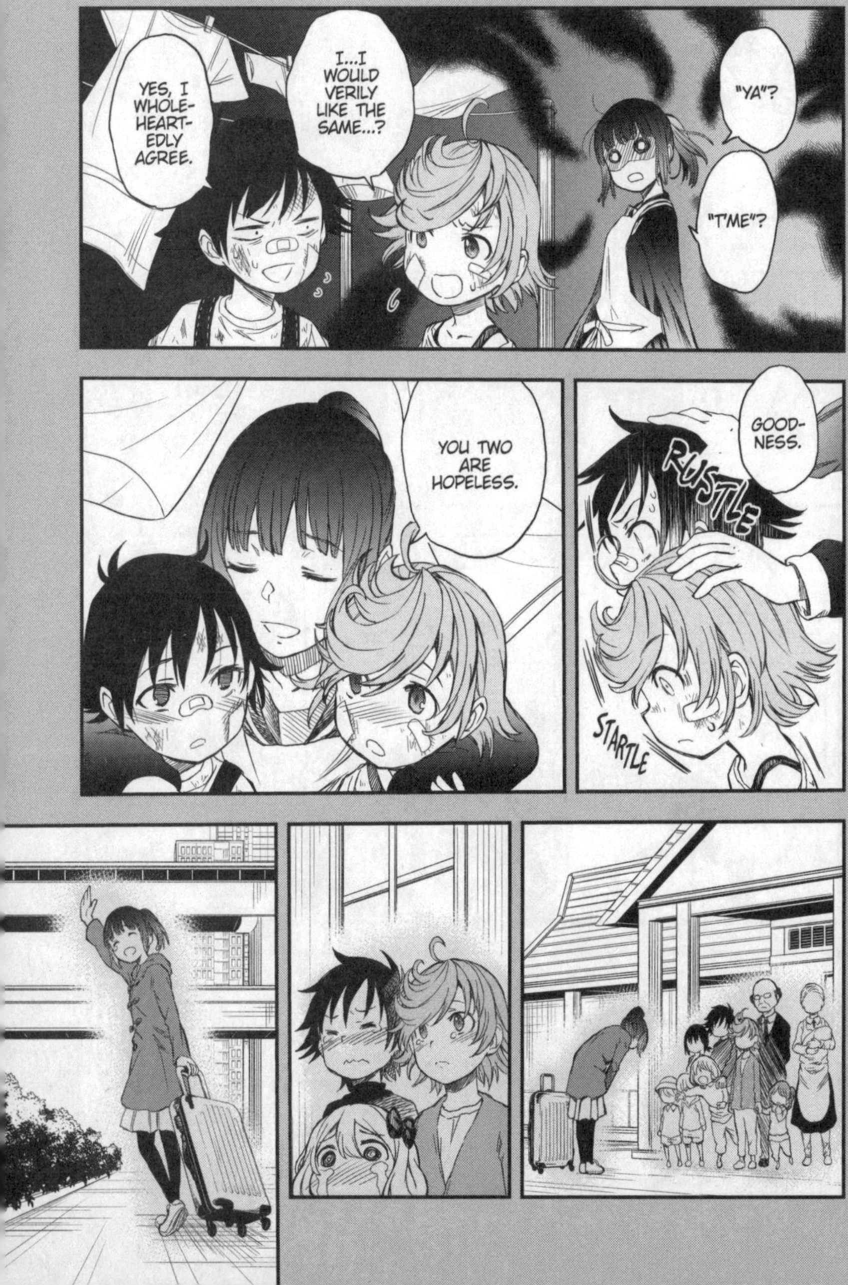
"YA"?
"T'ME"?
I...I WOULD VERILY LIKE THE SAME...?
YES, I WHOLE-HEART-EDLY AGREE.
GOOD-NESS.
RUSTLE
STARTLE
YOU TWO ARE HOPELESS.

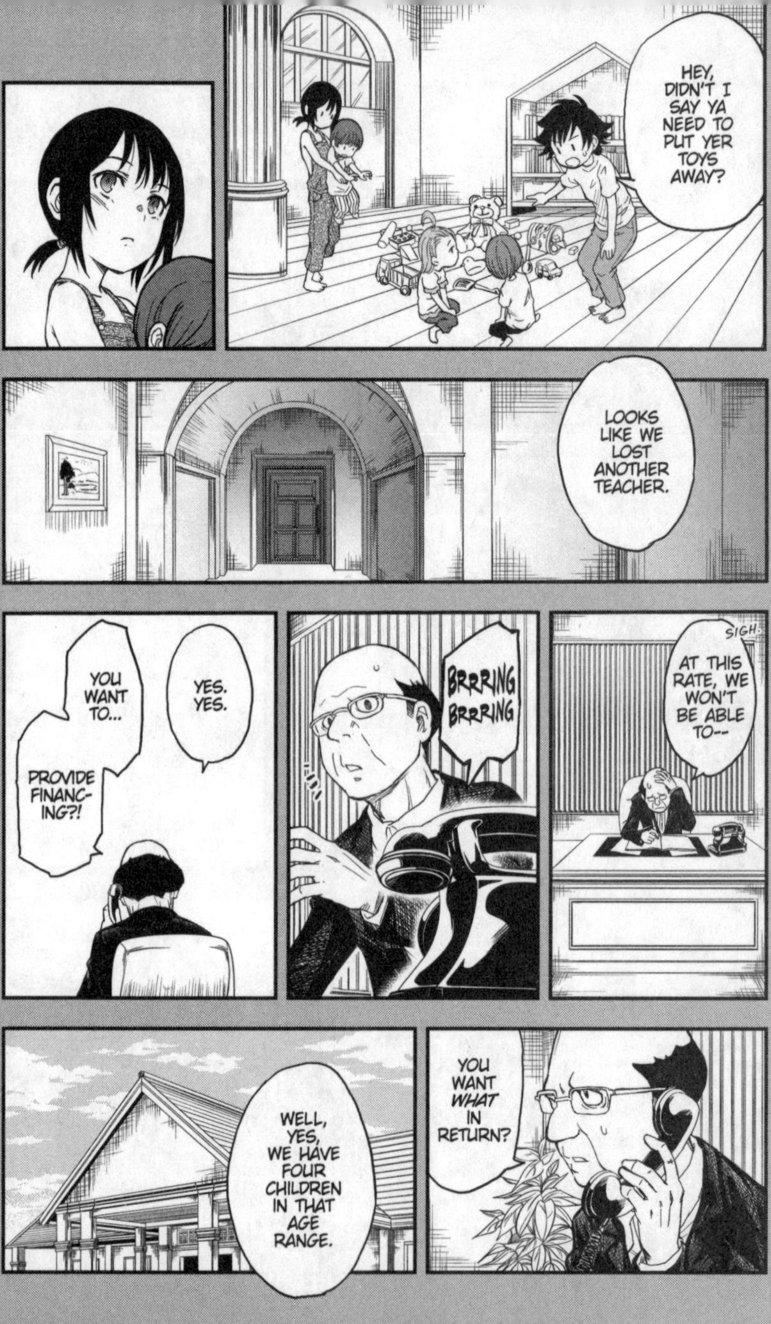
HEY, DIDN'T I SAY YA NEED TO PUT YER TOYS AWAY?
LOOKS LIKE WE LOST ANOTHER TEACHER.
SIGH.
AT THIS RATE, WE WON'T BE ABLE TO--
BRRRING BRRRING
YES. YES.
YOU WANT TO...
PROVIDE FINANCING?!
YOU WANT *WHAT* IN RETURN?
WELL, YES, WE HAVE FOUR CHILDREN IN THAT AGE RANGE.

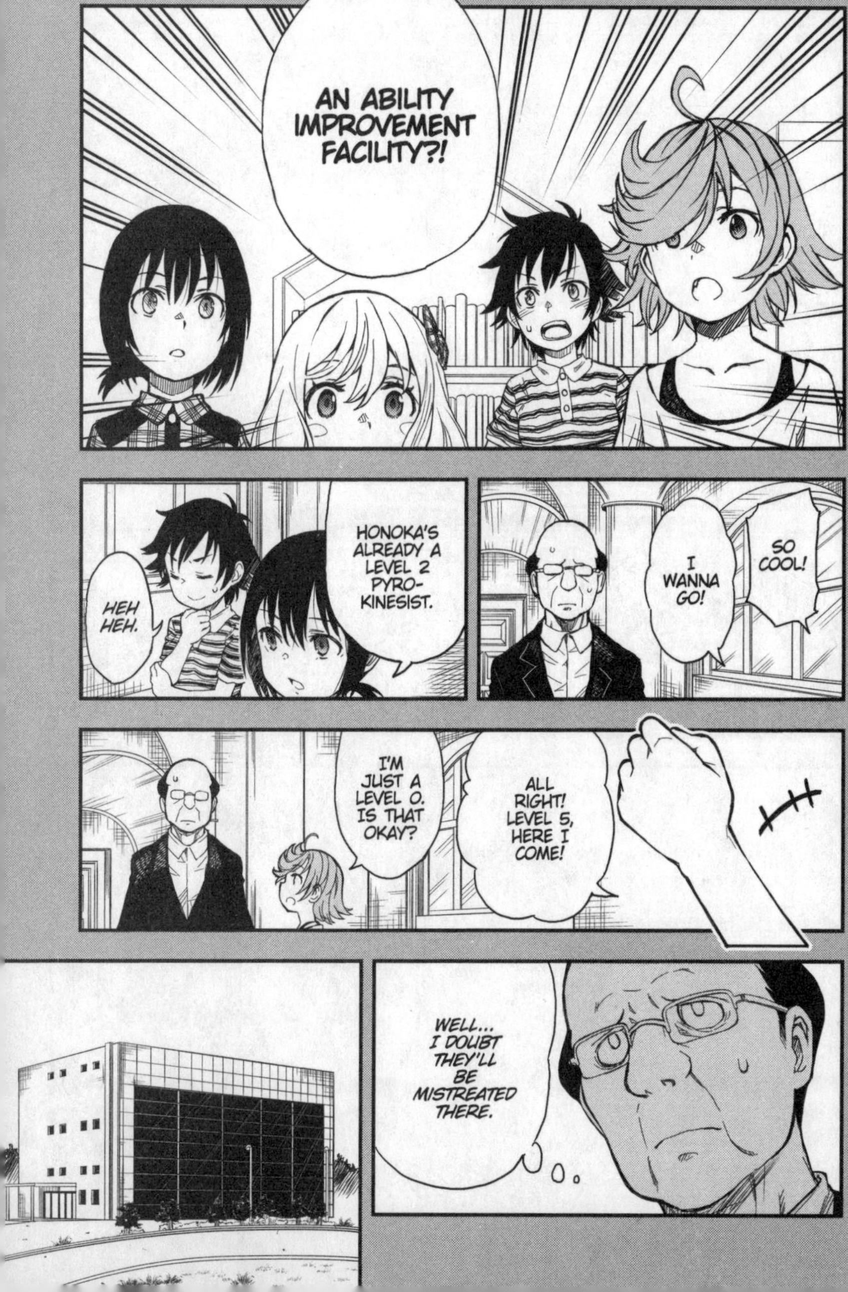
AN ABILITY IMPROVEMENT FACILITY?!
SO COOL!
I WANNA GO!
HONOKA'S ALREADY A LEVEL 2 PYRO-KINESIST.
HEH HEH.
ALL RIGHT! LEVEL 5, HERE I COME!
I'M JUST A LEVEL 0. IS THAT OKAY?
WELL... I DOUBT THEY'LL BE MISTREATED THERE.

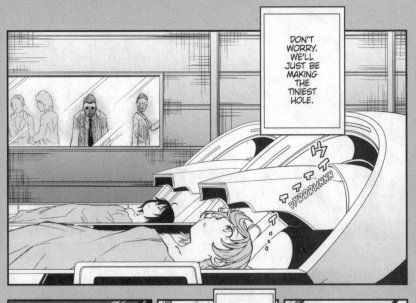

DON'T WORRY. WE'LL JUST BE MAKING THE TINIEST HOLE.

WE CAN'T GATHER ACCURATE DATA IF WE INJURE YOU, AFTER ALL.

CLOSE

YAY, YAY! I'VE FINALLY BECOME A LEVEL 2!

OH, NICE...

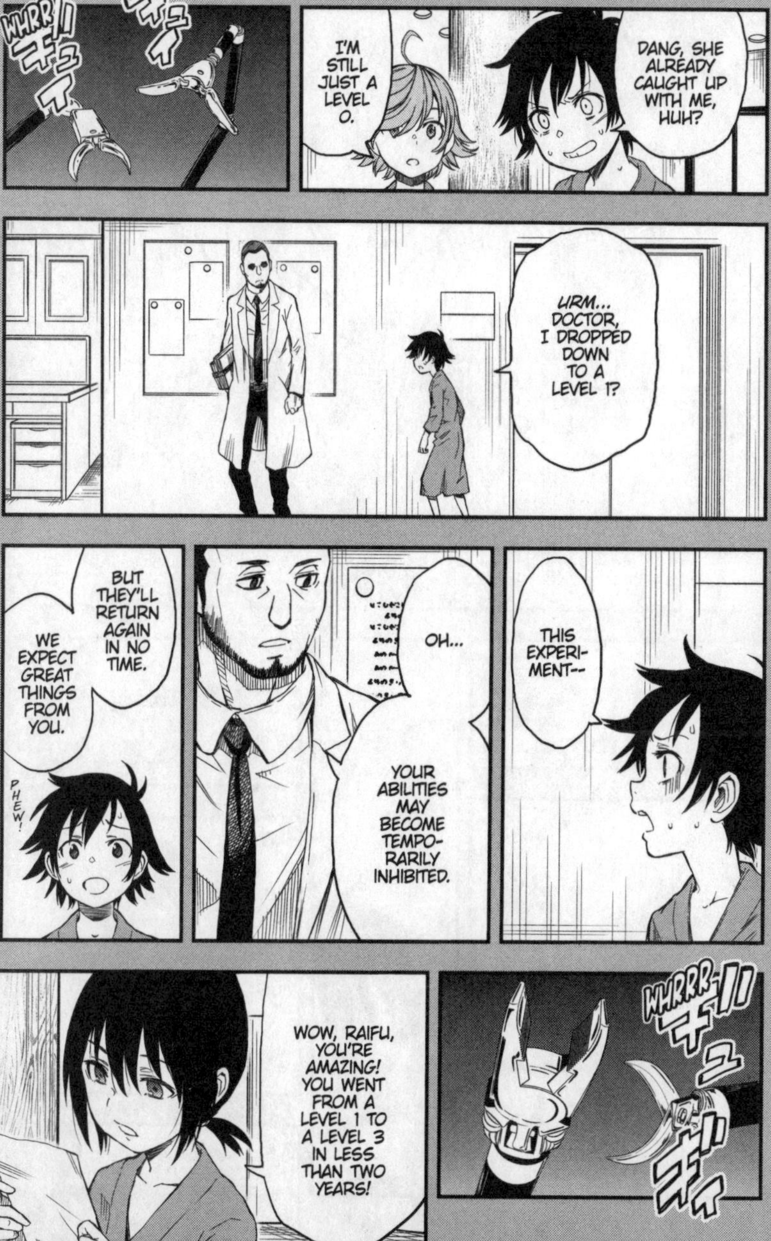
DANG, SHE ALREADY CAUGHT UP WITH ME, HUH?
I'M STILL JUST A LEVEL 0.
WHRR!!
WHRR!!
URM... DOCTOR, I DROPPED DOWN TO A LEVEL 1?
THIS EXPERIMENT--
OH...
YOUR ABILITIES MAY BECOME TEMPORARILY INHIBITED.
BUT THEY'LL RETURN AGAIN IN NO TIME.
WE EXPECT GREAT THINGS FROM YOU.
PHEW!
WHRRR!!
WOW, RAIFU, YOU'RE AMAZING! YOU WENT FROM A LEVEL 1 TO A LEVEL 3 IN LESS THAN TWO YEARS!

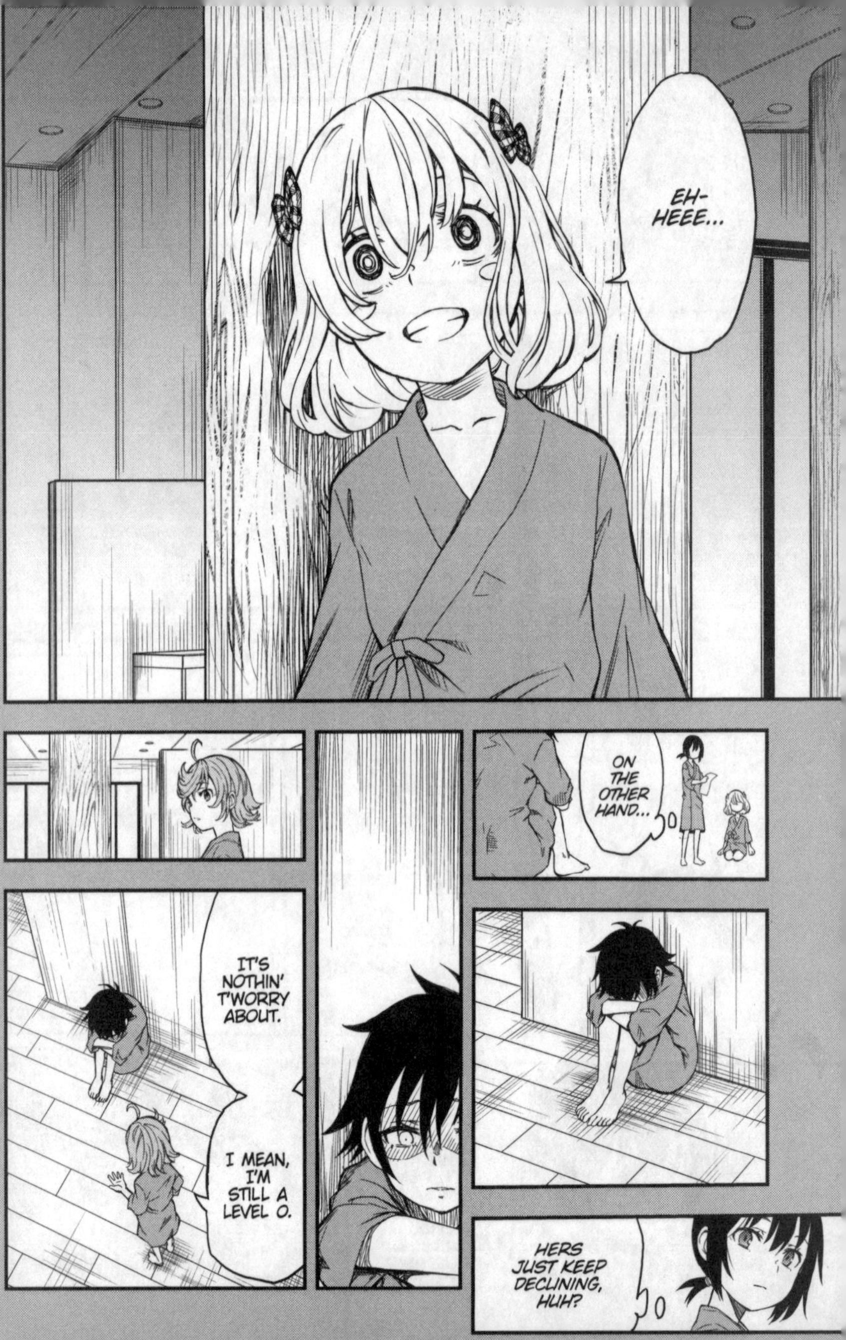
EH-HEEE...
ON THE OTHER HAND...
HERS JUST KEEP DECLINING, HUH?
IT'S NOTHIN' T'WORRY ABOUT.
I MEAN, I'M STILL A LEVEL 0.

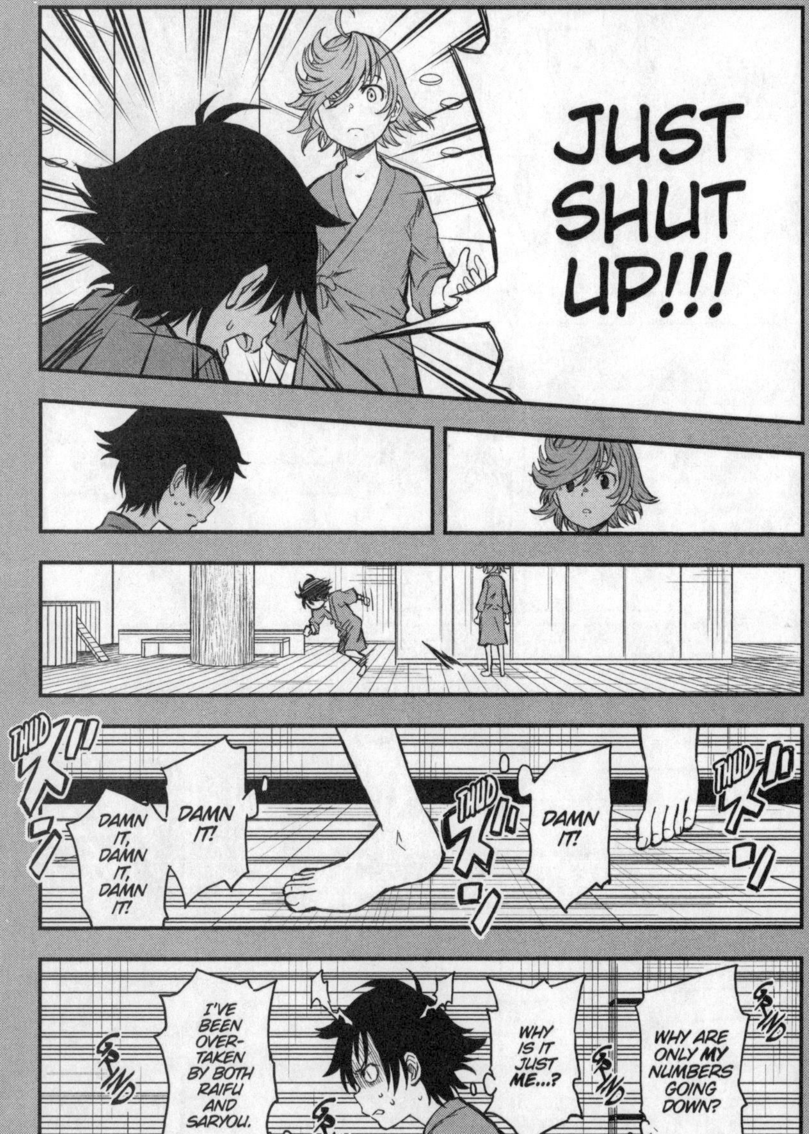

JUST SHUT UP!!!
THUD
DAMN IT!
THUD
DAMN IT!
DAMN IT, DAMN IT, DAMN IT!
THUD
GRIND
WHY ARE ONLY MY NUMBERS GOING DOWN?
GRIND
WHY IS IT JUST ME...?
GRIND
I'VE BEEN OVER-TAKEN BY BOTH RAIFU AND SARYOU.
GRIND

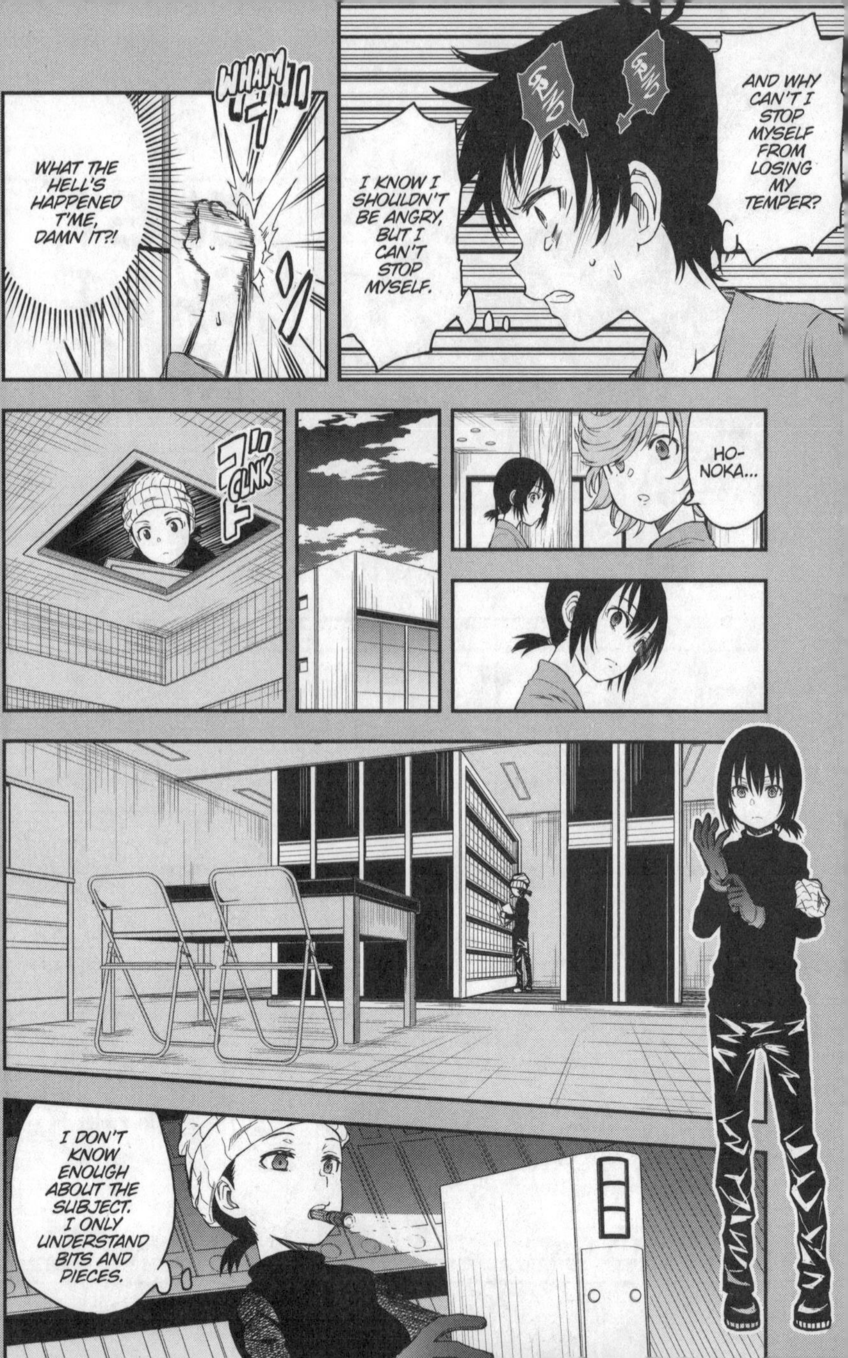
GRIND
GRIND
AND WHY CAN'T I STOP MYSELF FROM LOSING MY TEMPER?
I KNOW I SHOULDN'T BE ANGRY, BUT I CAN'T STOP MYSELF.
WHAM
WHAT THE HELL'S HAPPENED T'ME, DAMN IT?!
HO-NOKA...
CLNK
I DON'T KNOW ENOUGH ABOUT THE SUBJECT. I ONLY UNDERSTAND BITS AND PIECES.

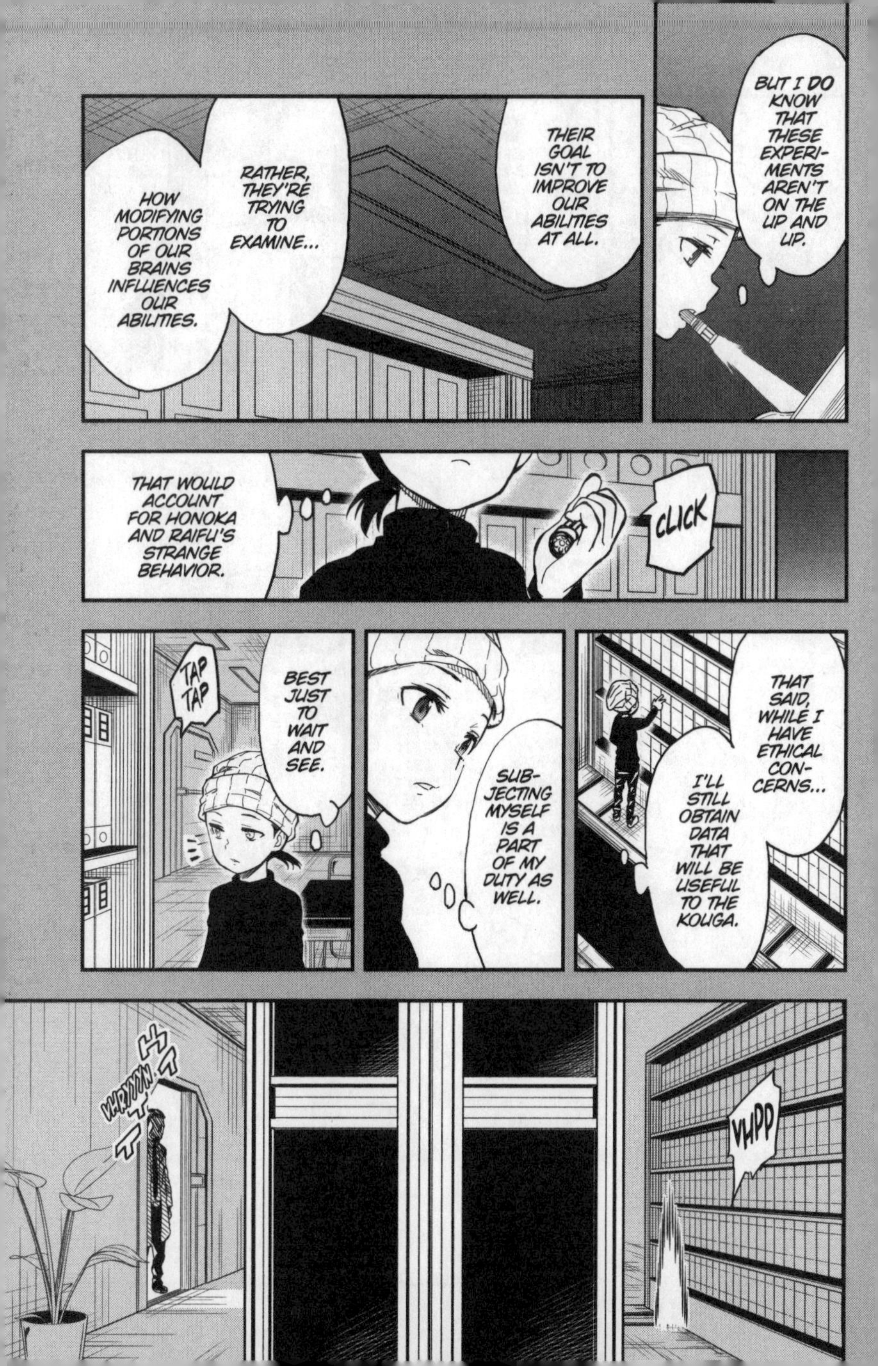
BUT I DO KNOW THAT THESE EXPERIMENTS AREN'T ON THE UP AND UP.
THEIR GOAL ISN'T TO IMPROVE OUR ABILITIES AT ALL.
RATHER, THEY'RE TRYING TO EXAMINE...
HOW MODIFYING PORTIONS OF OUR BRAINS INFLUENCES OUR ABILITIES.
CLICK
THAT WOULD ACCOUNT FOR HONOKA AND RAIFU'S STRANGE BEHAVIOR.
THAT SAID, WHILE I HAVE ETHICAL CONCERNS...
I'LL STILL OBTAIN DATA THAT WILL BE USEFUL TO THE KOUGA.
SUBJECTING MYSELF IS A PART OF MY DUTY AS WELL.
BEST JUST TO WAIT AND SEE.
TAP TAP
VHPP
VHRYYYN

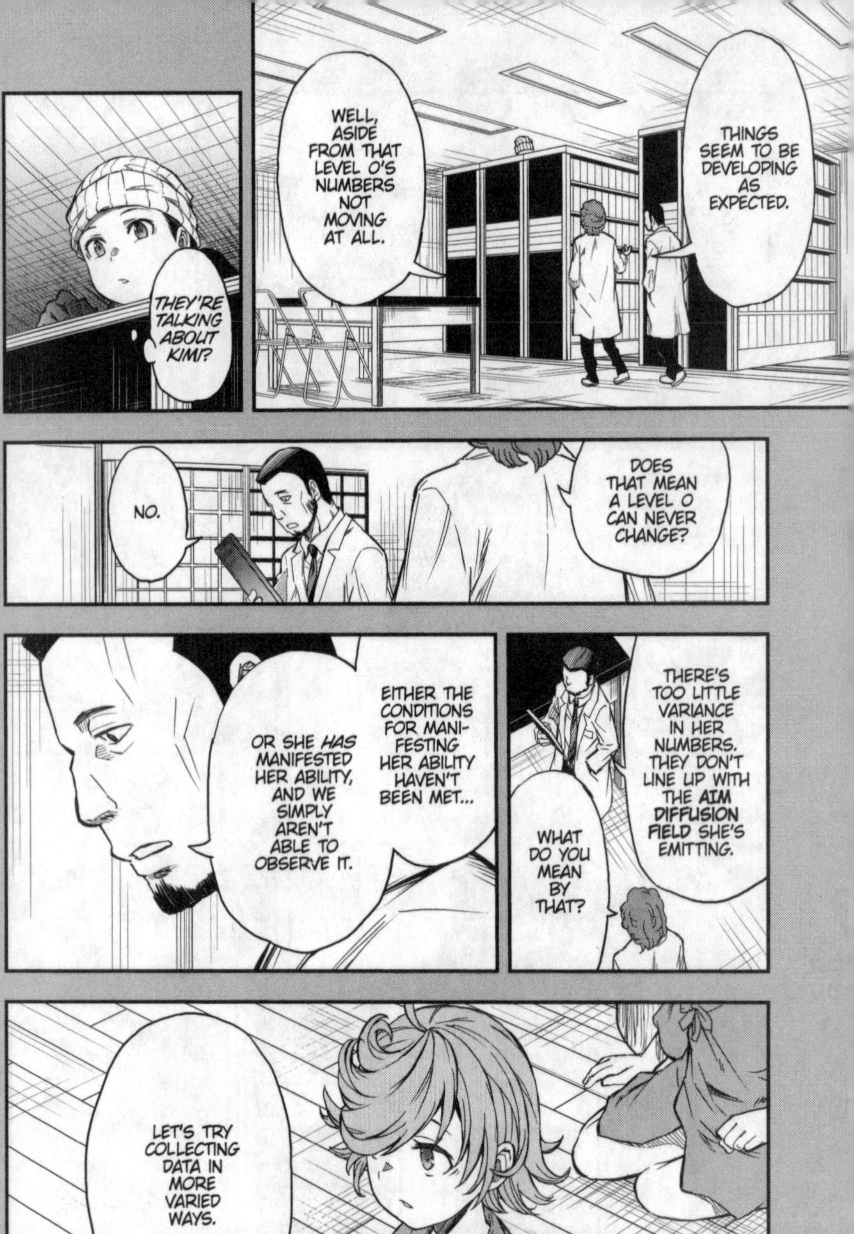
THINGS SEEM TO BE DEVELOPING AS EXPECTED.
WELL, ASIDE FROM THAT LEVEL 0'S NUMBERS NOT MOVING AT ALL.
THEY'RE TALKING ABOUT KIMI?
DOES THAT MEAN A LEVEL 0 CAN NEVER CHANGE?
NO.
THERE'S TOO LITTLE VARIANCE IN HER NUMBERS. THEY DON'T LINE UP WITH THE AIM DIFFUSION FIELD SHE'S EMITTING.
WHAT DO YOU MEAN BY THAT?
EITHER THE CONDITIONS FOR MANI-FESTING HER ABILITY HAVEN'T BEEN MET...
OR SHE *HAS* MANIFESTED HER ABILITY, AND WE SIMPLY AREN'T ABLE TO OBSERVE IT.
LET'S TRY COLLECTING DATA IN MORE VARIED WAYS.

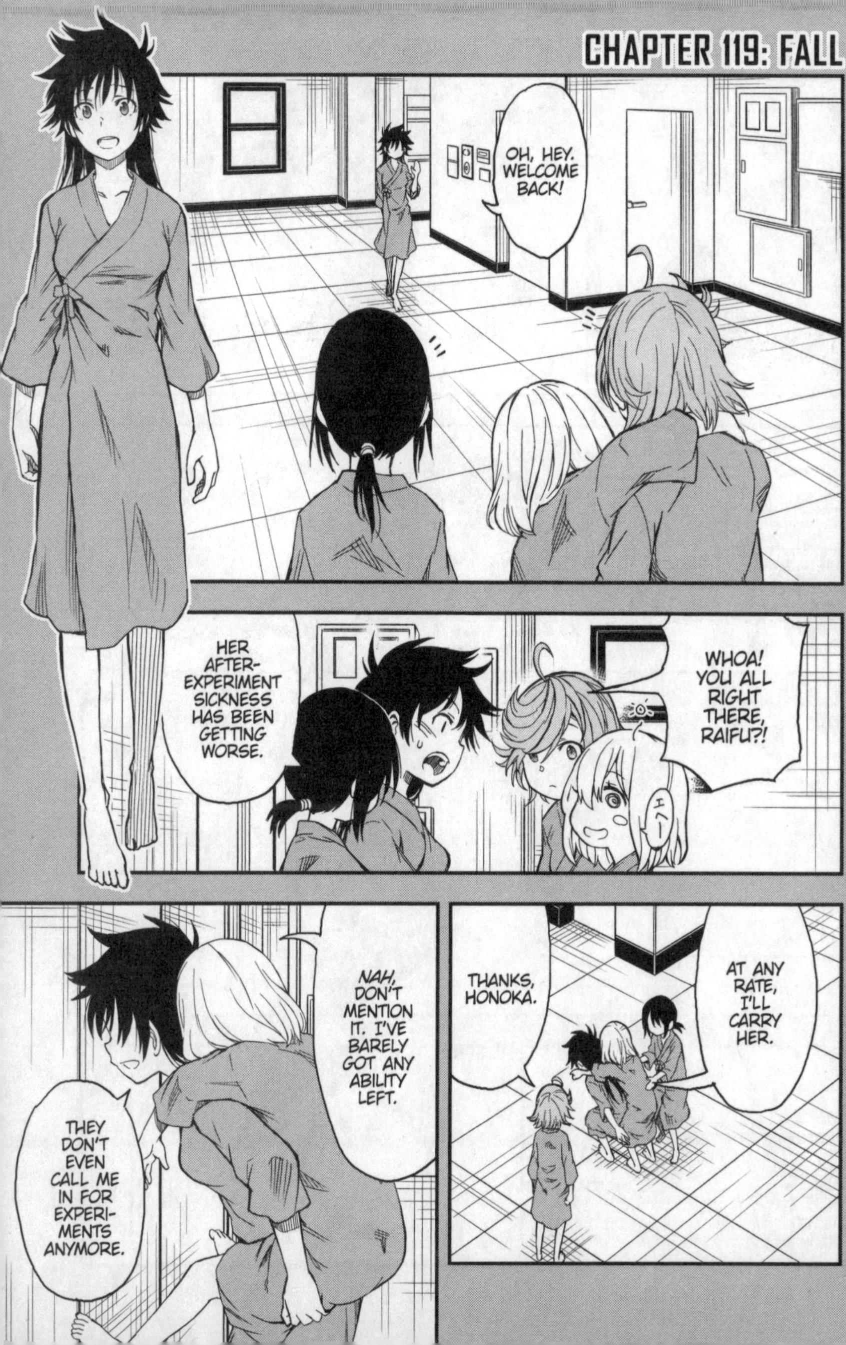
CHAPTER 119: FALL
OH, HEY. WELCOME BACK!
WHOA! YOU ALL RIGHT THERE, RAIFU?!
エヘー
HER AFTER-EXPERIMENT SICKNESS HAS BEEN GETTING WORSE.
AT ANY RATE, I'LL CARRY HER.
THANKS, HONOKA.
NAH, DON'T MENTION IT. I'VE BARELY GOT ANY ABILITY LEFT.
THEY DON'T EVEN CALL ME IN FOR EXPERIMENTS ANYMORE.

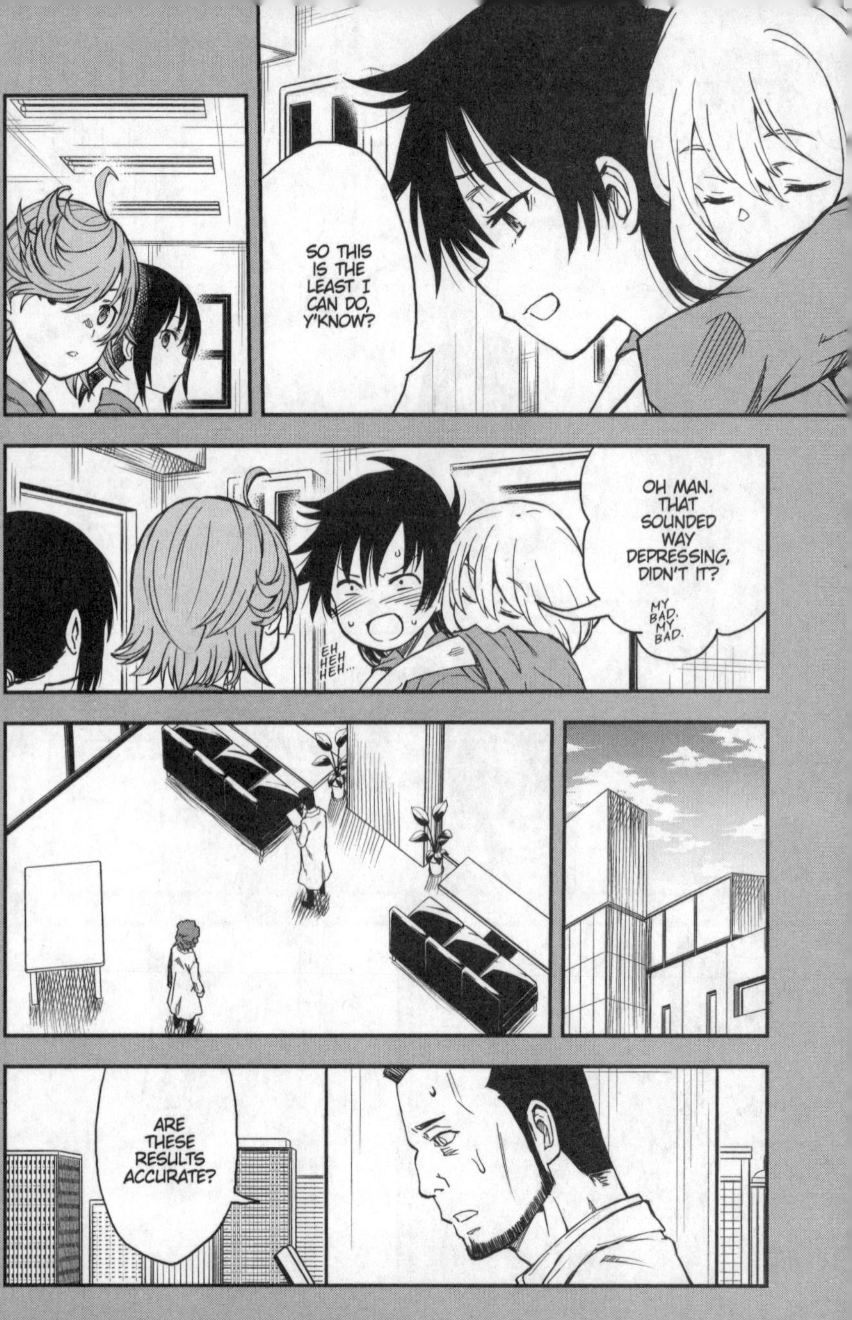
SO THIS IS THE LEAST I CAN DO, Y'KNOW?
OH MAN. THAT SOUNDED WAY DEPRESSING, DIDN'T IT?
MY BAD, MY BAD.
EH HEH HEH...
ARE THESE RESULTS ACCURATE?

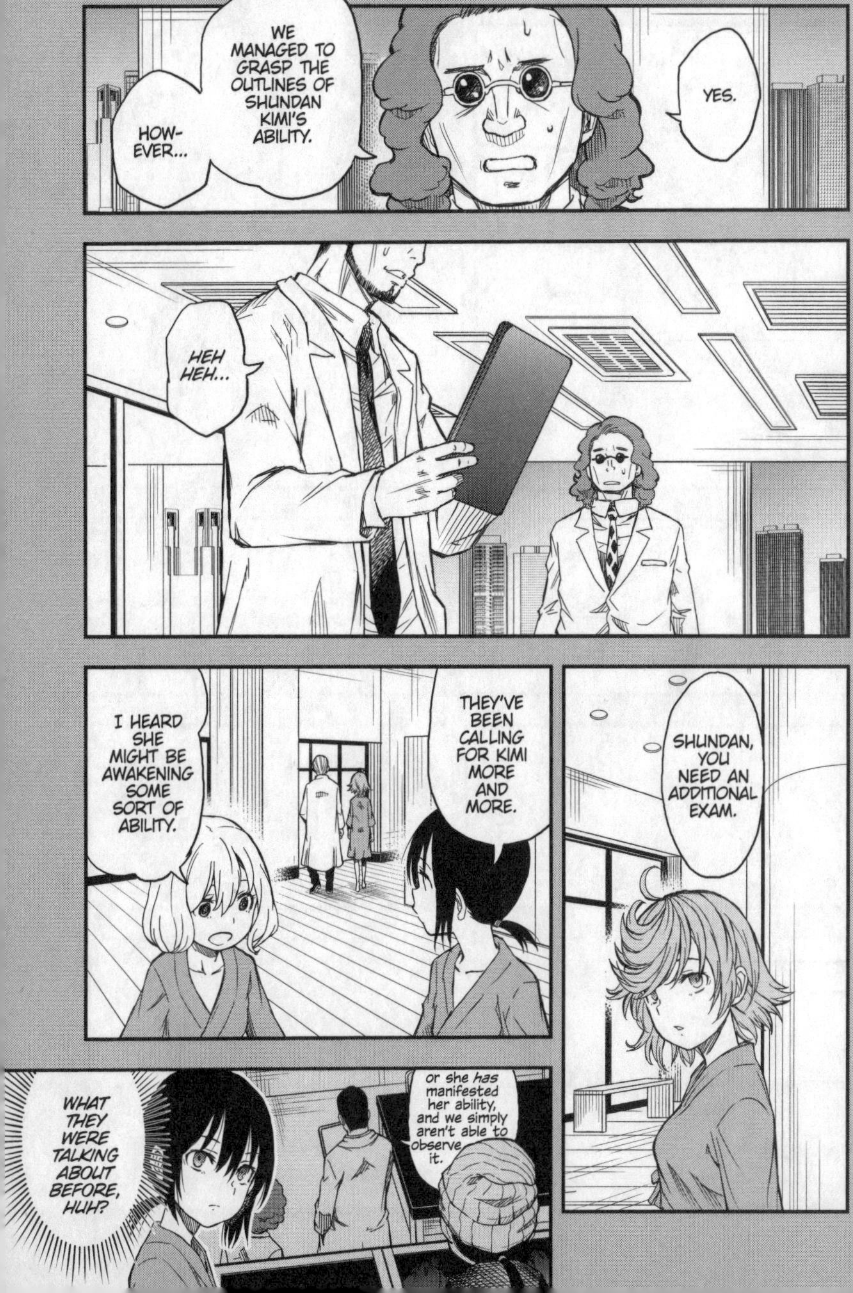
YES.
WE MANAGED TO GRASP THE OUTLINES OF SHUNDAN KIMI'S ABILITY.
HOW-EVER...
HEH HEH...
SHUNDAN, YOU NEED AN ADDITIONAL EXAM.
THEY'VE BEEN CALLING FOR KIMI MORE AND MORE.
I HEARD SHE MIGHT BE AWAKENING SOME SORT OF ABILITY.
or she *has* manifested her ability, and we simply aren't able to observe it.
WHAT THEY WERE TALKING ABOUT BEFORE, HUH?

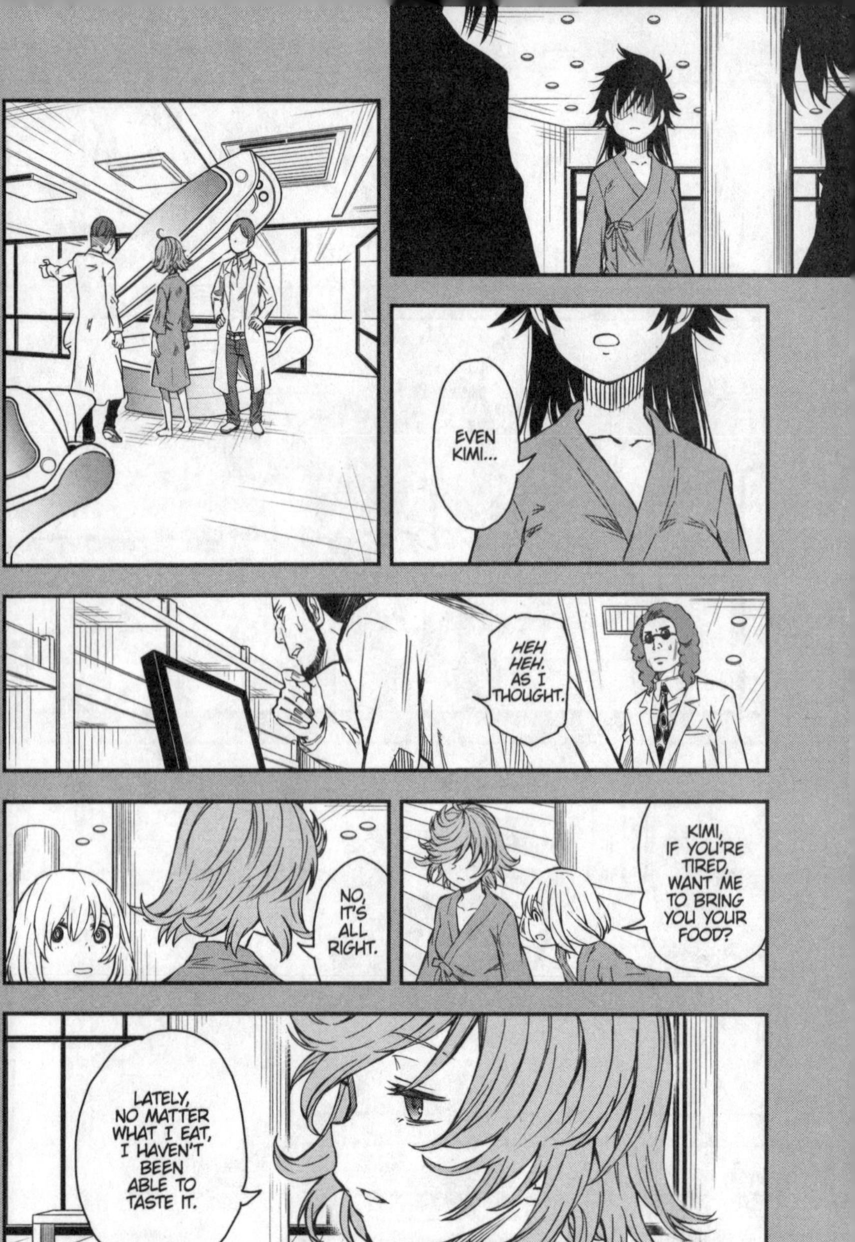
EVEN KIMI...
HEH HEH. AS I THOUGHT.
KIMI, IF YOU'RE TIRED, WANT ME TO BRING YOU YOUR FOOD?
NO, IT'S ALL RIGHT.
LATELY, NO MATTER WHAT I EAT, I HAVEN'T BEEN ABLE TO TASTE IT.

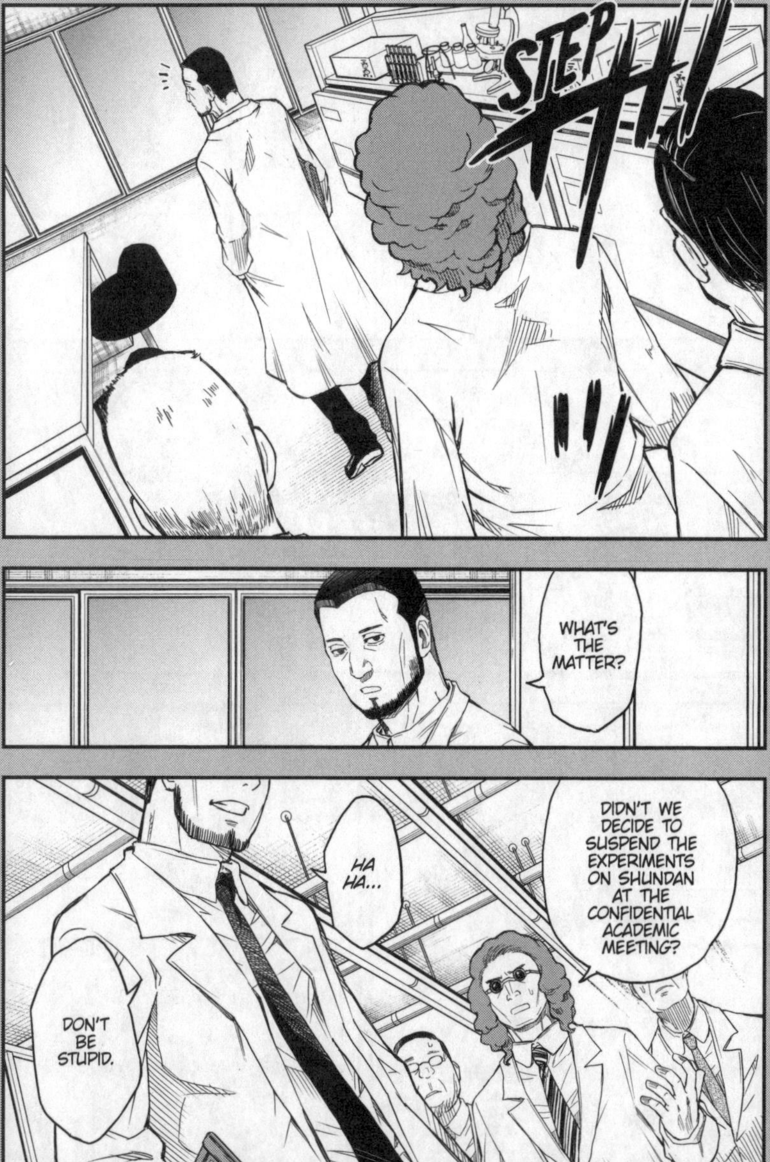
STEP!!
WHAT'S THE MATTER?
DIDN'T WE DECIDE TO SUSPEND THE EXPERIMENTS ON SHUNDAN AT THE CONFIDENTIAL ACADEMIC MEETING?
HA HA...
DON'T BE STUPID.

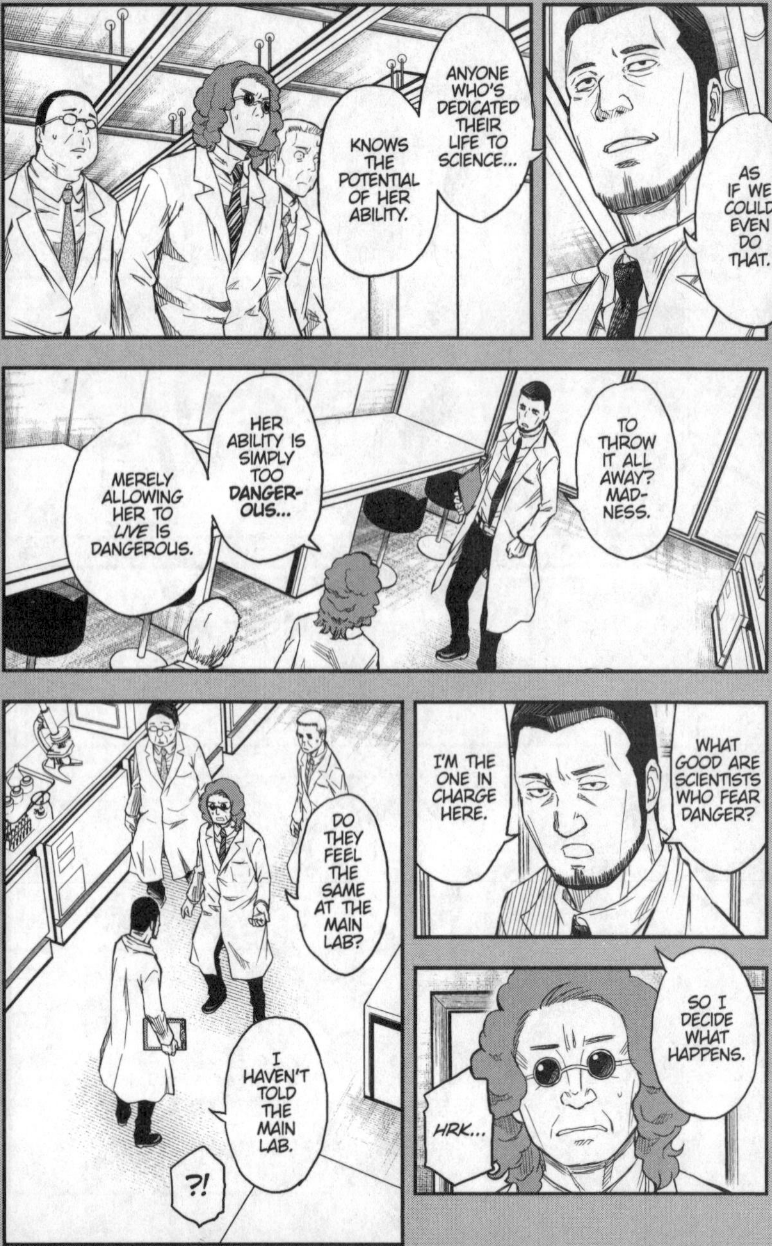
AS IF WE COULD EVEN DO THAT.
ANYONE WHO'S DEDICATED THEIR LIFE TO SCIENCE...
KNOWS THE POTENTIAL OF HER ABILITY.
TO THROW IT ALL AWAY? MAD-NESS.
HER ABILITY IS SIMPLY TOO DANGER-OUS...
MERELY ALLOWING HER TO *LIVE* IS DANGEROUS.
WHAT GOOD ARE SCIENTISTS WHO FEAR DANGER?
I'M THE ONE IN CHARGE HERE.
SO I DECIDE WHAT HAPPENS.
HRK...
DO THEY FEEL THE SAME AT THE MAIN LAB?
I HAVEN'T TOLD THE MAIN LAB.
?!

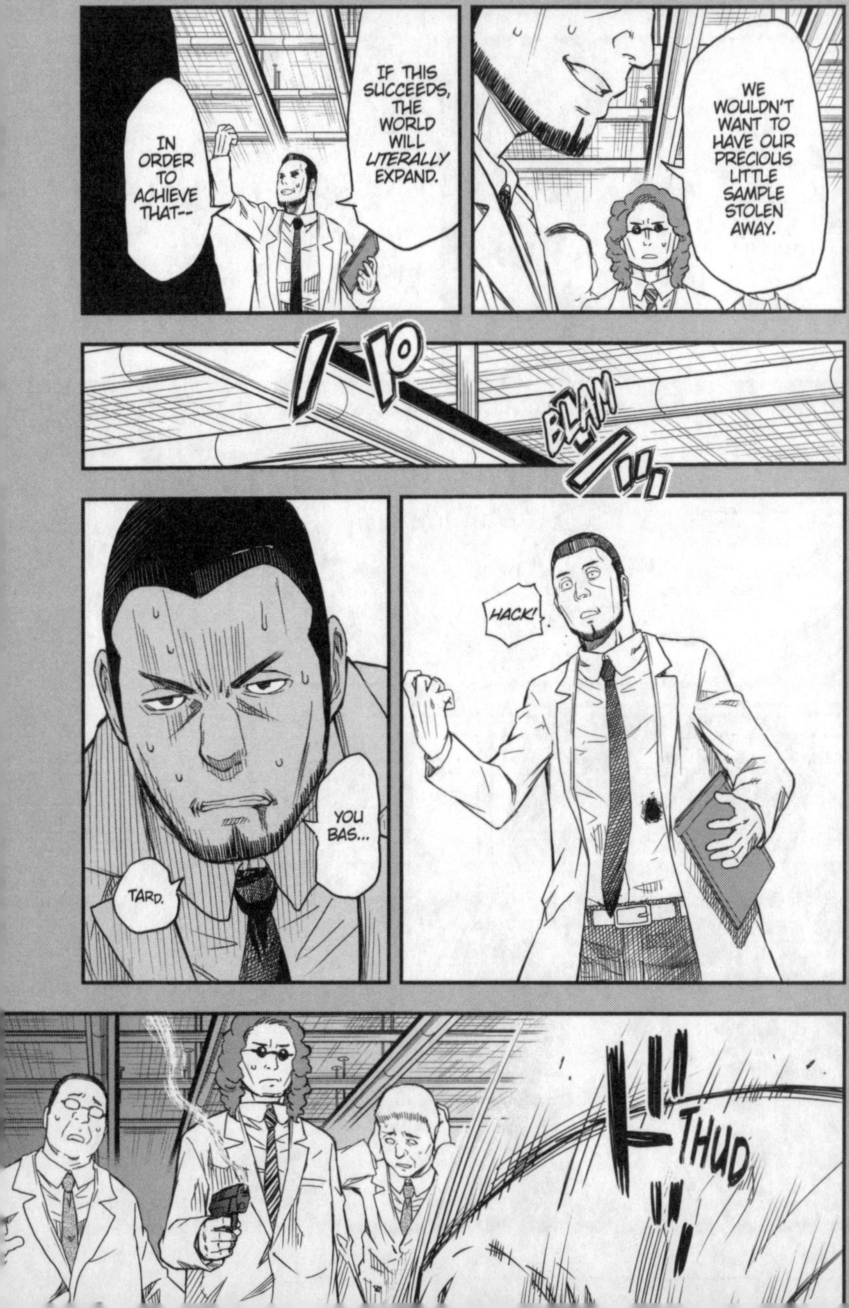
WE WOULDN'T WANT TO HAVE OUR PRECIOUS LITTLE SAMPLE STOLEN AWAY.
IF THIS SUCCEEDS, THE WORLD WILL *LITERALLY* EXPAND.
IN ORDER TO ACHIEVE THAT--
BLAM
HACK!
YOU BAS...
TARD.
THUD

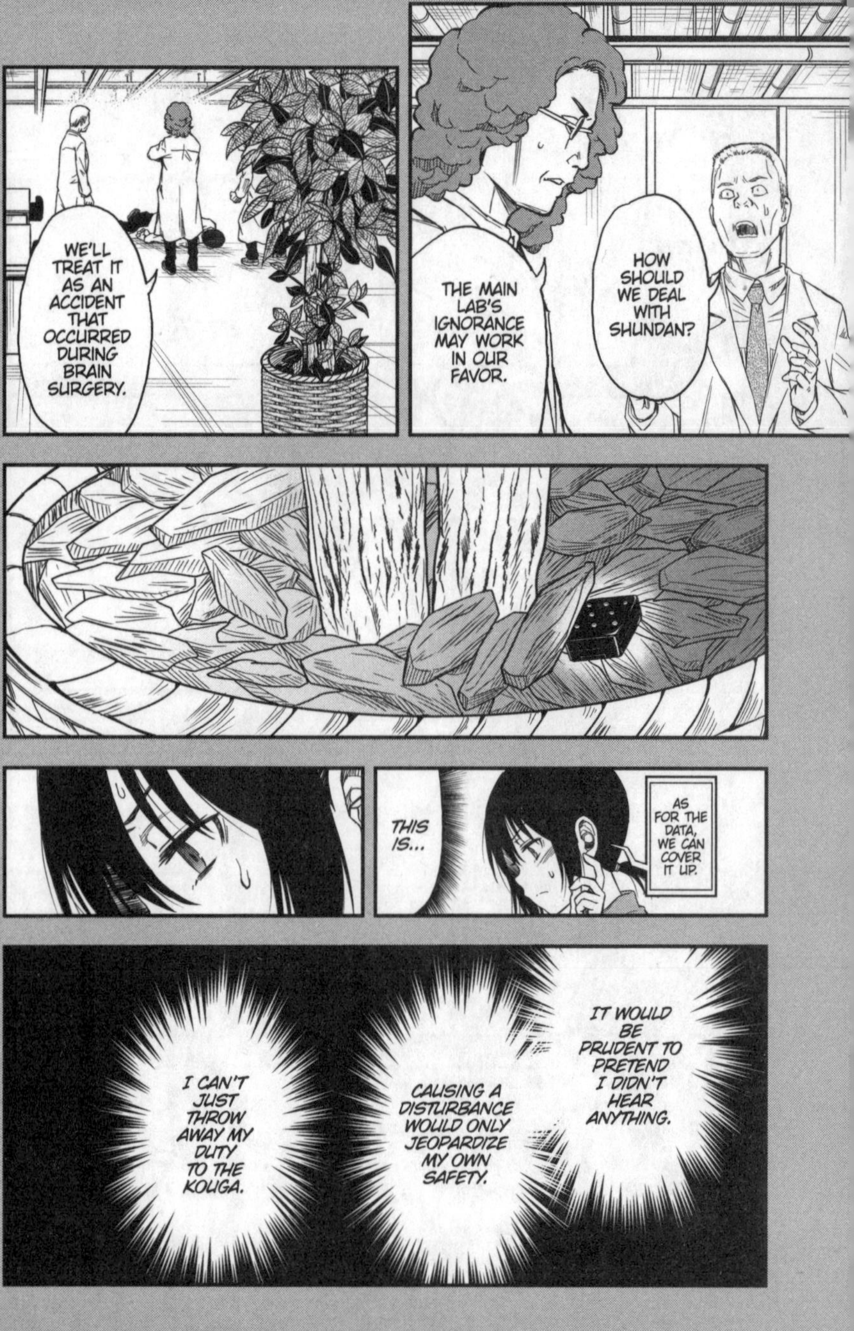
HOW SHOULD WE DEAL WITH SHUNDAN?
THE MAIN LAB'S IGNORANCE MAY WORK IN OUR FAVOR.
WE'LL TREAT IT AS AN ACCIDENT THAT OCCURRED DURING BRAIN SURGERY.
AS FOR THE DATA, WE CAN COVER IT UP.
THIS IS...
IT WOULD BE PRUDENT TO PRETEND I DIDN'T HEAR ANYTHING.
CAUSING A DISTURBANCE WOULD ONLY JEOPARDIZE MY OWN SAFETY.
I CAN'T JUST THROW AWAY MY DUTY TO THE KOUGA.

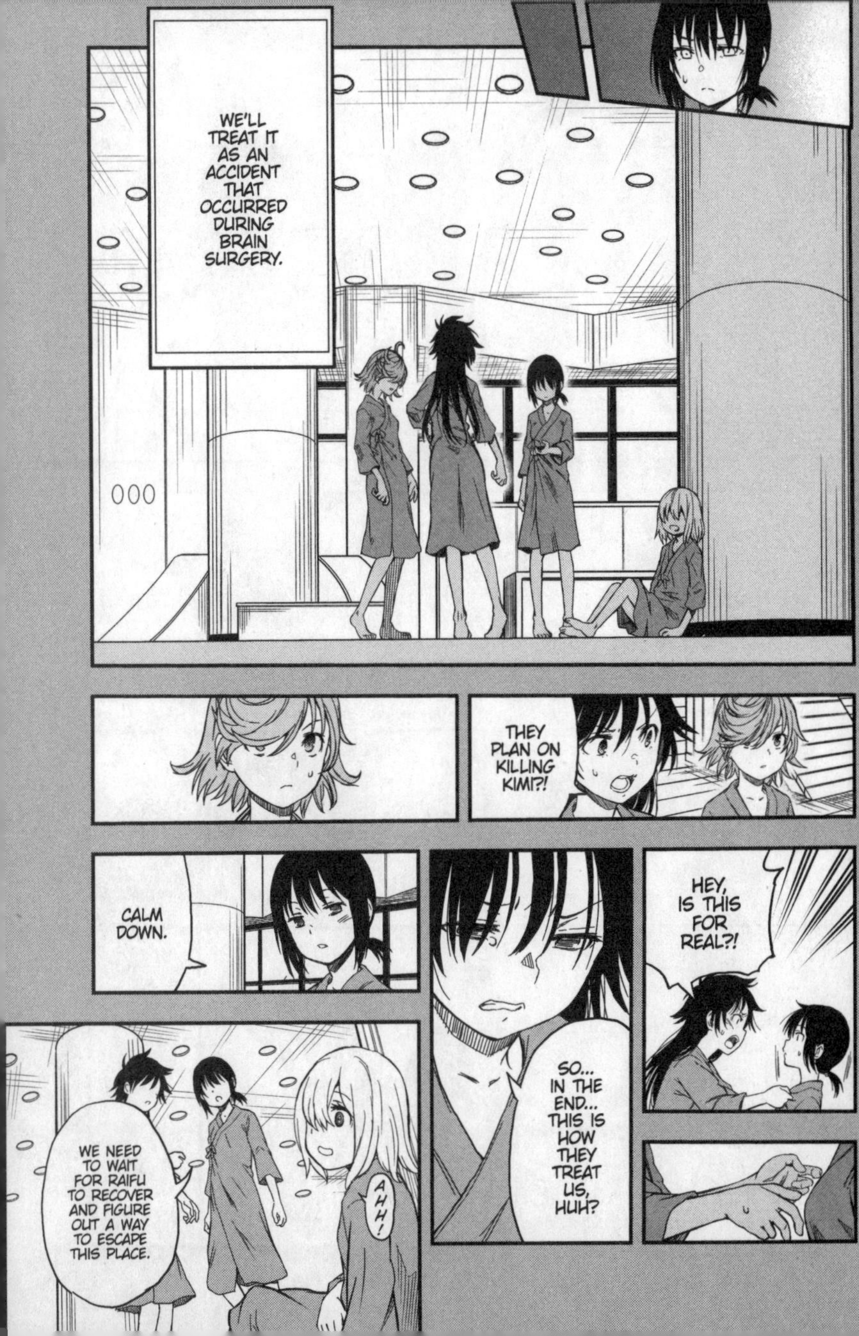
WE'LL TREAT IT AS AN ACCIDENT THAT OCCURRED DURING BRAIN SURGERY.
THEY PLAN ON KILLING KIMI?!
HEY, IS THIS FOR REAL?!
SO... IN THE END... THIS IS HOW THEY TREAT US, HUH?
CALM DOWN.
WE NEED TO WAIT FOR RAIFU TO RECOVER AND FIGURE OUT A WAY TO ESCAPE THIS PLACE.
AHH!

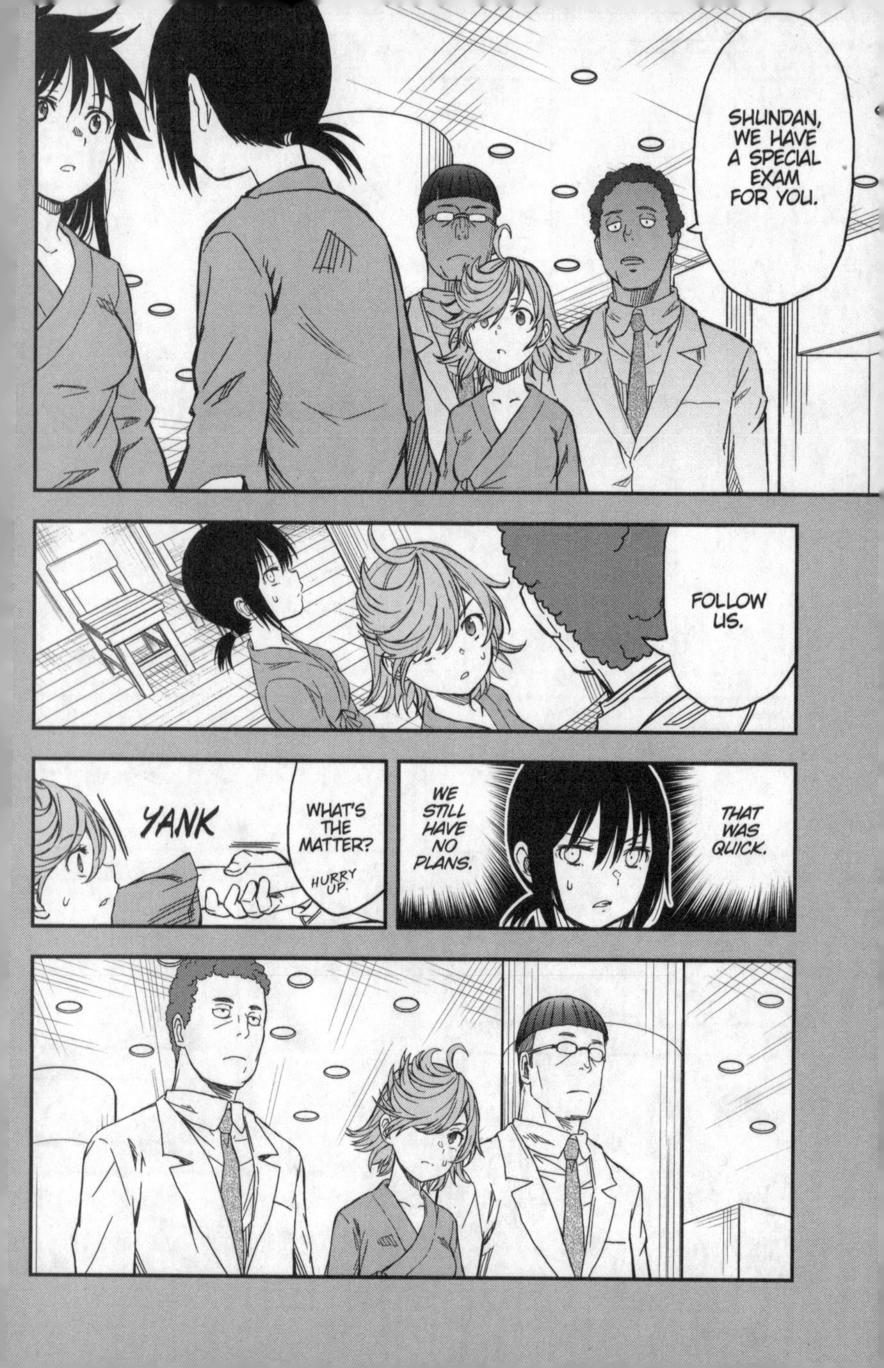
SHUNDAN, WE HAVE A SPECIAL EXAM FOR YOU.
FOLLOW US.
THAT WAS QUICK.
WE STILL HAVE NO PLANS.
WHAT'S THE MATTER?
HURRY UP.
YANK

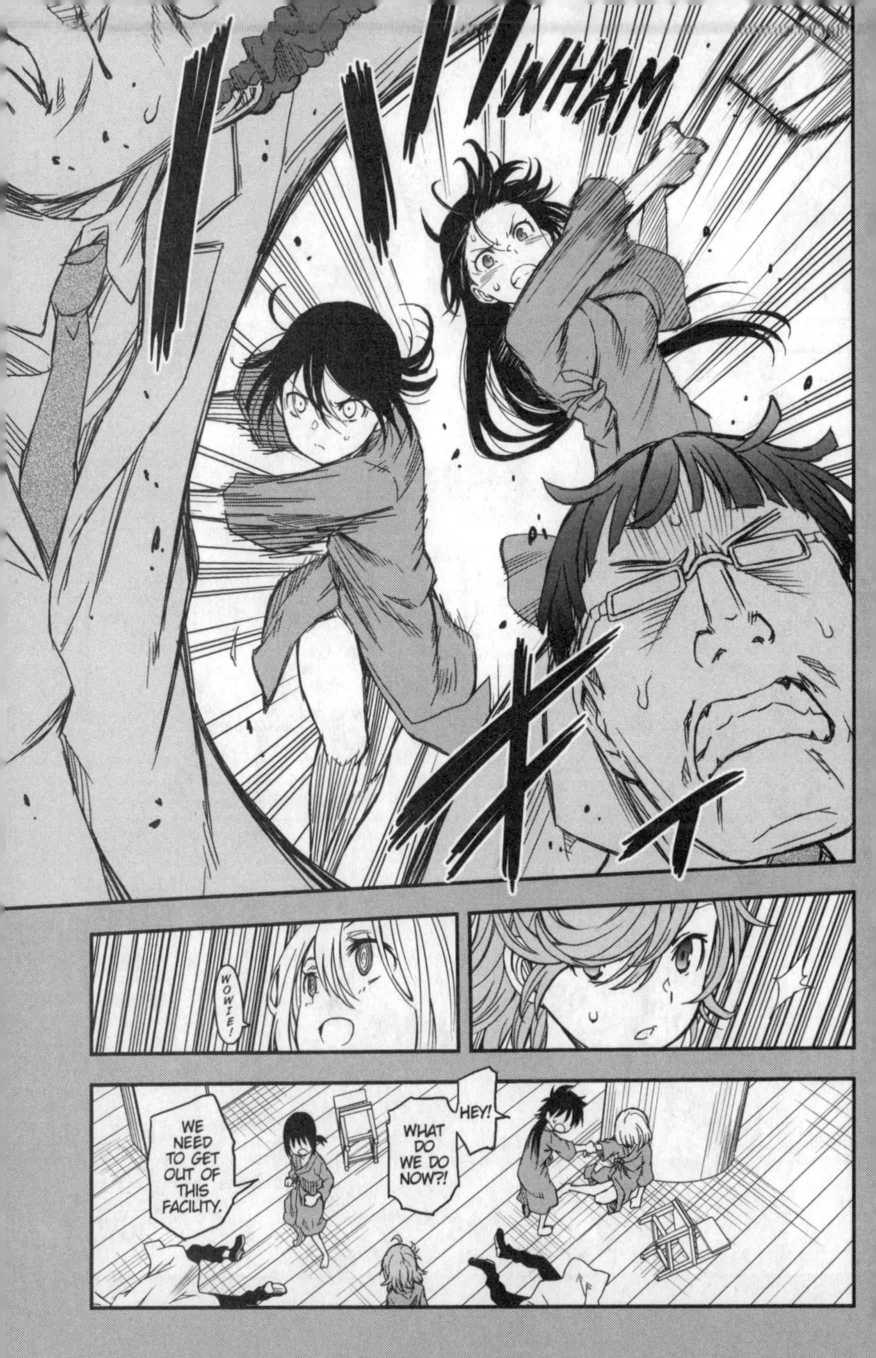
WHAM
WOWIE!
HEY!
WHAT DO WE DO NOW?!
WE NEED TO GET OUT OF THIS FACILITY.

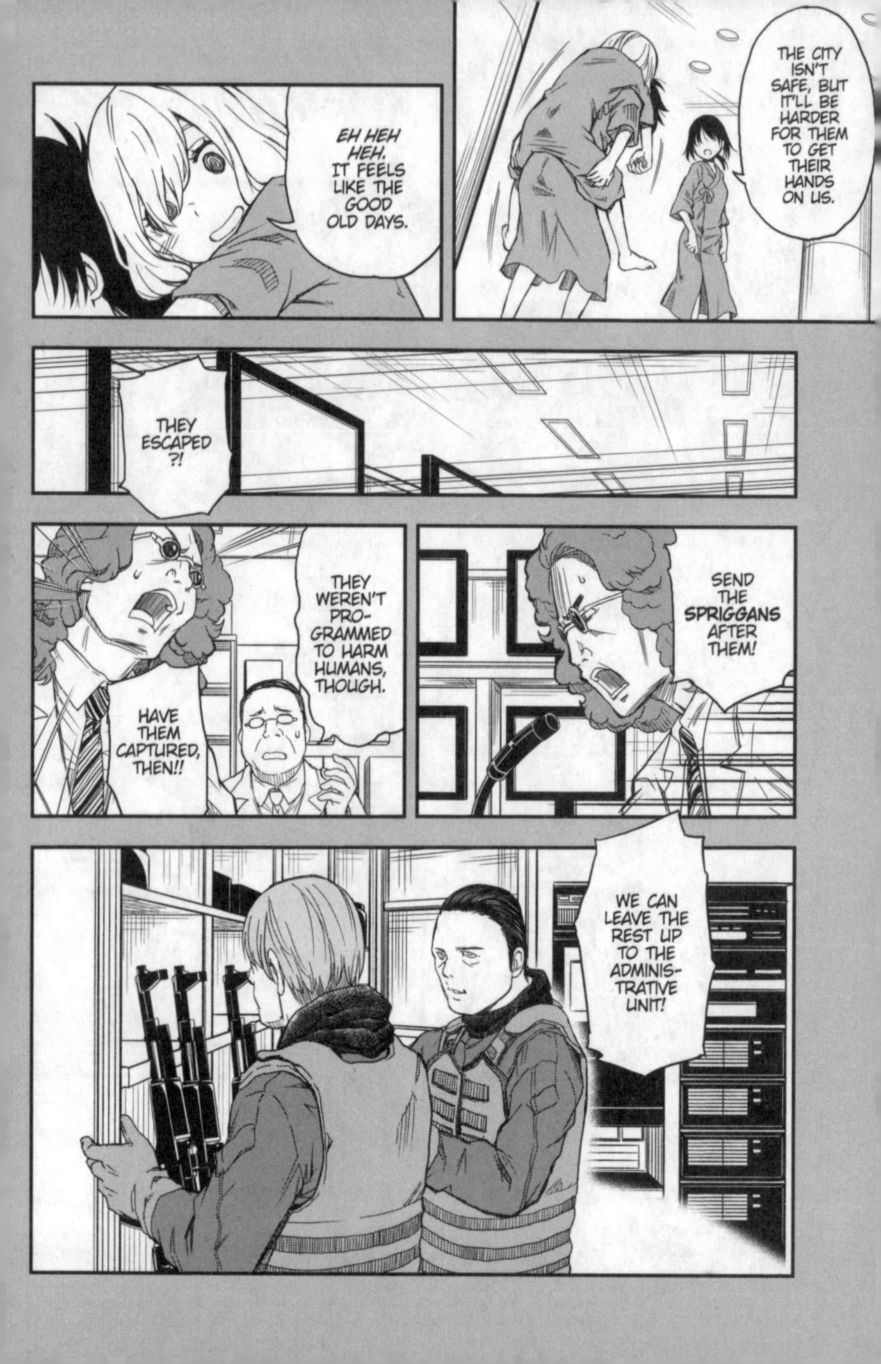
THE CITY ISN'T SAFE, BUT IT'LL BE HARDER FOR THEM TO GET THEIR HANDS ON US.
EH HEH HEH. IT FEELS LIKE THE GOOD OLD DAYS.
THEY ESCAPED?!
SEND THE SPRIGGANS AFTER THEM!
THEY WEREN'T PRO-GRAMMED TO HARM HUMANS, THOUGH.
HAVE THEM CAPTURED, THEN!!
WE CAN LEAVE THE REST UP TO THE ADMINIS-TRATIVE UNIT!

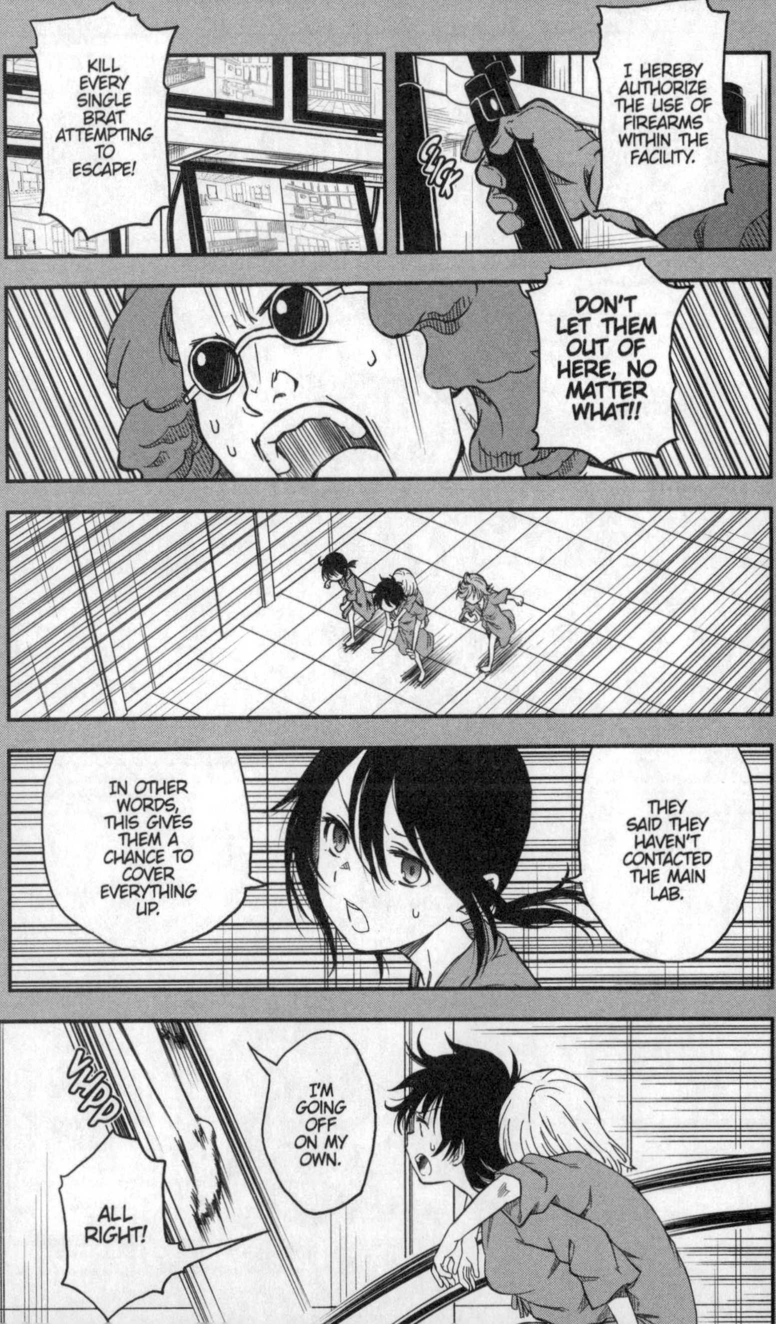
I HEREBY AUTHORIZE THE USE OF FIREARMS WITHIN THE FACILITY.
CLICK
KILL EVERY SINGLE BRAT ATTEMPTING TO ESCAPE!
DON'T LET THEM OUT OF HERE, NO MATTER WHAT!!
THEY SAID THEY HAVEN'T CONTACTED THE MAIN LAB.
IN OTHER WORDS, THIS GIVES THEM A CHANCE TO COVER EVERYTHING UP.
I'M GOING OFF ON MY OWN.
VHPP
ALL RIGHT!

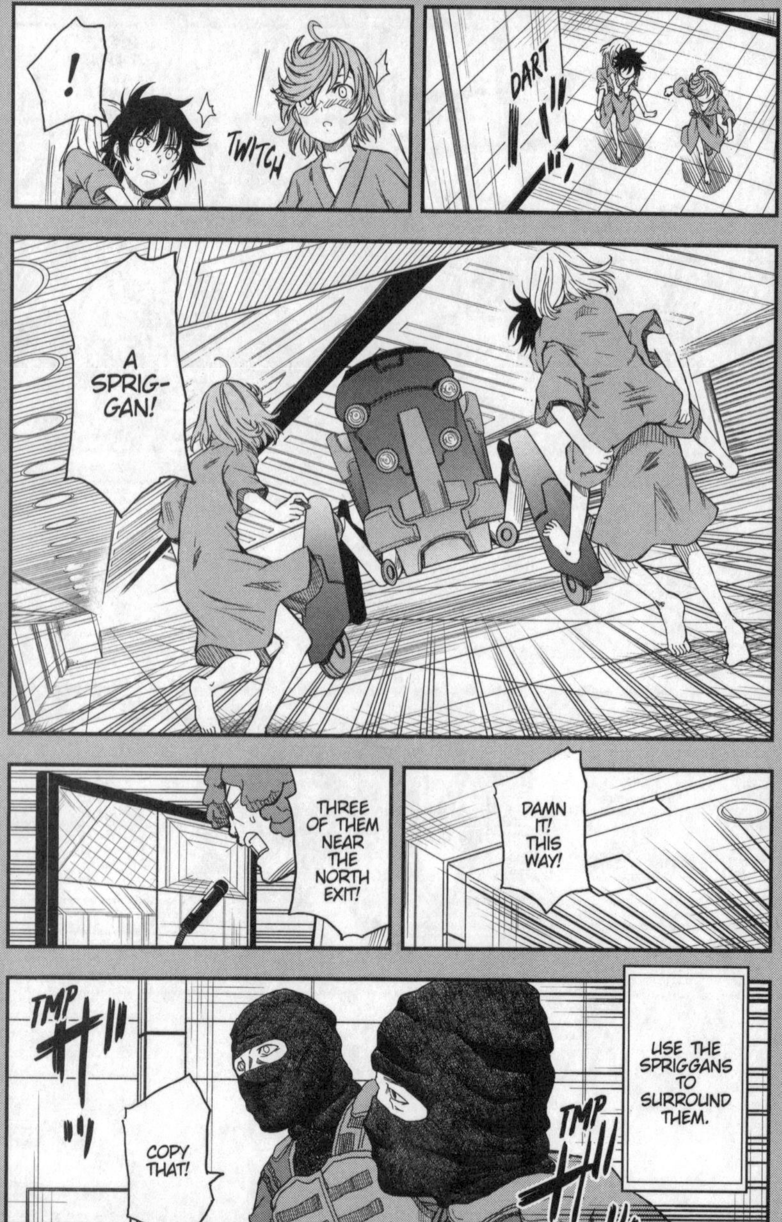
DART
!
TWITCH
A SPRIG-GAN!
DAMN IT! THIS WAY!
THREE OF THEM NEAR THE NORTH EXIT!
USE THE SPRIGGANS TO SURROUND THEM.
TMP
COPY THAT!
TMP

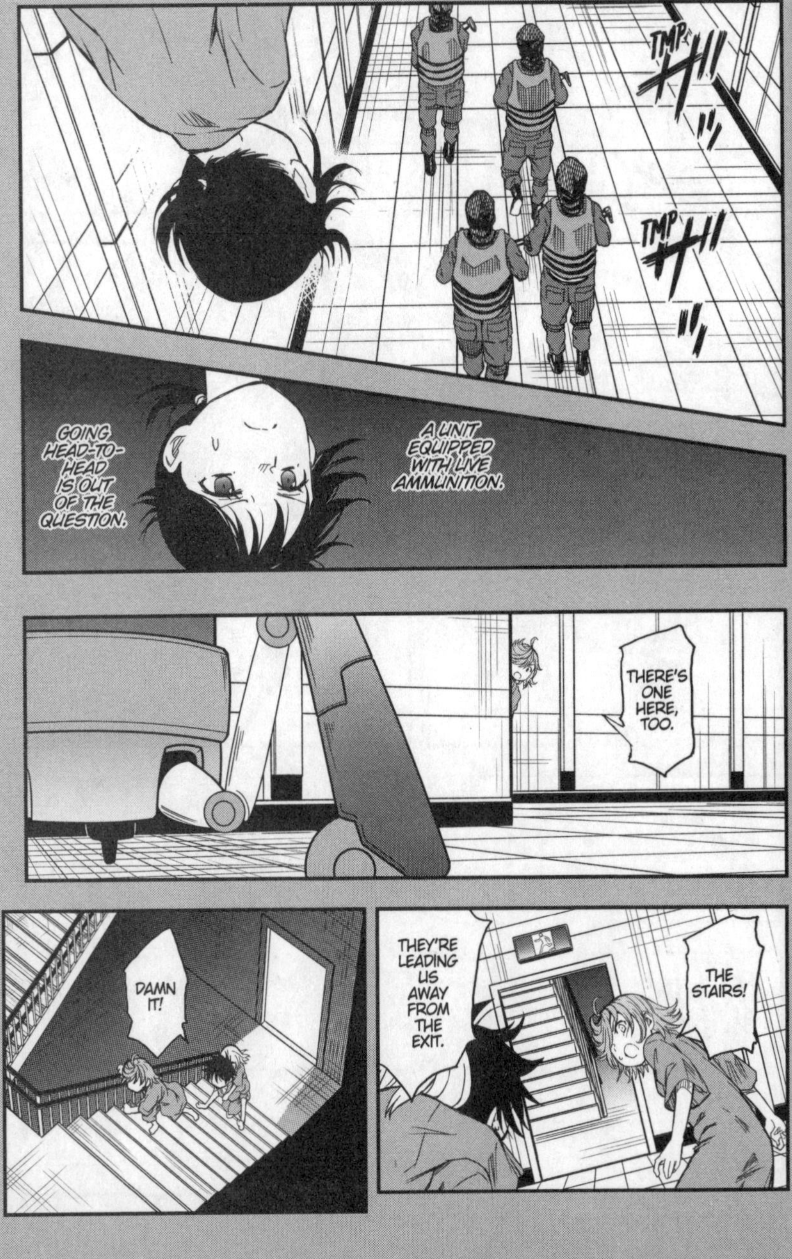
TMP
TMP
A UNIT EQUIPPED WITH LIVE AMMUNITION.
GOING HEAD-TO-HEAD IS OUT OF THE QUESTION.
THERE'S ONE HERE, TOO.
THE STAIRS!
THEY'RE LEADING US AWAY FROM THE EXIT.
DAMN IT!

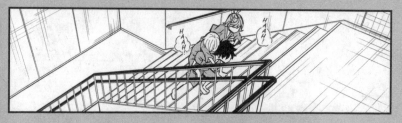

KIMI... YOU'RE SOME SORTA ESPER, TOO?

AND HERE I THOUGHT...

YOU WERE JUST LIKE ME.

I WAS THROWN AWAY BY PARENTS WHOSE FACES I DON'T EVEN KNOW...

THEN CALLED A LEECH ON ACADEMY CITY'S RESOURCES.

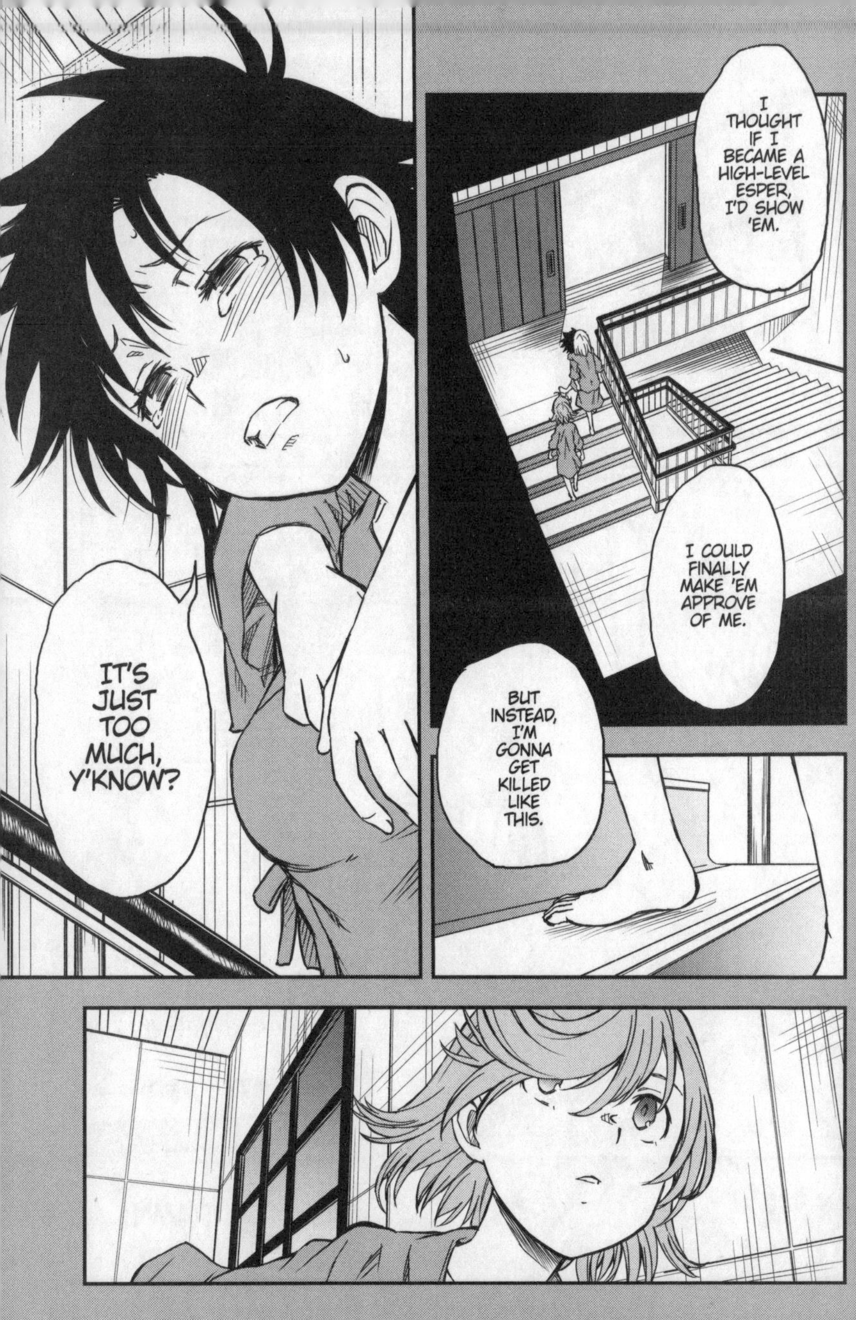
I THOUGHT IF I BECAME A HIGH-LEVEL ESPER, I'D SHOW 'EM.
I COULD FINALLY MAKE 'EM APPROVE OF ME.
BUT INSTEAD, I'M GONNA GET KILLED LIKE THIS.
IT'S JUST TOO MUCH, Y'KNOW?

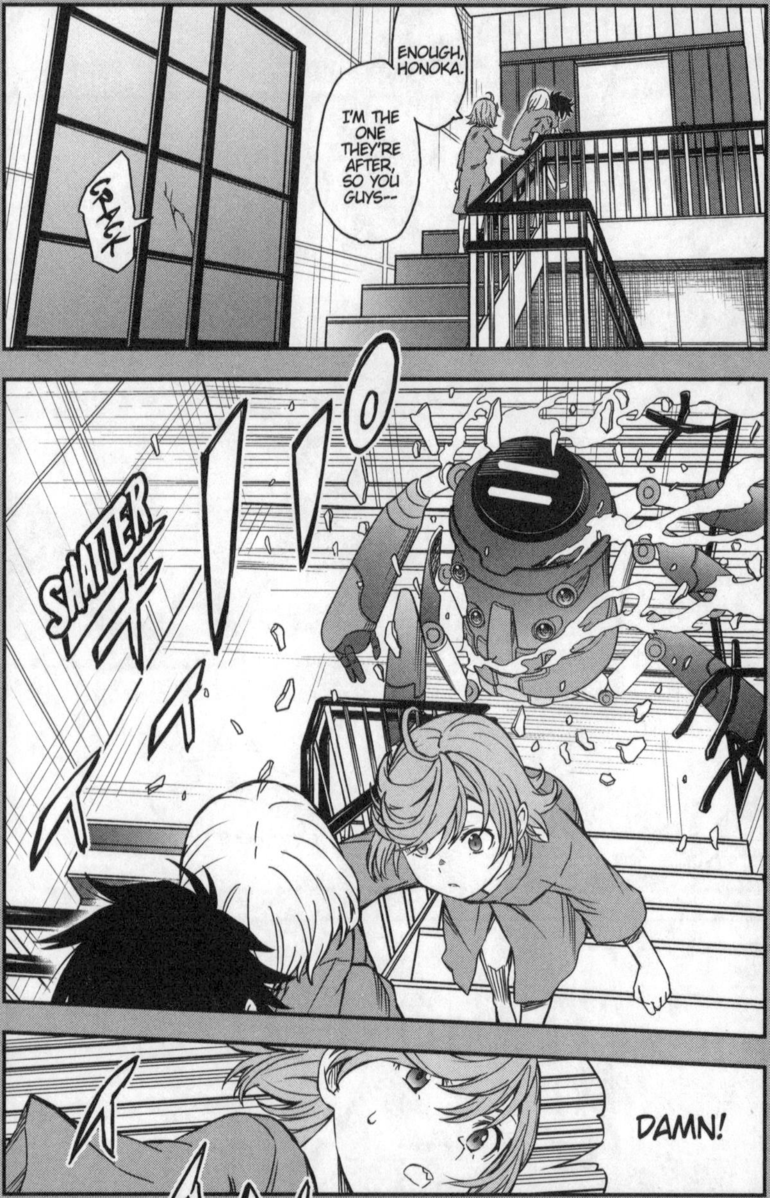
ENOUGH, HONOKA.
I'M THE ONE THEY'RE AFTER, SO YOU GUYS--
CRACK
SHATTER
DAMN!

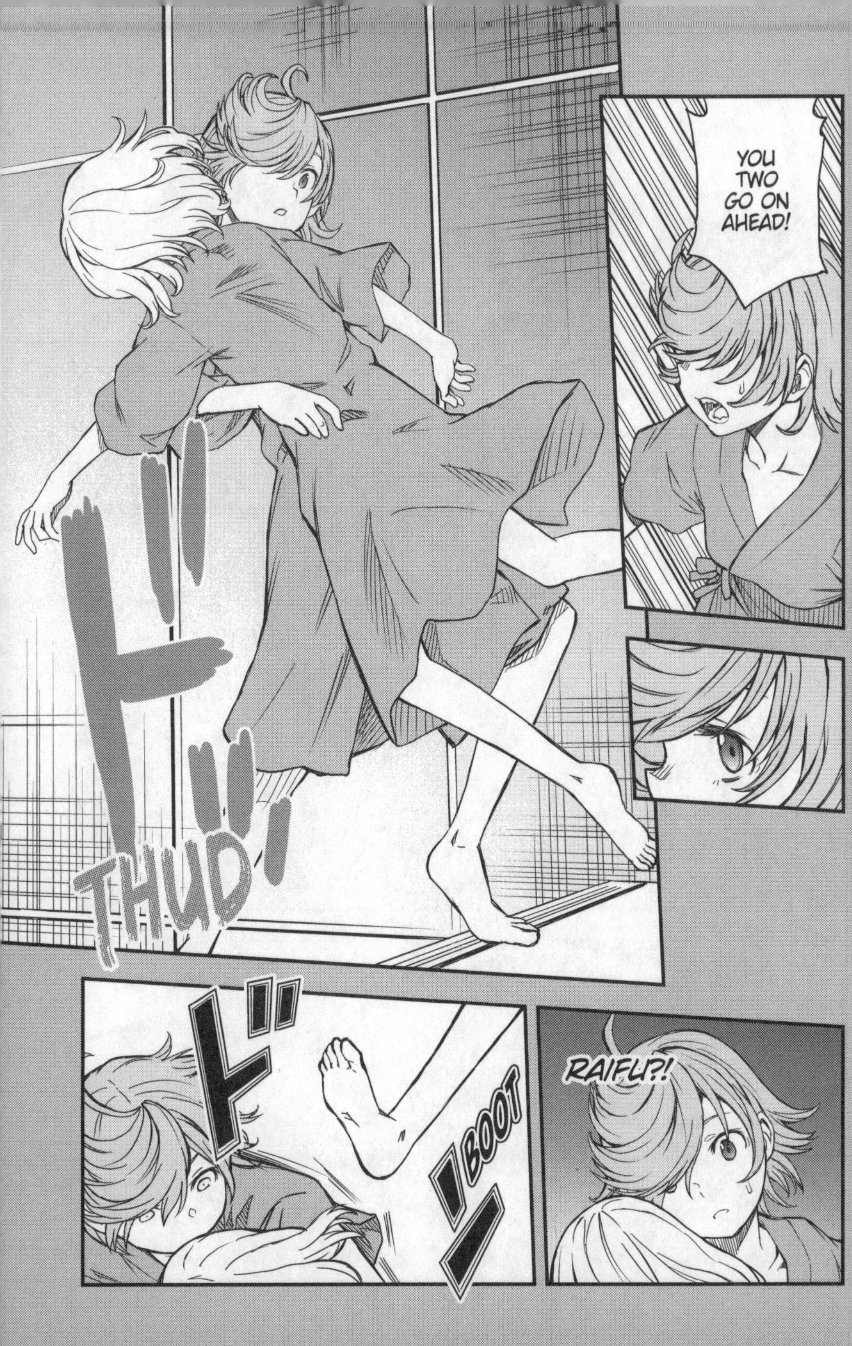
YOU TWO GO ON AHEAD!
ド
THUD
RAIFU?!
ド
BOOT

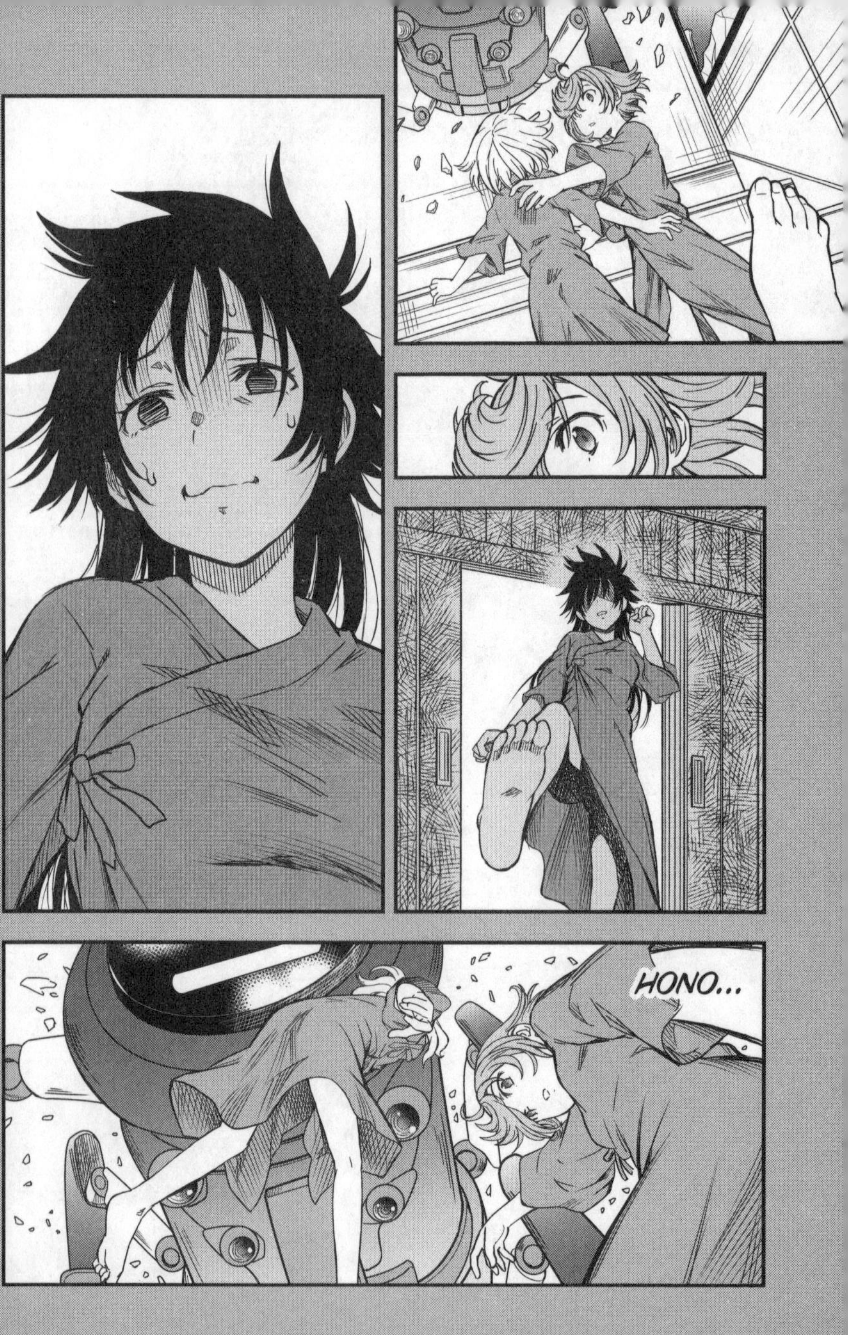
HONO...

CHAPTER 120: DISCERNMENT

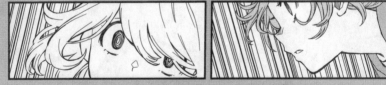

DART

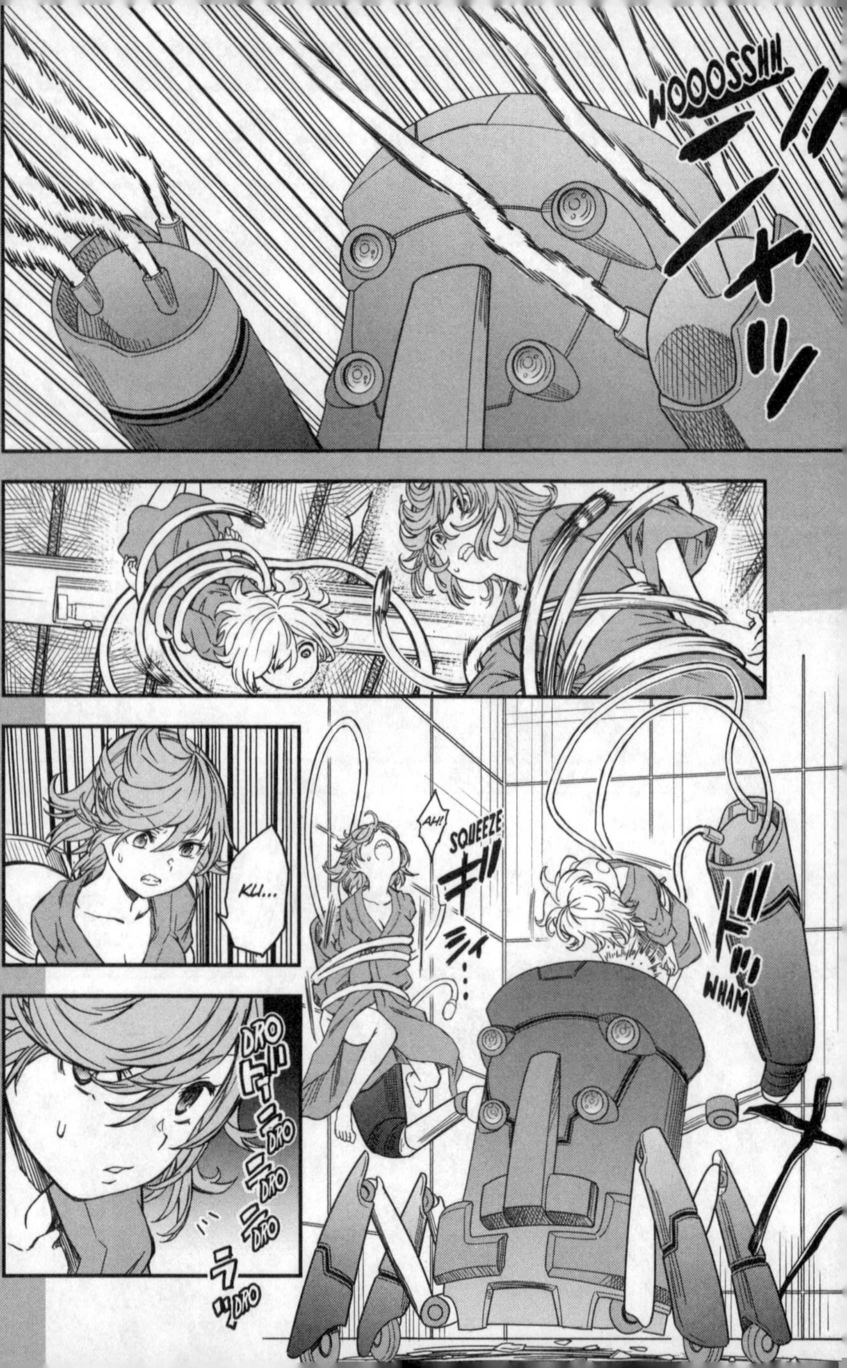
WOOOSSHH
AH!
SQUEEZE
WHAM
KU...
DRO
DRO
DRO
DRO
DRO

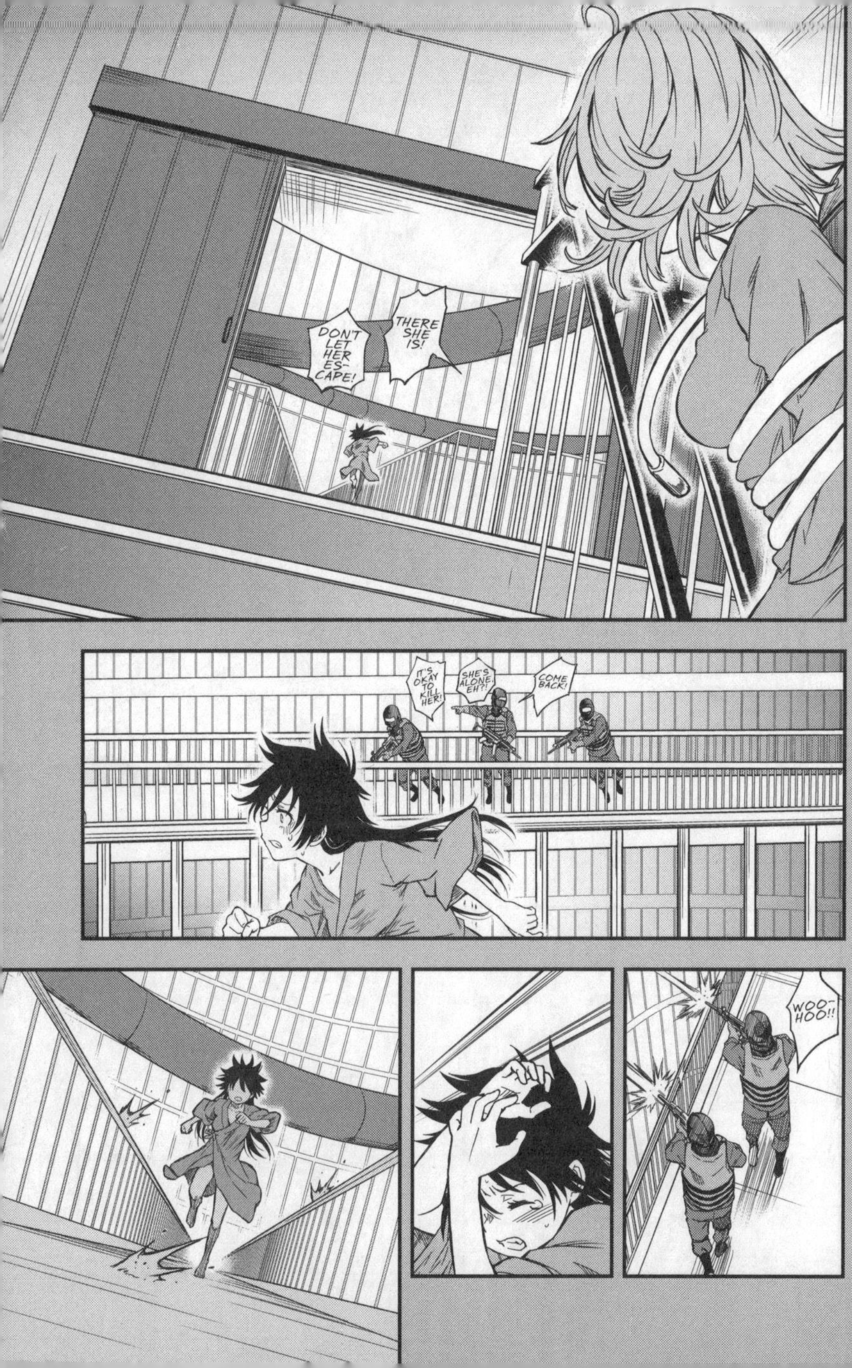
THERE SHE IS!
DON'T LET HER ES-CAPE!
COME BACK!
SHE'S ALONE, EH?!
IT'S OKAY TO KILL HER!
WOO-HOO!!

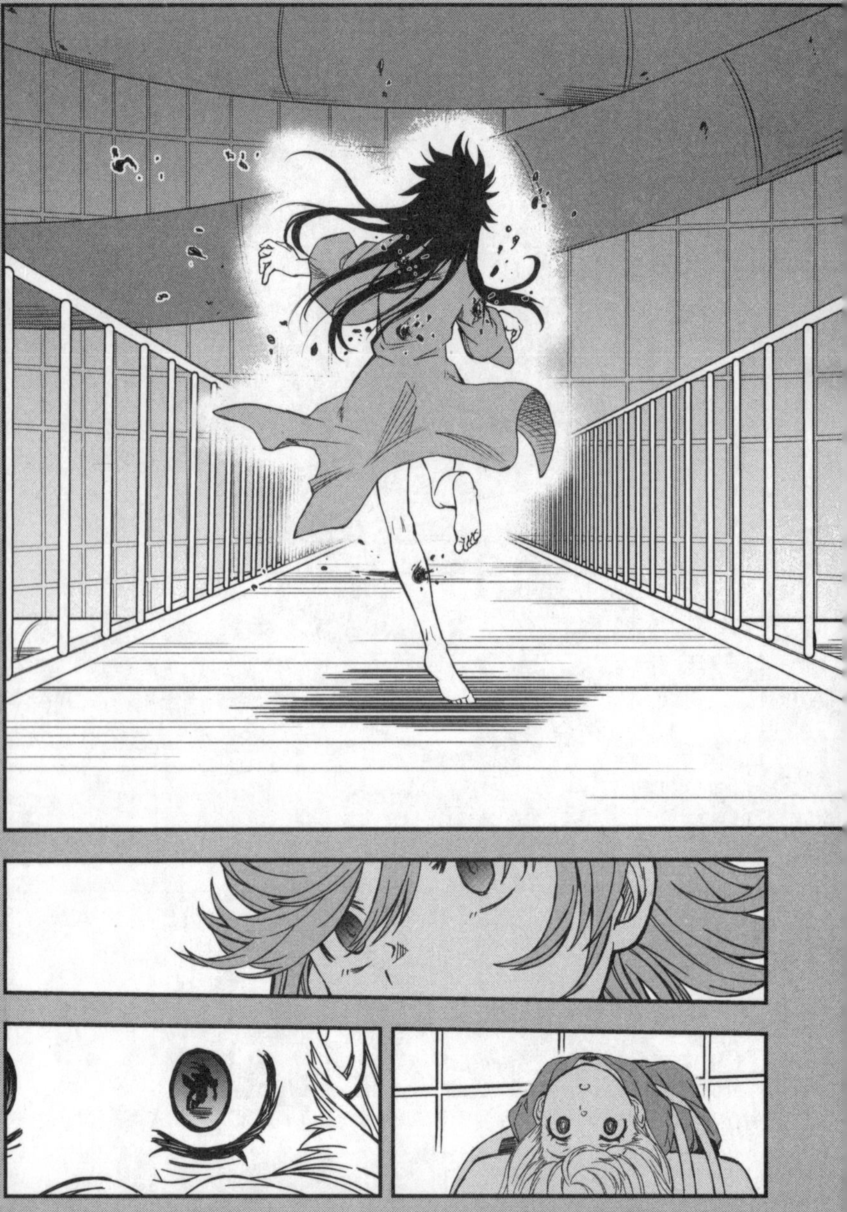

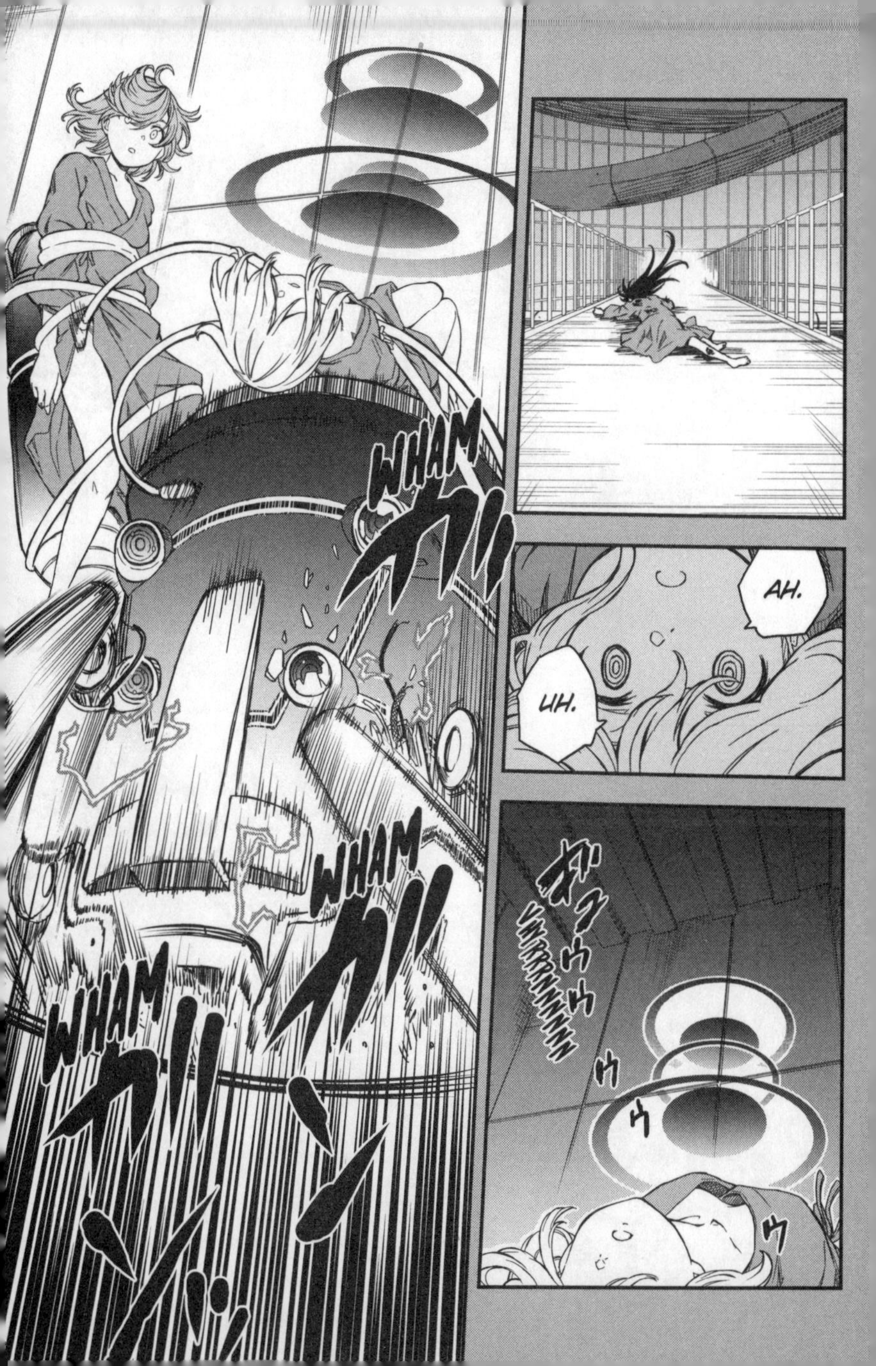
AH.
UH.
VWRRRNNNNNN
WHAM
WHAM
WHAM

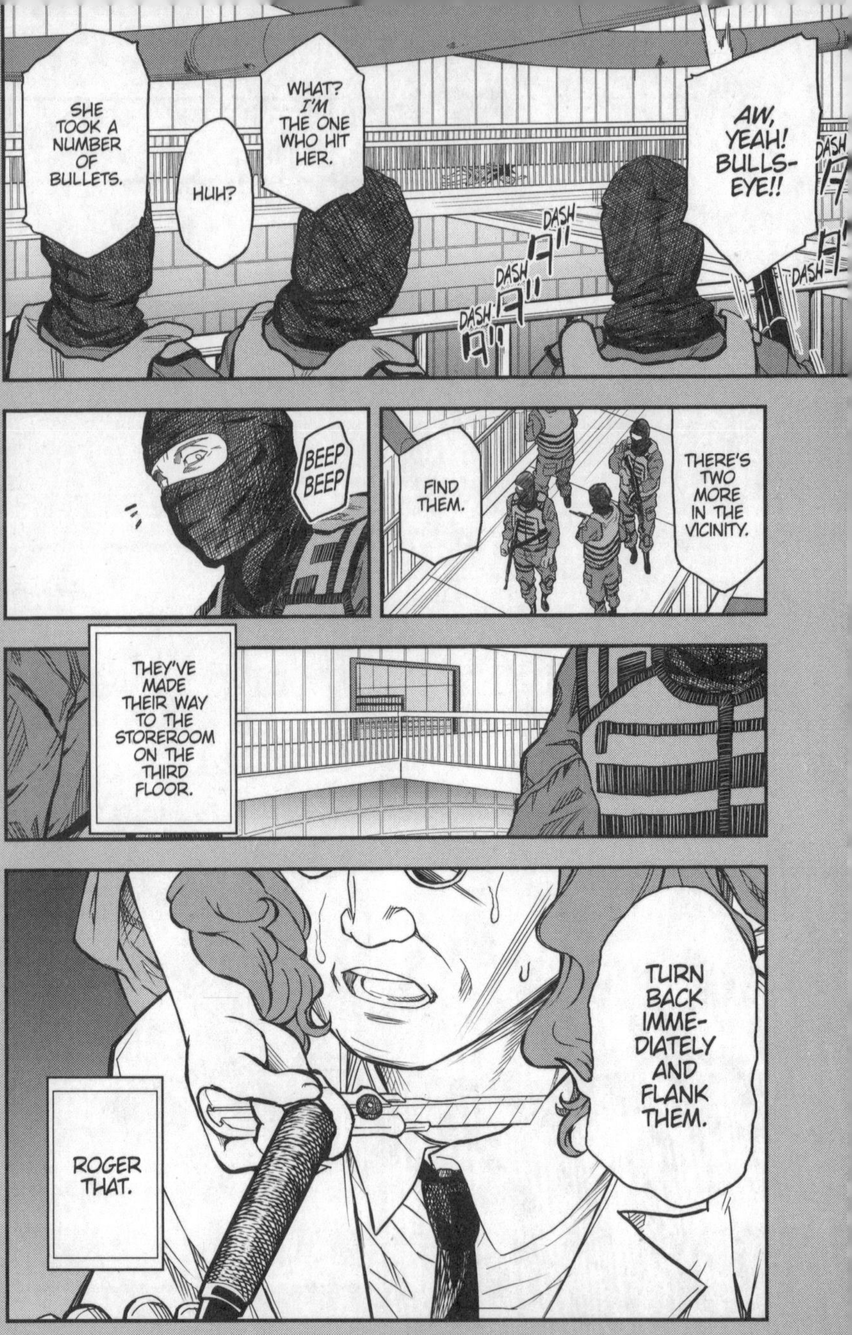
AW, YEAH! BULLS-EYE!!
DASH DASH
WHAT? *I'M* THE ONE WHO HIT HER.
DASH DASH DASH
HUH?
SHE TOOK A NUMBER OF BULLETS.
THERE'S TWO MORE IN THE VICINITY.
FIND THEM.
BEEP BEEP
THEY'VE MADE THEIR WAY TO THE STOREROOM ON THE THIRD FLOOR.
TURN BACK IMME-DIATELY AND FLANK THEM.
ROGER THAT.

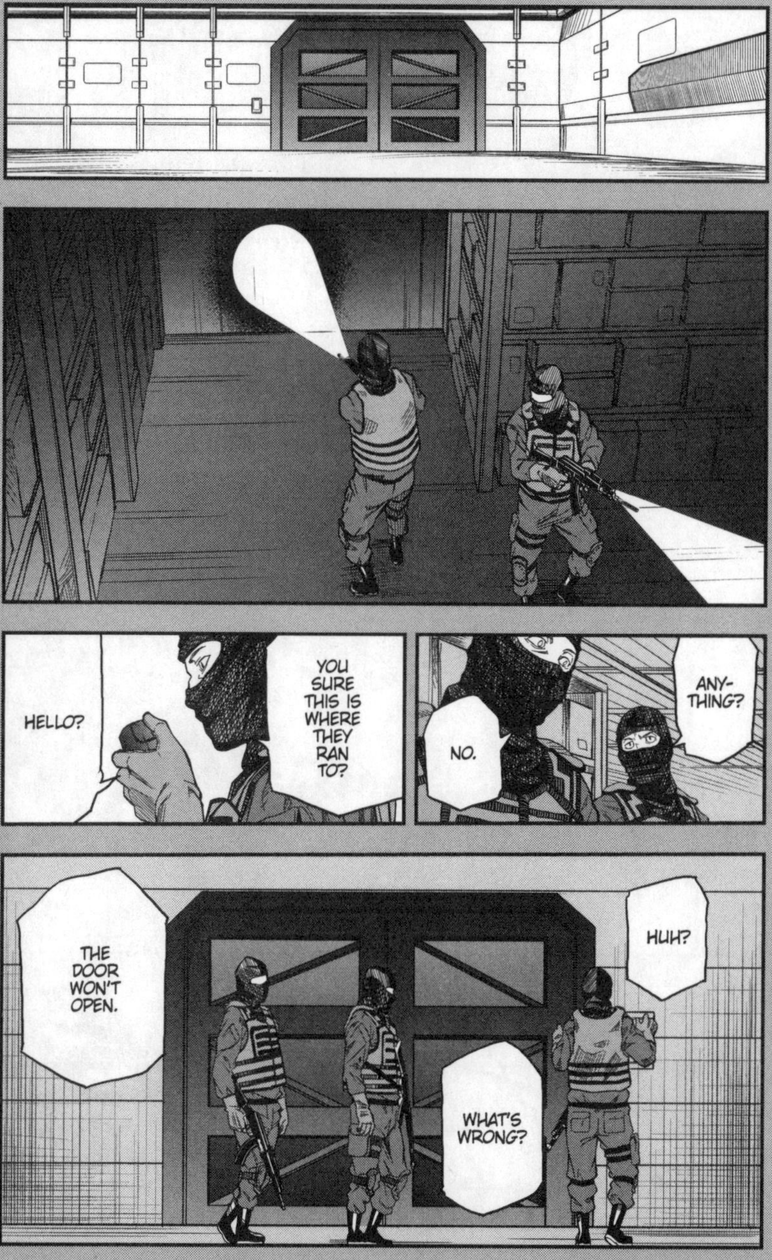
ANY-THING?
NO.
YOU SURE THIS IS WHERE THEY RAN TO?
HELLO?
HUH?
THE DOOR WON'T OPEN.
WHAT'S WRONG?

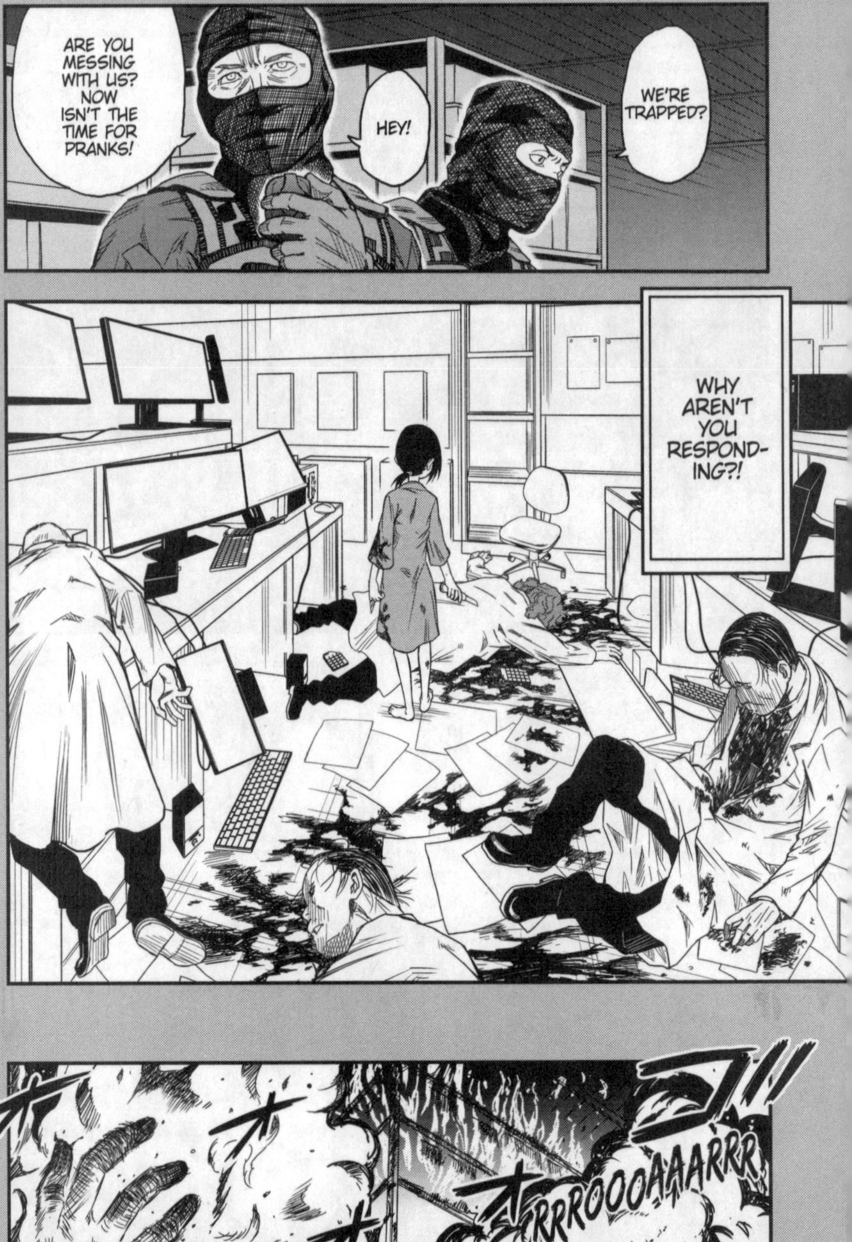
WE'RE TRAPPED?
HEY!
ARE YOU MESSING WITH US? NOW ISN'T THE TIME FOR PRANKS!
WHY AREN'T YOU RESPONDING?!
RRROOOAAARRR

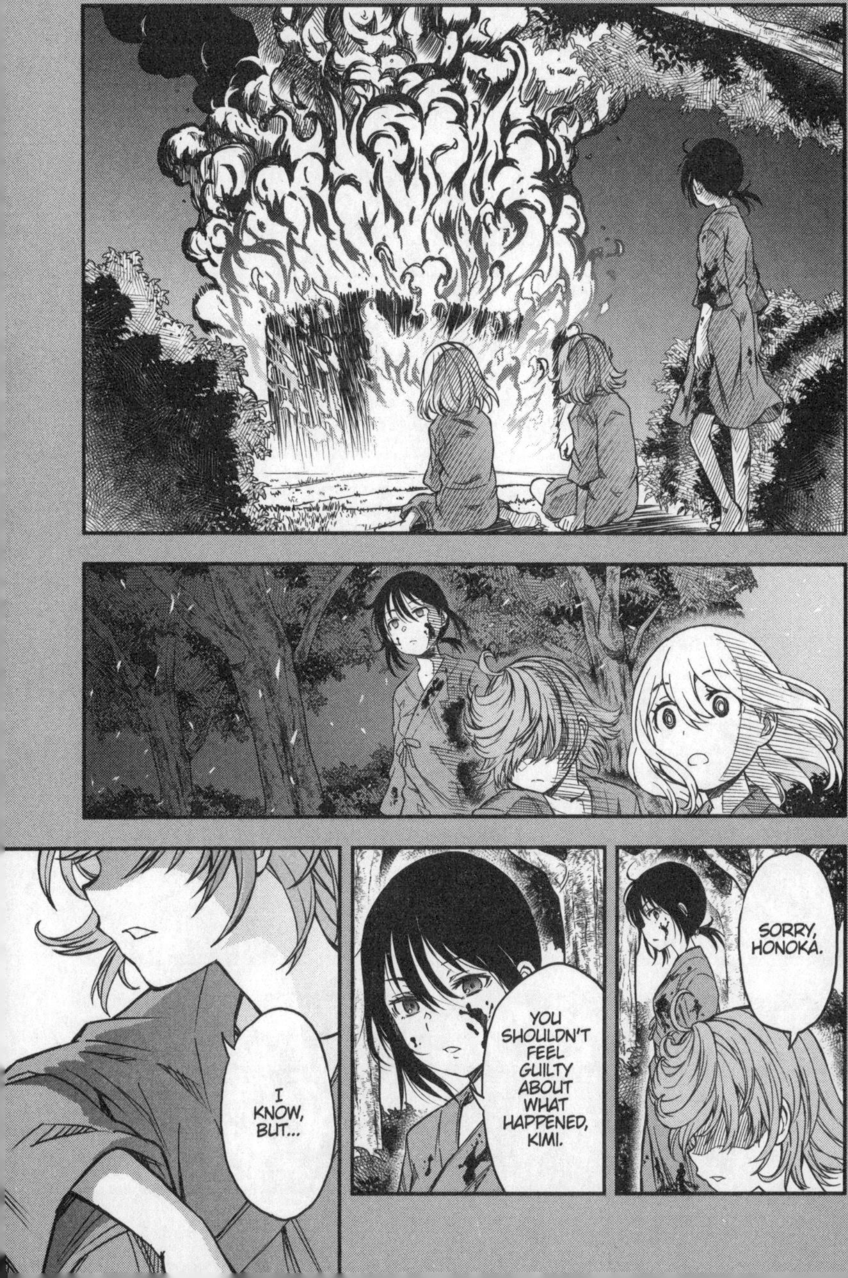
SORRY, HONOKA.
YOU SHOULDN'T FEEL GUILTY ABOUT WHAT HAPPENED, KIMI.
I KNOW, BUT...

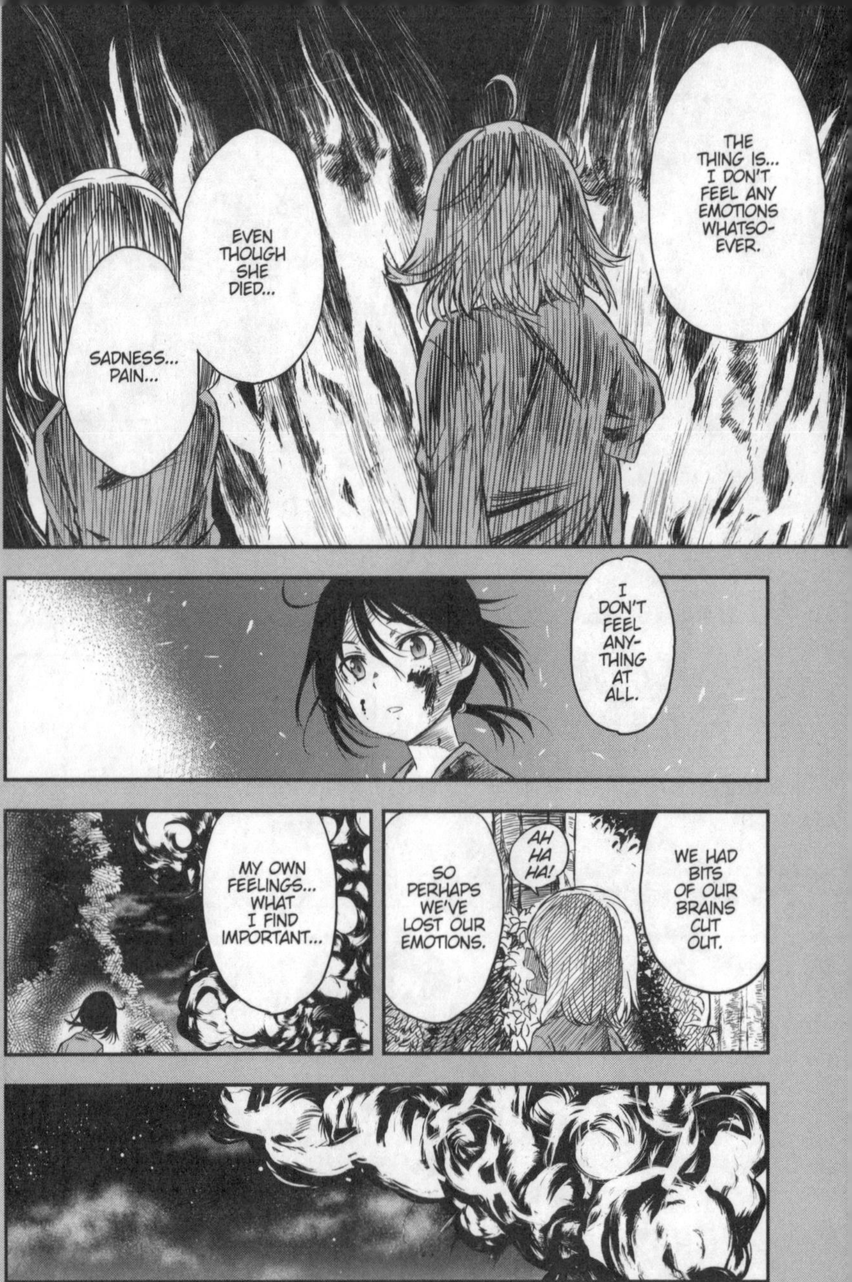
THE THING IS... I DON'T FEEL ANY EMOTIONS WHATSO-EVER.
EVEN THOUGH SHE DIED...
SADNESS... PAIN...
I DON'T FEEL ANY-THING AT ALL.
WE HAD BITS OF OUR BRAINS CUT OUT.
AH HA HA!
SO PERHAPS WE'VE LOST OUR EMOTIONS.
MY OWN FEELINGS... WHAT I FIND IMPORTANT...

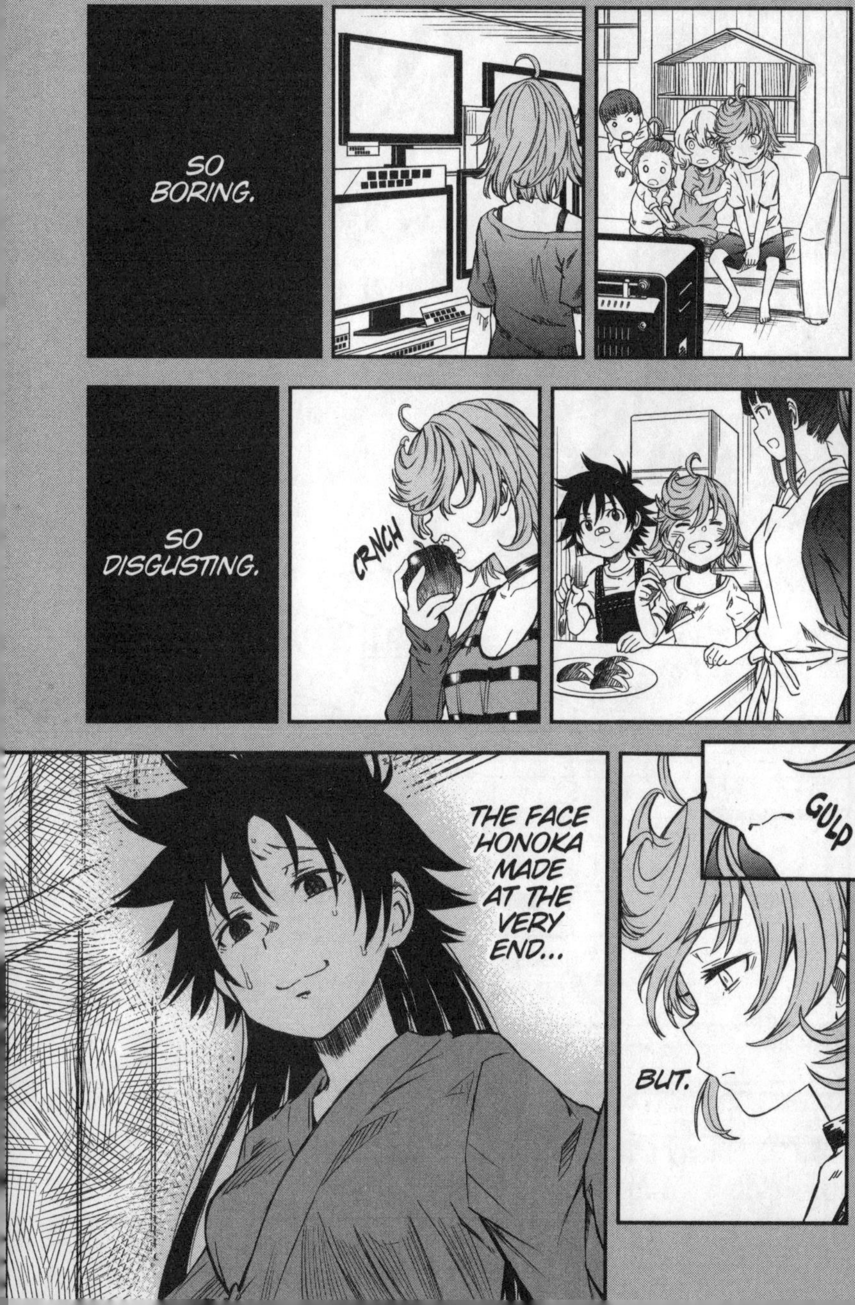
SO BORING.
CRNCH
SO DISGUSTING.
GULP
BUT.
THE FACE HONOKA MADE AT THE VERY END...

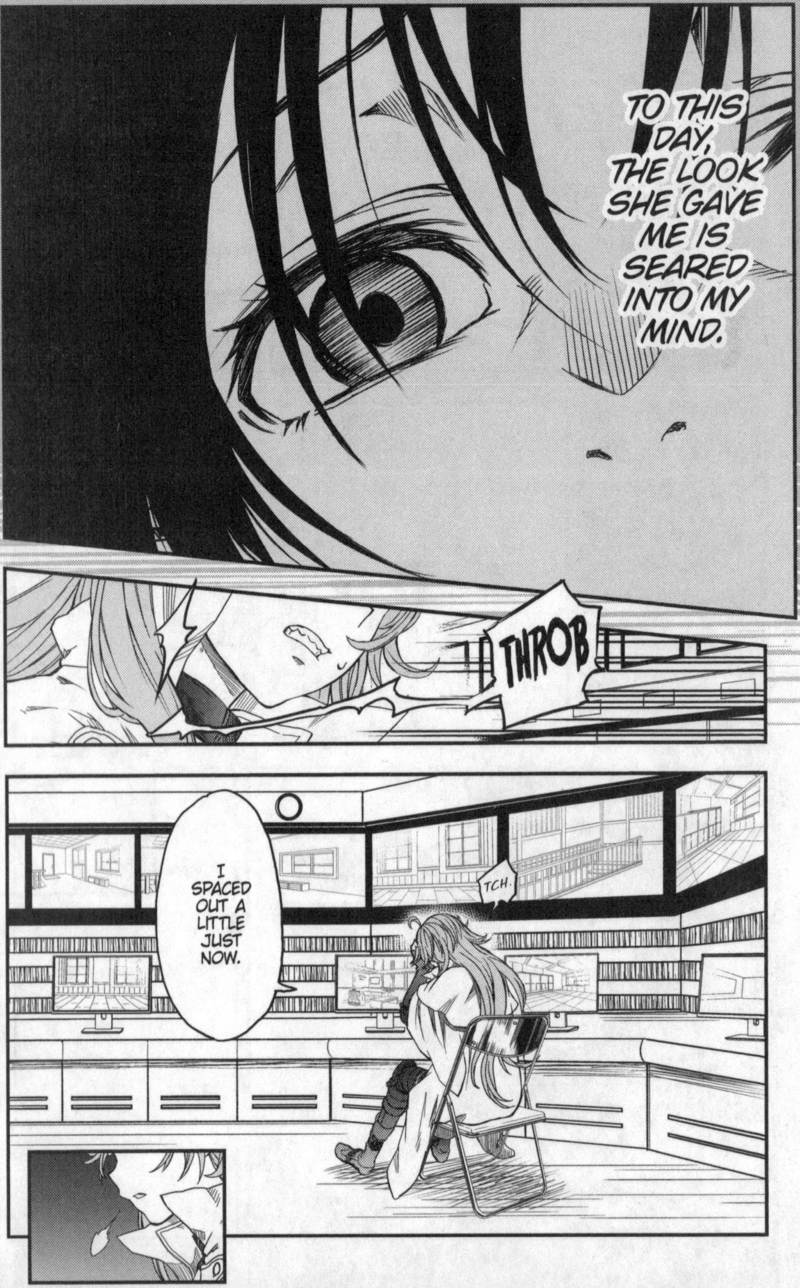
TO THIS DAY, THE LOOK SHE GAVE ME IS SEARED INTO MY MIND.
THROB
TCH.
I SPACED OUT A LITTLE JUST NOW.

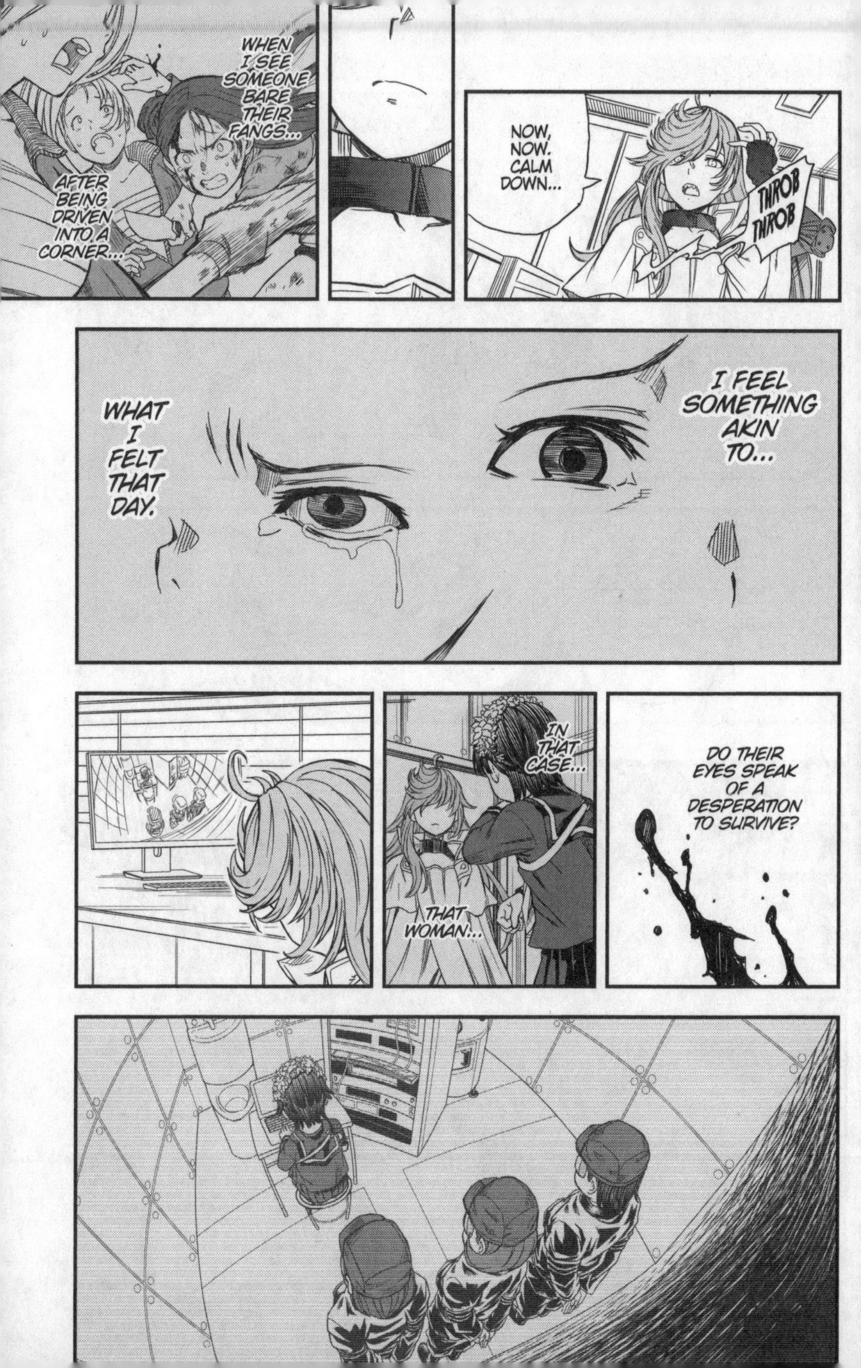
NOW, NOW. CALM DOWN...
THROB THROB
WHEN I SEE SOMEONE BARE THEIR FANGS...
AFTER BEING DRIVEN INTO A CORNER...
I FEEL SOMETHING AKIN TO...
WHAT I FELT THAT DAY.
DO THEIR EYES SPEAK OF A DESPERATION TO SURVIVE?
IN THAT CASE...
THAT WOMAN...

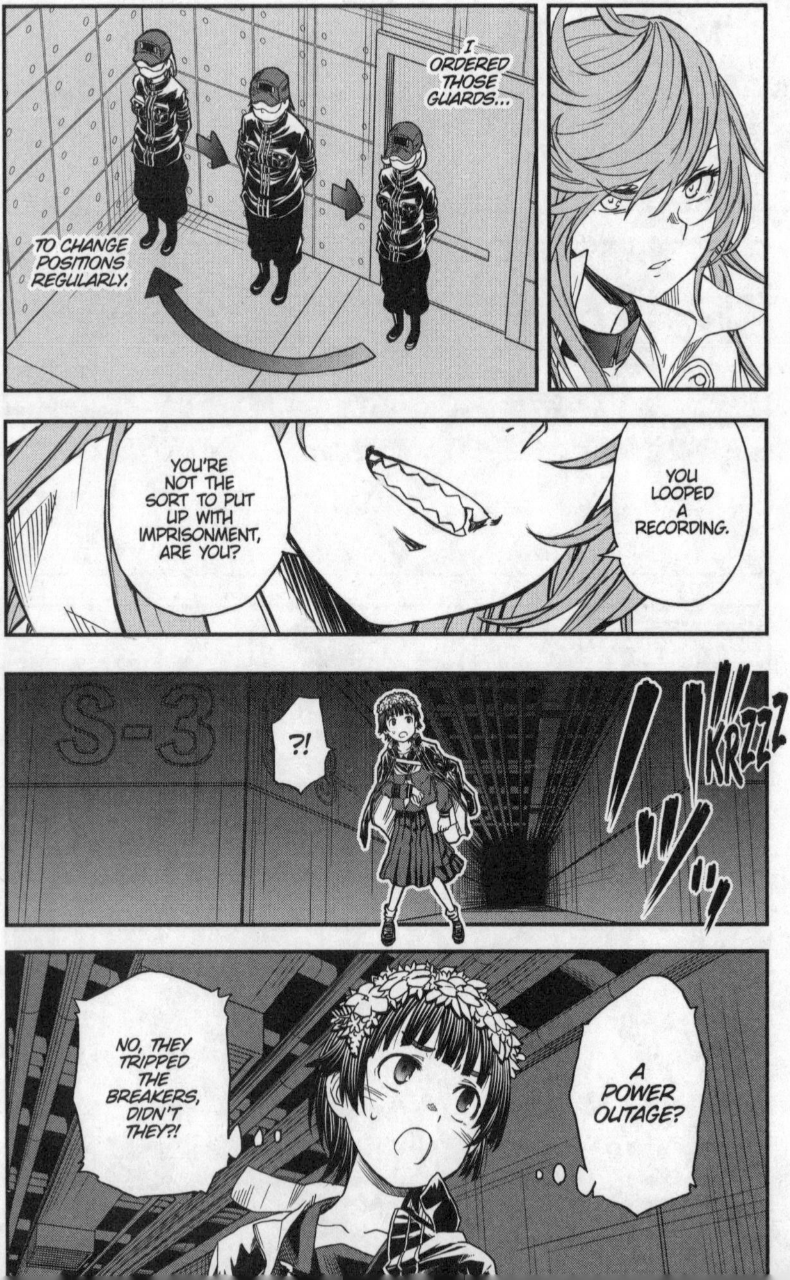
I ORDERED THOSE GUARDS...
TO CHANGE POSITIONS REGULARLY.
YOU LOOPED A RECORDING.
YOU'RE NOT THE SORT TO PUT UP WITH IMPRISONMENT, ARE YOU?
KRZZZ
?!
S-3
A POWER OUTAGE?
NO, THEY TRIPPED THE BREAKERS, DIDN'T THEY?!

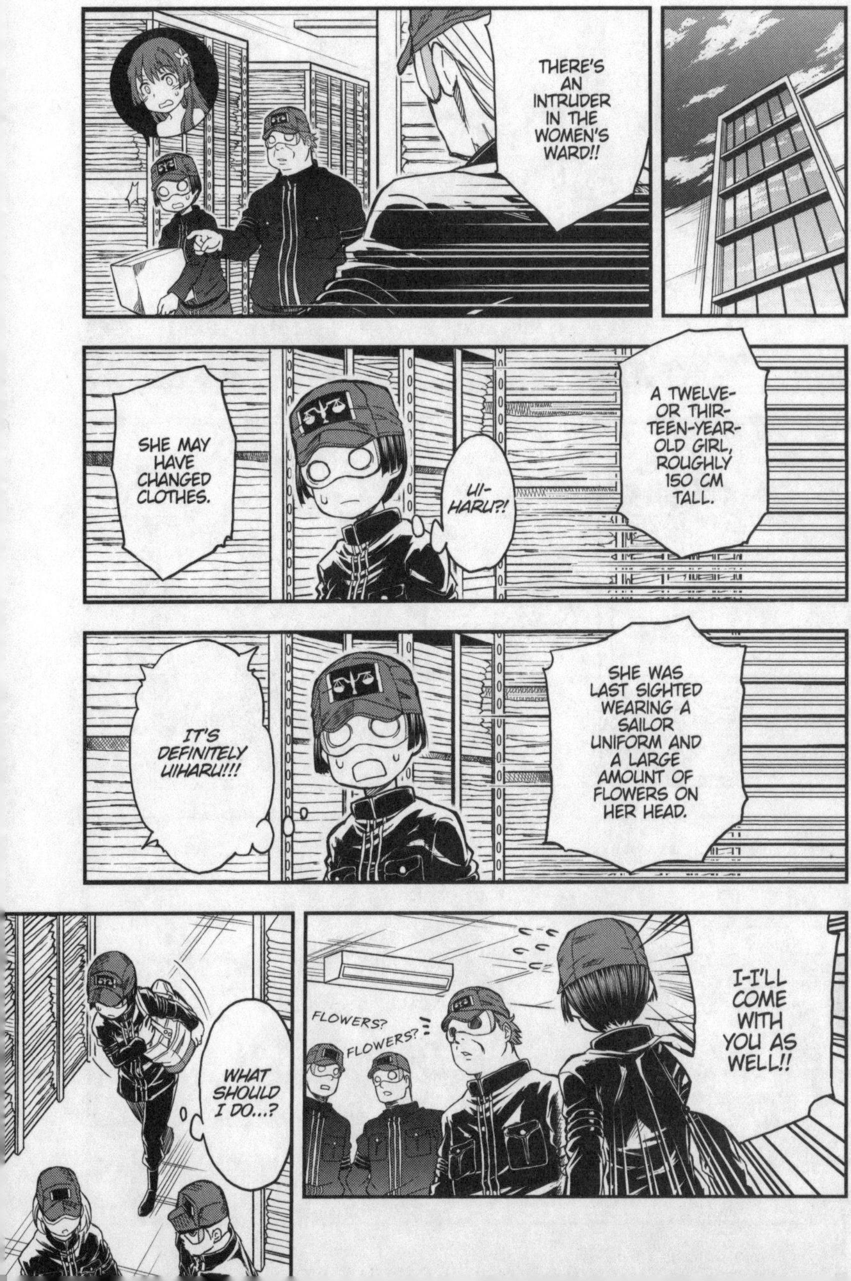
THERE'S AN INTRUDER IN THE WOMEN'S WARD!!
A TWELVE- OR THIRTEEN-YEAR-OLD GIRL, ROUGHLY 150 CM TALL.
UI-HARU?!
SHE MAY HAVE CHANGED CLOTHES.
SHE WAS LAST SIGHTED WEARING A SAILOR UNIFORM AND A LARGE AMOUNT OF FLOWERS ON HER HEAD.
IT'S DEFINITELY UIHARU!!!
I-I'LL COME WITH YOU AS WELL!!
FLOWERS?
FLOWERS?
WHAT SHOULD I DO...?

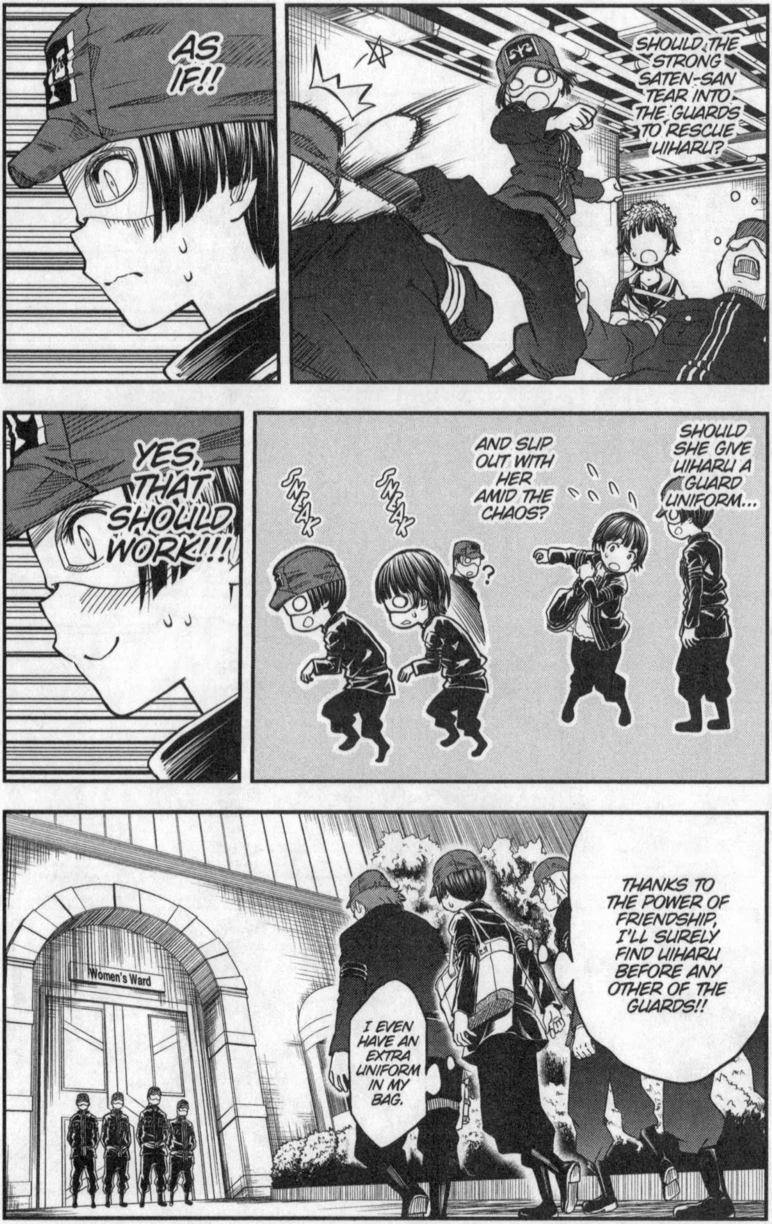
SHOULD THE STRONG SATEN-SAN TEAR INTO THE GUARDS TO RESCUE UIHARU?
AS IF!!
SHOULD SHE GIVE UIHARU A GUARD UNIFORM...
AND SLIP OUT WITH HER AMID THE CHAOS?
SNEAK
SNEAK
YES, THAT SHOULD WORK!!!
THANKS TO THE POWER OF FRIENDSHIP, I'LL SURELY FIND UIHARU BEFORE ANY OTHER OF THE GUARDS!!
I EVEN HAVE AN EXTRA UNIFORM IN MY BAG.
Women's Ward

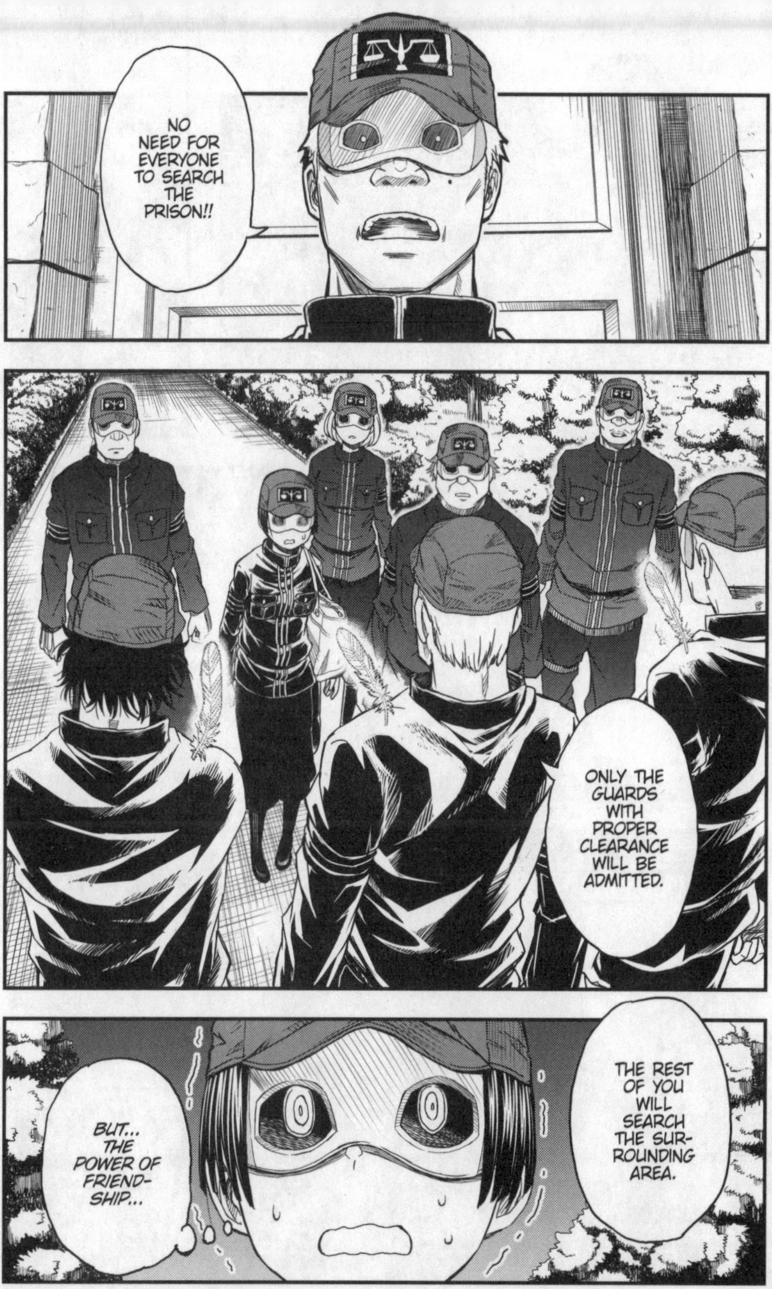
NO NEED FOR EVERYONE TO SEARCH THE PRISON!!
ONLY THE GUARDS WITH PROPER CLEARANCE WILL BE ADMITTED.
THE REST OF YOU WILL SEARCH THE SUR-ROUNDING AREA.
BUT... THE POWER OF FRIEND-SHIP...

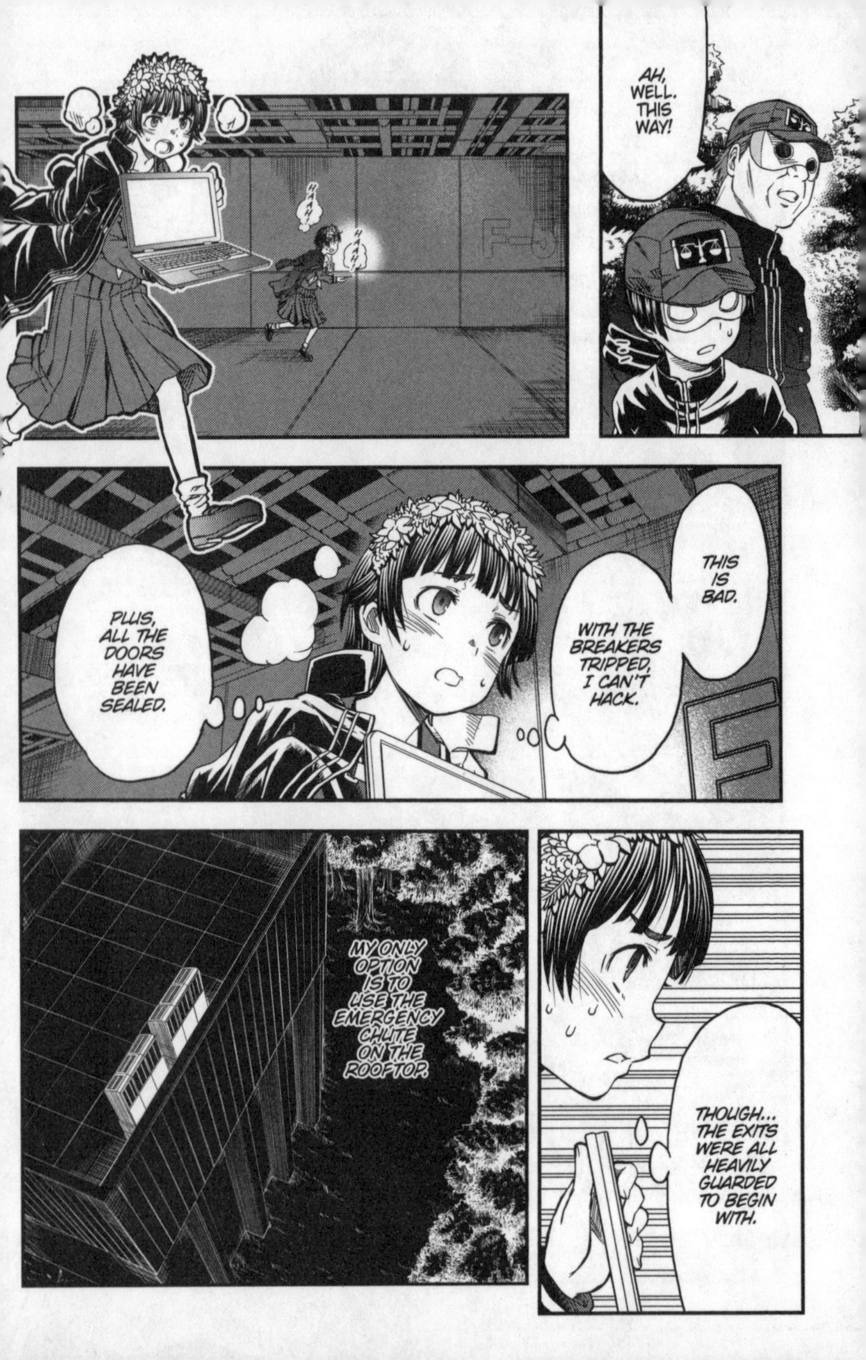
AH, WELL. THIS WAY!
HAAH!
HAAH!
THIS IS BAD.
WITH THE BREAKERS TRIPPED, I CAN'T HACK.
PLUS, ALL THE DOORS HAVE BEEN SEALED.
THOUGH... THE EXITS WERE ALL HEAVILY GUARDED TO BEGIN WITH.
MY ONLY OPTION IS TO USE THE EMERGENCY CHUTE ON THE ROOFTOP.

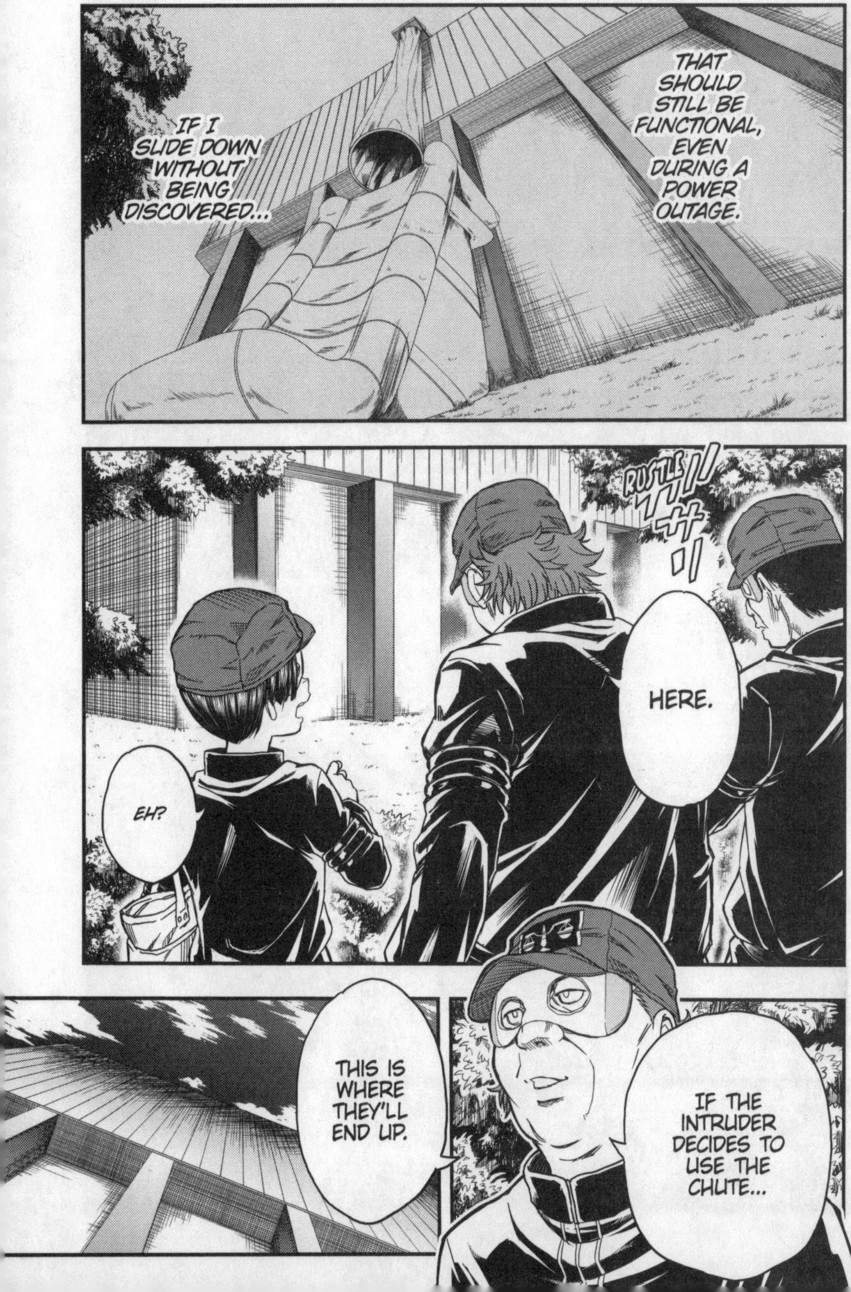
THAT SHOULD STILL BE FUNCTIONAL, EVEN DURING A POWER OUTAGE.
IF I SLIDE DOWN WITHOUT BEING DISCOVERED...
RUSTLE
HERE.
EH?
IF THE INTRUDER DECIDES TO USE THE CHUTE...
THIS IS WHERE THEY'LL END UP.

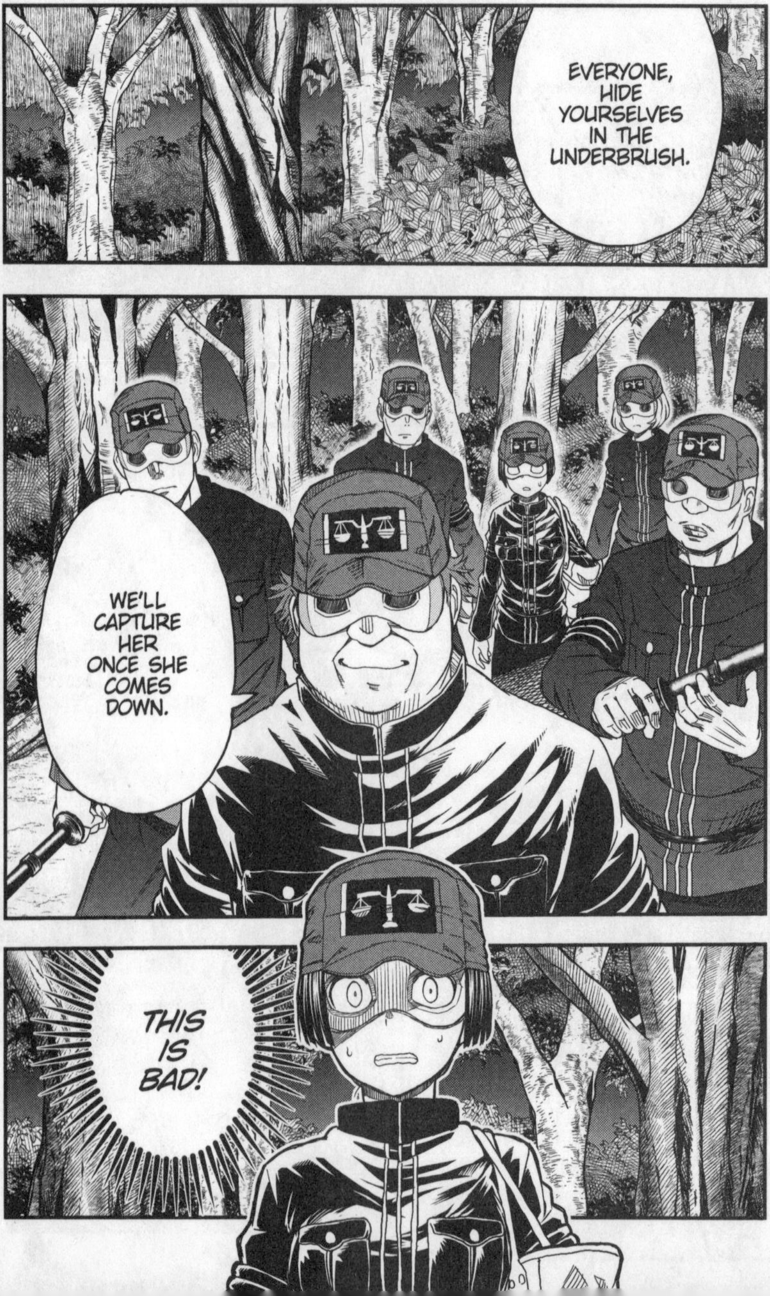
EVERYONE, HIDE YOURSELVES IN THE UNDERBRUSH.
WE'LL CAPTURE HER ONCE SHE COMES DOWN.
THIS IS BAD!

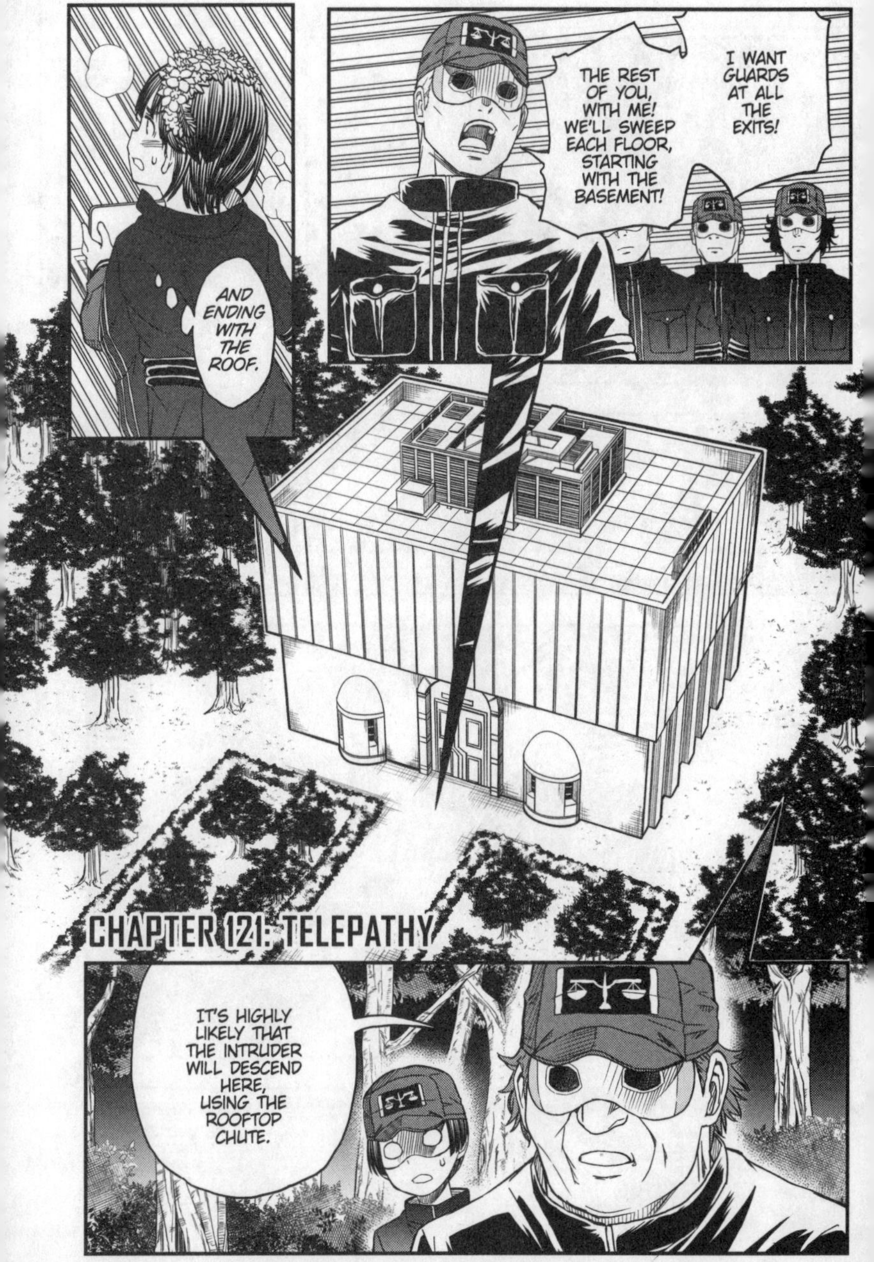
I WANT GUARDS AT ALL THE EXITS!
THE REST OF YOU, WITH ME! WE'LL SWEEP EACH FLOOR, STARTING WITH THE BASEMENT!
AND ENDING WITH THE ROOF.
CHAPTER 121: TELEPATHY
IT'S HIGHLY LIKELY THAT THE INTRUDER WILL DESCEND HERE, USING THE ROOFTOP CHUTE.

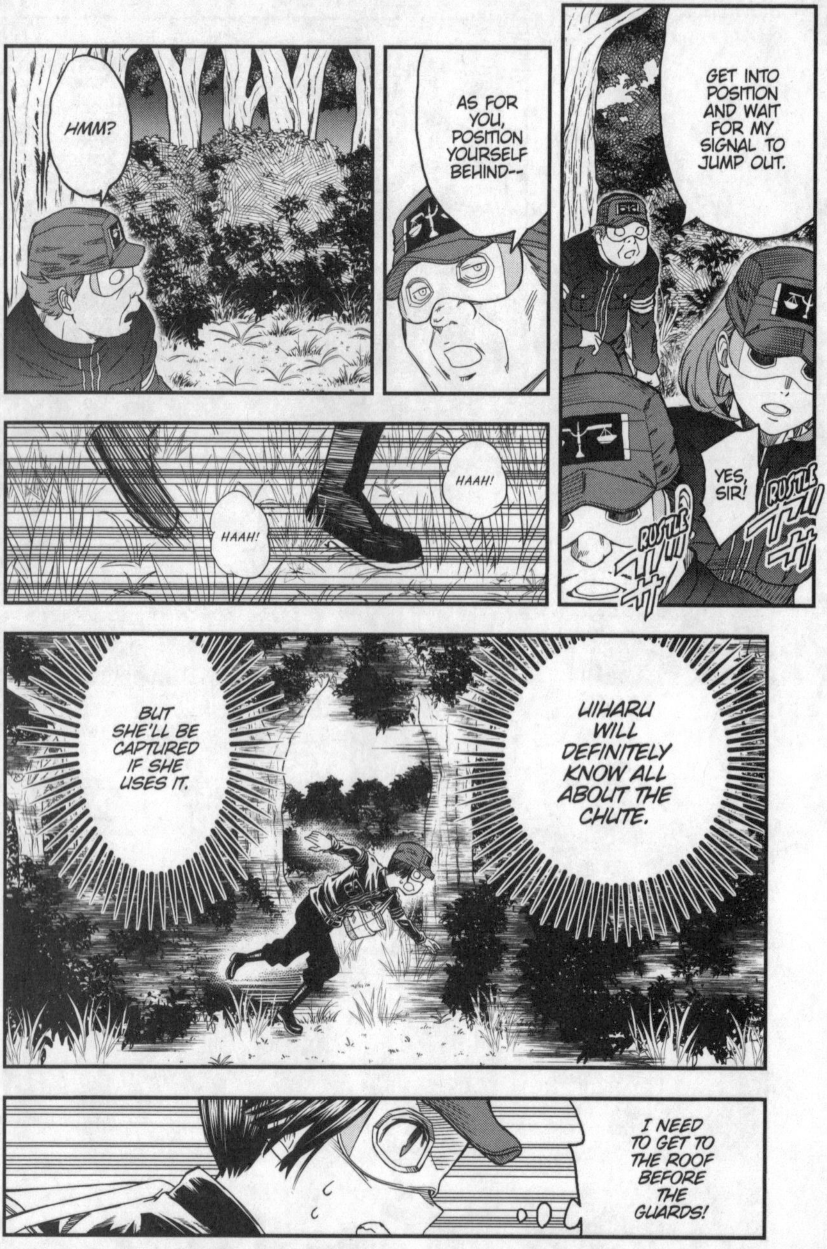
GET INTO POSITION AND WAIT FOR MY SIGNAL TO JUMP OUT.
YES, SIR!
RUSTLE
RUSTLE
AS FOR YOU, POSITION YOURSELF BEHIND--
HMM?
HAAH!
HAAH!
UIHARU WILL DEFINITELY KNOW ALL ABOUT THE CHUTE.
BUT SHE'LL BE CAPTURED IF SHE USES IT.
I NEED TO GET TO THE ROOF BEFORE THE GUARDS!

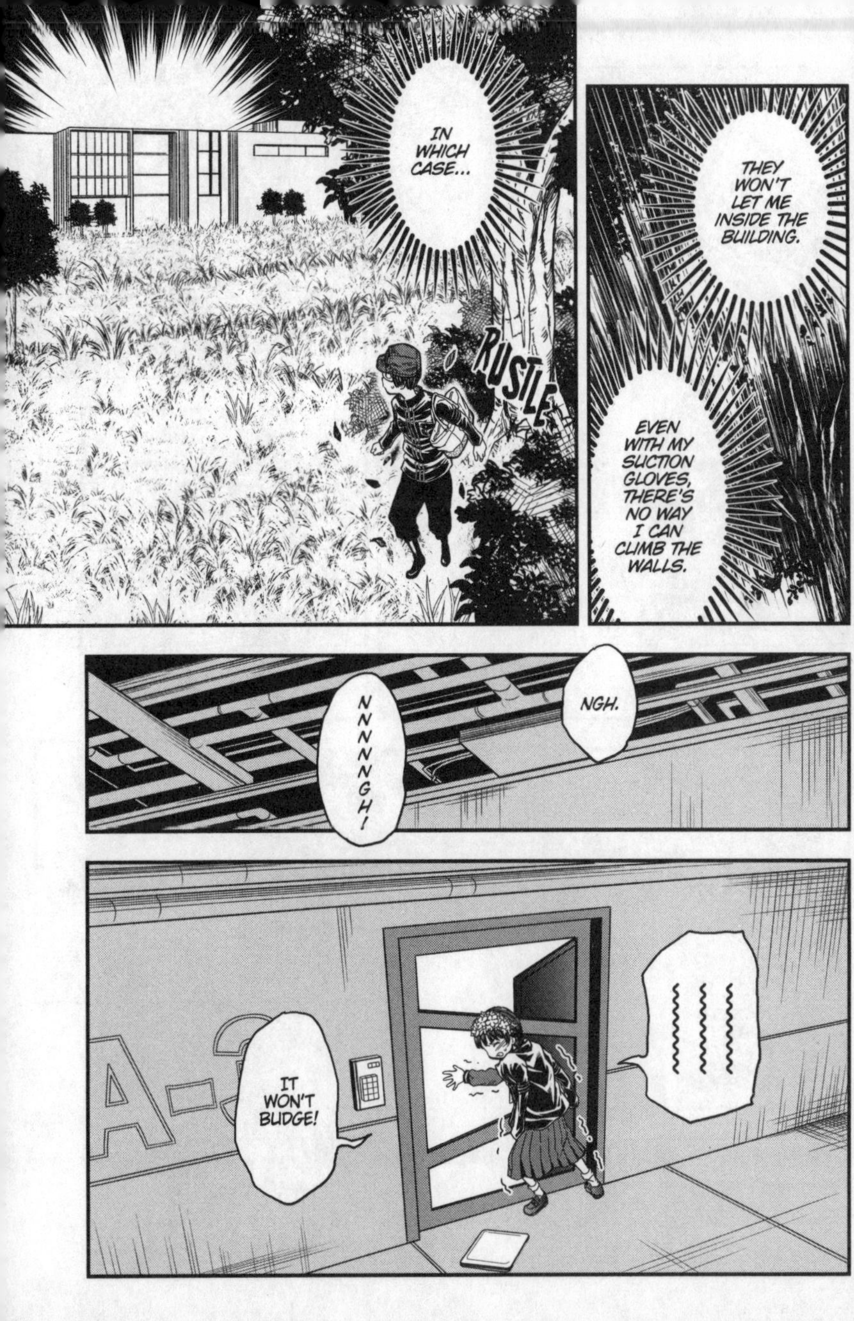
THEY WON'T LET ME INSIDE THE BUILDING.
EVEN WITH MY SUCTION GLOVES, THERE'S NO WAY I CAN CLIMB THE WALLS.
IN WHICH CASE...
RUSTLE
NGH.
NNNNNGH!
IT WON'T BUDGE!

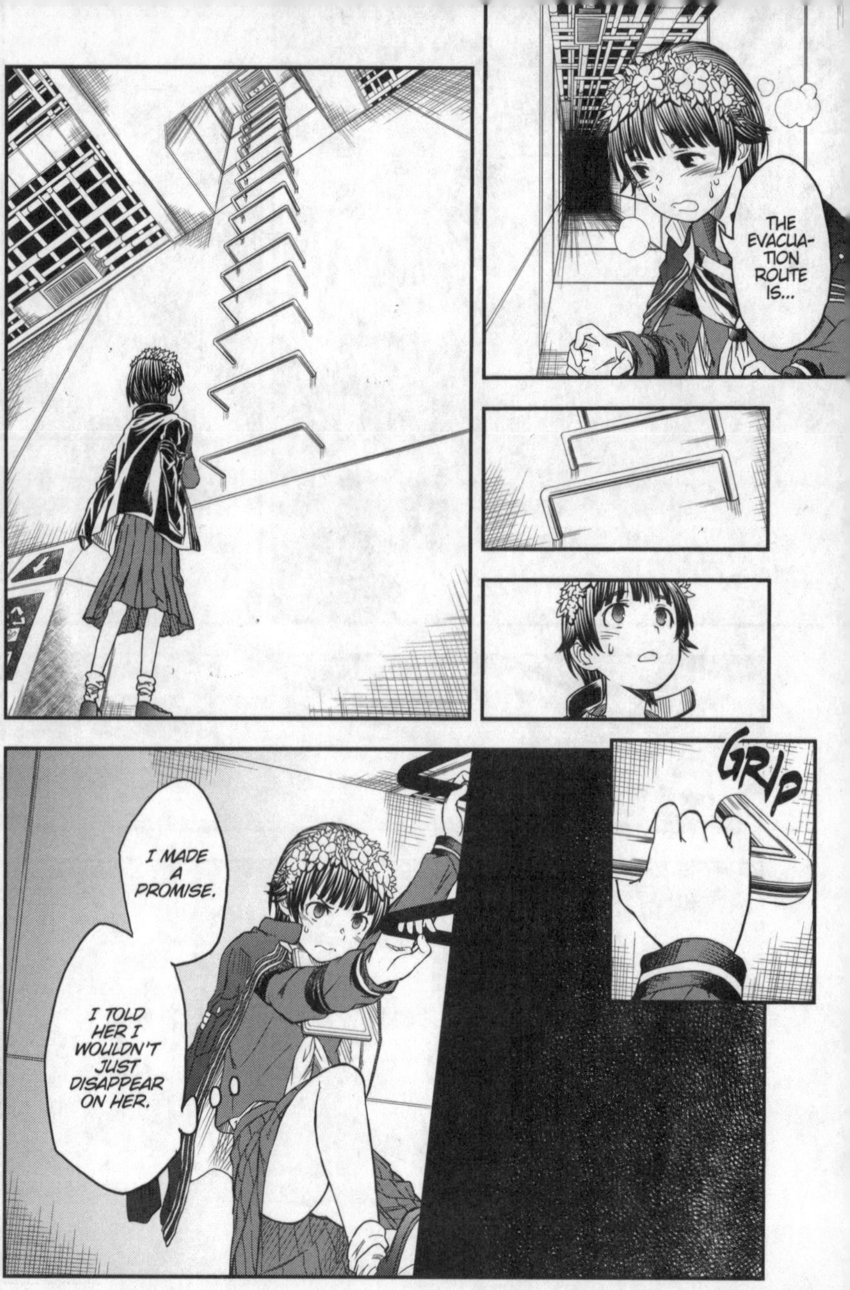
THE EVACUATION-TION ROUTE IS...
GRIP
I MADE A PROMISE.
I TOLD HER I WOULDN'T JUST DISAPPEAR ON HER.

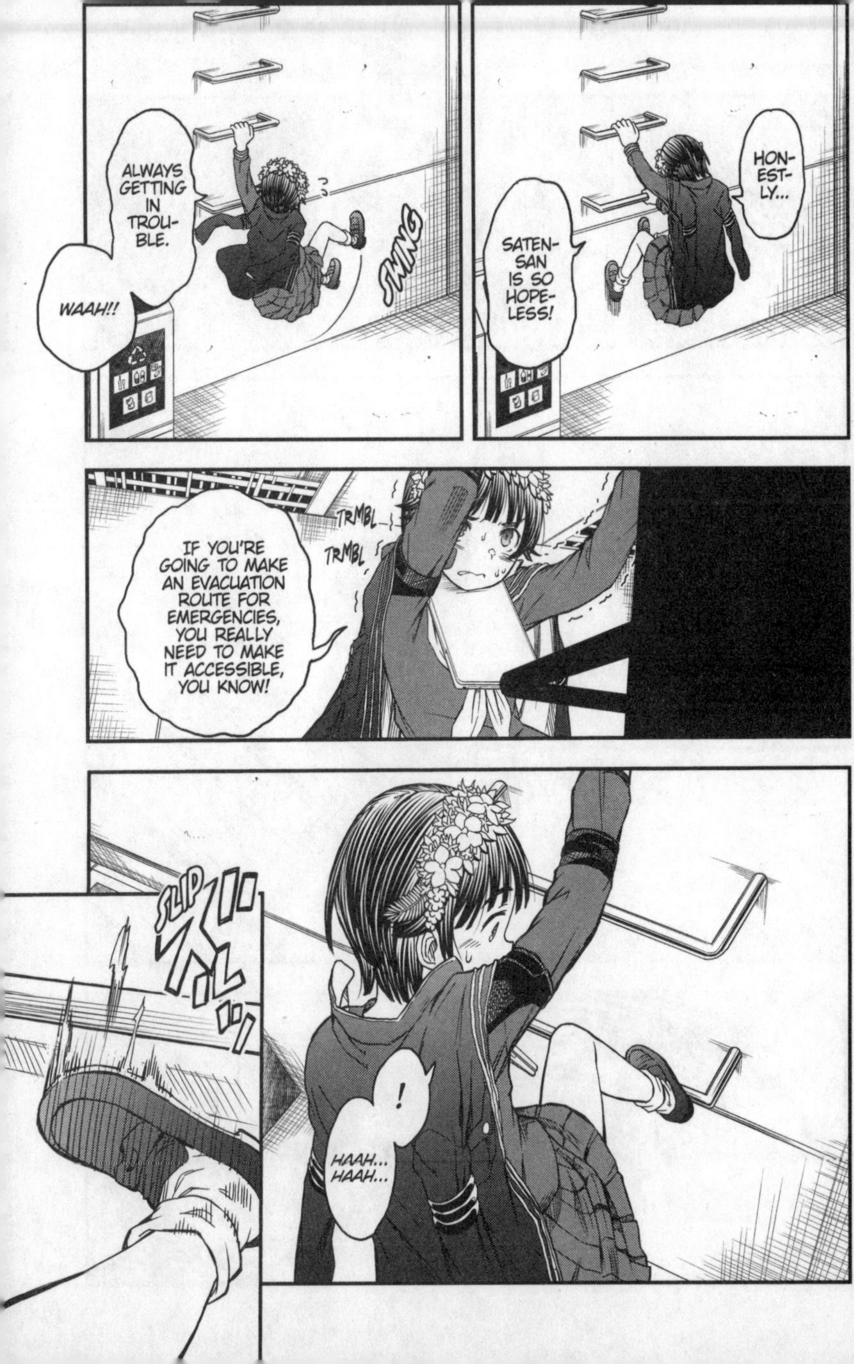
HONEST-LY...
SATEN-SAN IS SO HOPELESS!
ALWAYS GETTING IN TROUBLE.
SWING
WAAH!!
TRMBL TRMBL
IF YOU'RE GOING TO MAKE AN EVACUATION ROUTE FOR EMERGENCIES, YOU REALLY NEED TO MAKE IT ACCESSIBLE, YOU KNOW!
!
HAAH... HAAH...
SLIP

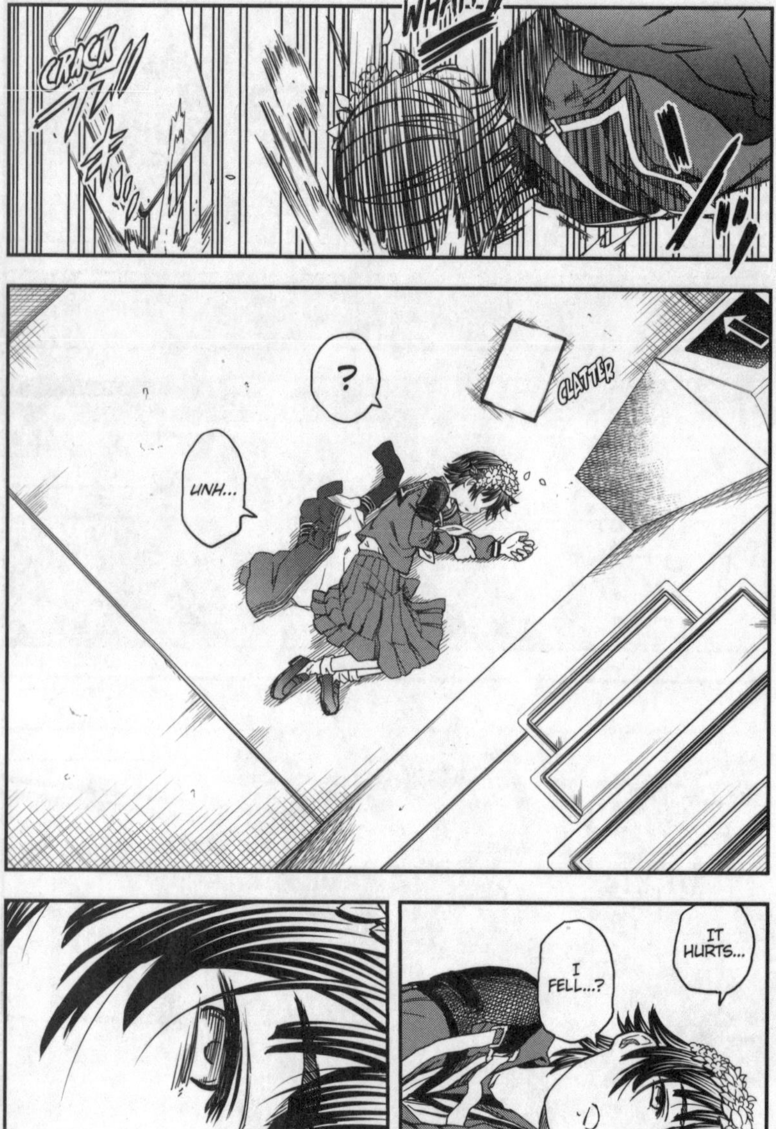
WHAM
CRACK
CLATTER
?
UNH...
IT HURTS...
I FELL...?

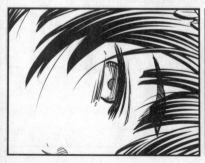

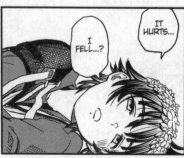

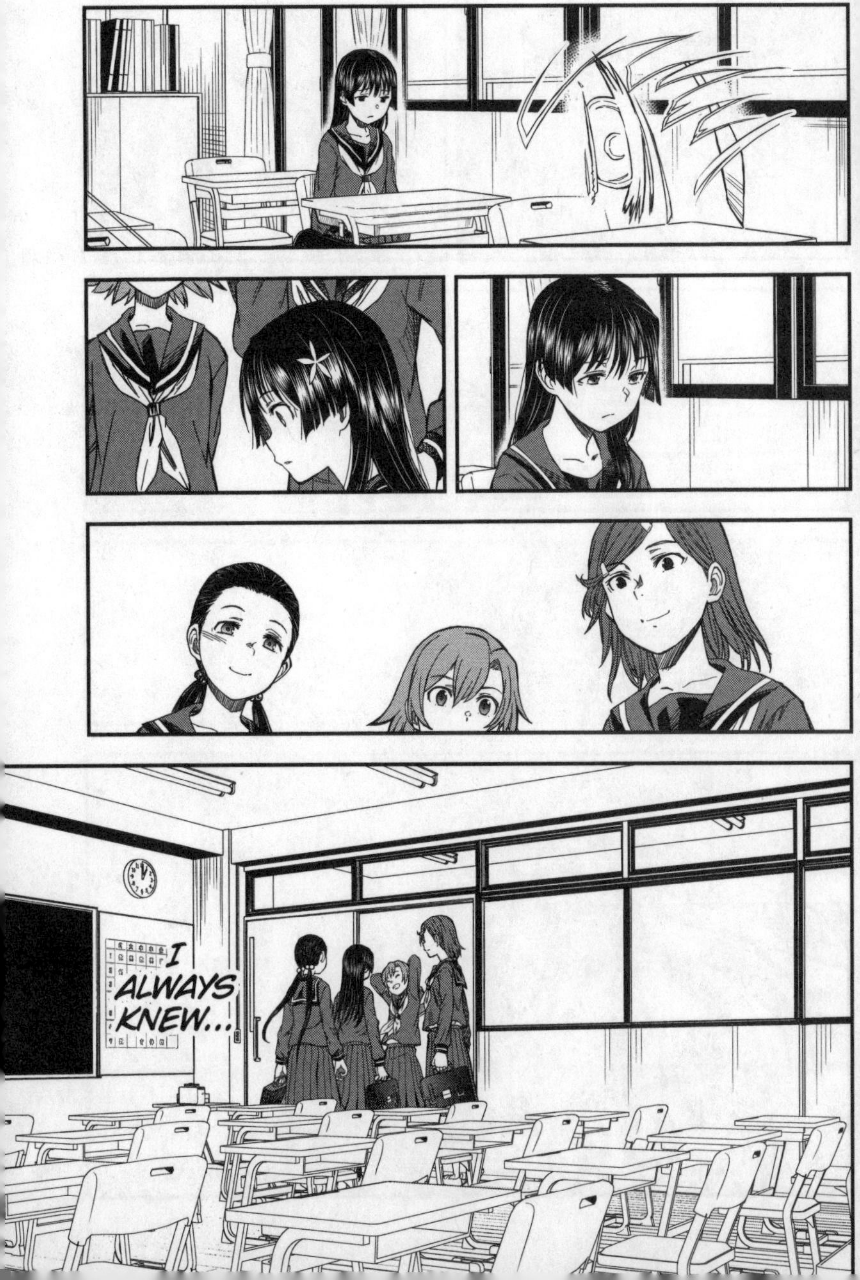
I ALWAYS KNEW...

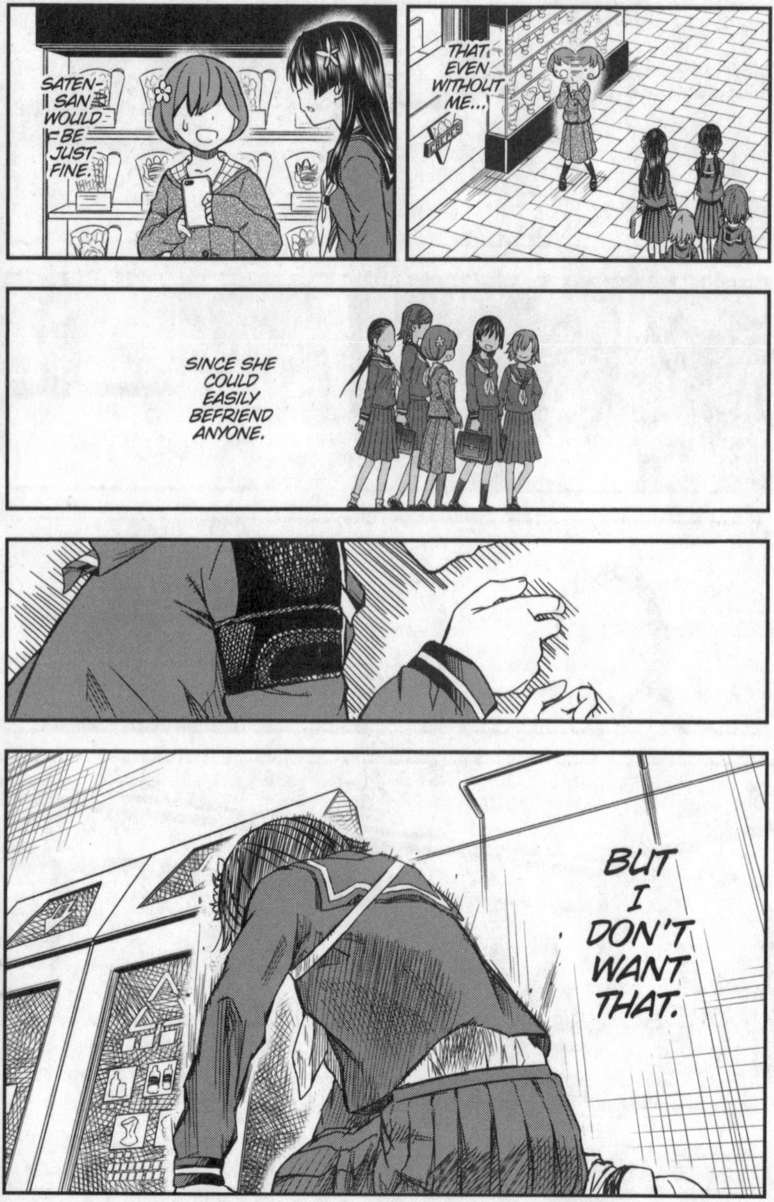
THAT EVEN WITHOUT ME...
SATEN-SAN WOULD BE JUST FINE.
SINCE SHE COULD EASILY BEFRIEND ANYONE.
BUT I DON'T WANT THAT.

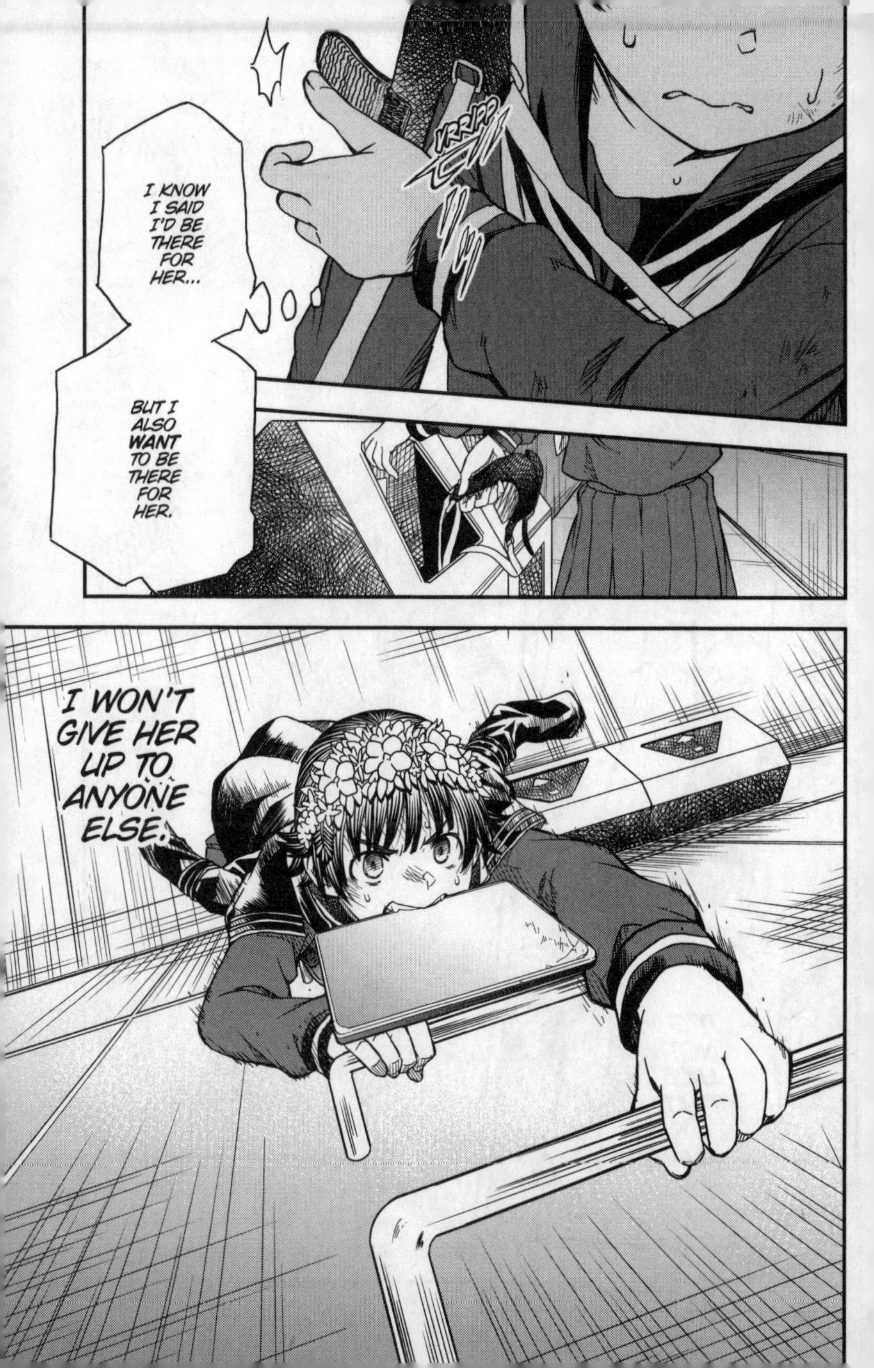
VRRIPP
I KNOW I SAID I'D BE THERE FOR HER...
BUT I ALSO WANT TO BE THERE FOR HER.
I WON'T GIVE HER UP TO ANYONE ELSE.

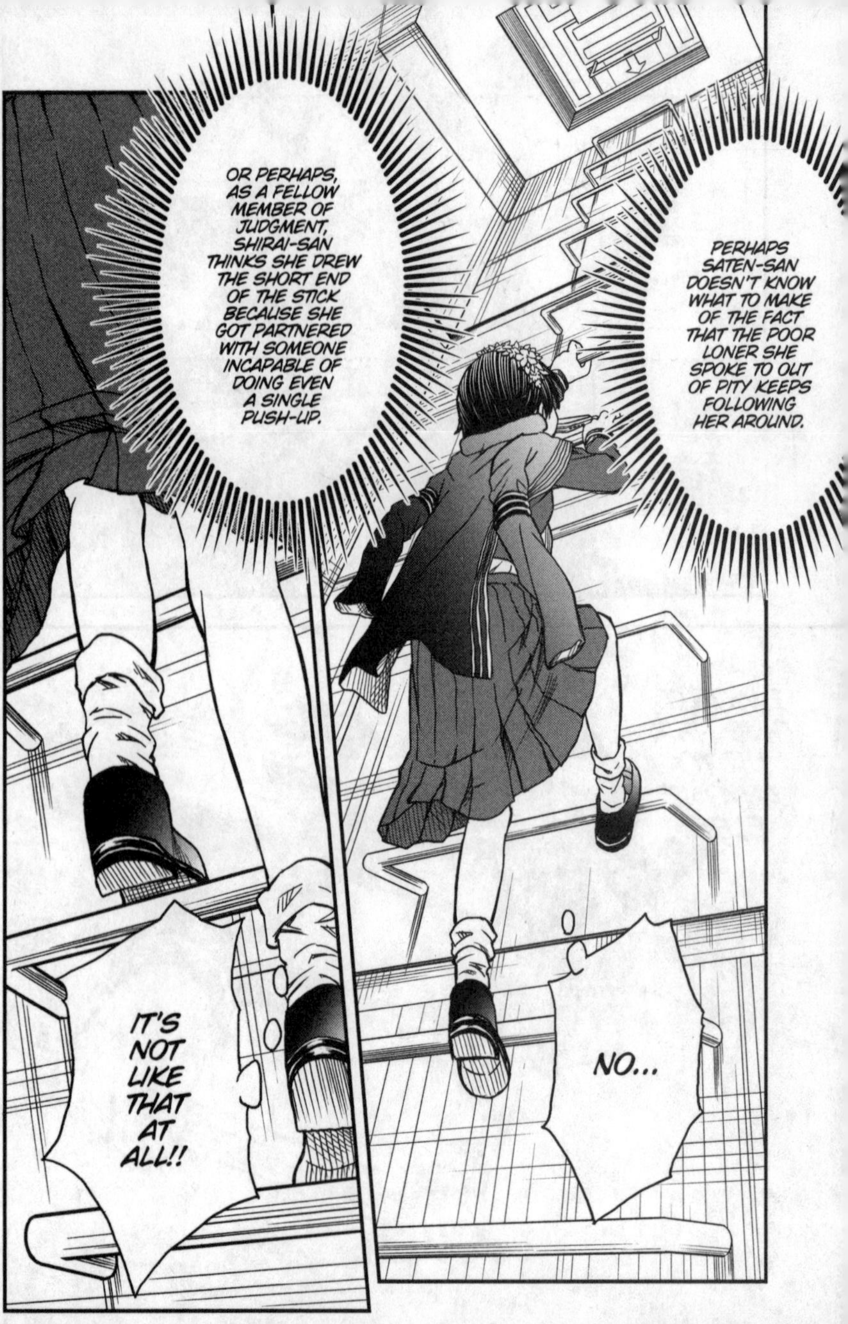
PERHAPS SATEN-SAN DOESN'T KNOW WHAT TO MAKE OF THE FACT THAT THE POOR LONER SHE SPOKE TO OUT OF PITY KEEPS FOLLOWING HER AROUND.
OR PERHAPS, AS A FELLOW MEMBER OF JUDGMENT, SHIRAI-SAN THINKS SHE DREW THE SHORT END OF THE STICK BECAUSE SHE GOT PARTNERED WITH SOMEONE INCAPABLE OF DOING EVEN A SINGLE PUSH-UP.
NO...
IT'S NOT LIKE THAT AT ALL!!

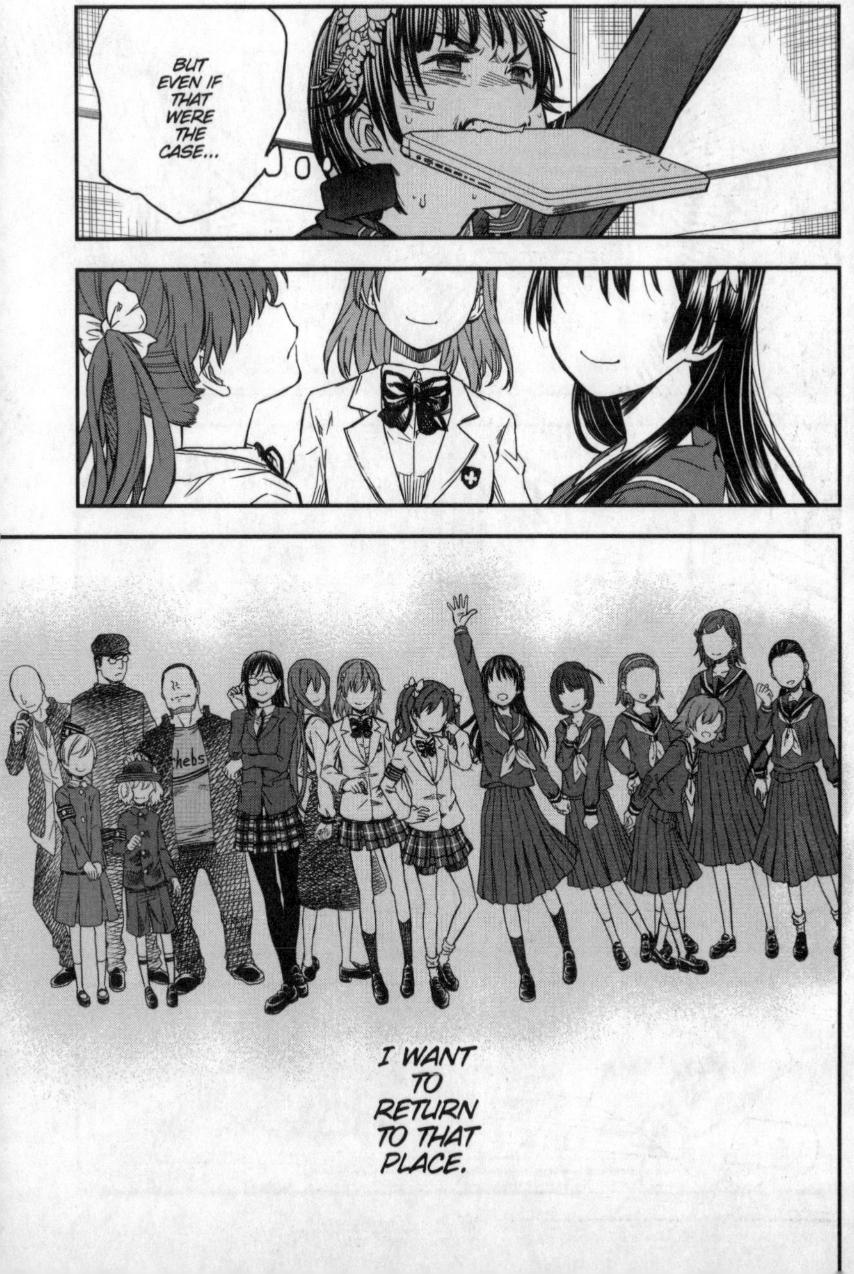
BUT EVEN IF THAT WERE THE CASE...
I WANT TO RETURN TO THAT PLACE.

NNNGGGGHHH!

SHOVE

TRMBL
TRMBL

CREAK   CREAK

HUH?
IT
WON'T
OPEN.

IS IT
LOCKED?
IT
SHOULDN'T
BE.

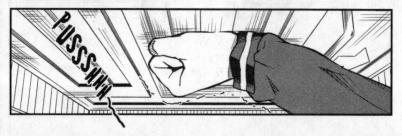

PUSSSNNN

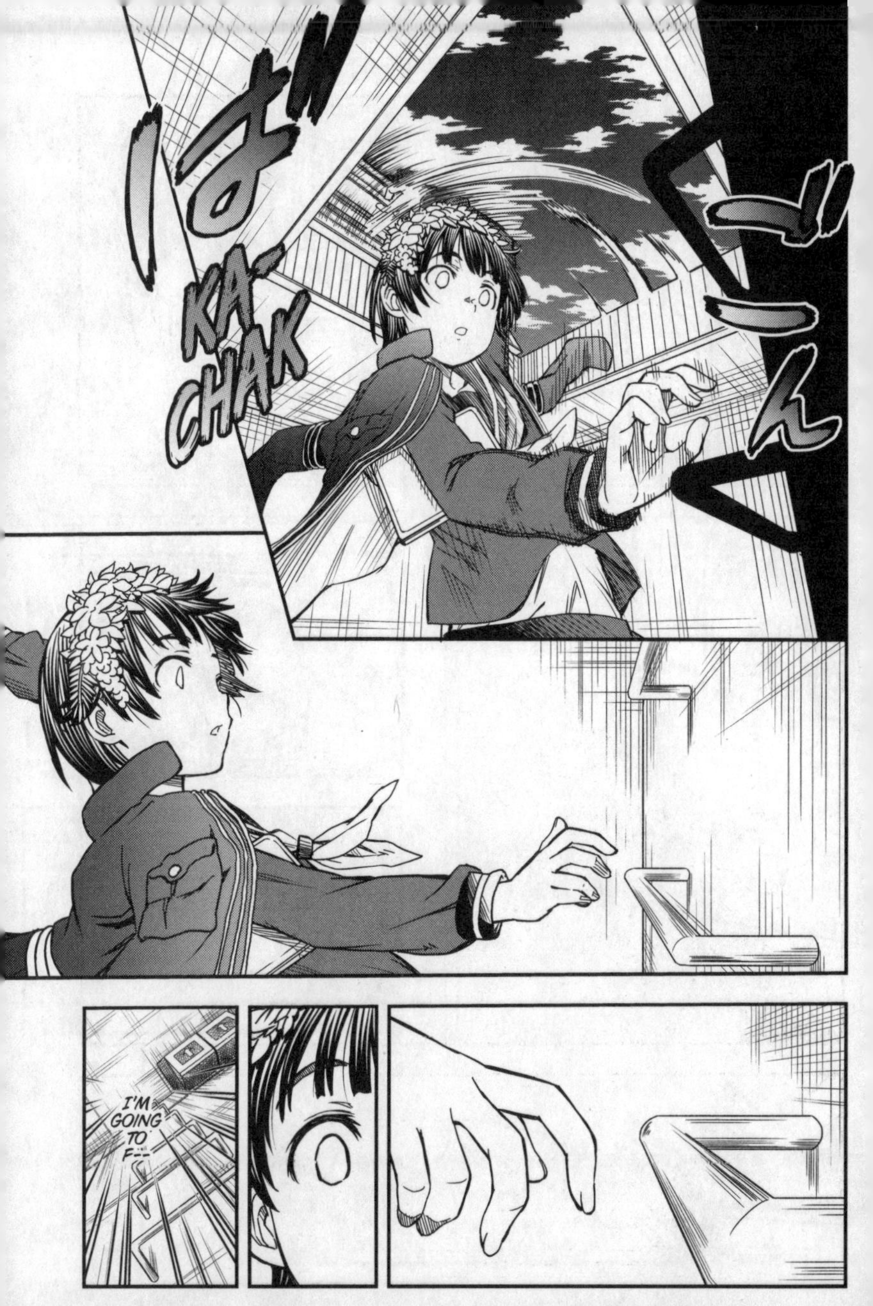
KA-CHAK
I'M GOING TO F--

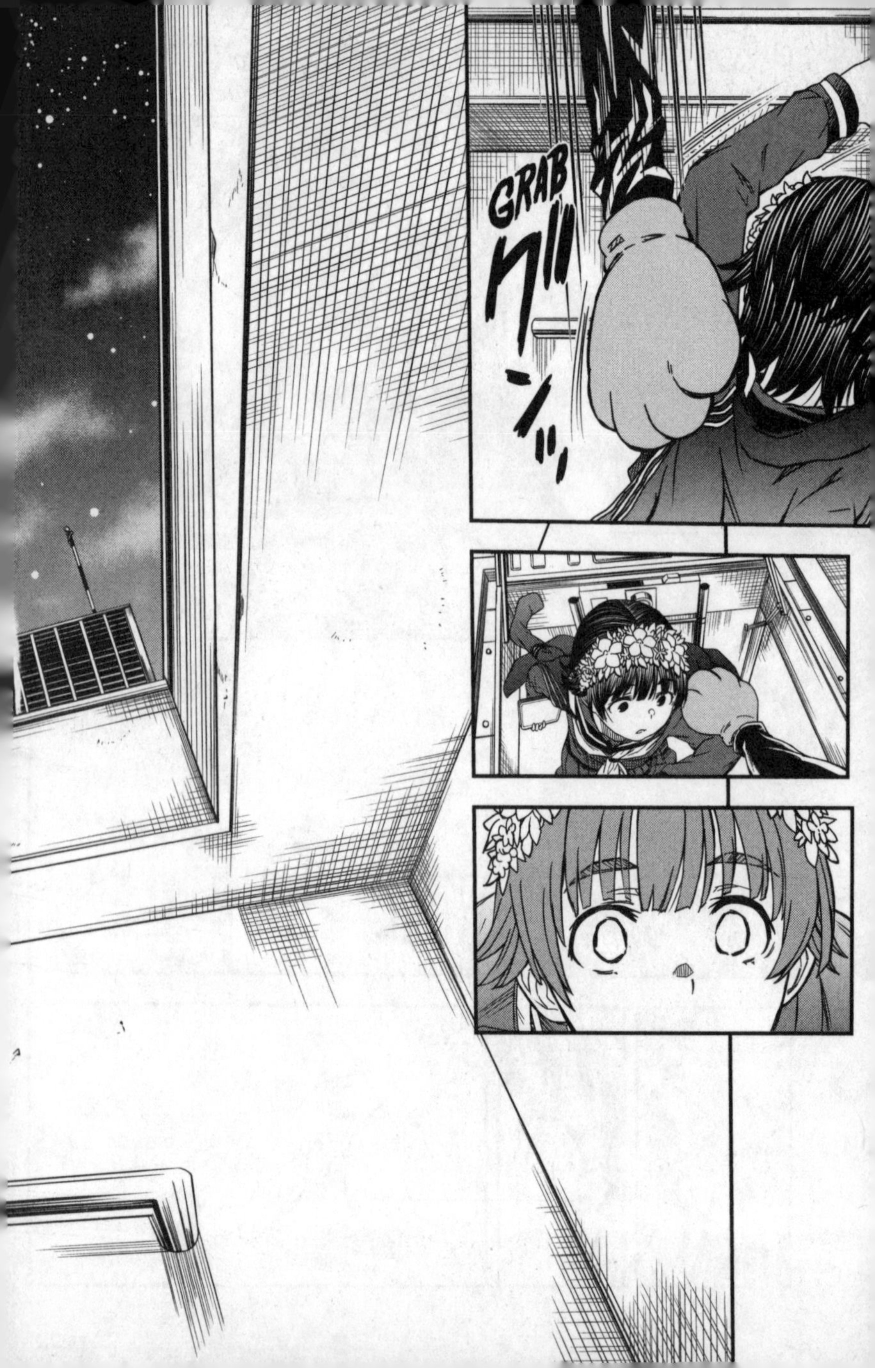
GRAB

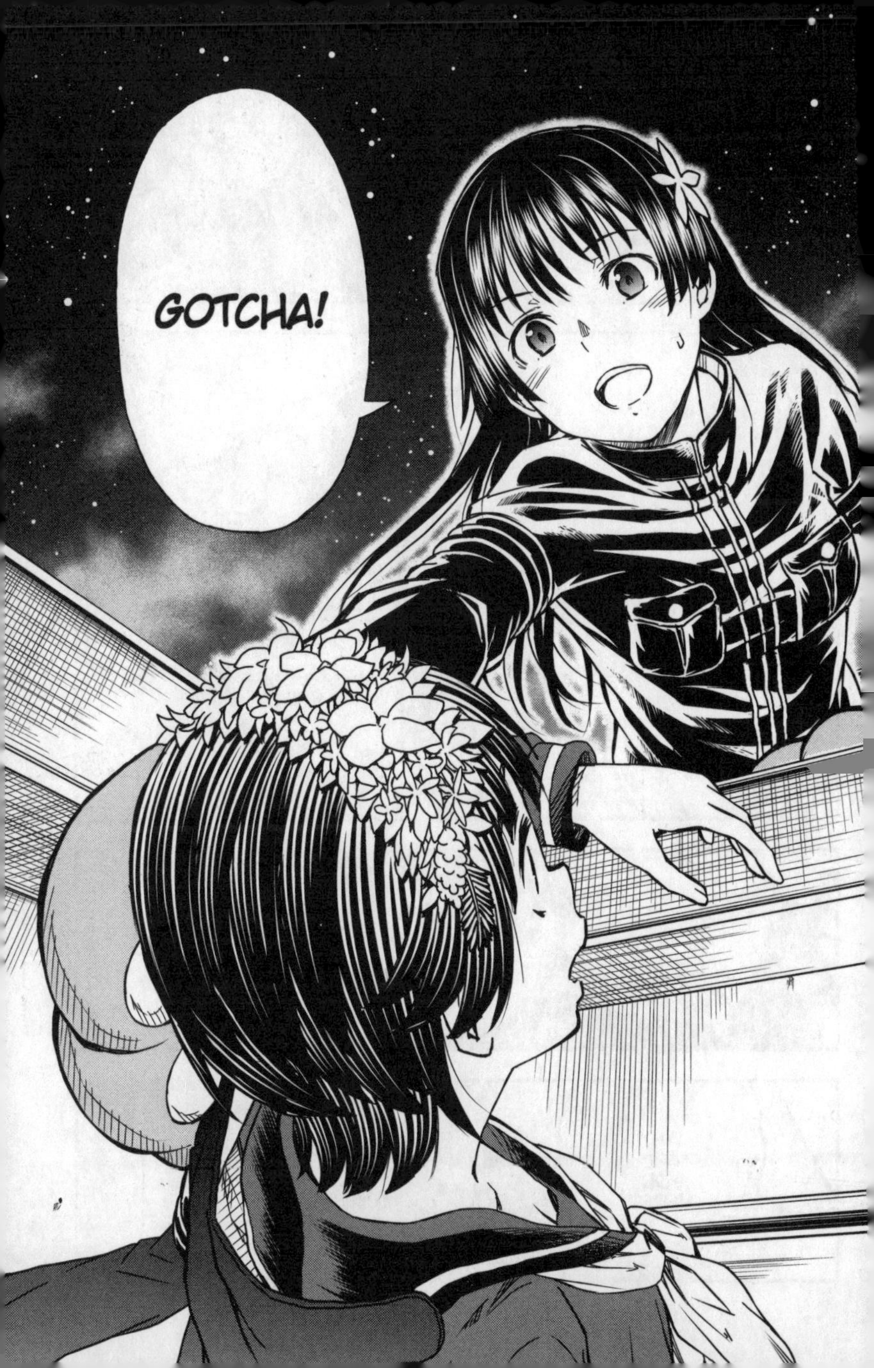
GOTCHA!

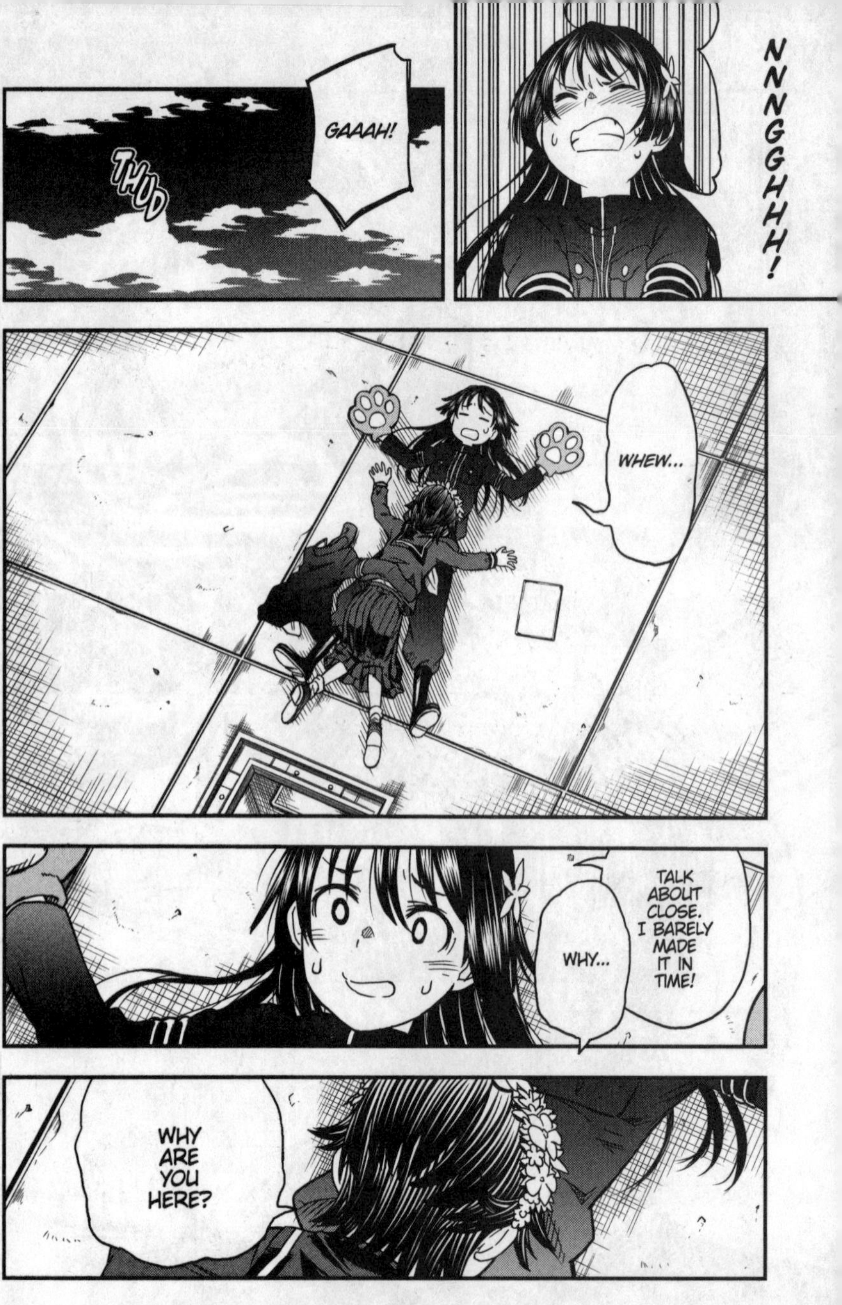
NNNGGHHH!
GAAAH!
THUD
WHEW...
TALK ABOUT CLOSE. I BARELY MADE IT IN TIME!
WHY...
WHY ARE YOU HERE?

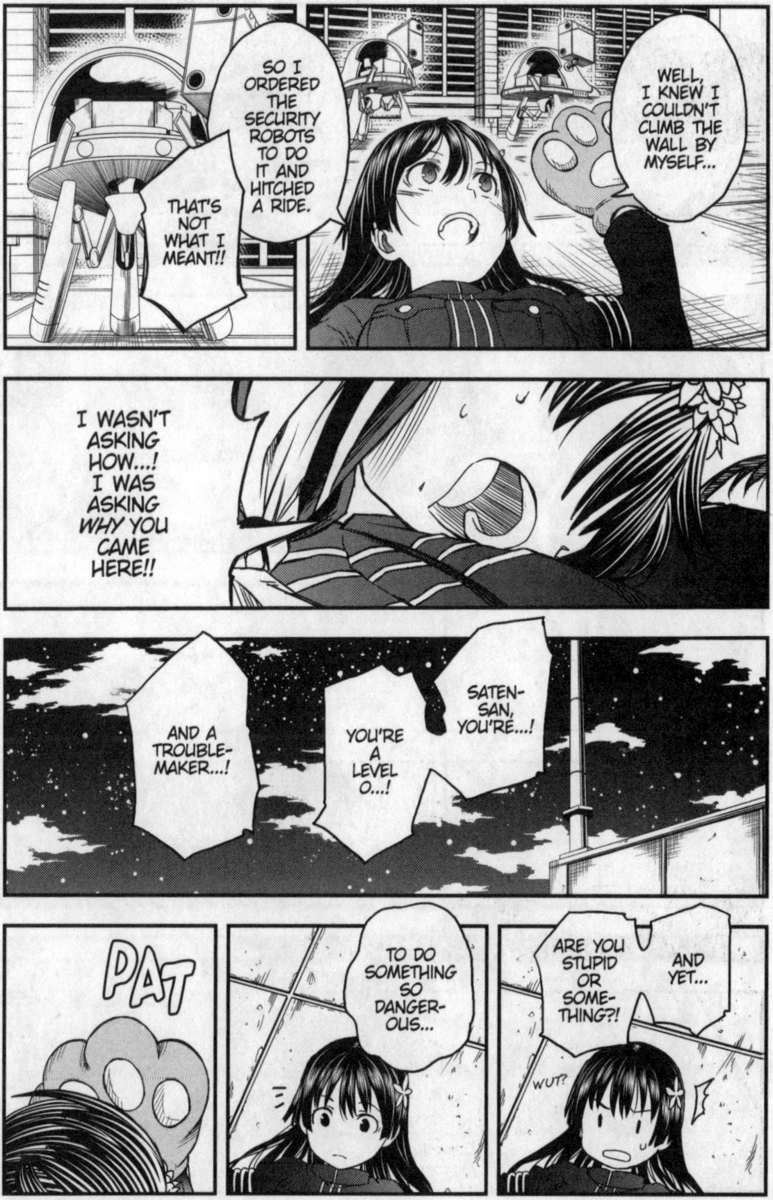
WELL, I KNEW I COULDN'T CLIMB THE WALL BY MYSELF...
SO I ORDERED THE SECURITY ROBOTS TO DO IT AND HITCHED A RIDE.
THAT'S NOT WHAT I MEANT!!
I WASN'T ASKING HOW...! I WAS ASKING *WHY* YOU CAME HERE!!
SATEN-SAN, YOU'RE...!
YOU'RE A LEVEL 0...!
AND A TROUBLE-MAKER...!
AND YET...
ARE YOU STUPID OR SOME-THING?!
WUT?
TO DO SOMETHING SO DANGER-OUS...
PAT

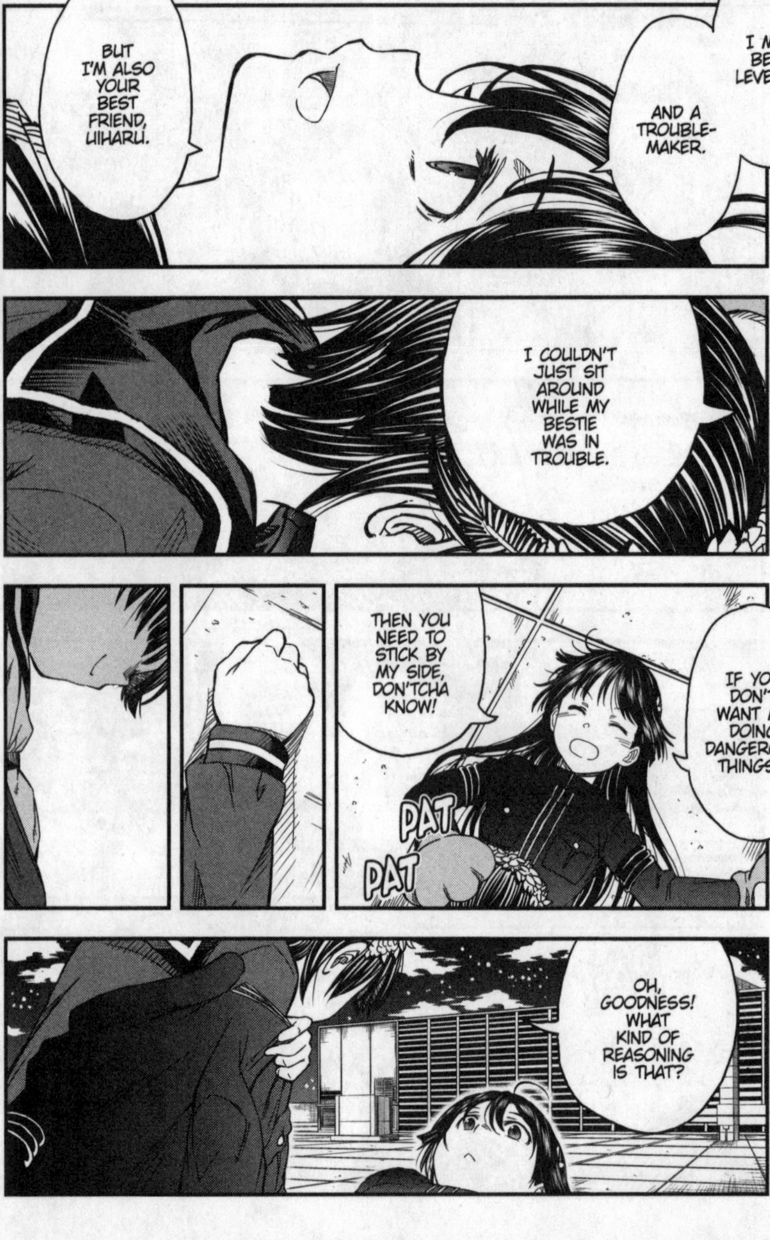
I MAY BE A LEVEL 0.
AND A TROUBLE-MAKER.
BUT I'M ALSO YOUR BEST FRIEND, UIHARU.
I COULDN'T JUST SIT AROUND WHILE MY BESTIE WAS IN TROUBLE.
IF YOU DON'T WANT ME DOING DANGEROUS THINGS...
THEN YOU NEED TO STICK BY MY SIDE, DON'TCHA KNOW!
PAT
PAT
OH, GOODNESS! WHAT KIND OF REASONING IS THAT?

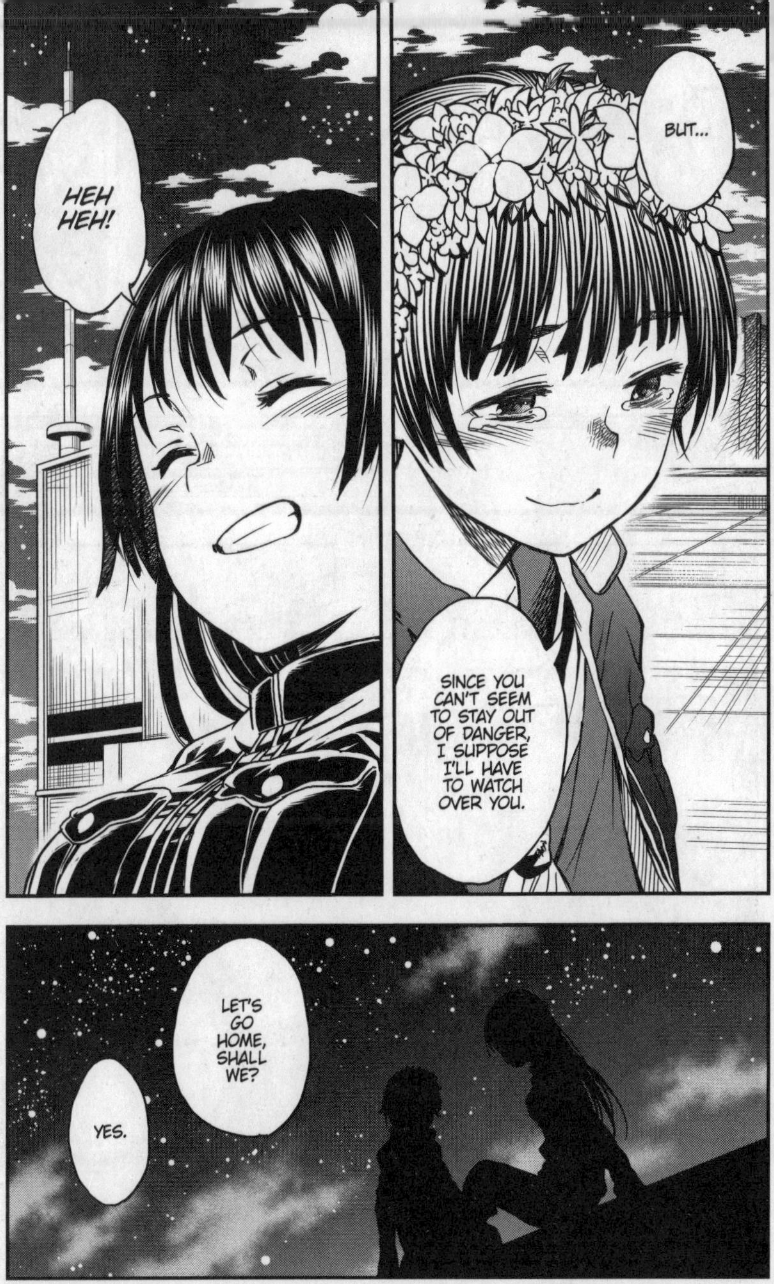
BUT...
SINCE YOU CAN'T SEEM TO STAY OUT OF DANGER, I SUPPOSE I'LL HAVE TO WATCH OVER YOU.
HEH HEH!
LET'S GO HOME, SHALL WE?
YES.

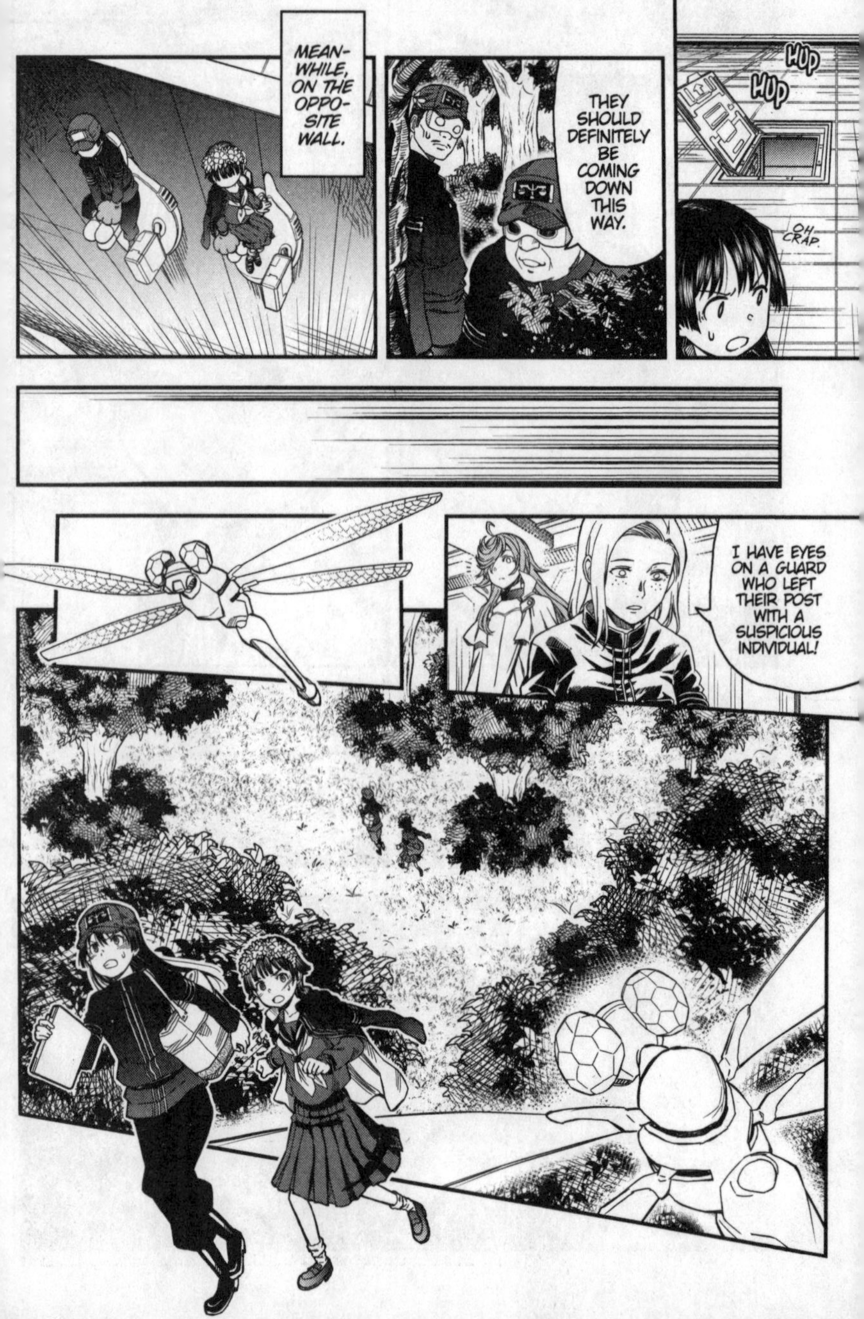
HUP
HUP
OH CRAP.
THEY SHOULD DEFINITELY BE COMING DOWN THIS WAY.
MEAN-WHILE, ON THE OPPO-SITE WALL.
I HAVE EYES ON A GUARD WHO LEFT THEIR POST WITH A SUSPICIOUS INDIVIDUAL!

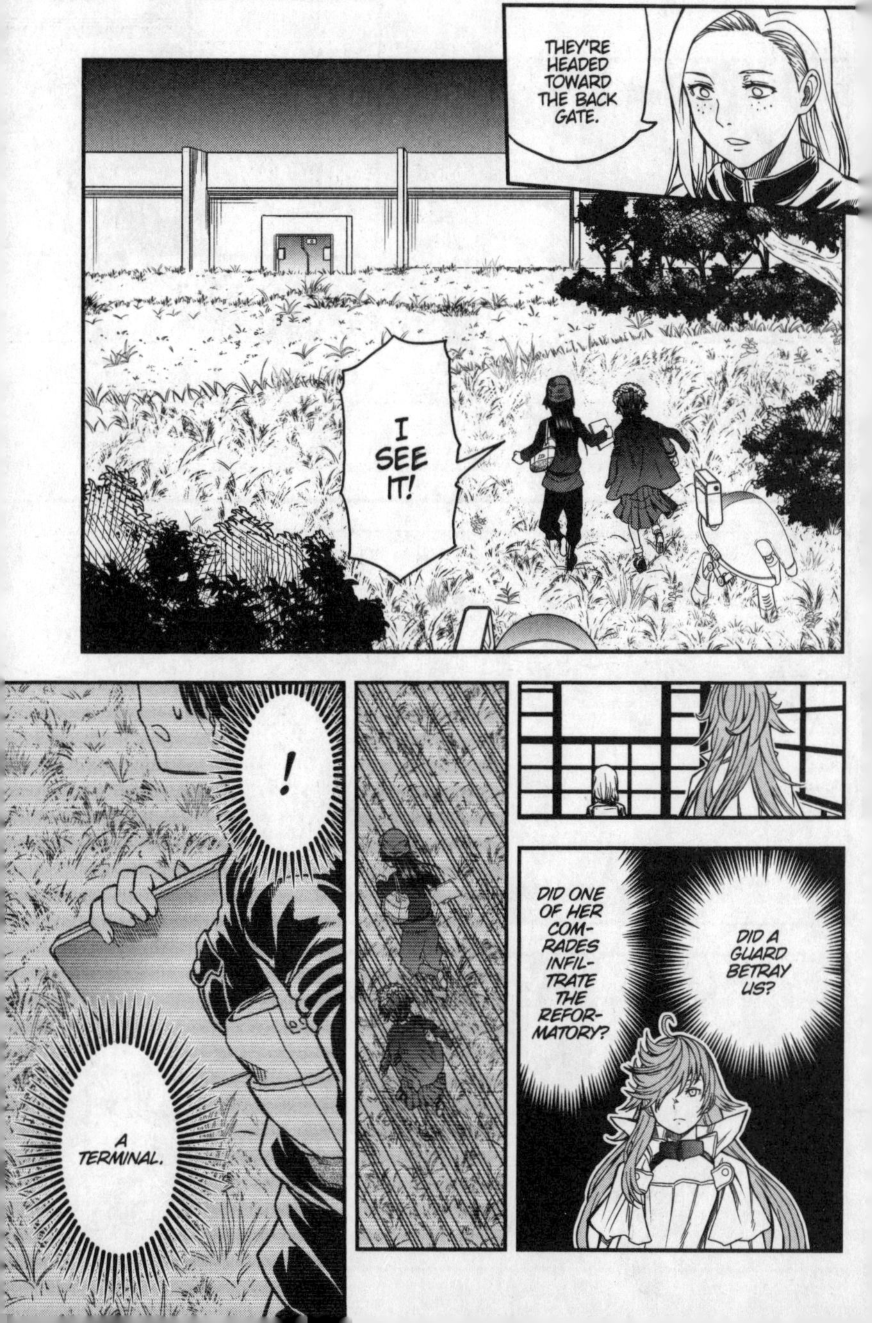
THEY'RE HEADED TOWARD THE BACK GATE.
I SEE IT!
DID A GUARD BETRAY US?
DID ONE OF HER COM-RADES INFIL-TRATE THE REFOR-MATORY?
!
A TERMINAL.

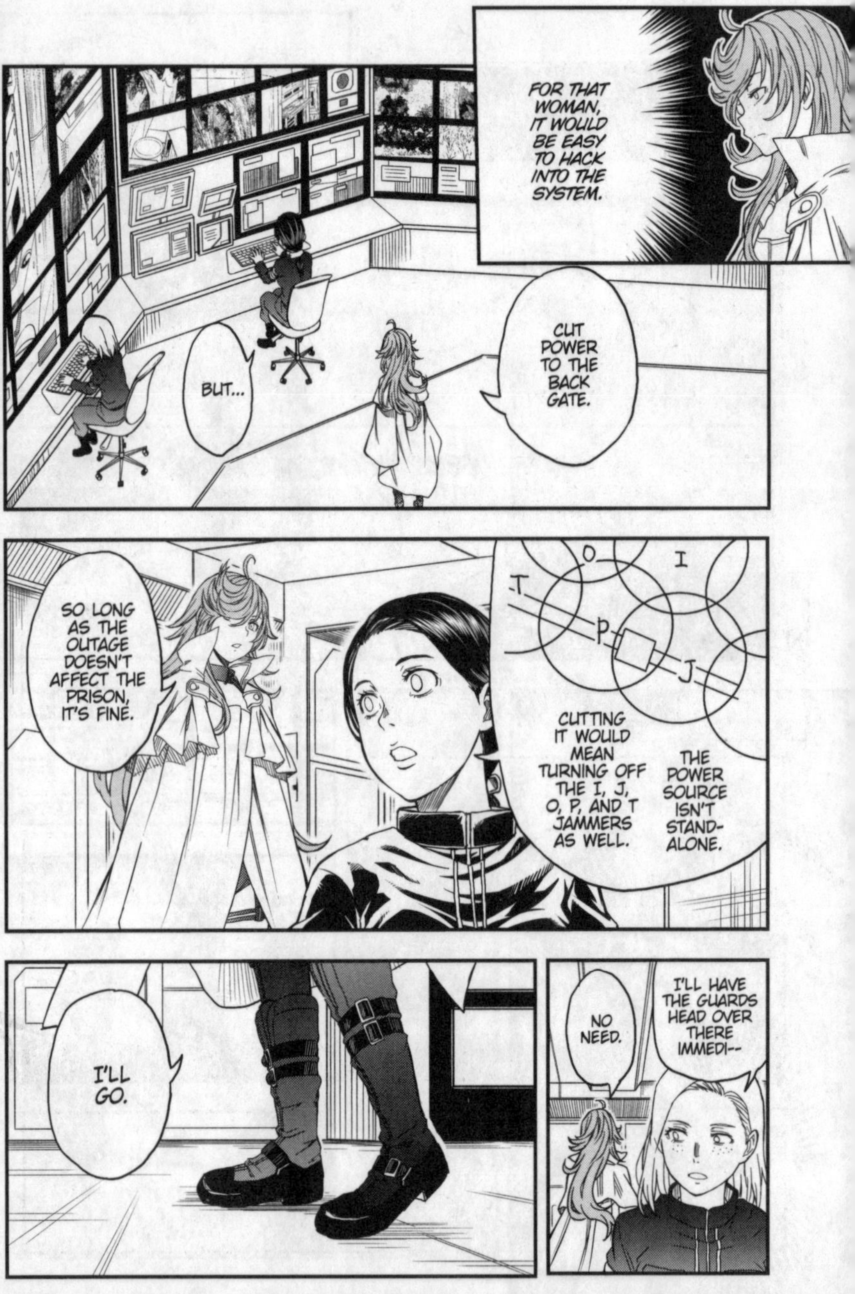
FOR THAT WOMAN, IT WOULD BE EASY TO HACK INTO THE SYSTEM.
CUT POWER TO THE BACK GATE.
BUT...
THE POWER SOURCE ISN'T STAND-ALONE.
CUTTING IT WOULD MEAN TURNING OFF THE I, J, O, P, AND T JAMMERS AS WELL.
SO LONG AS THE OUTAGE DOESN'T AFFECT THE PRISON, IT'S FINE.
I'LL HAVE THE GUARDS HEAD OVER THERE IMMEDI--
NO NEED.
I'LL GO.

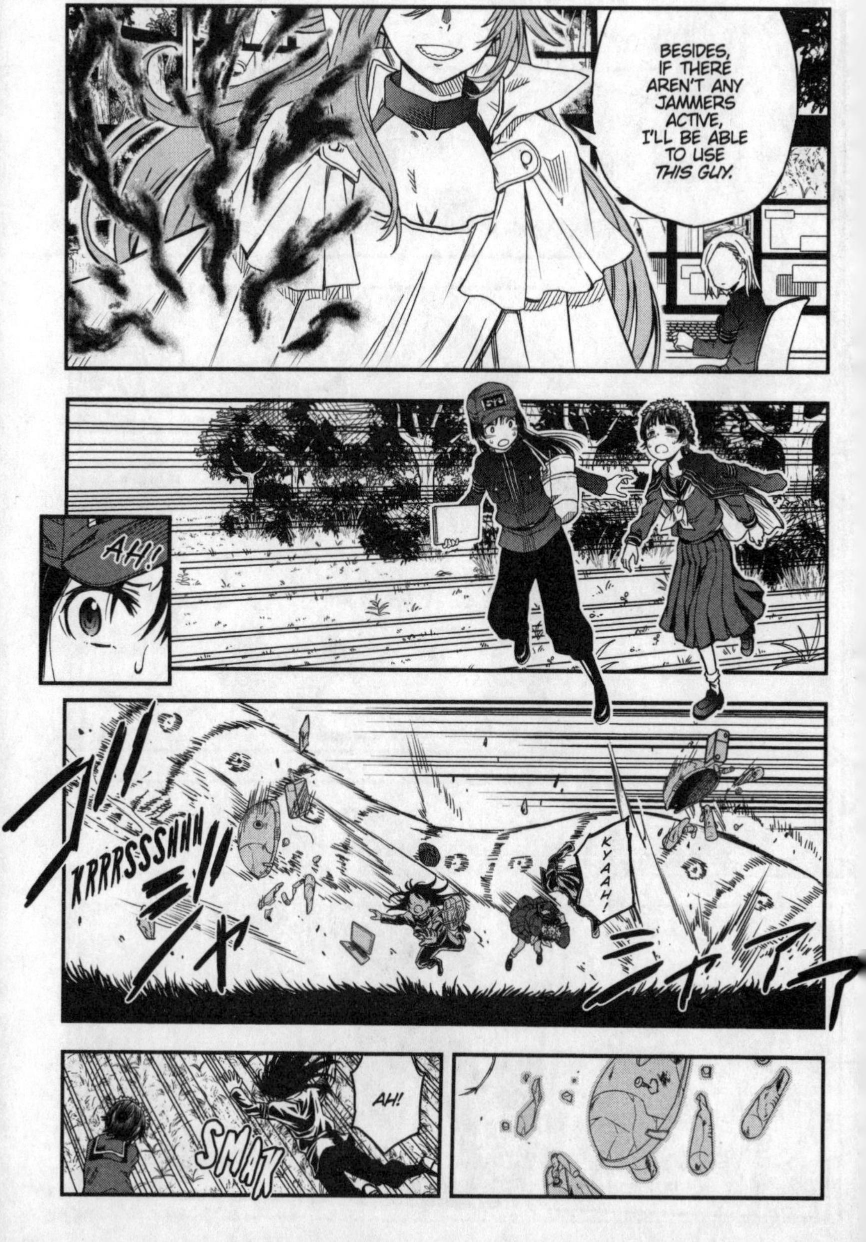
BESIDES, IF THERE AREN'T ANY JAMMERS ACTIVE, I'LL BE ABLE TO USE *THIS GUY.*
AH!
KYAAAH!
KRRRSSSHHH
AH!
SMAK

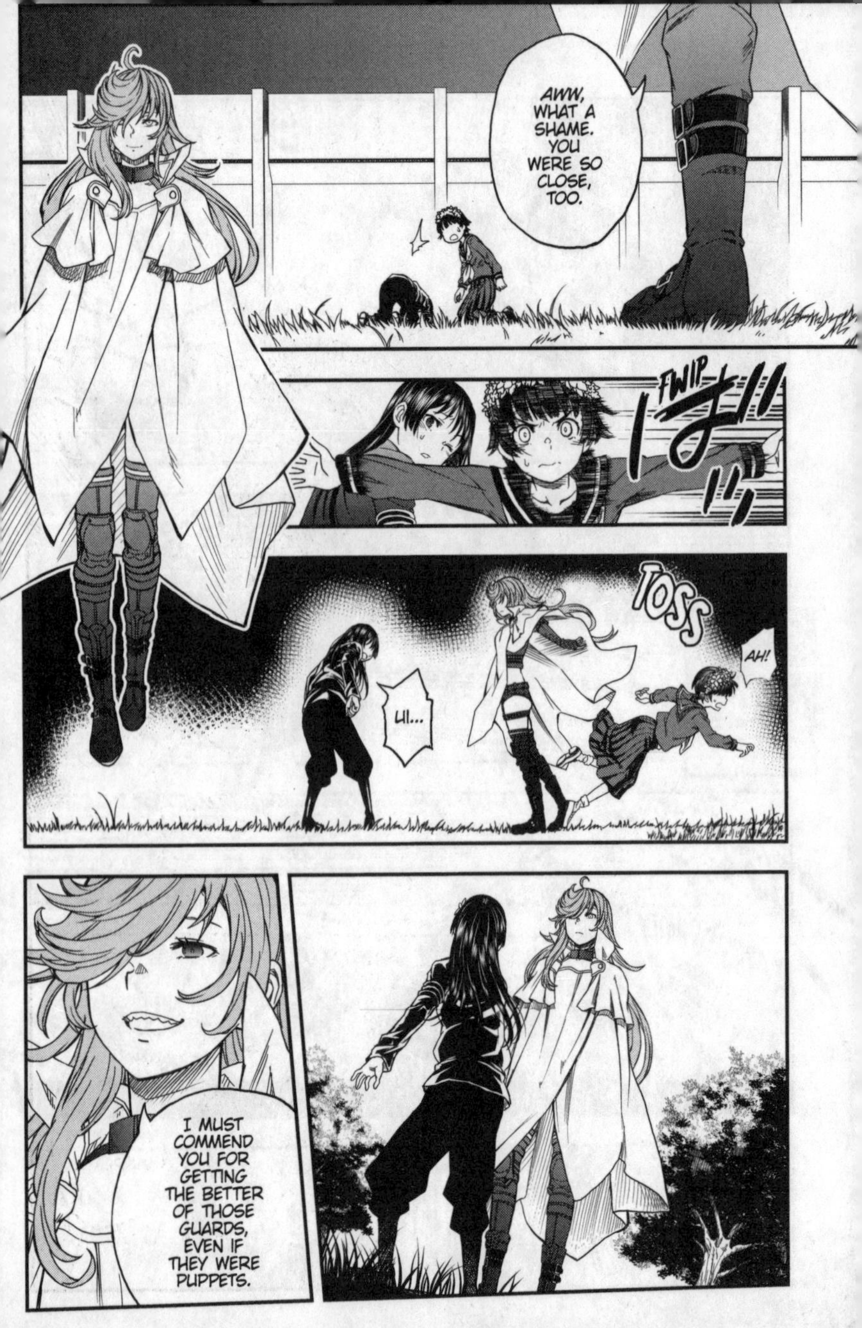
AWW, WHAT A SHAME. YOU WERE SO CLOSE, TOO.
FWIP
TOSS
AH!
UI...
I MUST COMMEND YOU FOR GETTING THE BETTER OF THOSE GUARDS, EVEN IF THEY WERE PUPPETS.

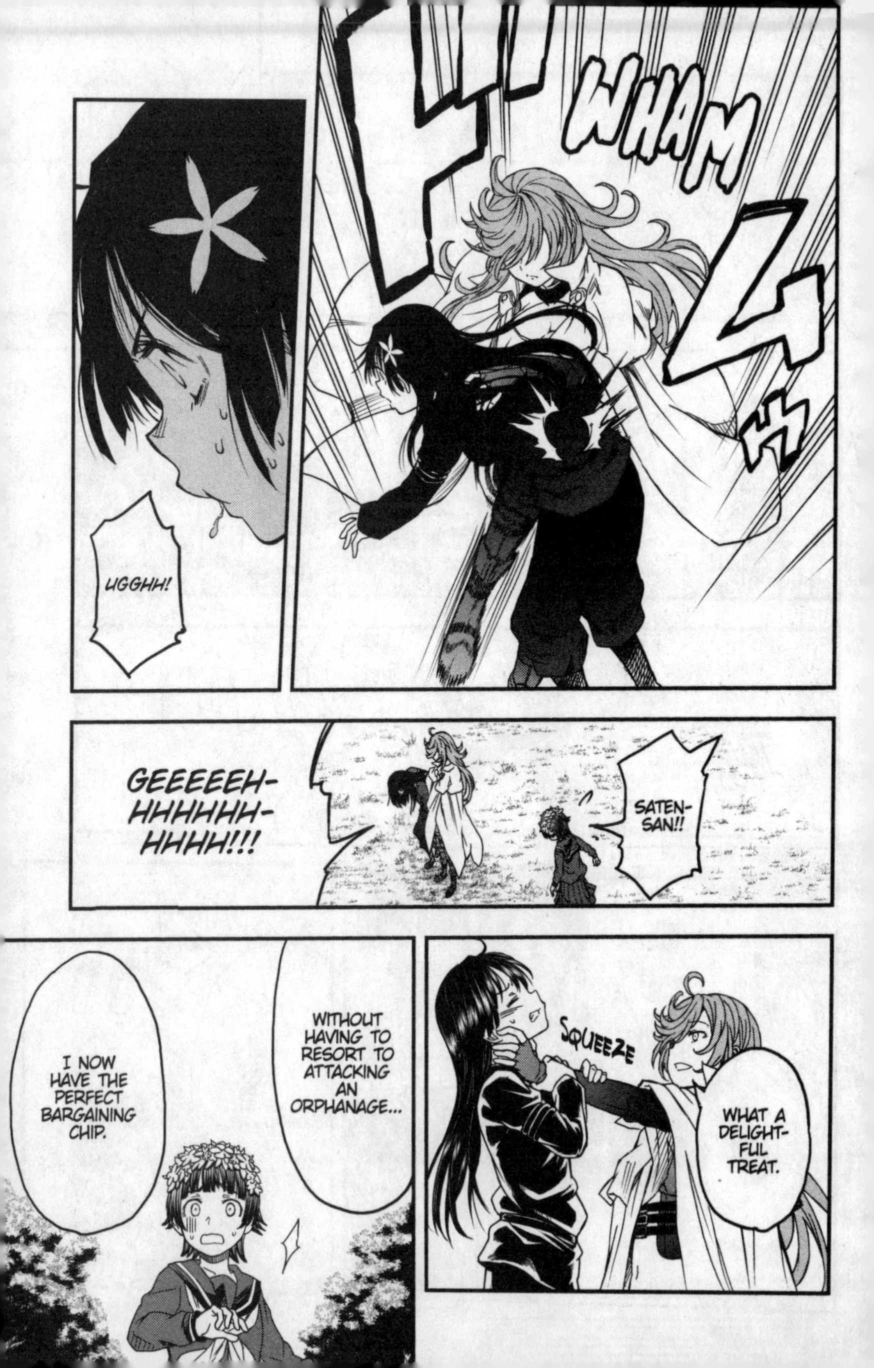
WHAM
UGGHH!
SATEN-SAN!!
GEEEEEH-HHHHHH-HHHH!!!
SQUEEZE
WHAT A DELIGHT-FUL TREAT.
WITHOUT HAVING TO RESORT TO ATTACKING AN ORPHANAGE...
I NOW HAVE THE PERFECT BARGAINING CHIP.

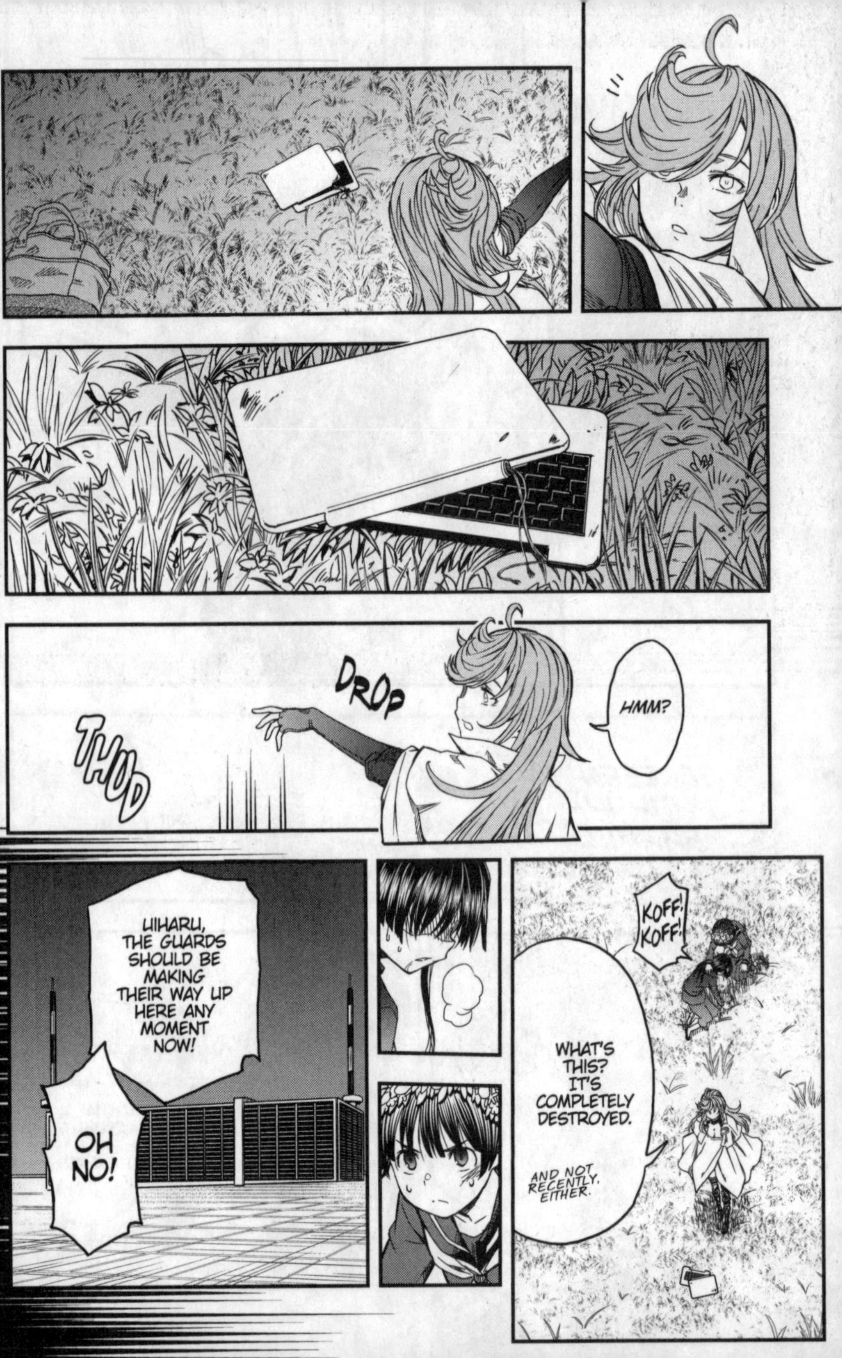
HMM?
DROP
THUD
KOFF! KOFF!
WHAT'S THIS? IT'S COMPLETELY DESTROYED.
AND NOT RECENTLY, EITHER.
UIHARU, THE GUARDS SHOULD BE MAKING THEIR WAY UP HERE ANY MOMENT NOW!
OH NO!

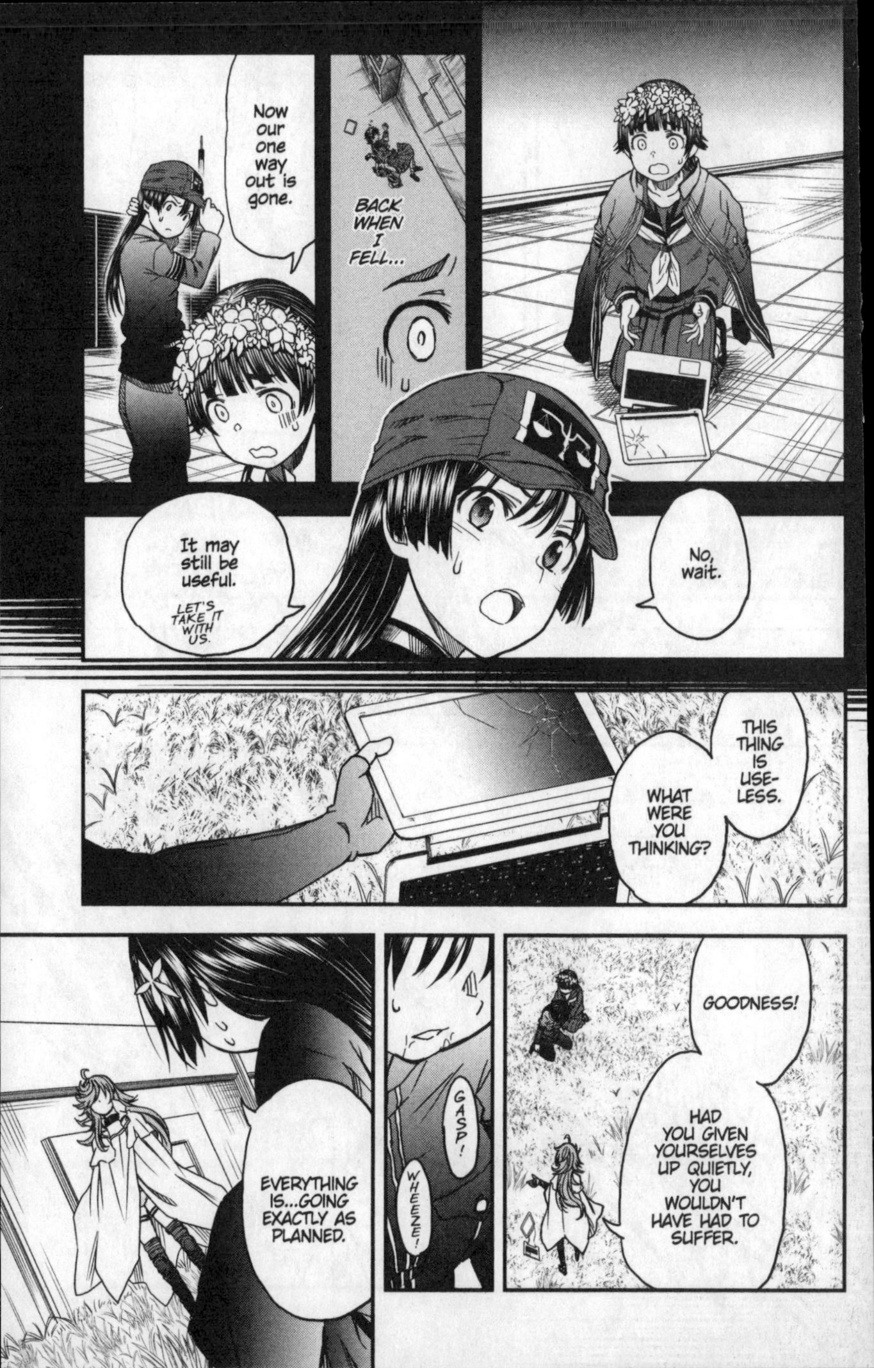
BACK WHEN I FELL...
Now our one way out is gone.
No, wait.
It may still be useful.
LET'S TAKE IT WITH US.
THIS THING IS USELESS.
WHAT WERE YOU THINKING?
GOODNESS!
HAD YOU GIVEN YOURSELVES UP QUIETLY, YOU WOULDN'T HAVE HAD TO SUFFER.
GASP!
WHEEZE!
EVERYTHING IS...GOING EXACTLY AS PLANNED.

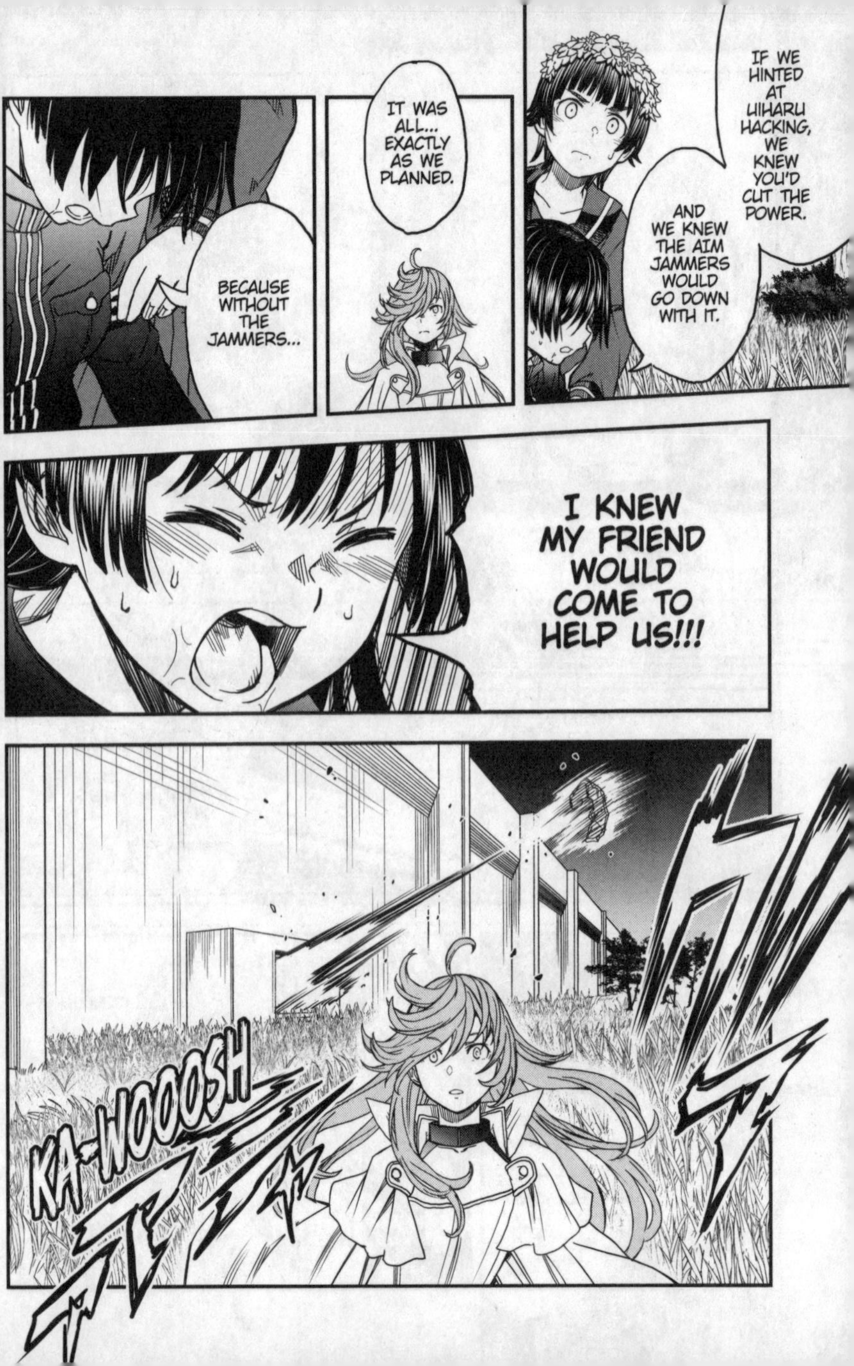
IF WE HINTED AT UIHARU HACKING, WE KNEW YOU'D CUT THE POWER.
AND WE KNEW THE AIM JAMMERS WOULD GO DOWN WITH IT.
IT WAS ALL... EXACTLY AS WE PLANNED.
BECAUSE WITHOUT THE JAMMERS...
I KNEW MY FRIEND WOULD COME TO HELP US!!!
KA-WOOOSH

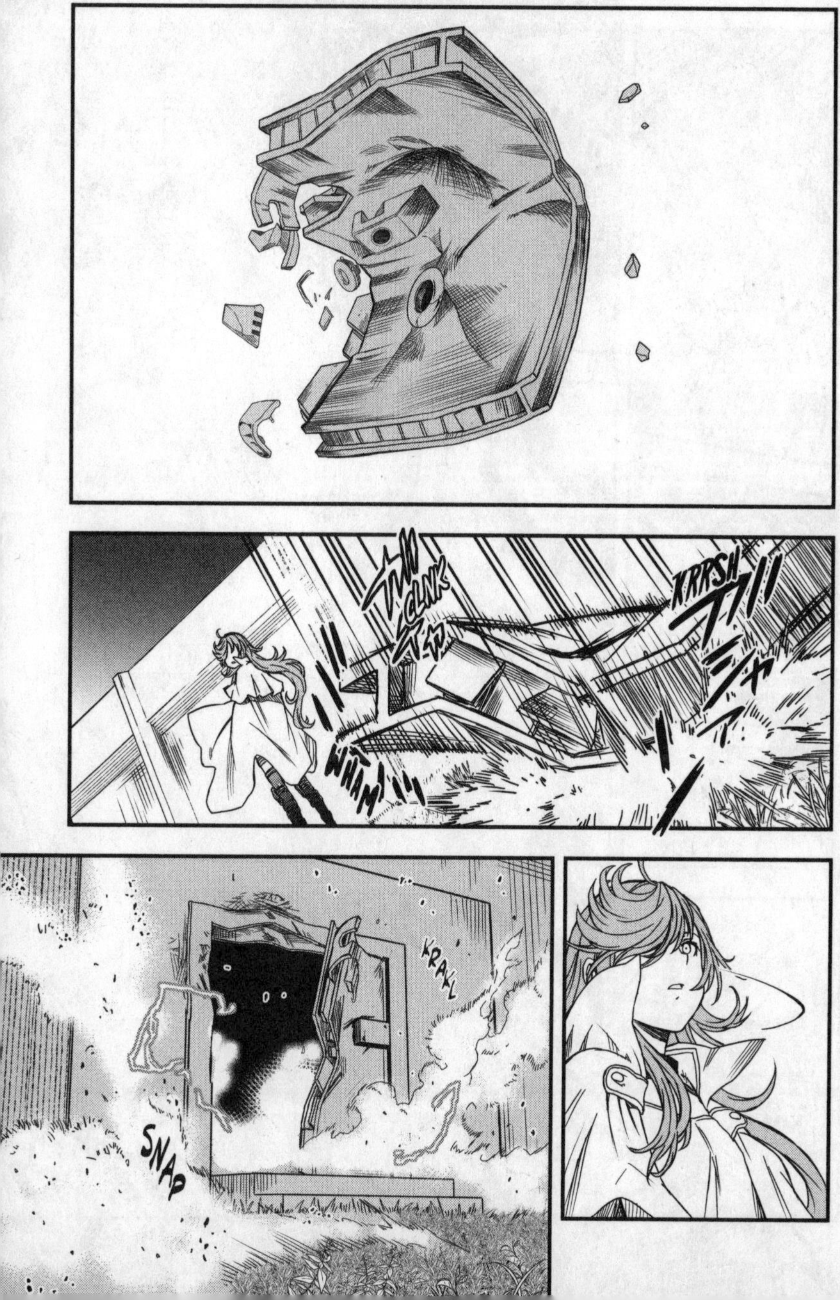
KRRSH
CLNK
WHAM
KRAKL
SNAP

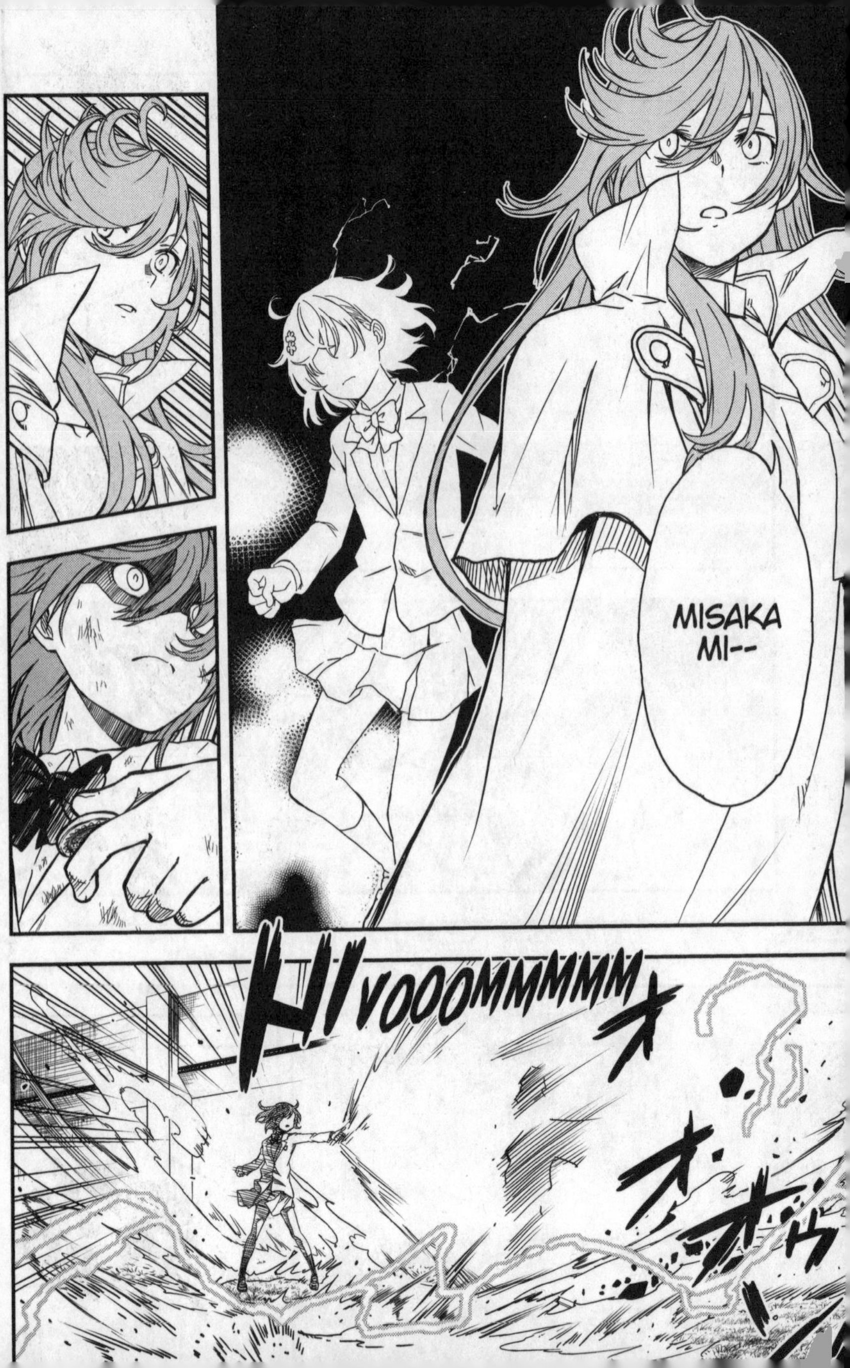
MISAKA MI--
VOOOMMMMMM

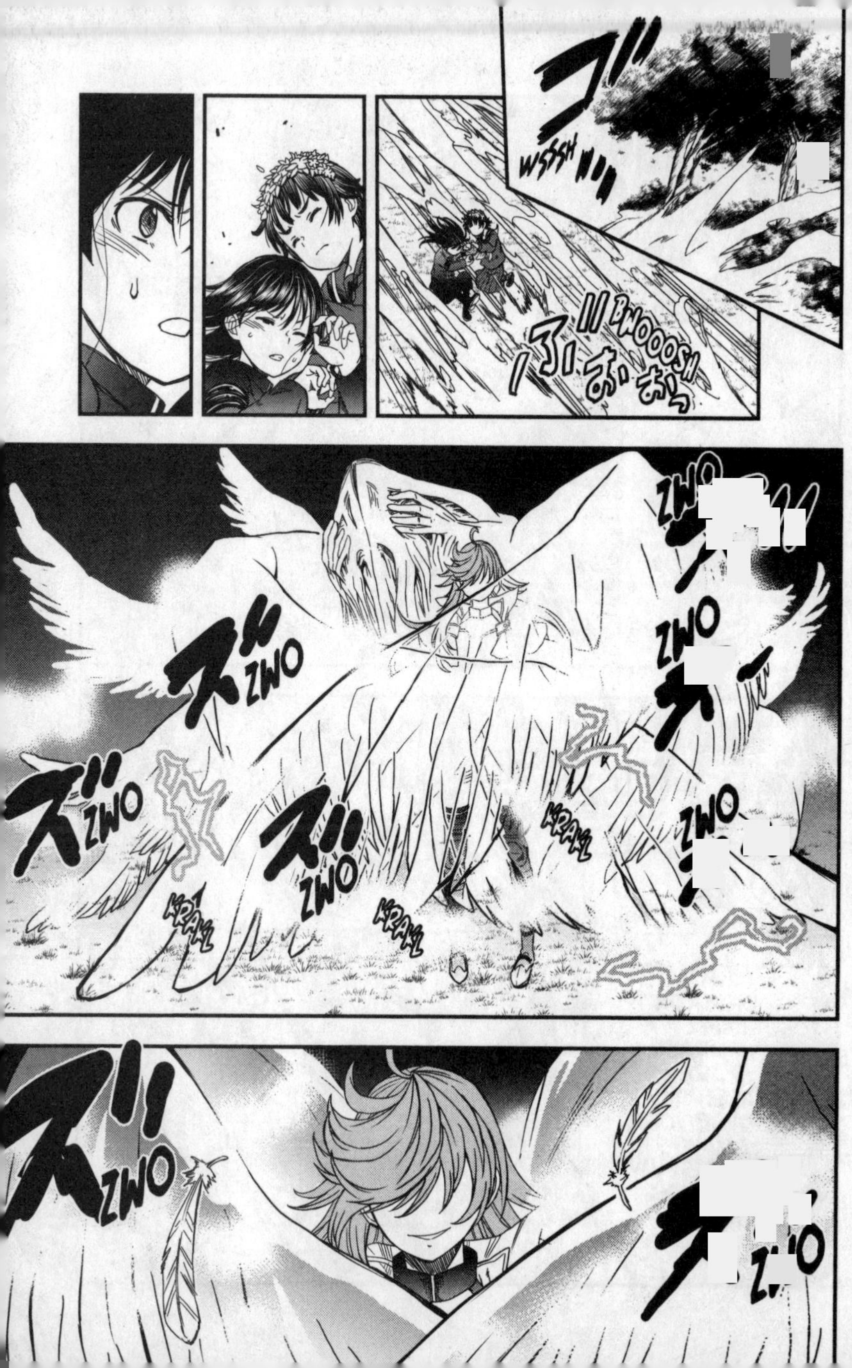
WSSSH
BWOOOSH
ZWO
ZWO
ZWO
KRAKL
ZWO
ZWO
KRAKL
ZWO
KRAKL
ZWO
ZWO

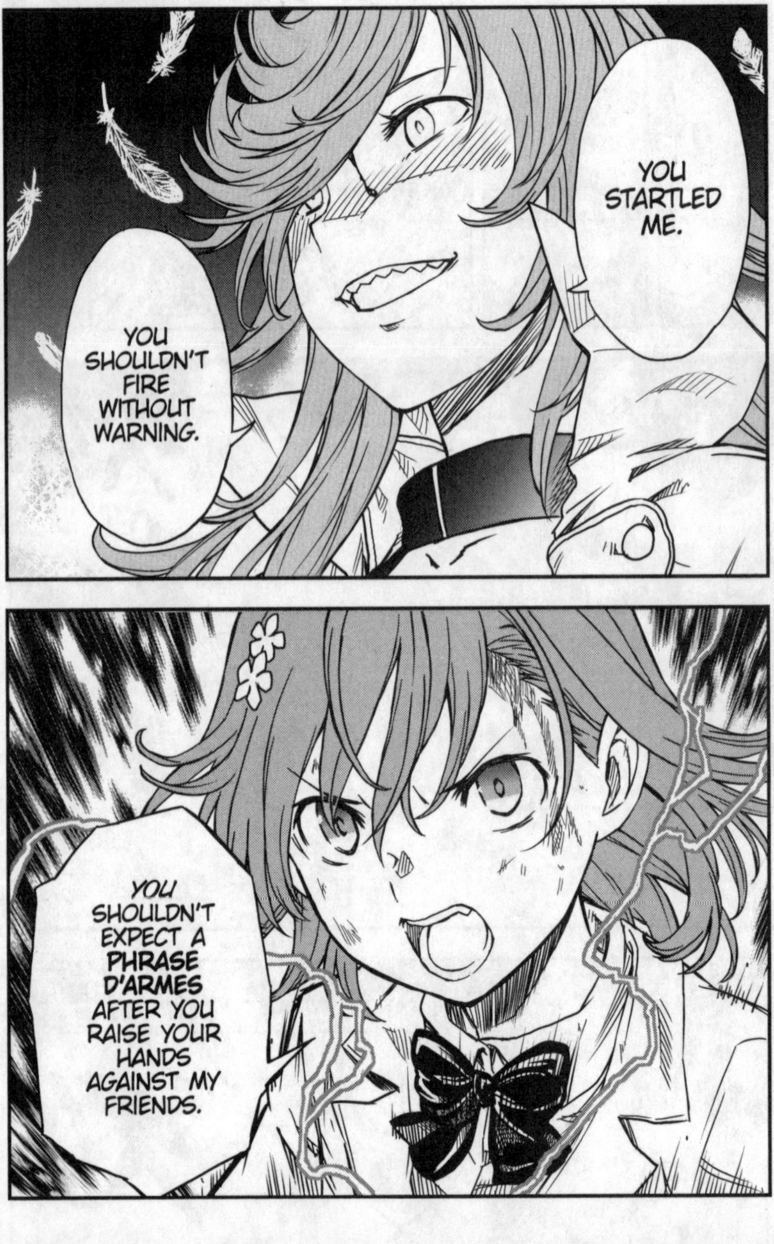
YOU STARTLED ME.
YOU SHOULDN'T FIRE WITHOUT WARNING.
YOU SHOULDN'T EXPECT A **PHRASE D'ARMES** AFTER YOU RAISE YOUR HANDS AGAINST MY FRIENDS.

CHAPTER 122: REPLICATION

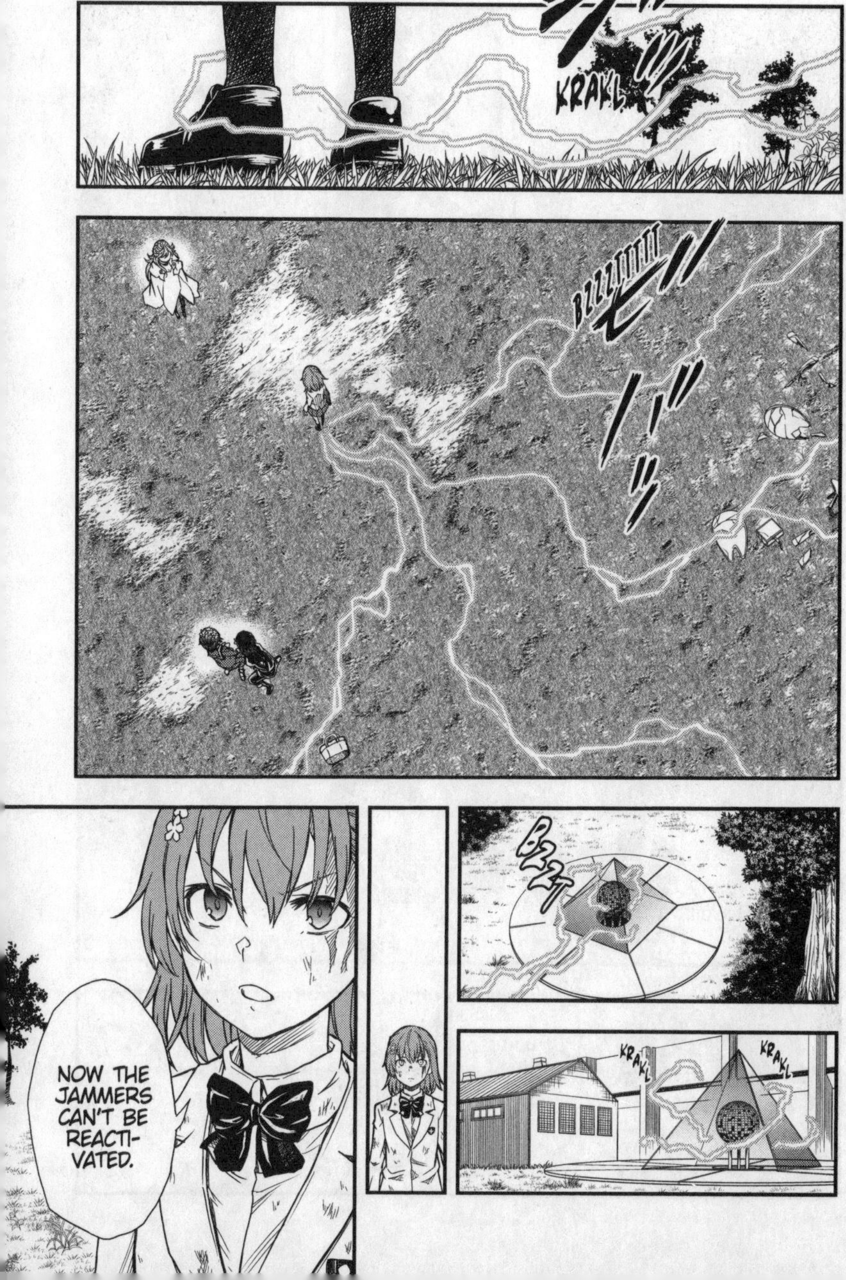
KRAKL
BZZZTTTTT
BZZT
KRAKL
KRAKL
NOW THE JAMMERS CAN'T BE REACTIVATED.

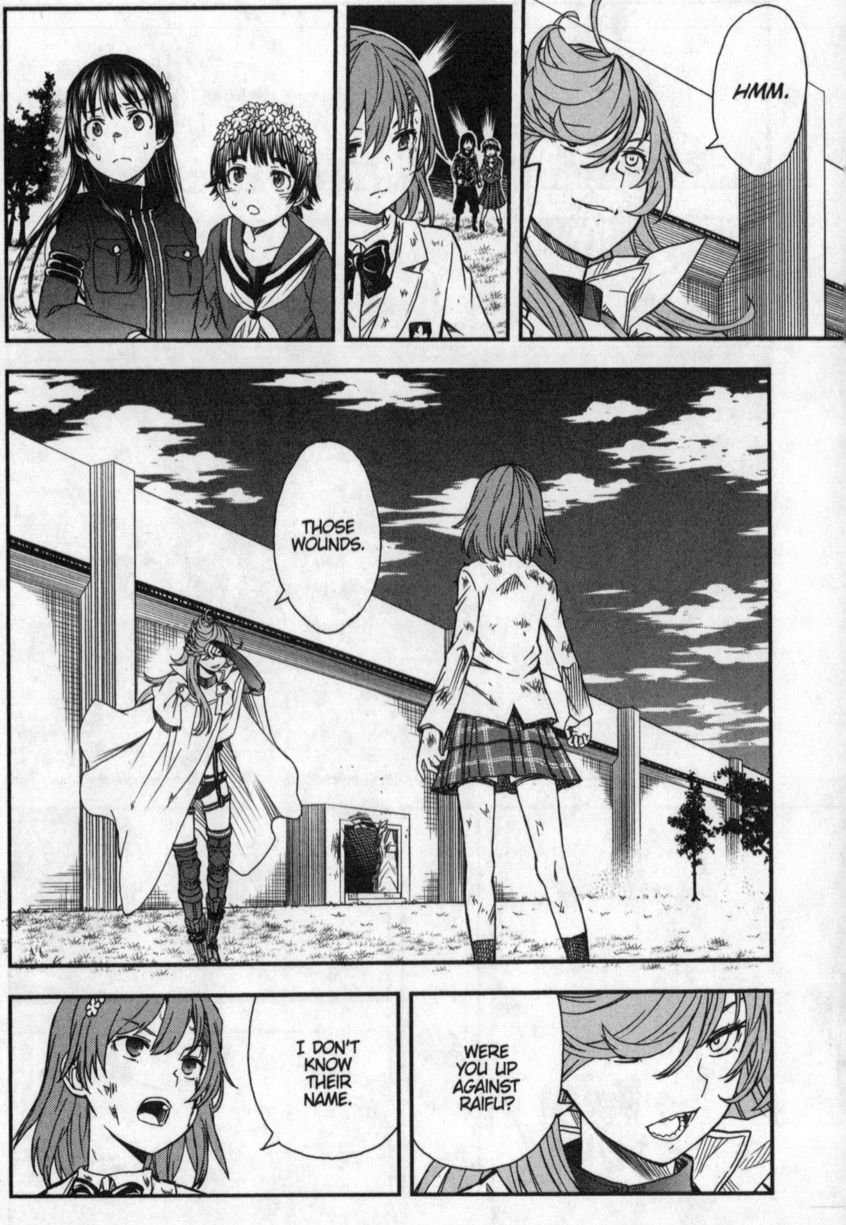
HMM.
THOSE WOUNDS.
WERE YOU UP AGAINST RAIFU?
I DON'T KNOW THEIR NAME.

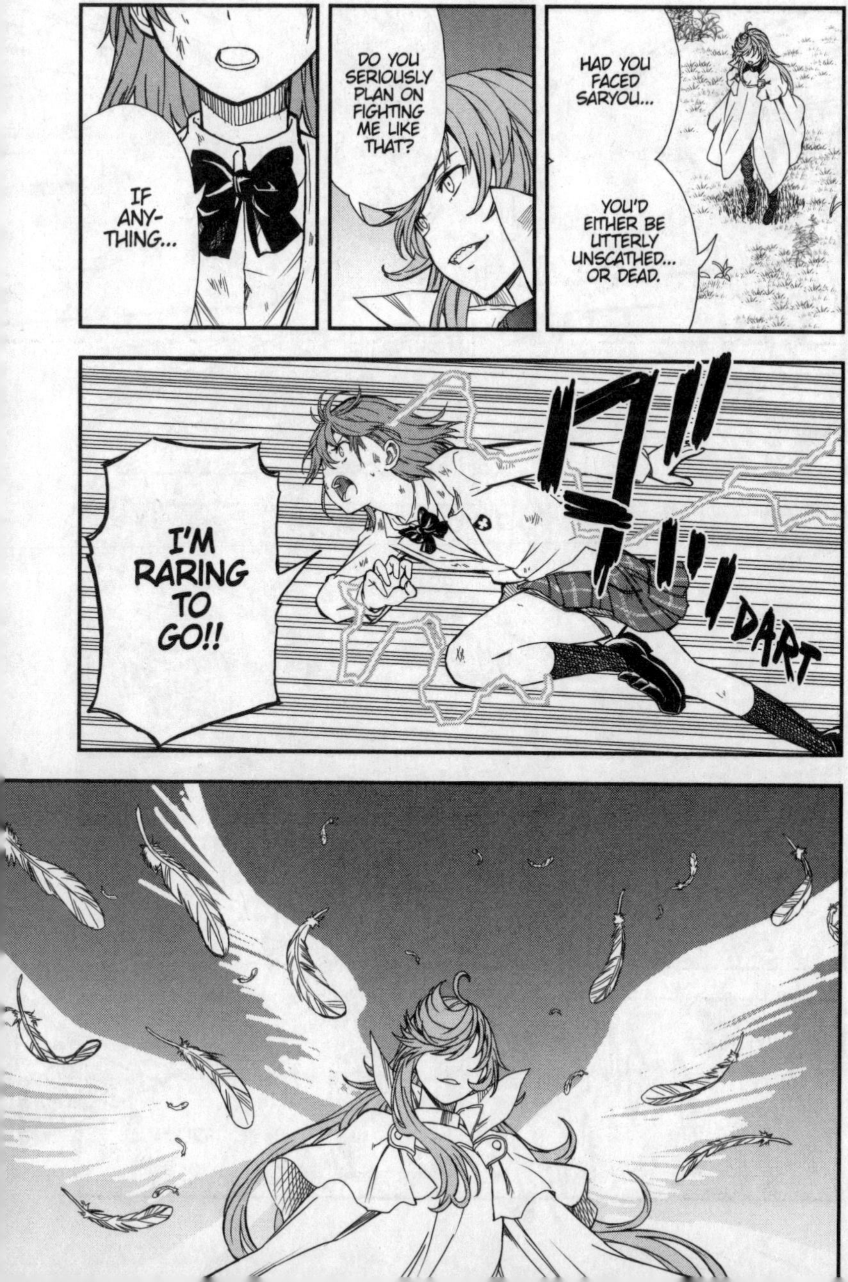
HAD YOU FACED SARYOU...
YOU'D EITHER BE UTTERLY UNSCATHED... OR DEAD.
DO YOU SERIOUSLY PLAN ON FIGHTING ME LIKE THAT?
IF ANY-THING...
DART
I'M RARING TO GO!!

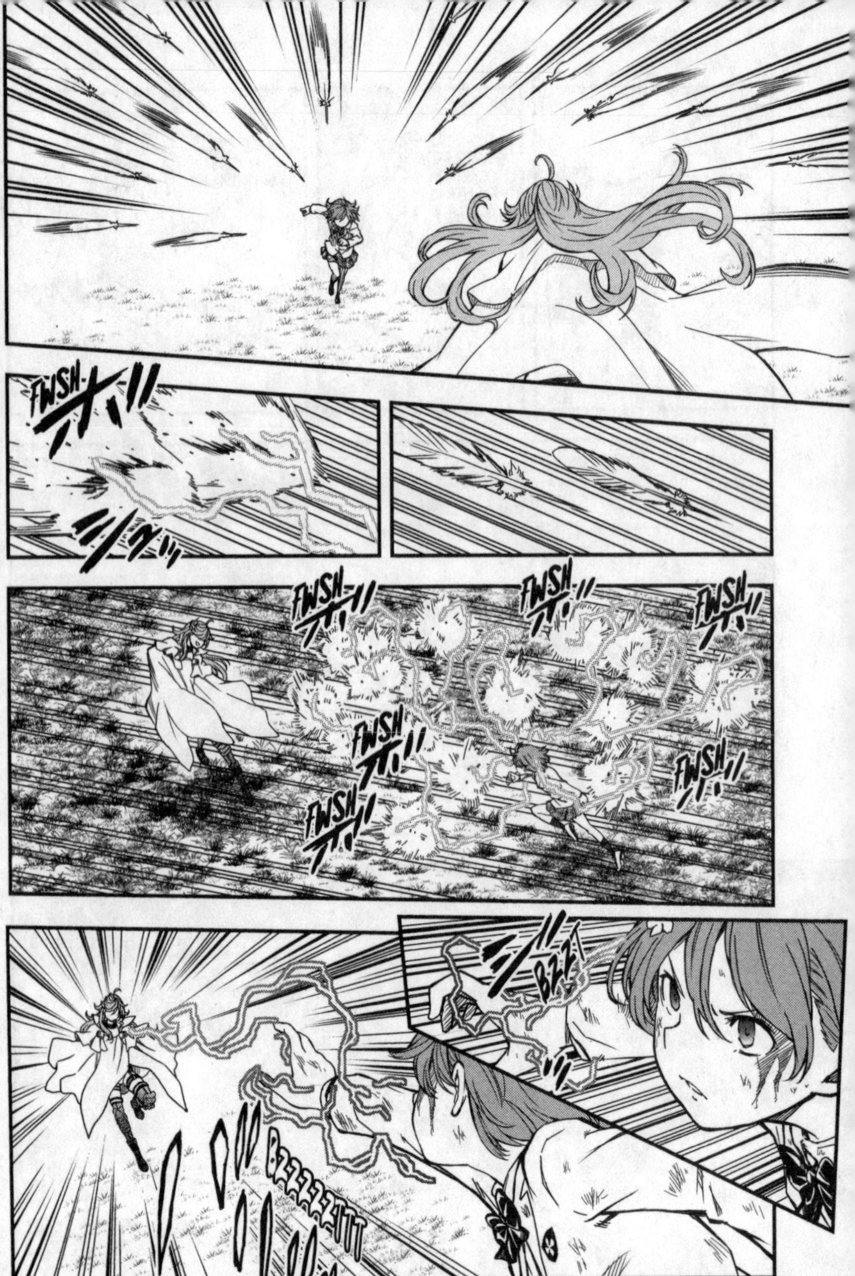
FWSH
FWSH
FWSH
FWSH
FWSH
FWSH
FWSH
BZZT
BZZZZTTT

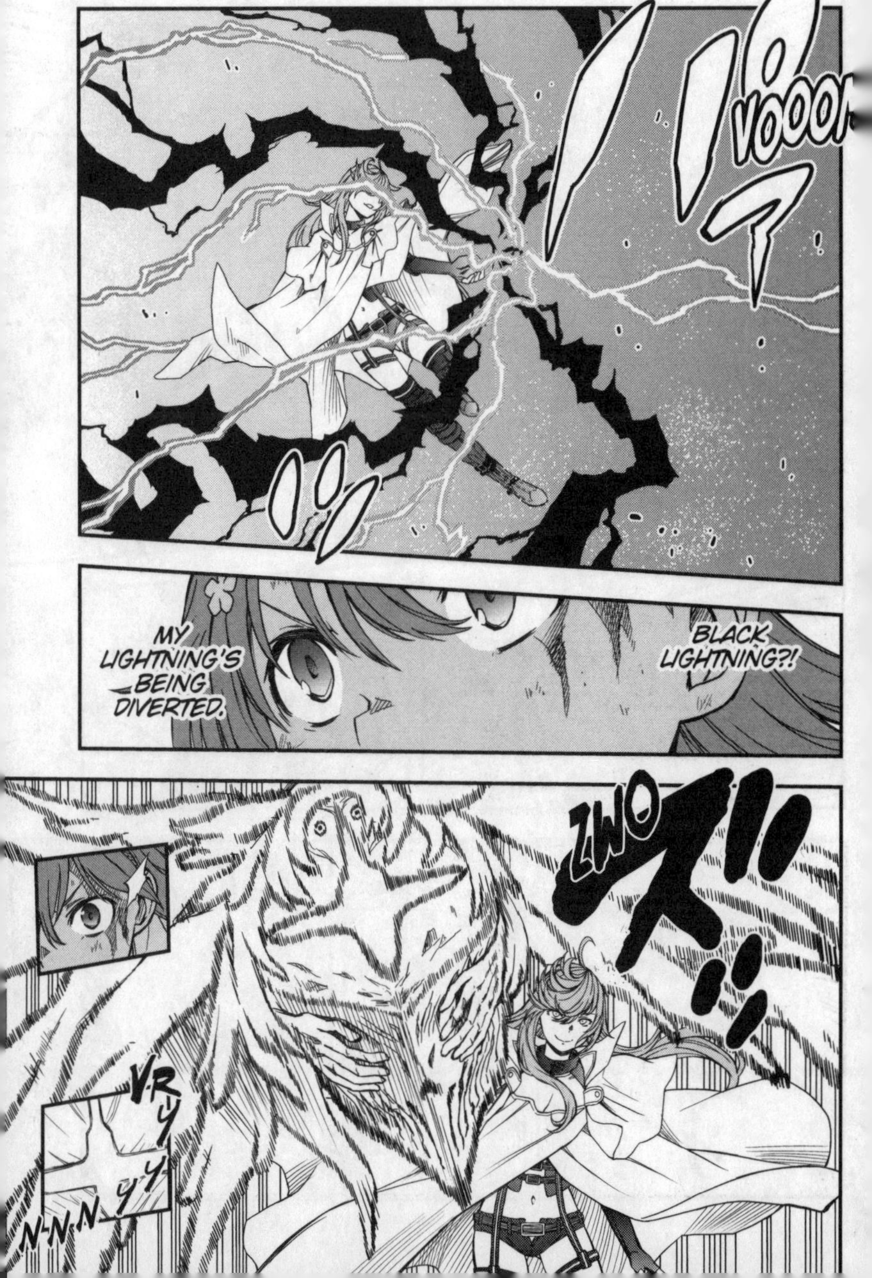
VOOO
BLACK LIGHTNING?!
MY LIGHTNING'S BEING DIVERTED.
ZWO
V-R-Y-Y-Y-N-N-N

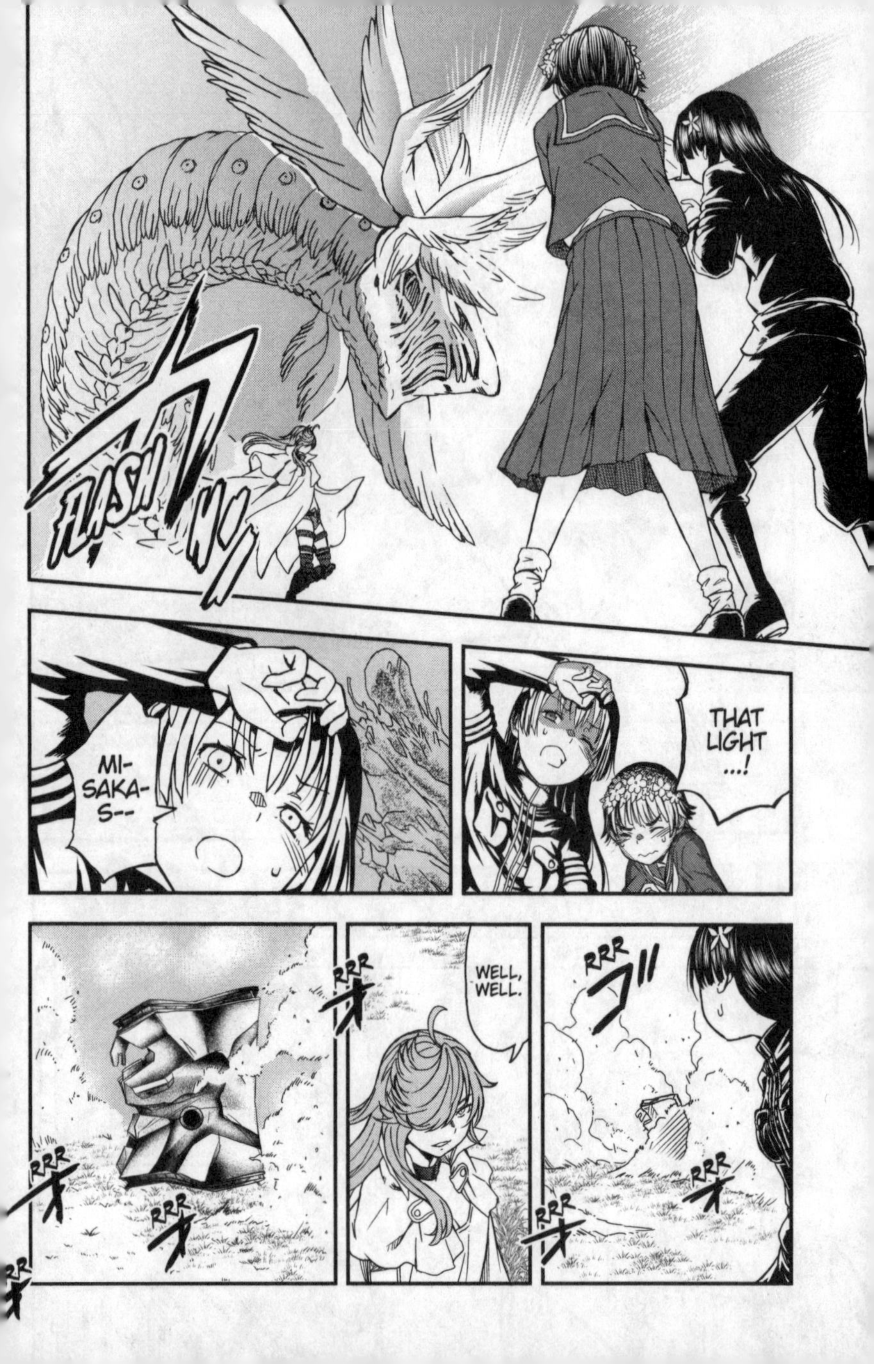
FLASH
THAT LIGHT ...!
MI-SAKAS-S--
RRR
RRR
RRR
WELL, WELL.
RRR
RRR
RRR
RRR

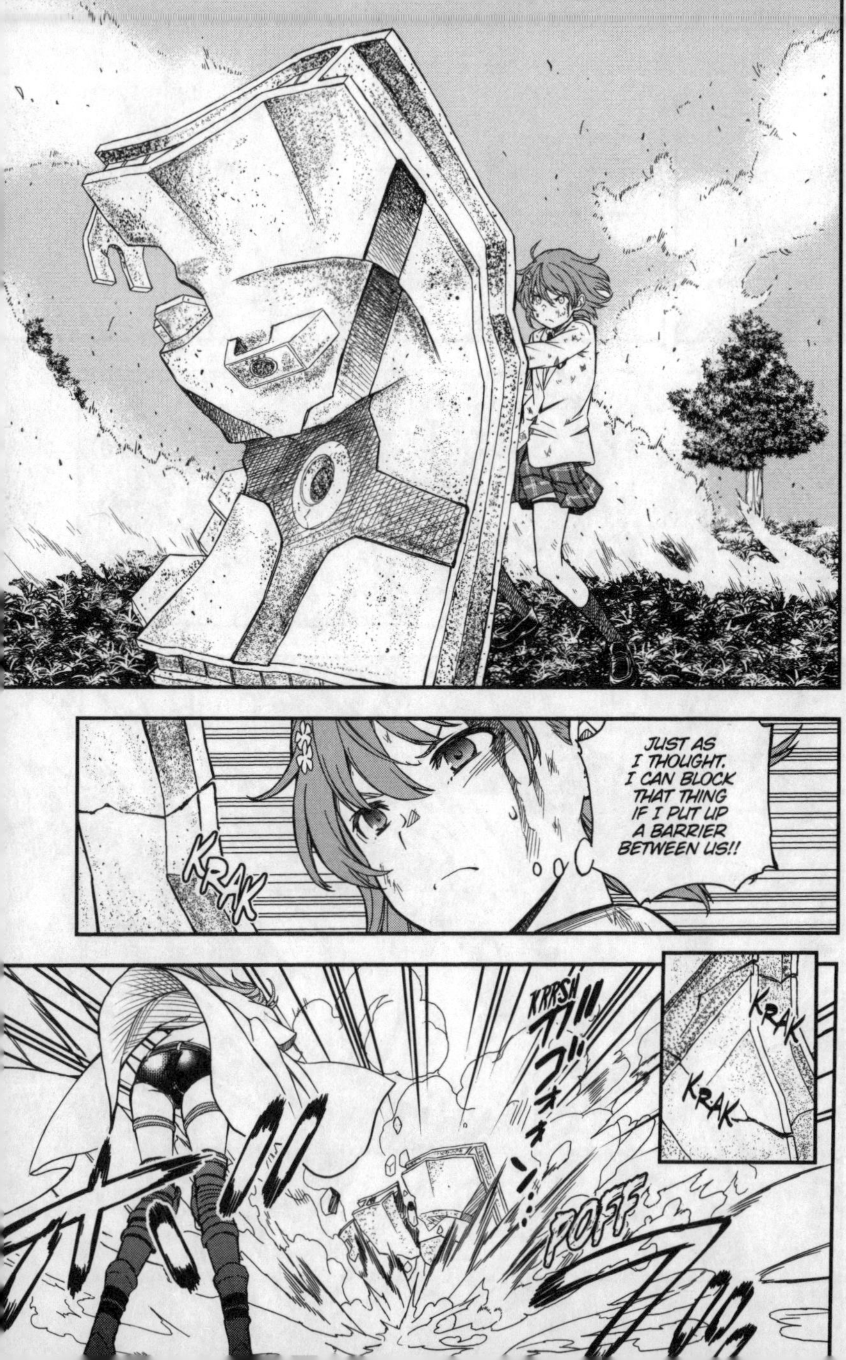
JUST AS I THOUGHT. I CAN BLOCK THAT THING IF I PUT UP A BARRIER BETWEEN US!!
KRAK
KRAK
KRAK
KRASH
POFF

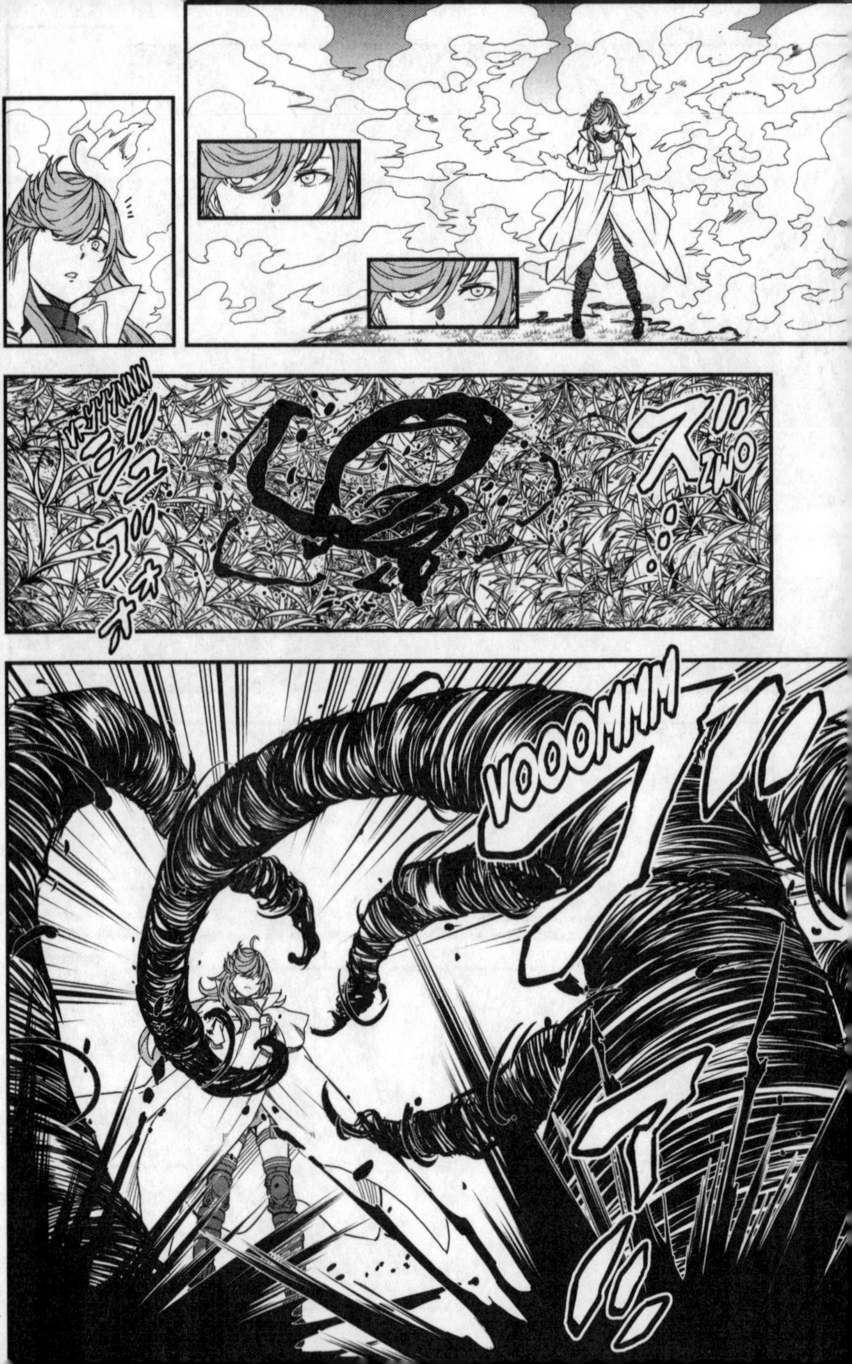
ZWO
VOOOMMM

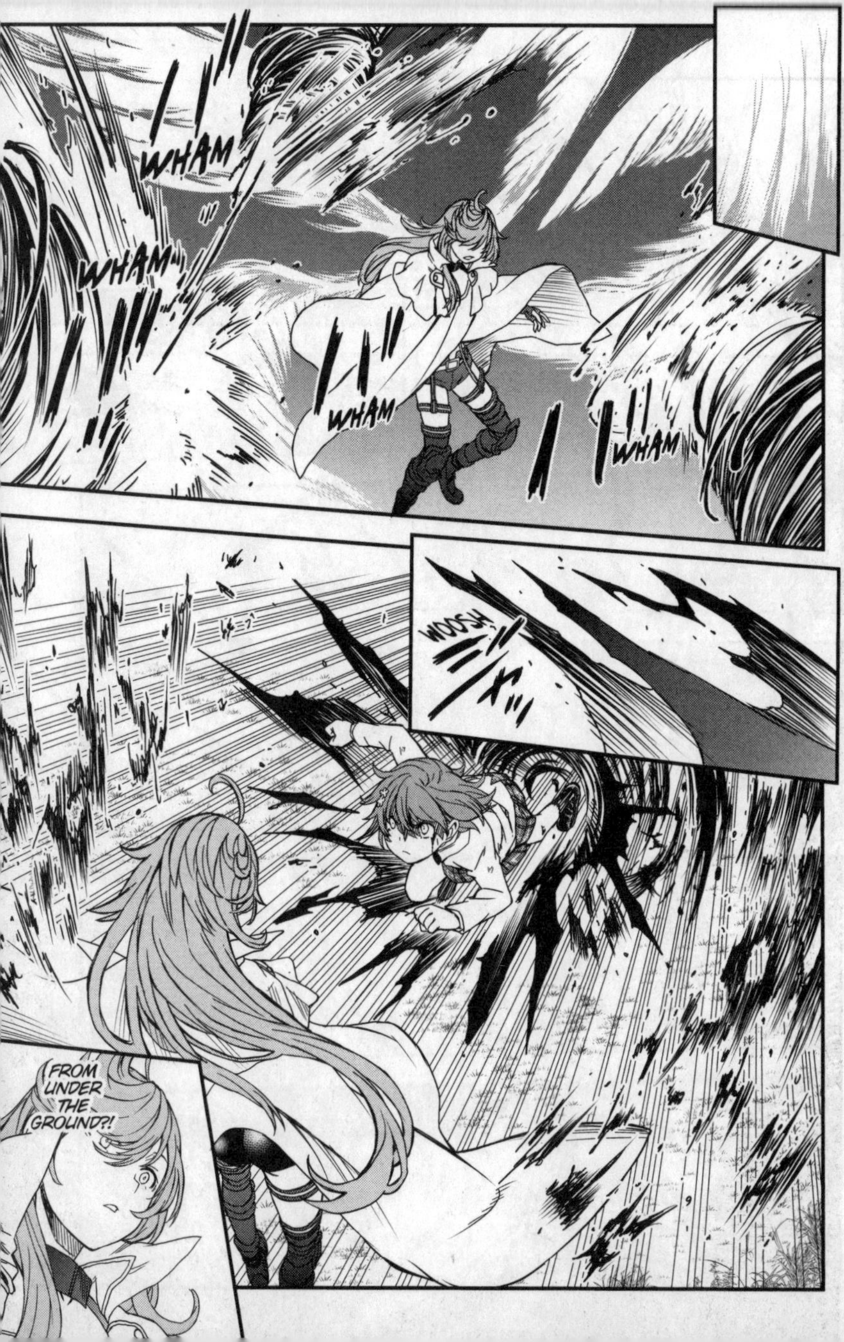
WHAM
WHAM
WHAM
WHAM
WOOSH
FROM UNDER THE GROUND?!

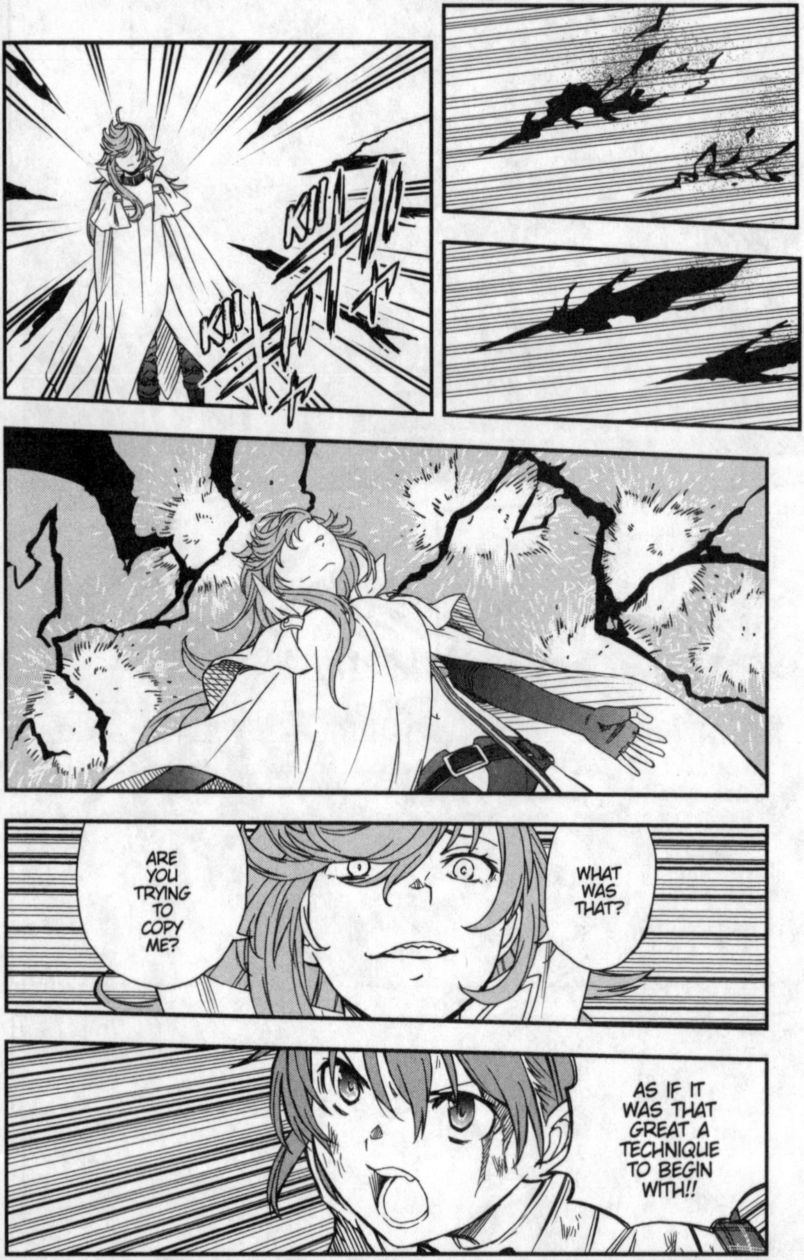
KII
KII
WHAT WAS THAT?
ARE YOU TRYING TO COPY ME?
AS IF IT WAS THAT GREAT A TECHNIQUE TO BEGIN WITH!!

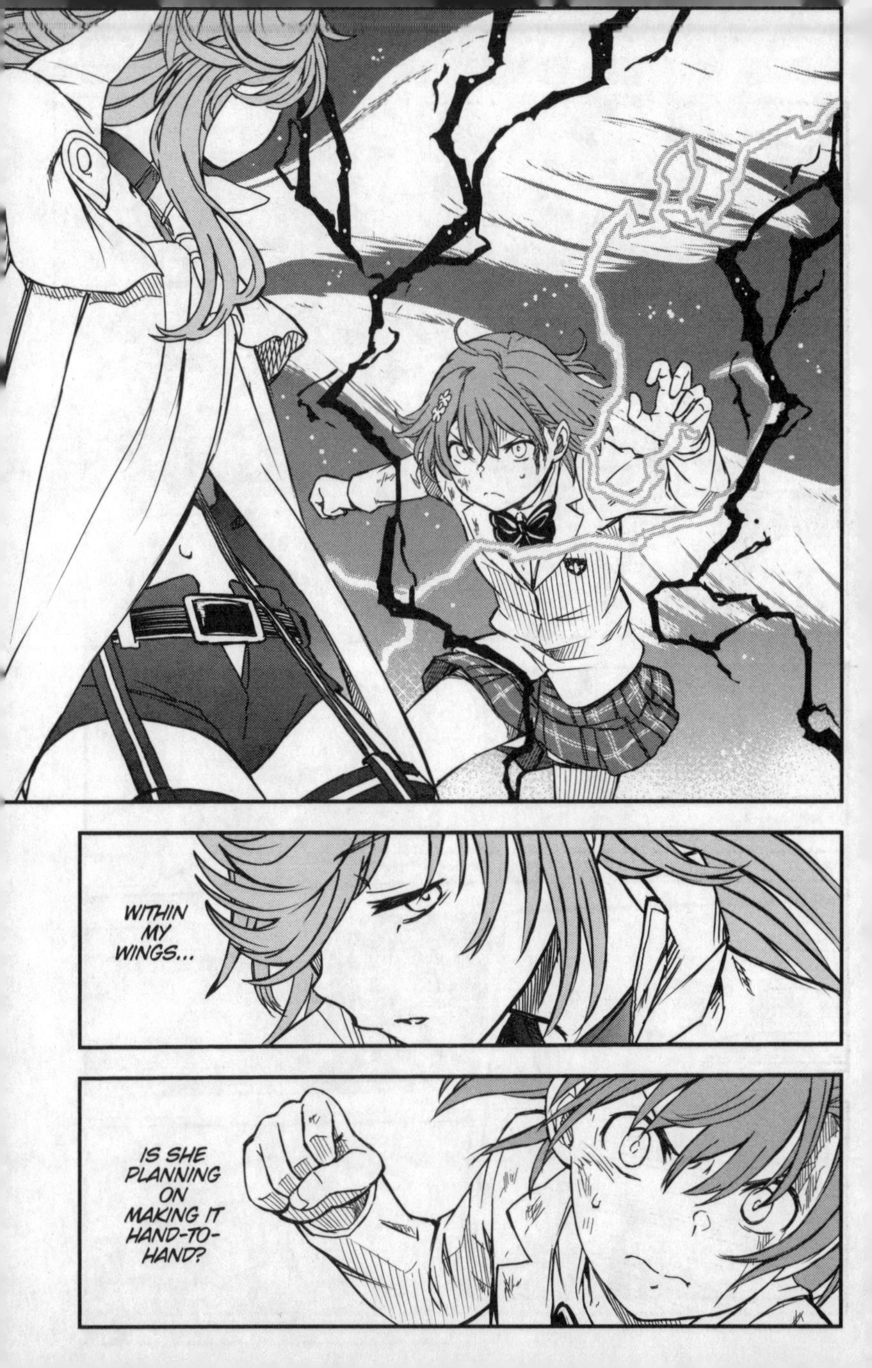
WITHIN MY WINGS...
IS SHE PLANNING ON MAKING IT HAND-TO-HAND?

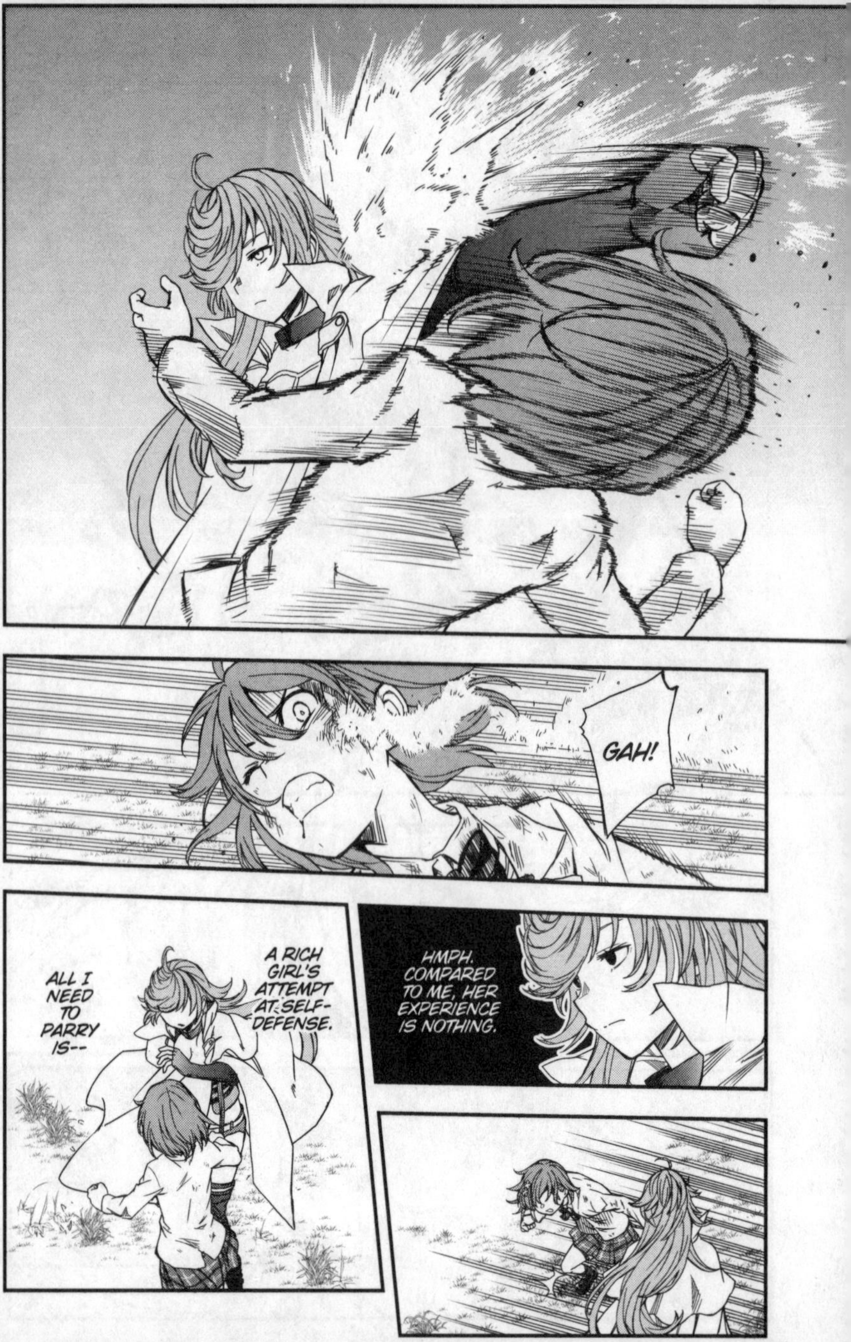
GAH!
HMPH. COMPARED TO ME, HER EXPERIENCE IS NOTHING.
A RICH GIRL'S ATTEMPT AT SELF-DEFENSE.
ALL I NEED TO PARRY IS--

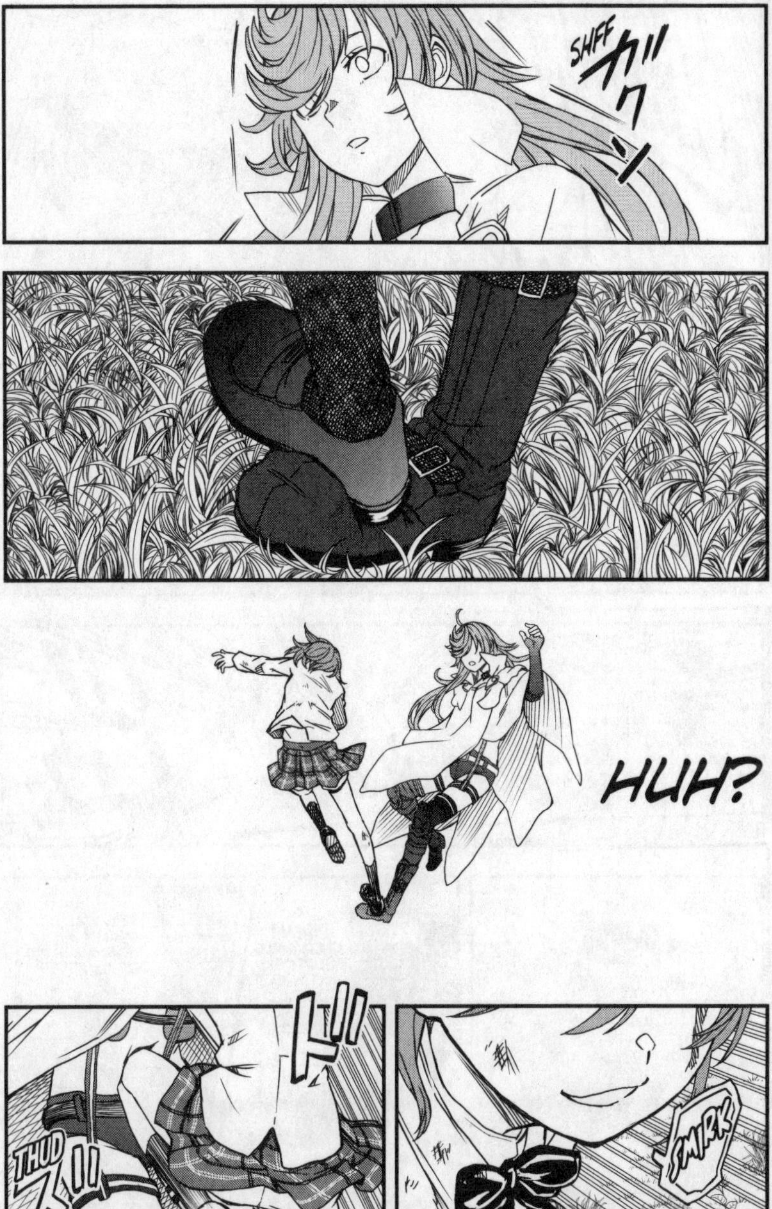
SHFF
ガクン
HUH?
SMIRK
ド!!
THUD
ズ!!

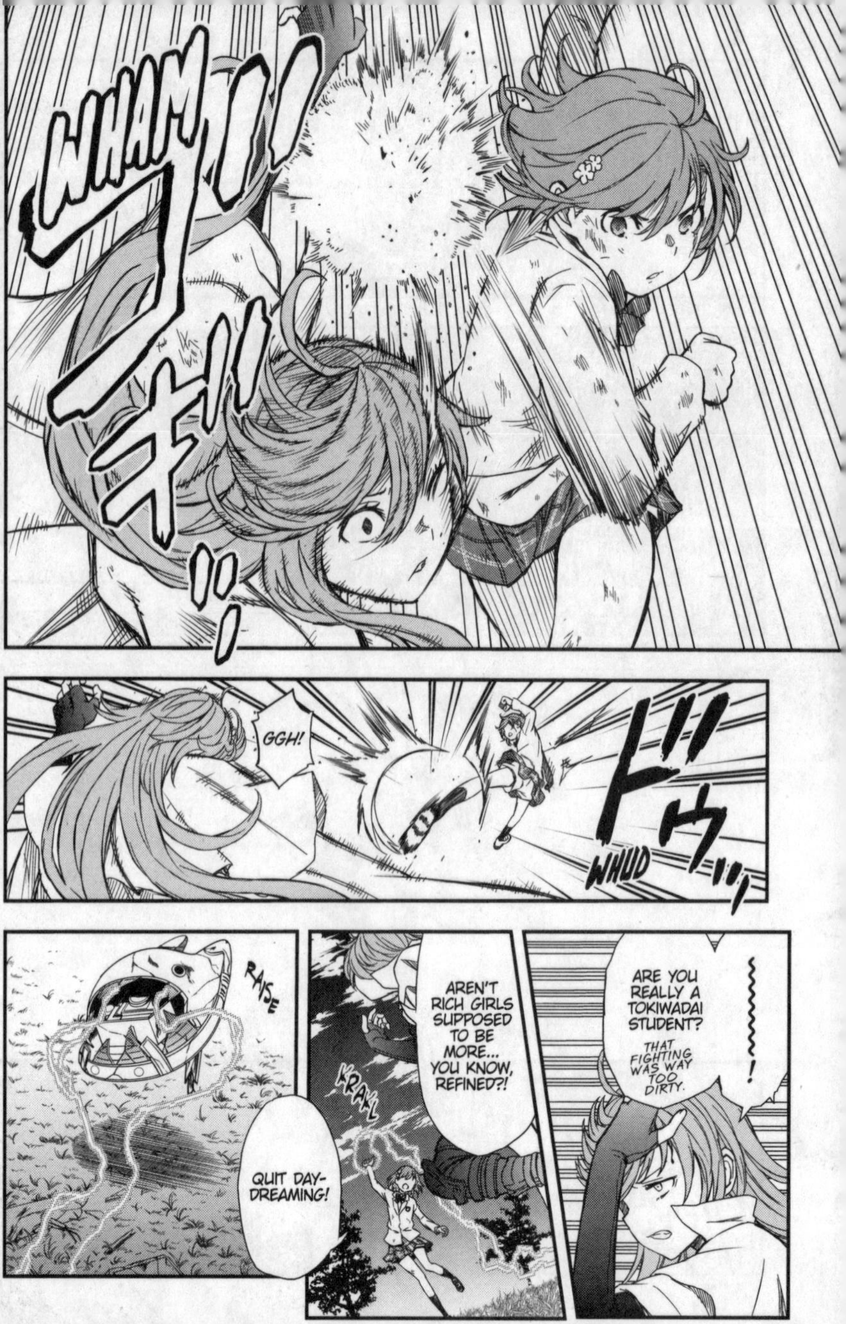
WHAM
GGH!
WHUD
ARE YOU REALLY A TOKIWADAI STUDENT?
THAT FIGHTING WAS WAY TOO DIRTY.
AREN'T RICH GIRLS SUPPOSED TO BE MORE... YOU KNOW, REFINED?!
KRAKL
QUIT DAY-DREAMING!
RAISE

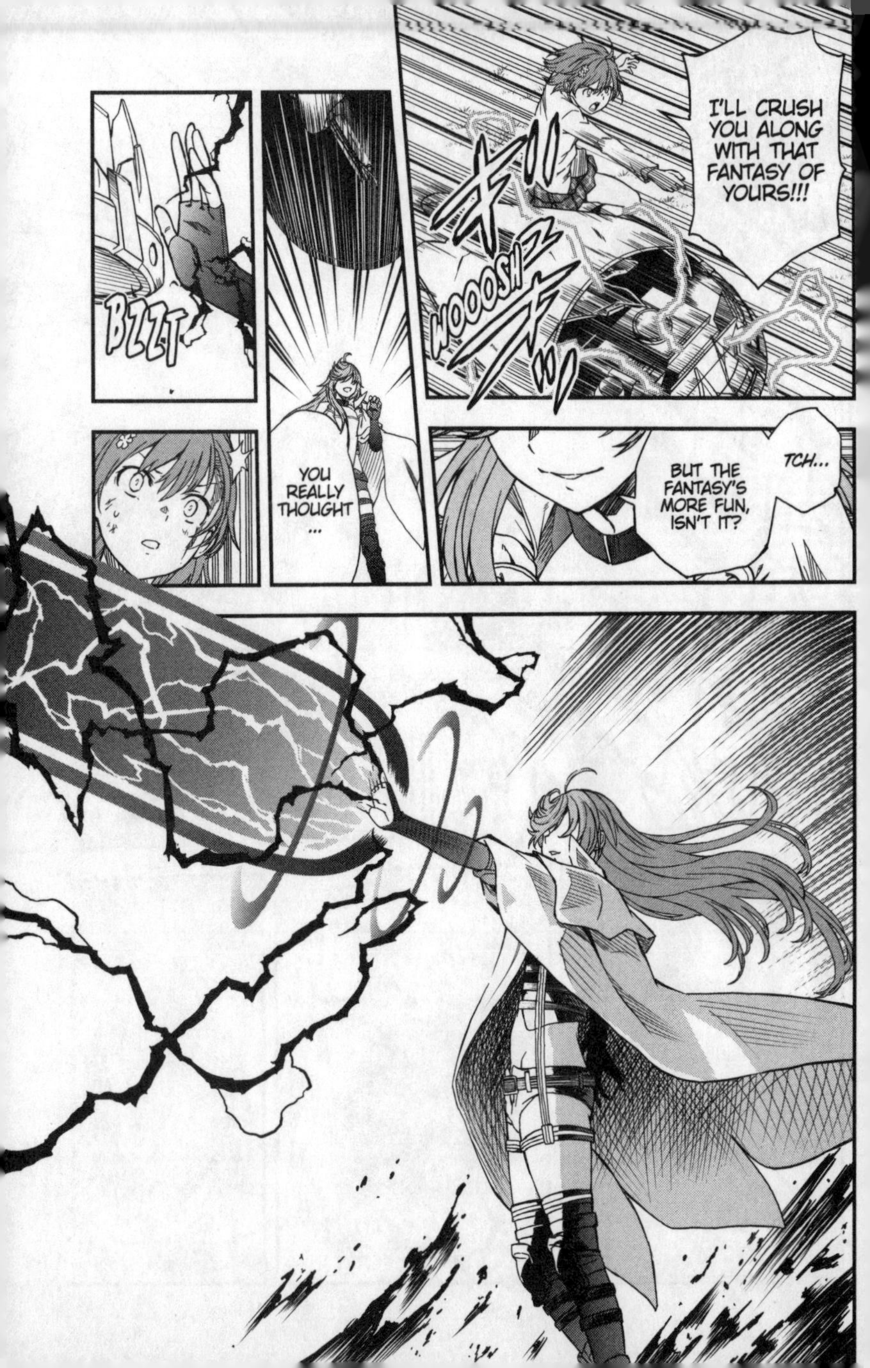
I'LL CRUSH YOU ALONG WITH THAT FANTASY OF YOURS!!!
WOOOSH
BZZT
TCH...
BUT THE FANTASY'S MORE FUN, ISN'T IT?
YOU REALLY THOUGHT ...

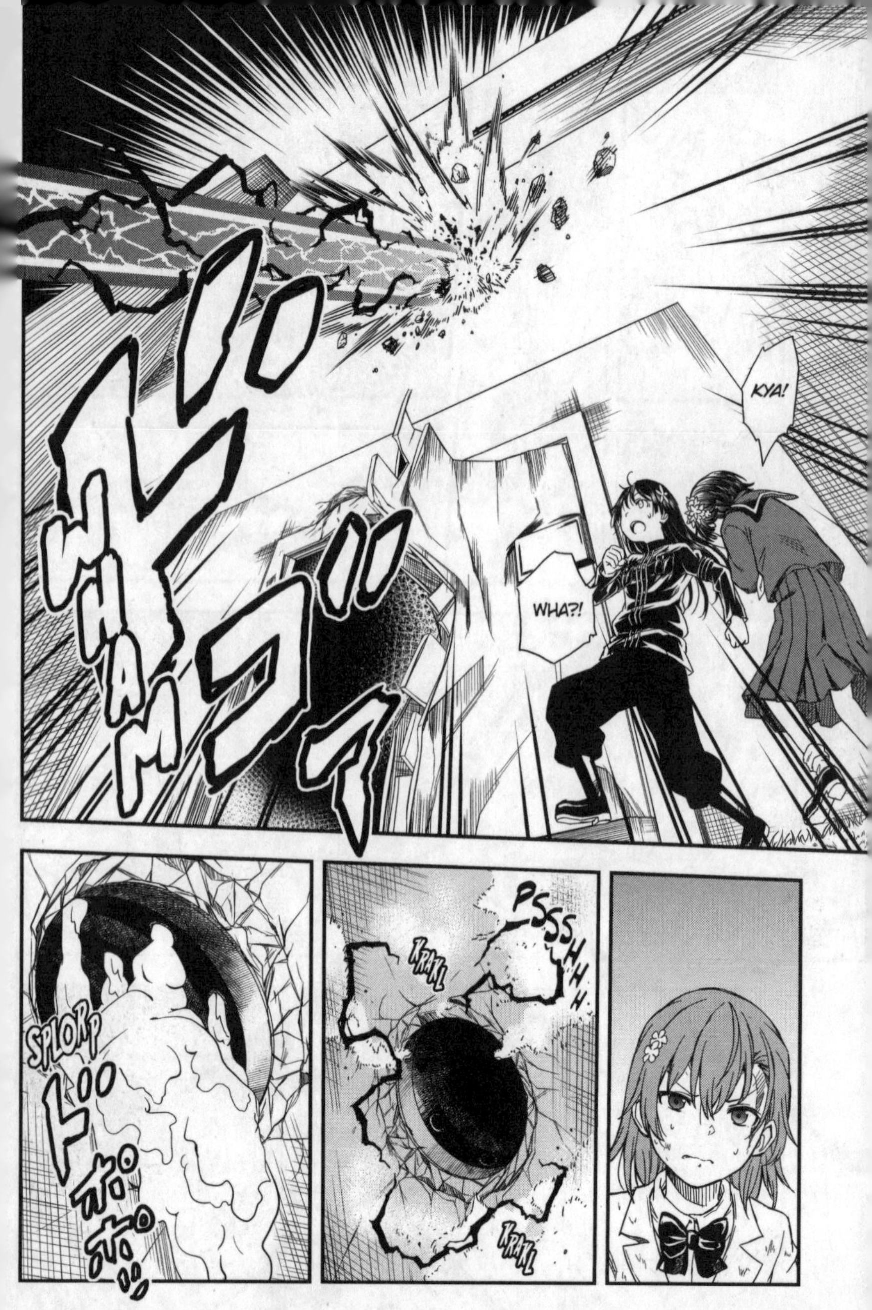
KYA!
WHA?!
WHAM
PSSSHHH
KRAKL
KRAKL
SPLORP

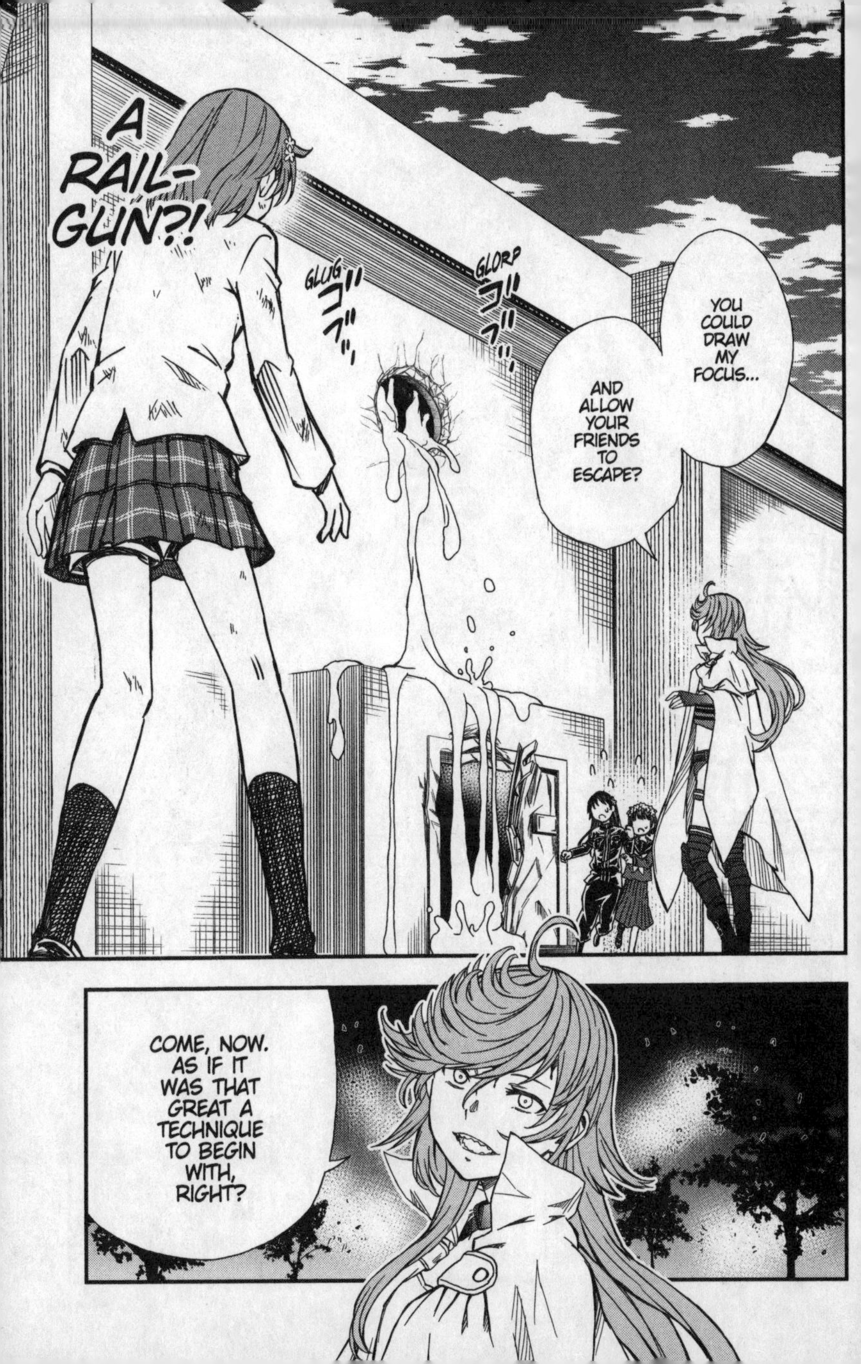

A RAIL-GUN?!
GLORP
GLUG
YOU COULD DRAW MY FOCUS...
AND ALLOW YOUR FRIENDS TO ESCAPE?
COME, NOW. AS IF IT WAS THAT GREAT A TECHNIQUE TO BEGIN WITH, RIGHT?

A Certain SCIENTIFIC Railgun

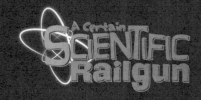

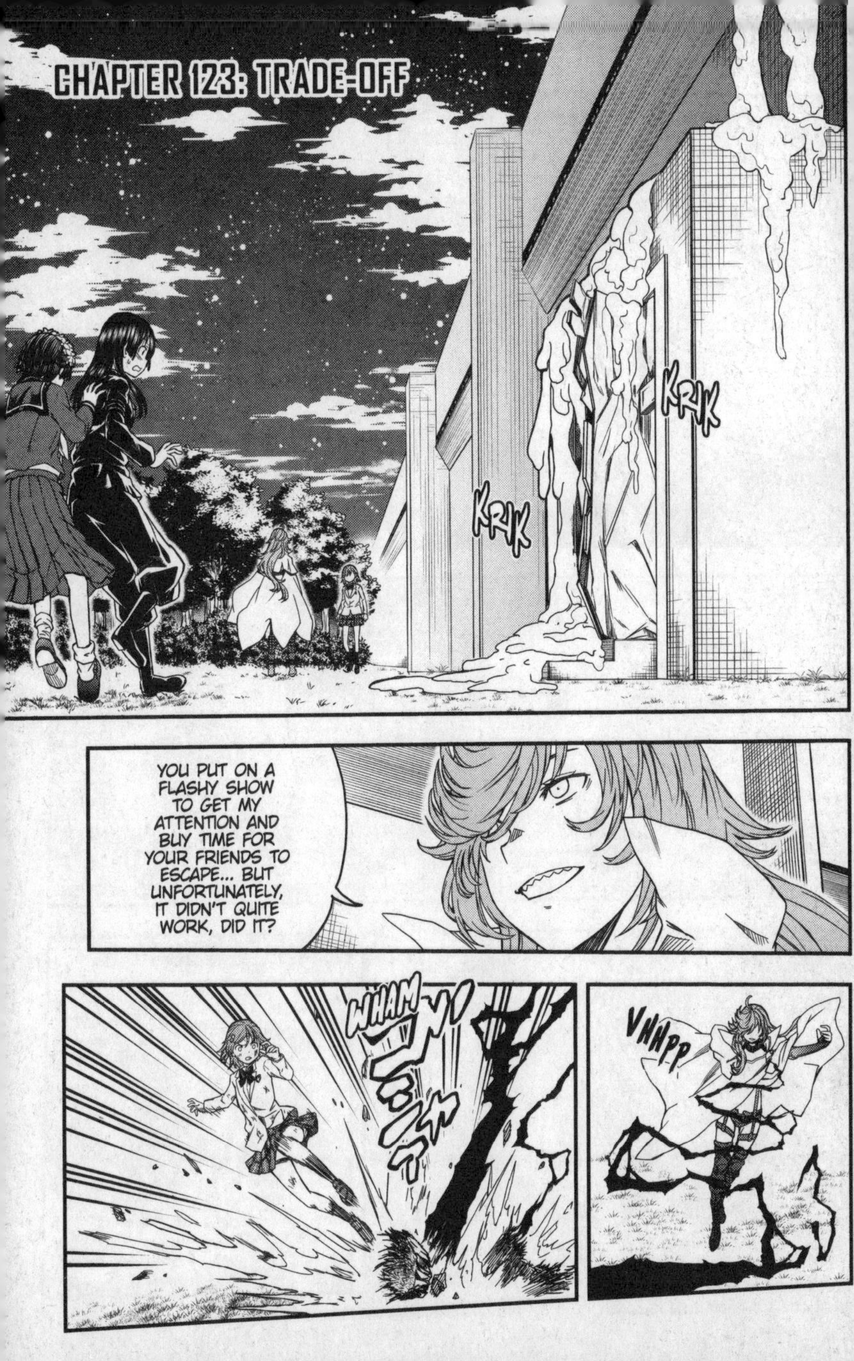
CHAPTER 123: TRADE-OFF
KRIK
KRIK
YOU PUT ON A FLASHY SHOW TO GET MY ATTENTION AND BUY TIME FOR YOUR FRIENDS TO ESCAPE... BUT UNFORTUNATELY, IT DIDN'T QUITE WORK, DID IT?
VNHPP
WHAM

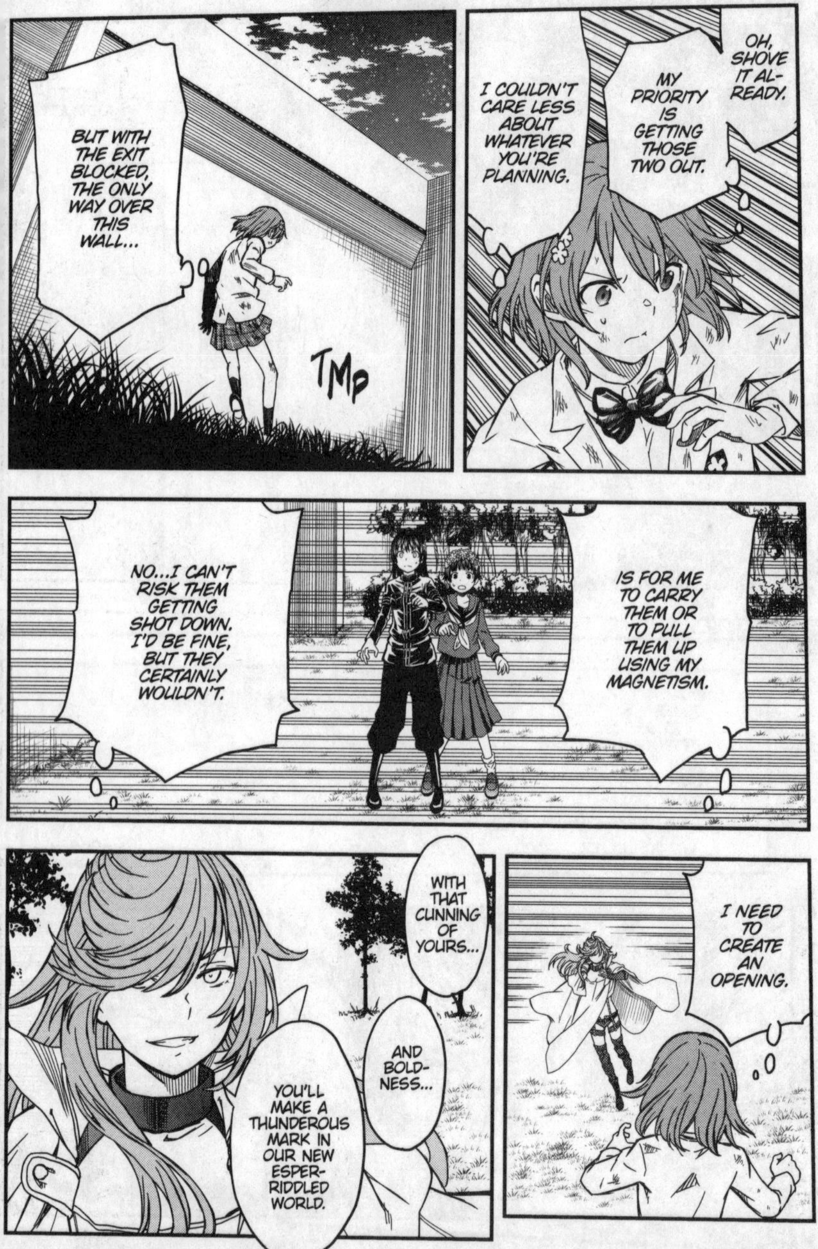
OH, SHOVE IT ALREADY.
MY PRIORITY IS GETTING THOSE TWO OUT.
I COULDN'T CARE LESS ABOUT WHATEVER YOU'RE PLANNING.
BUT WITH THE EXIT BLOCKED, THE ONLY WAY OVER THIS WALL...
TMP
IS FOR ME TO CARRY THEM OR TO PULL THEM UP USING MY MAGNETISM.
NO...I CAN'T RISK THEM GETTING SHOT DOWN. I'D BE FINE, BUT THEY CERTAINLY WOULDN'T.
I NEED TO CREATE AN OPENING.
WITH THAT CUNNING OF YOURS...
AND BOLDNESS...
YOU'LL MAKE A THUNDEROUS MARK IN OUR NEW ESPER-RIDDLED WORLD.

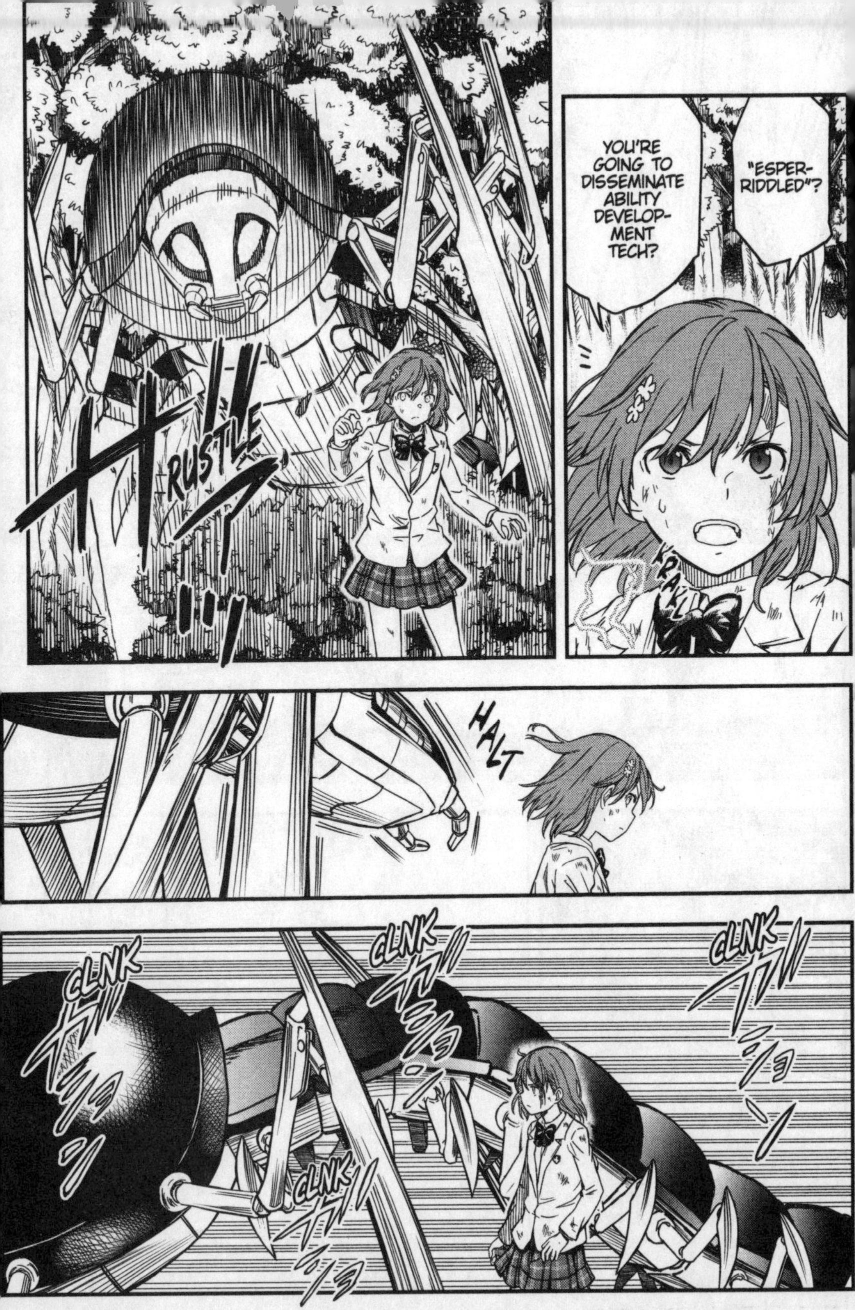
"ESPER-RIDDLED"?
YOU'RE GOING TO DISSEMINATE ABILITY DEVELOPMENT TECH?
KRAKL
RUSTLE
HALT
CLNK
CLNK
CLNK
CLNK

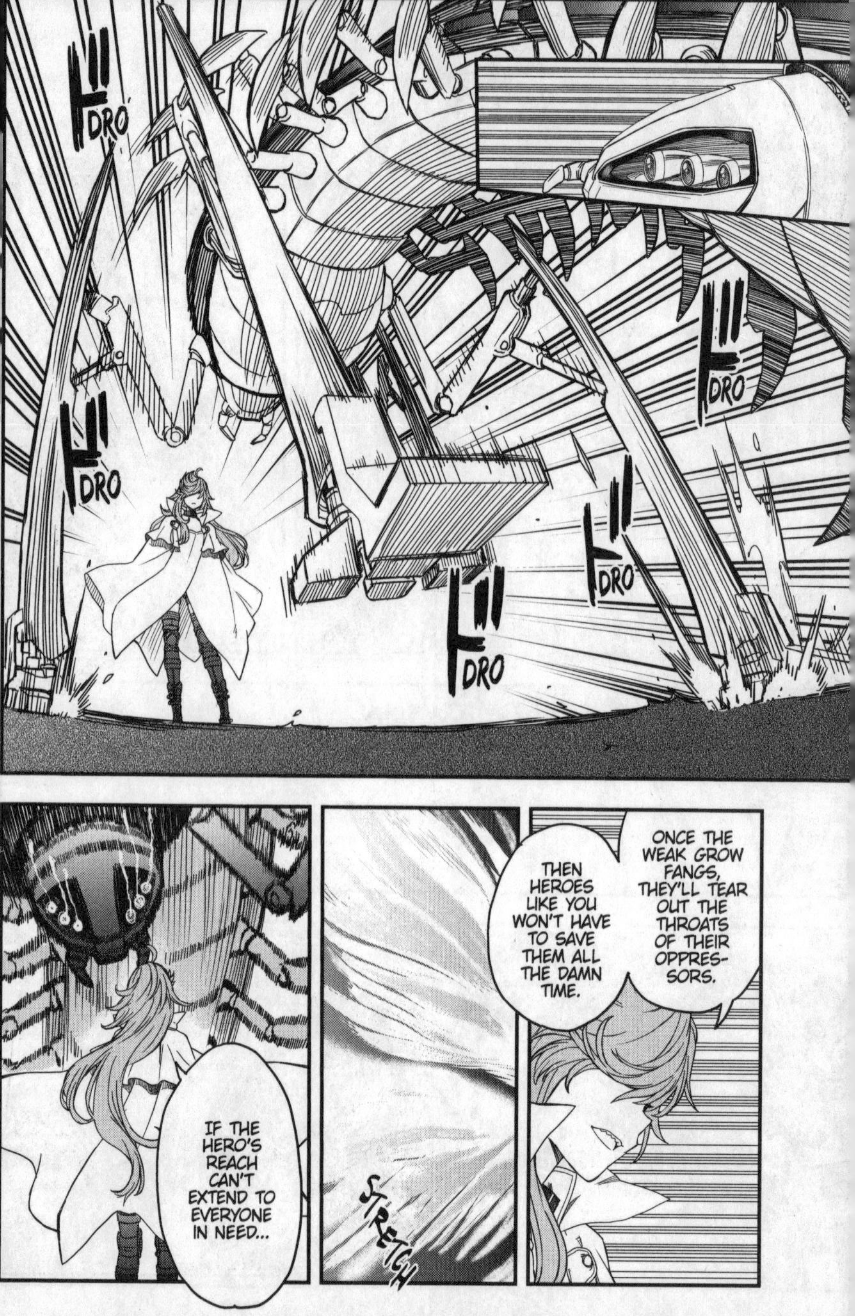

DRO
DRO
DRO
DRO
DRO
ONCE THE WEAK GROW FANGS, THEY'LL TEAR OUT THE THROATS OF THEIR OPPRES-SORS.
THEN HEROES LIKE YOU WON'T HAVE TO SAVE THEM ALL THE DAMN TIME.
STRETCH
IF THE HERO'S REACH CAN'T EXTEND TO EVERYONE IN NEED...

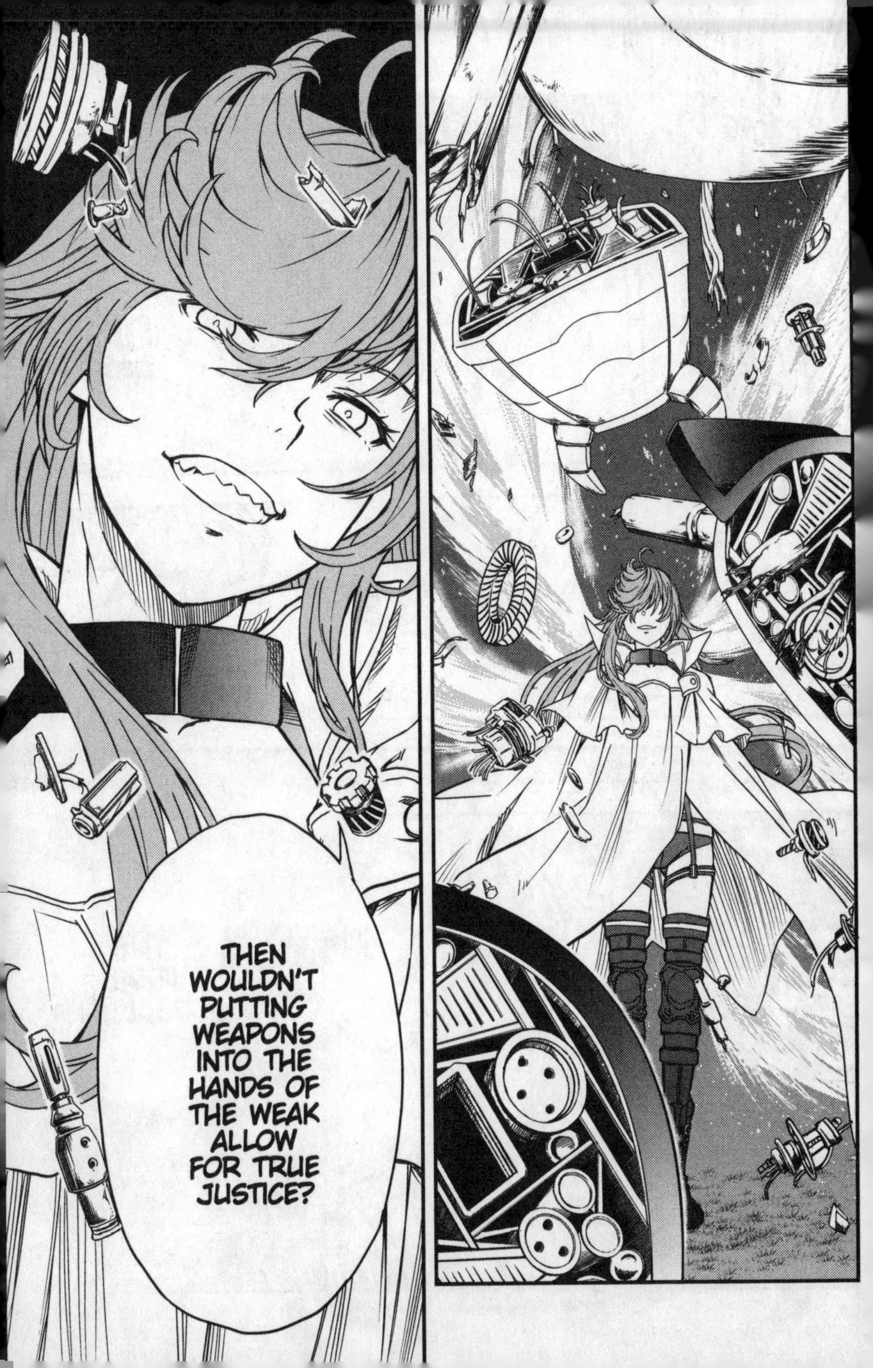
THEN WOULDN'T PUTTING WEAPONS INTO THE HANDS OF THE WEAK ALLOW FOR TRUE JUSTICE?

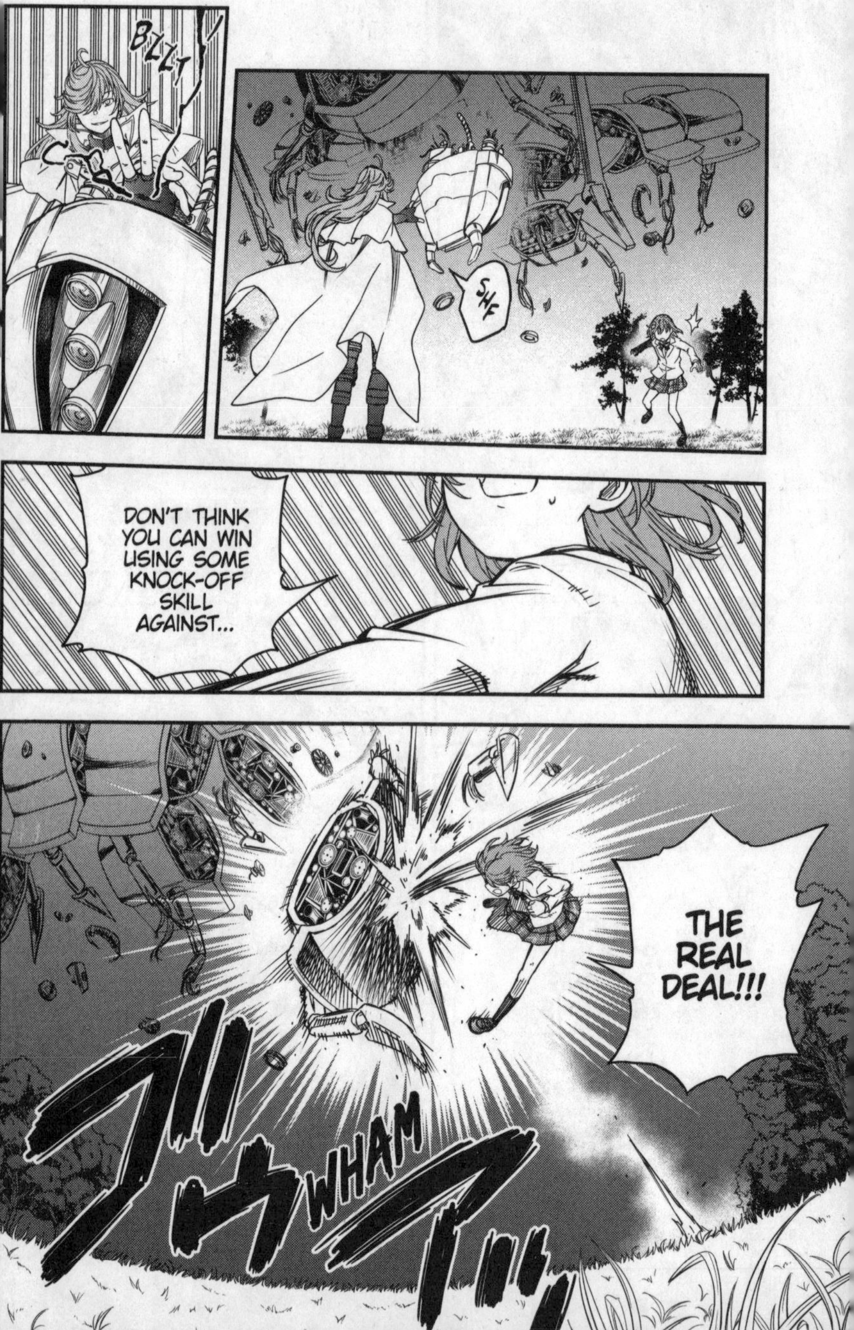
SHF
BZZT
DON'T THINK YOU CAN WIN USING SOME KNOCK-OFF SKILL AGAINST...
THE REAL DEAL!!!
WHAM

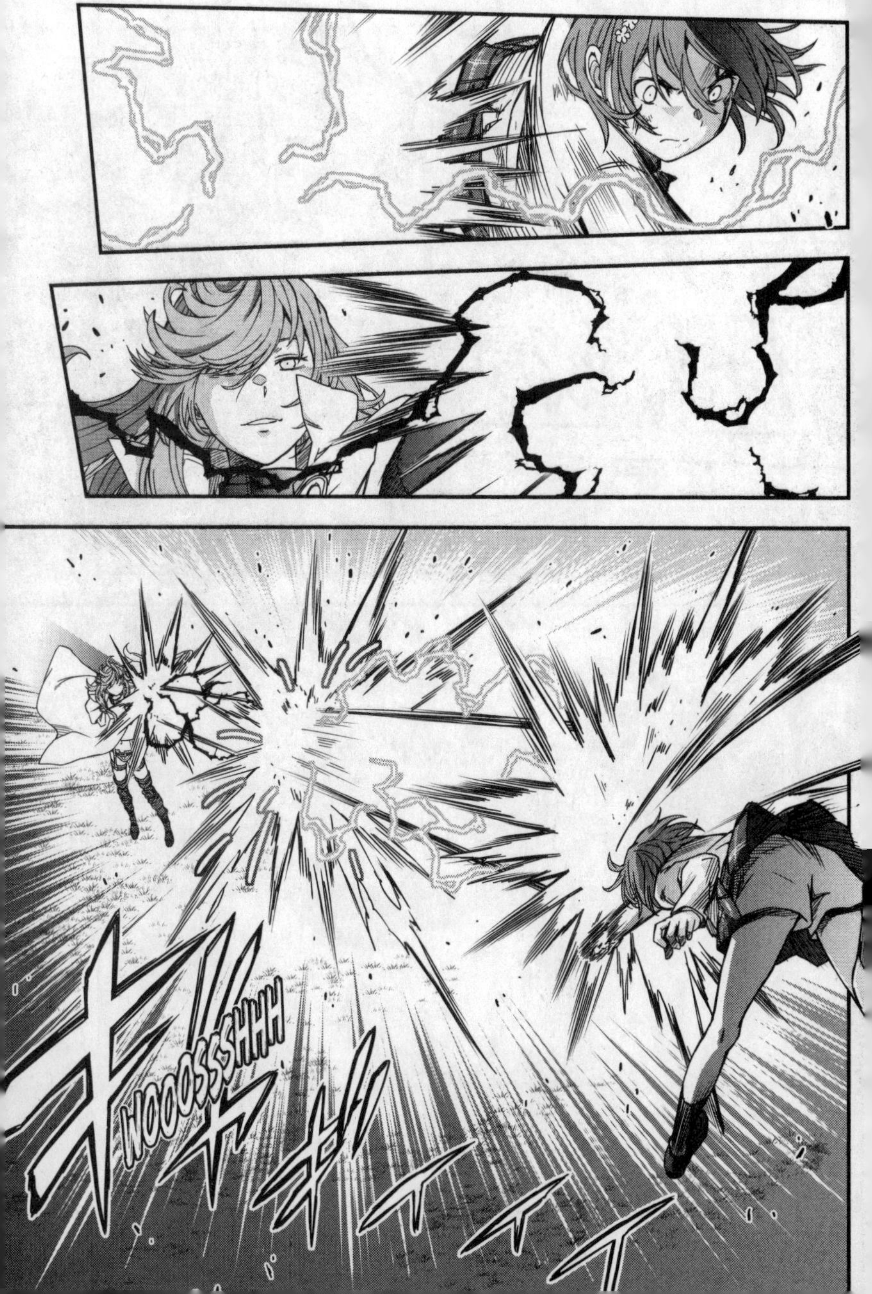
WOOOSSSHHH

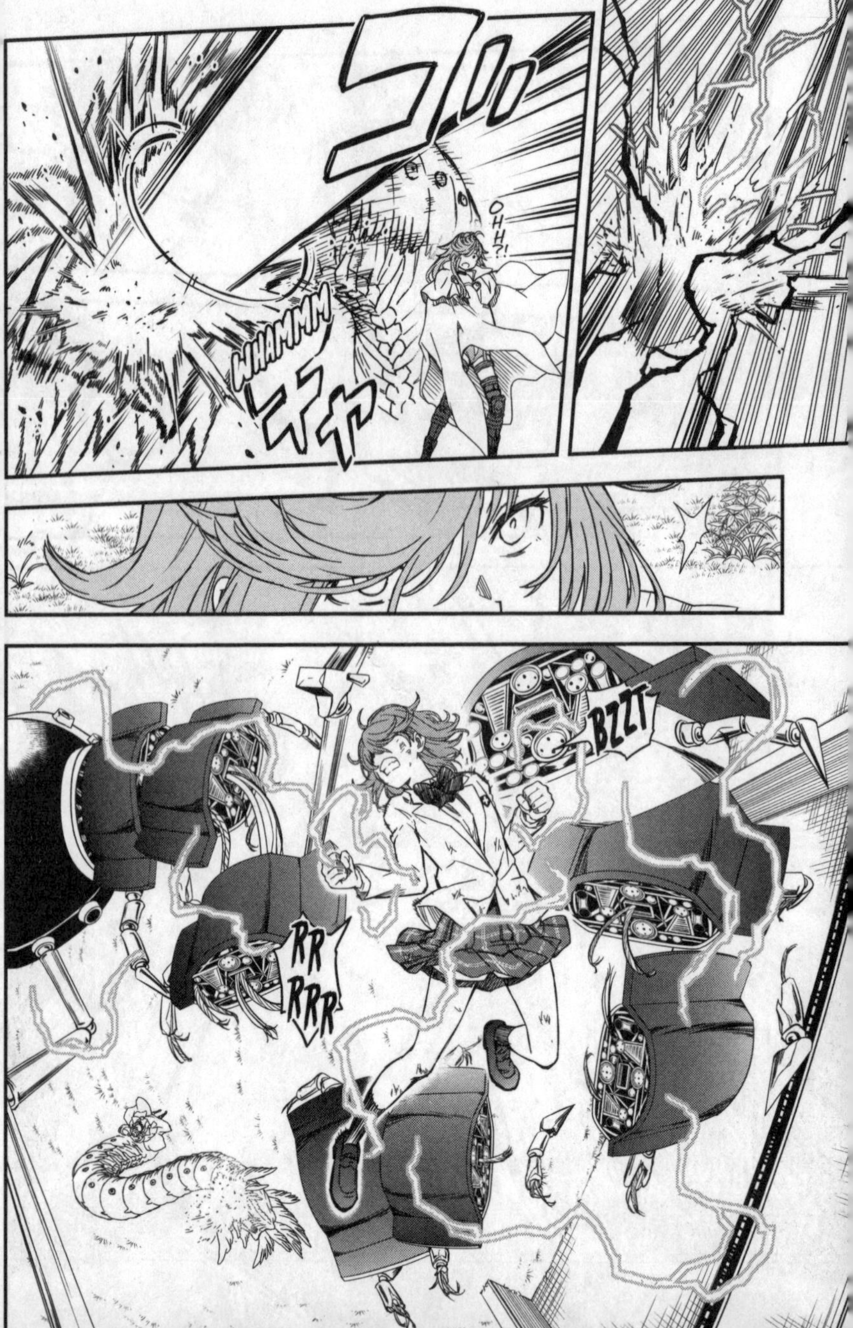
OHH?!
WHAMMM
BZZT
RR RRR

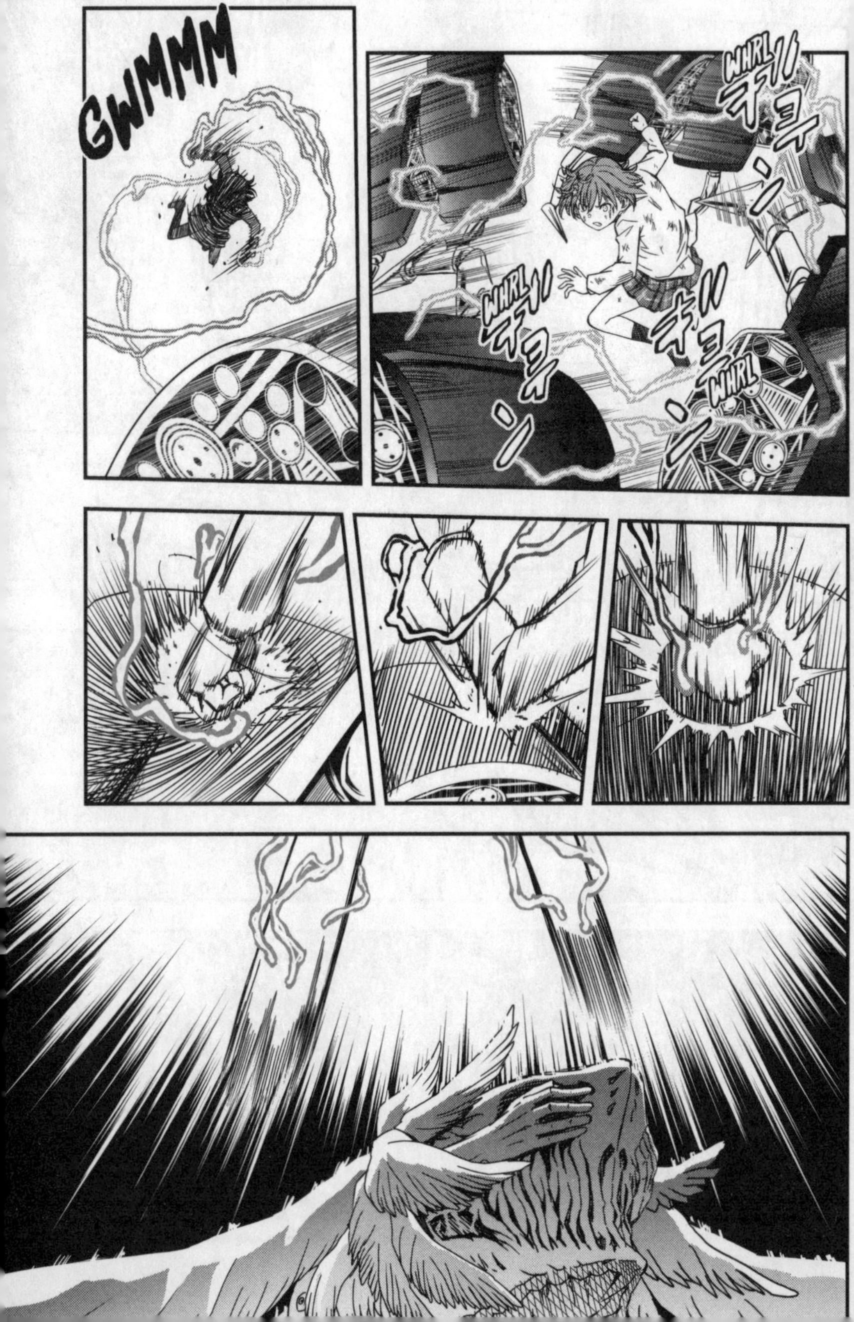
WHRL
WHRL
WHRL
GWMMM

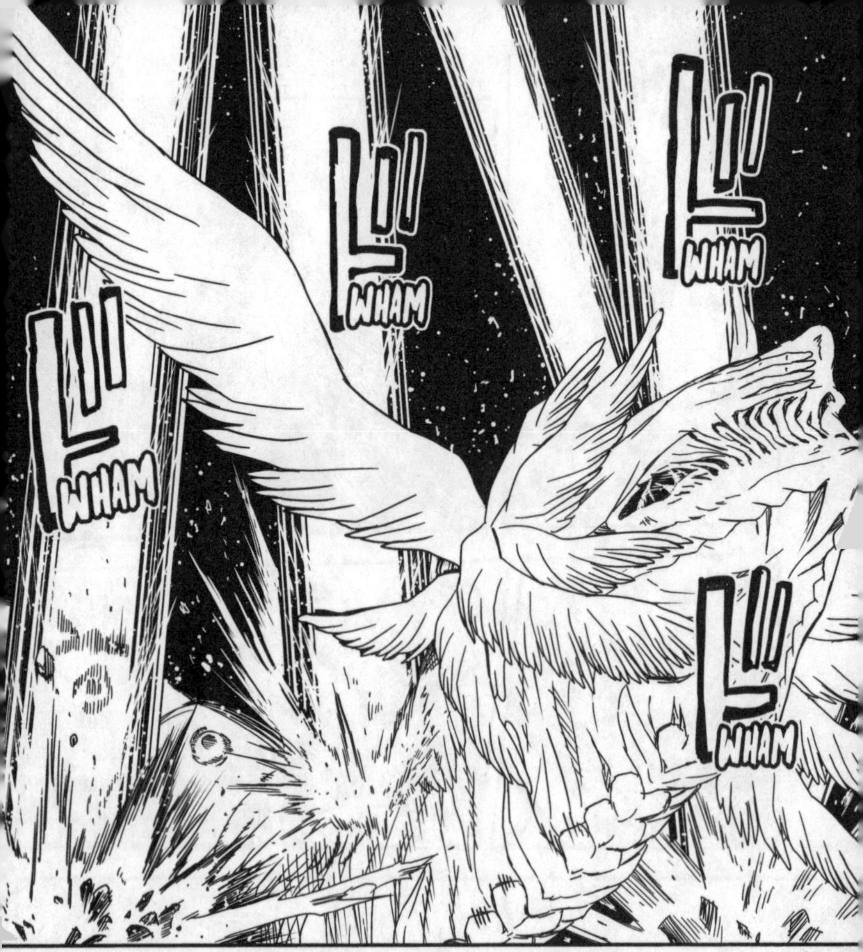
WHAM
WHAM
WHAM
WHAM
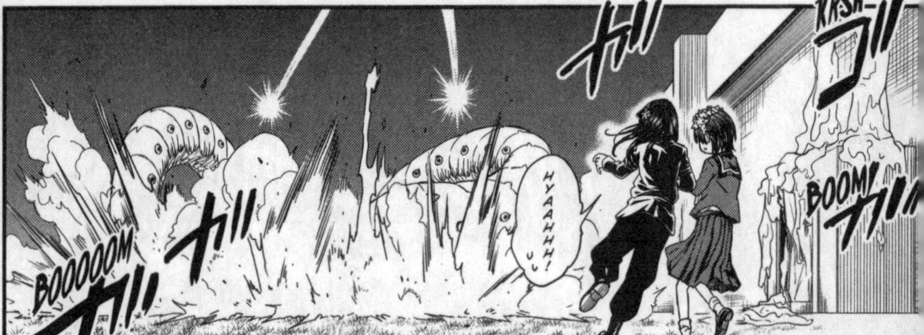
KRSH—
BOOM!
HYAAHHH!
BOOOOOM

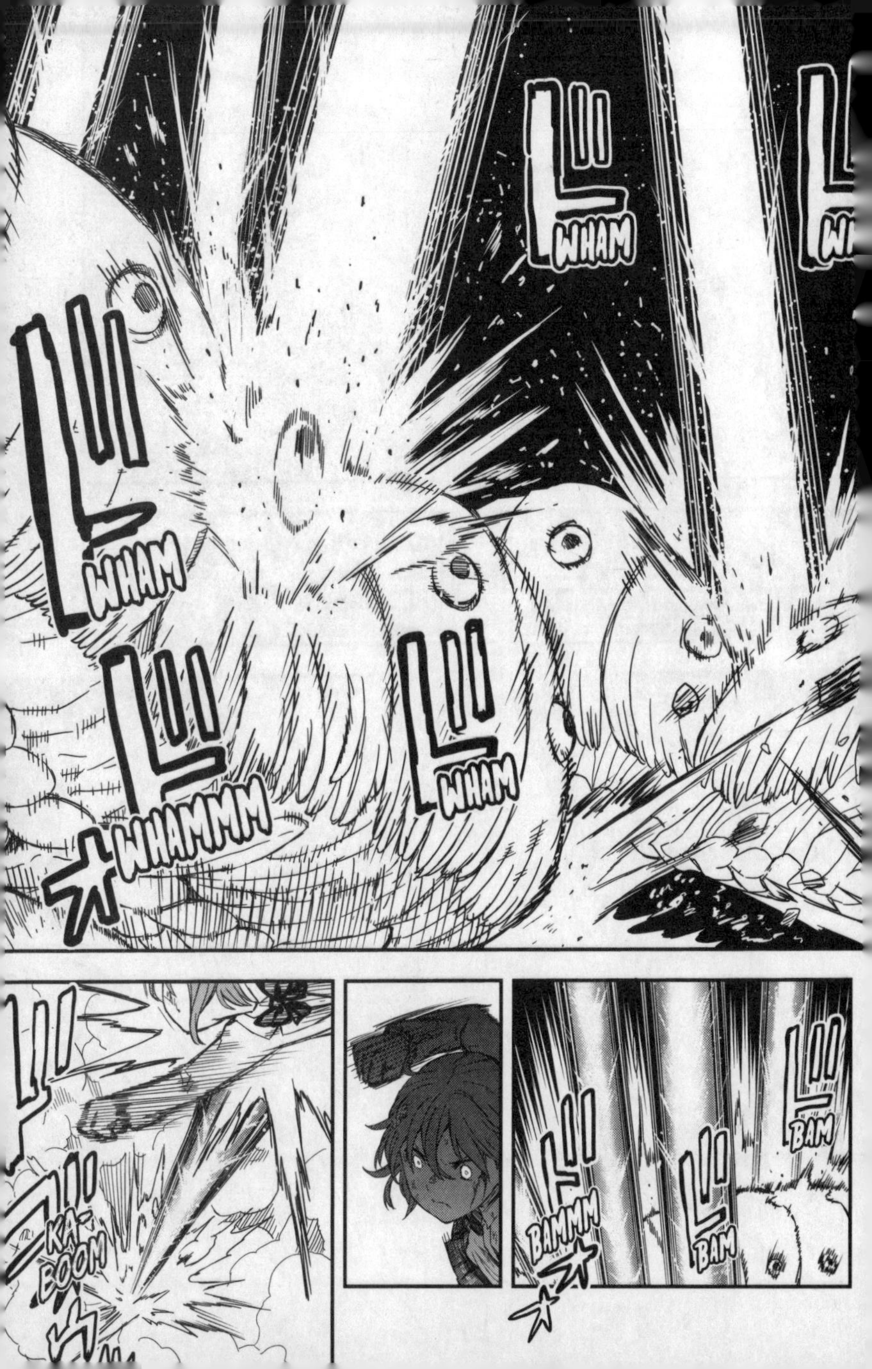
WHAM
WHAM
WHAM
WHAMMM
BAM
BAMMM
BAM
KA-
BOOM

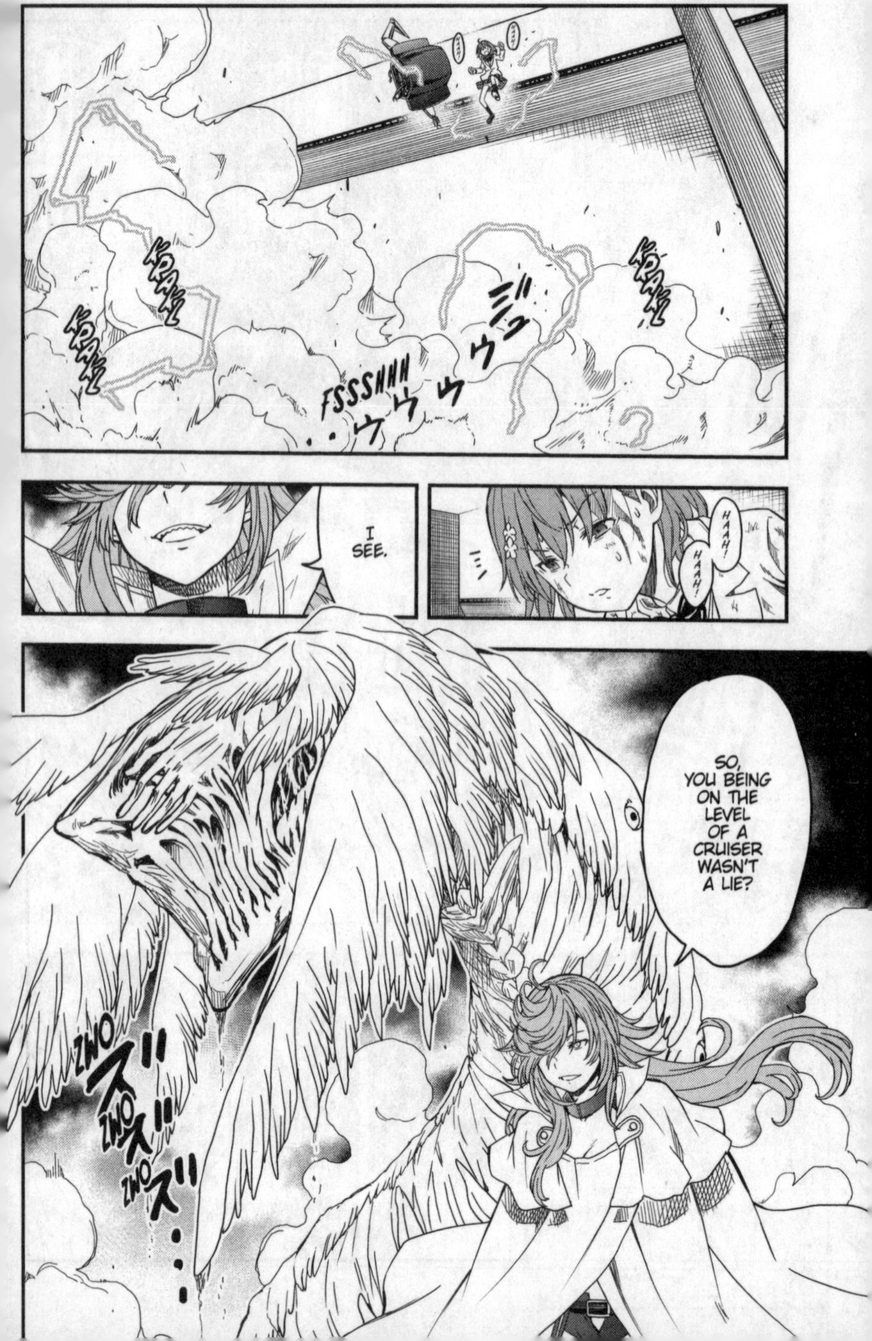
KRAK!
ジュウウウ...
FSSSHHH
KRAK!
KRAK!
HAAH!
HAAH!
I SEE.
SO, YOU BEING ON THE LEVEL OF A CRUISER WASN'T A LIE?
ZWO ズ ZWO ズ ZWO ズ...

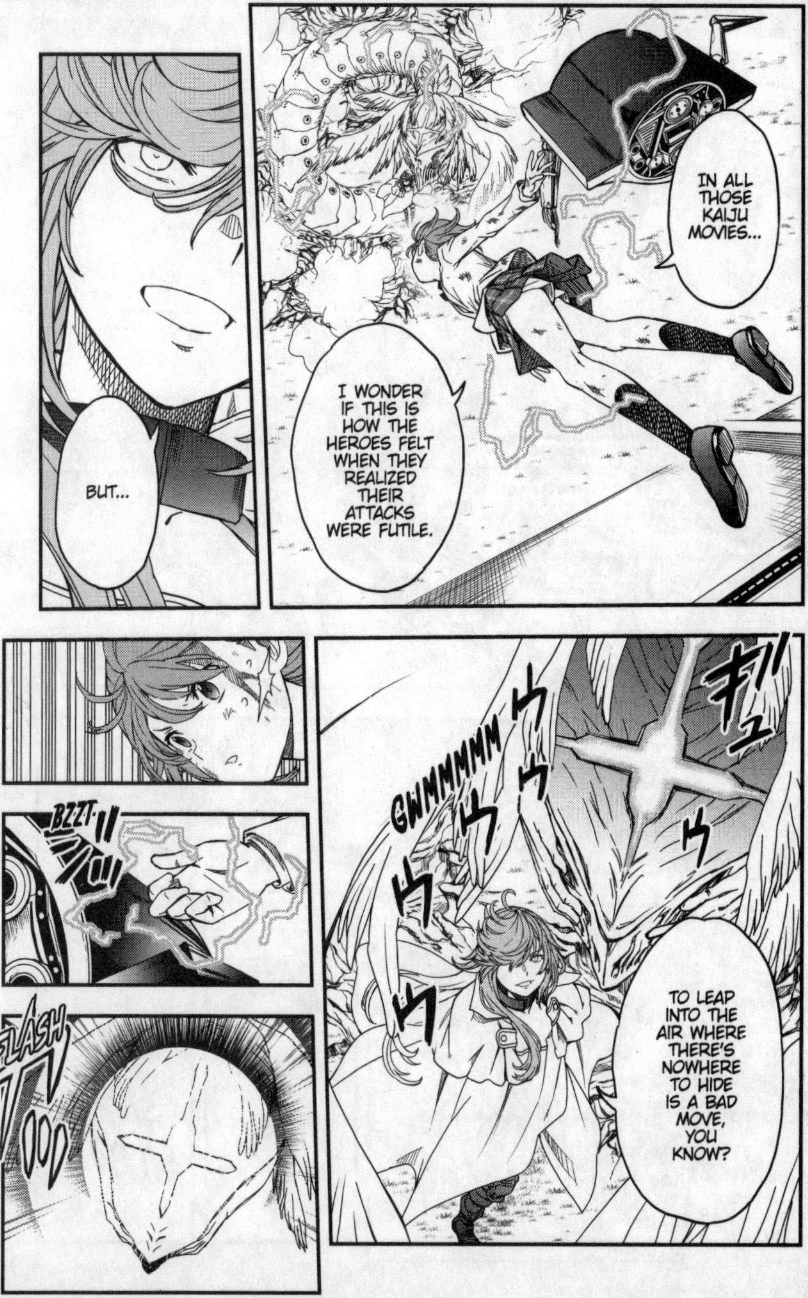
IN ALL THOSE KAIJU MOVIES...
I WONDER IF THIS IS HOW THE HEROES FELT WHEN THEY REALIZED THEIR ATTACKS WERE FUTILE.
BUT...
GWMMMMM
TO LEAP INTO THE AIR WHERE THERE'S NOWHERE TO HIDE IS A BAD MOVE, YOU KNOW?
BZZT
FLASH

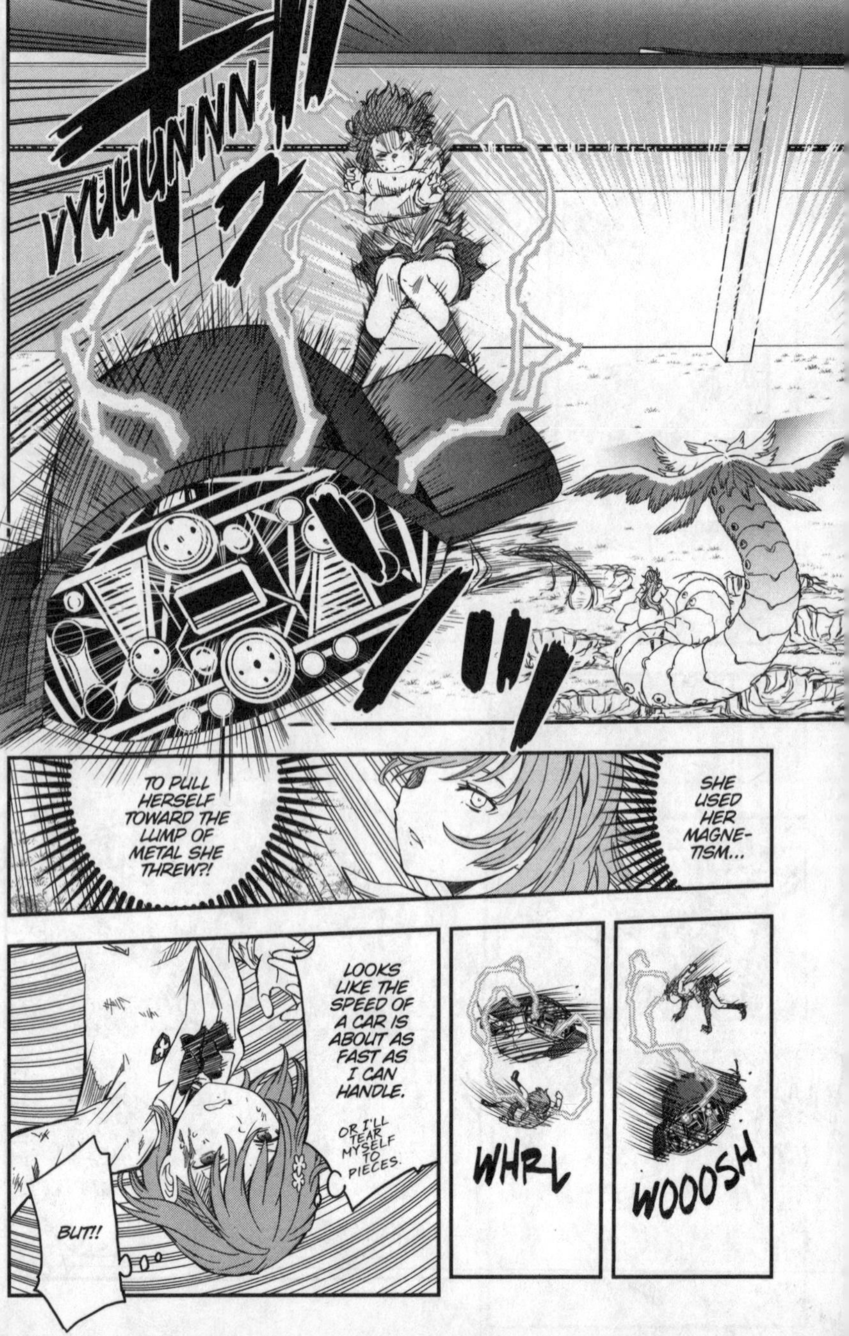
VYUUUNNN
SHE USED HER MAGNETISM...
TO PULL HERSELF TOWARD THE LUMP OF METAL SHE THREW?!
WOOOSH
WHRL
LOOKS LIKE THE SPEED OF A CAR IS ABOUT AS FAST AS I CAN HANDLE.
OR I'LL TEAR MYSELF TO PIECES.
BUT!!

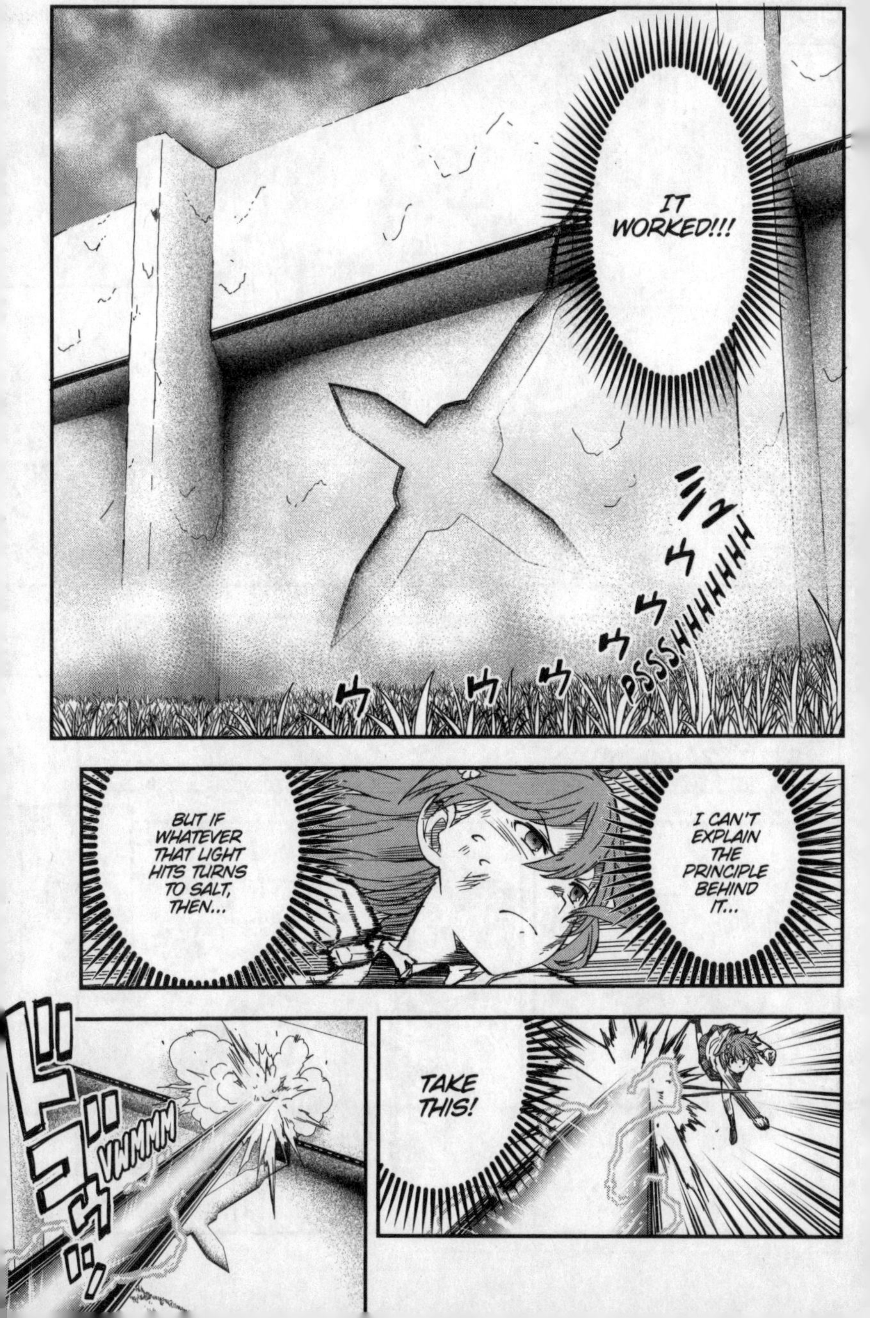
IT WORKED!!!
PSSSHHHHHHH
I CAN'T EXPLAIN THE PRINCIPLE BEHIND IT...
BUT IF WHATEVER THAT LIGHT HITS TURNS TO SALT, THEN...
TAKE THIS!
VWMMM

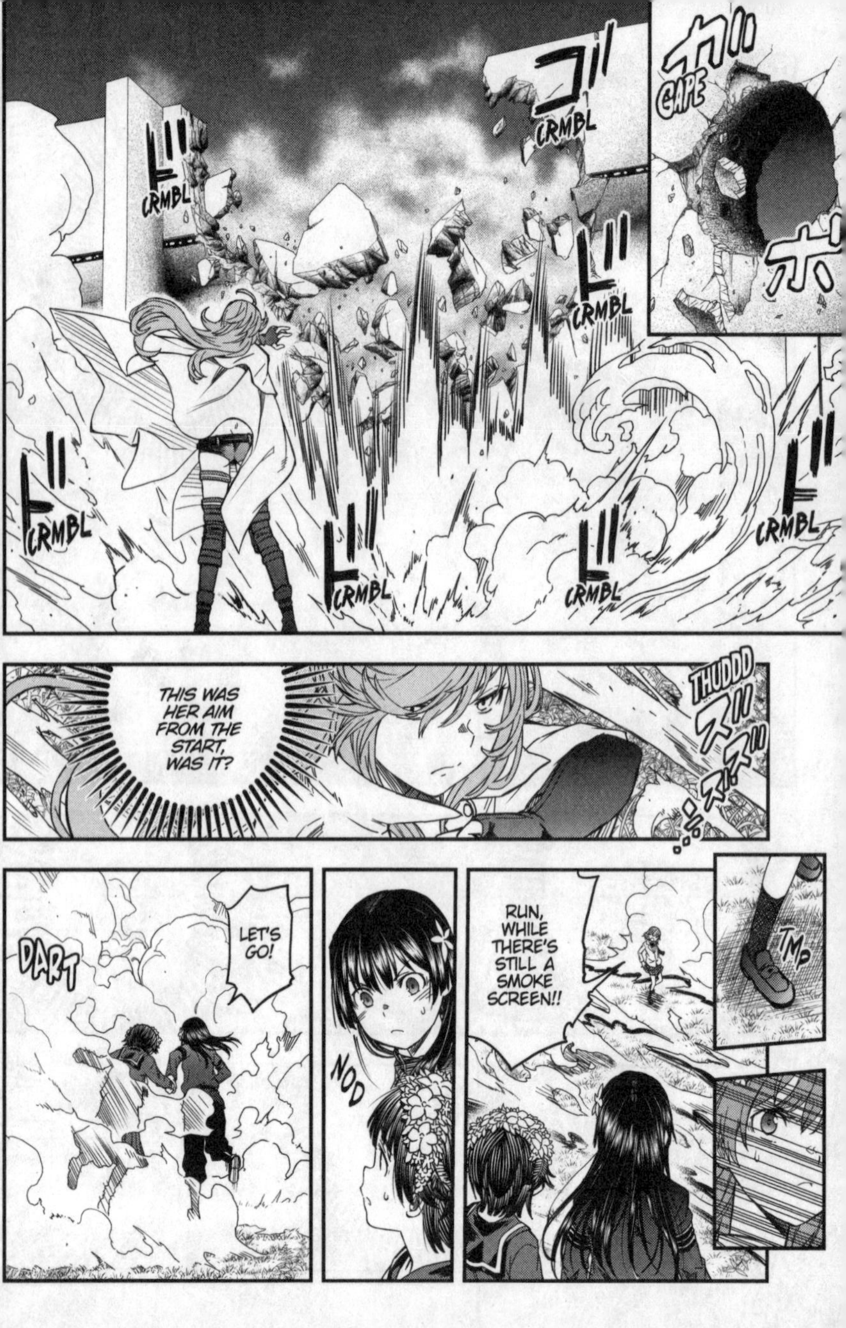
GAPE
CRMBL
CRMBL
CRMBL
CRMBL
CRMBL
CRMBL
CRMBL
THUDDD
THIS WAS HER AIM FROM THE START, WAS IT?
TMP
RUN, WHILE THERE'S STILL A SMOKE SCREEN!!
NOD
LET'S GO!
DART

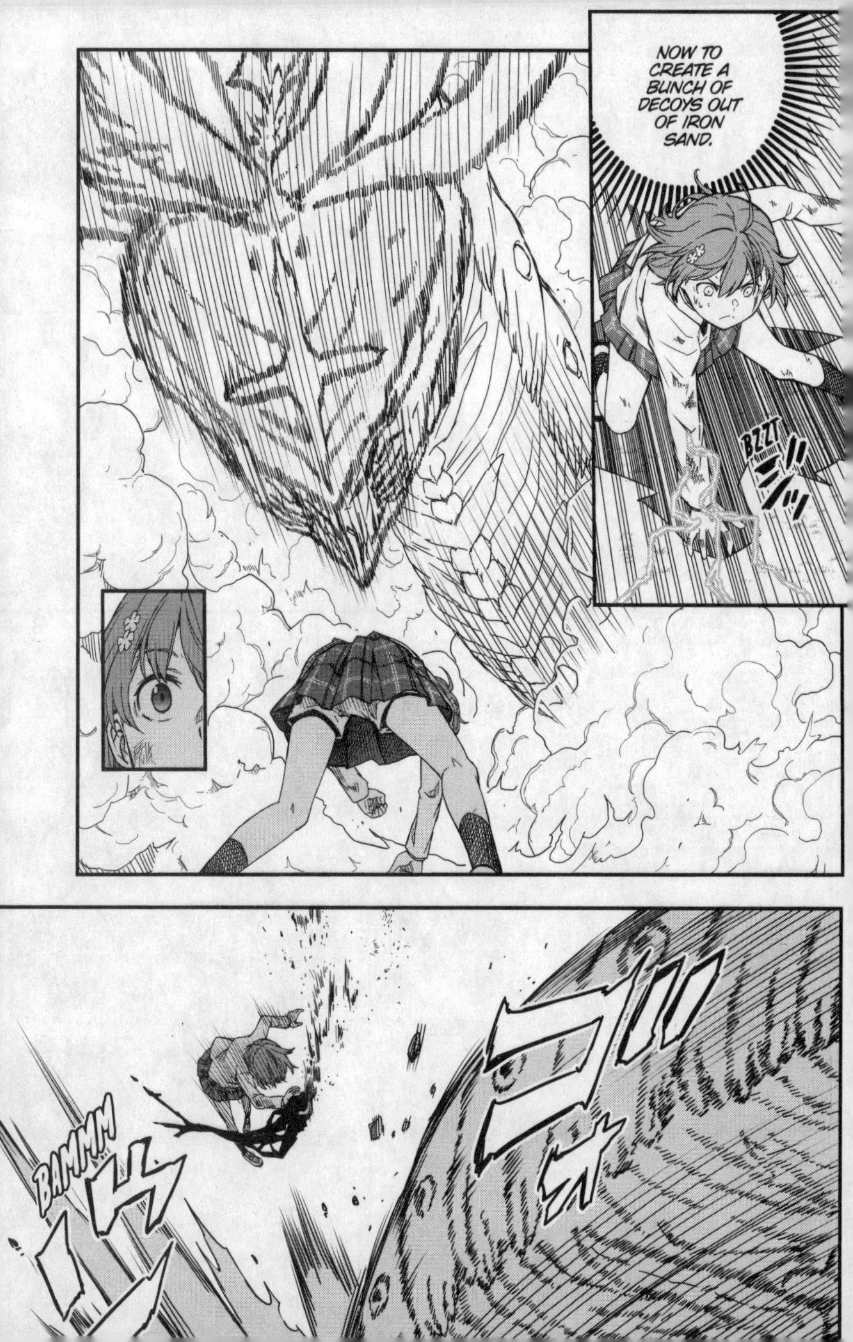
NOW TO CREATE A BUNCH OF DECOYS OUT OF IRON SAND.
BZZT
BAMMM

A Certain SCIENTIFIC Railgun

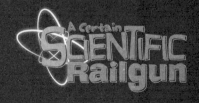

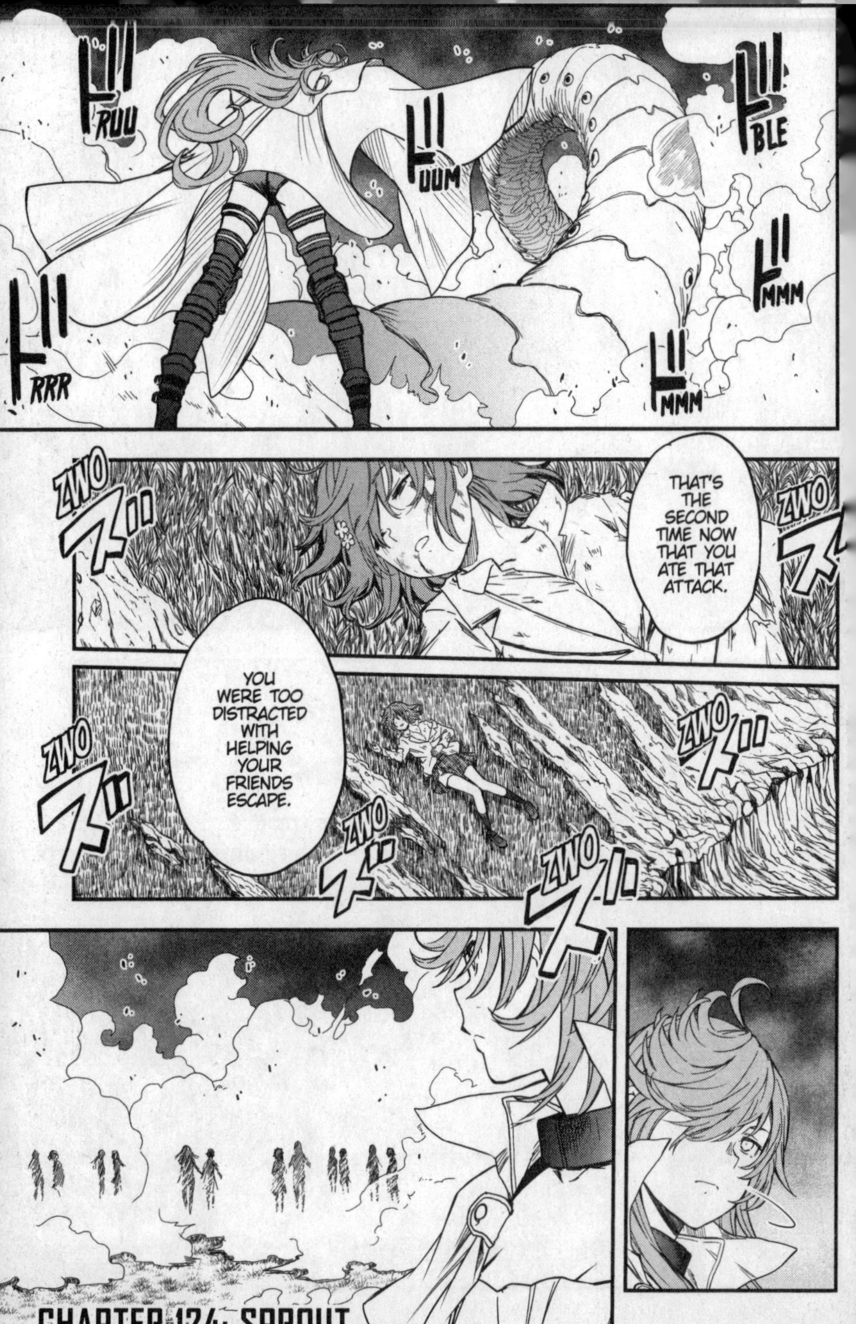
BLE
MMM
MMM
UUM
RUU
RRR
ZWO
THAT'S THE SECOND TIME NOW THAT YOU ATE THAT ATTACK.
ZWO
ZWO
YOU WERE TOO DISTRACTED WITH HELPING YOUR FRIENDS ESCAPE.
ZWO
ZWO
ZWO

CHAPTER 124: SPROUT

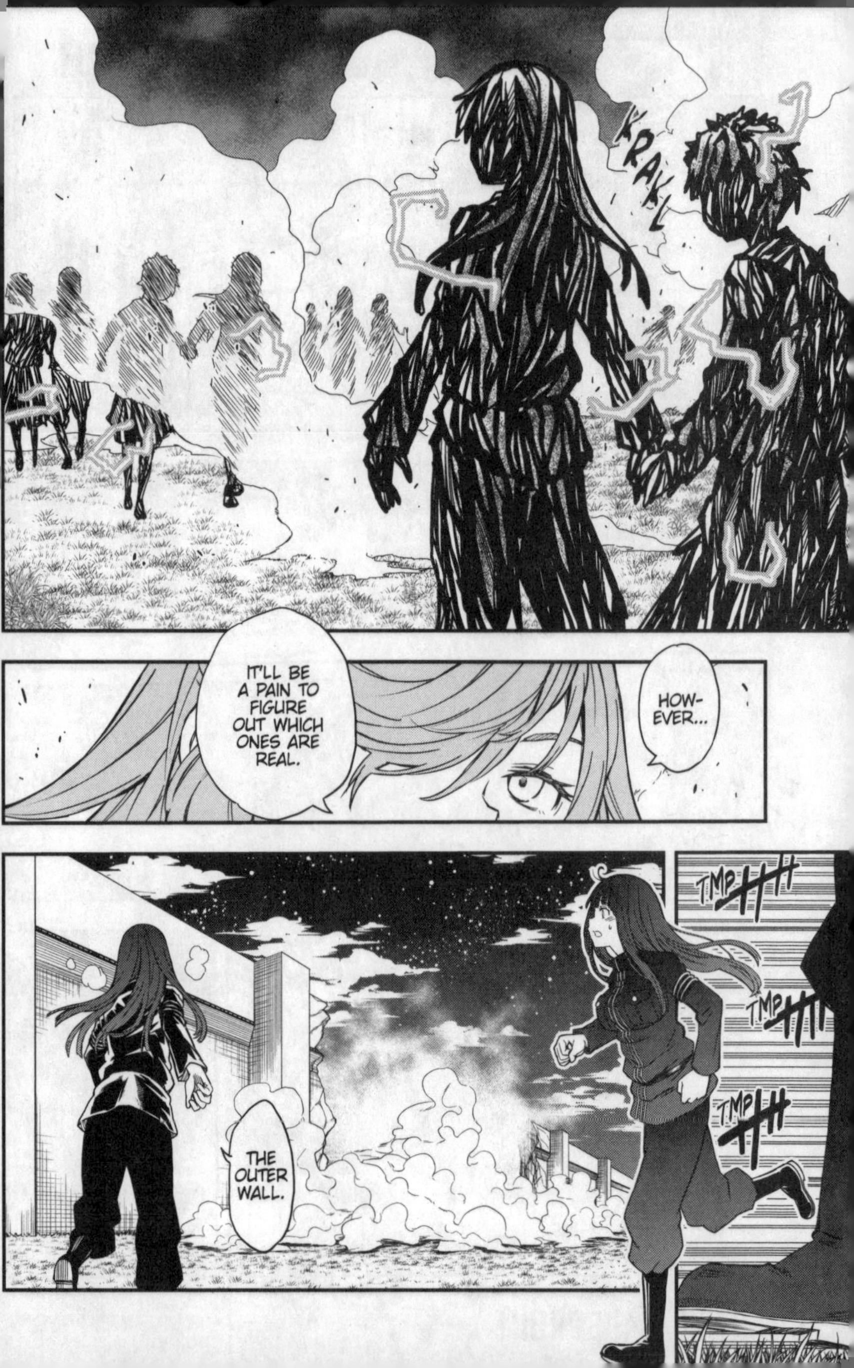
KRAKL
HOW-EVER...
IT'LL BE A PAIN TO FIGURE OUT WHICH ONES ARE REAL.
TMP
TMP
TMP
THE OUTER WALL.

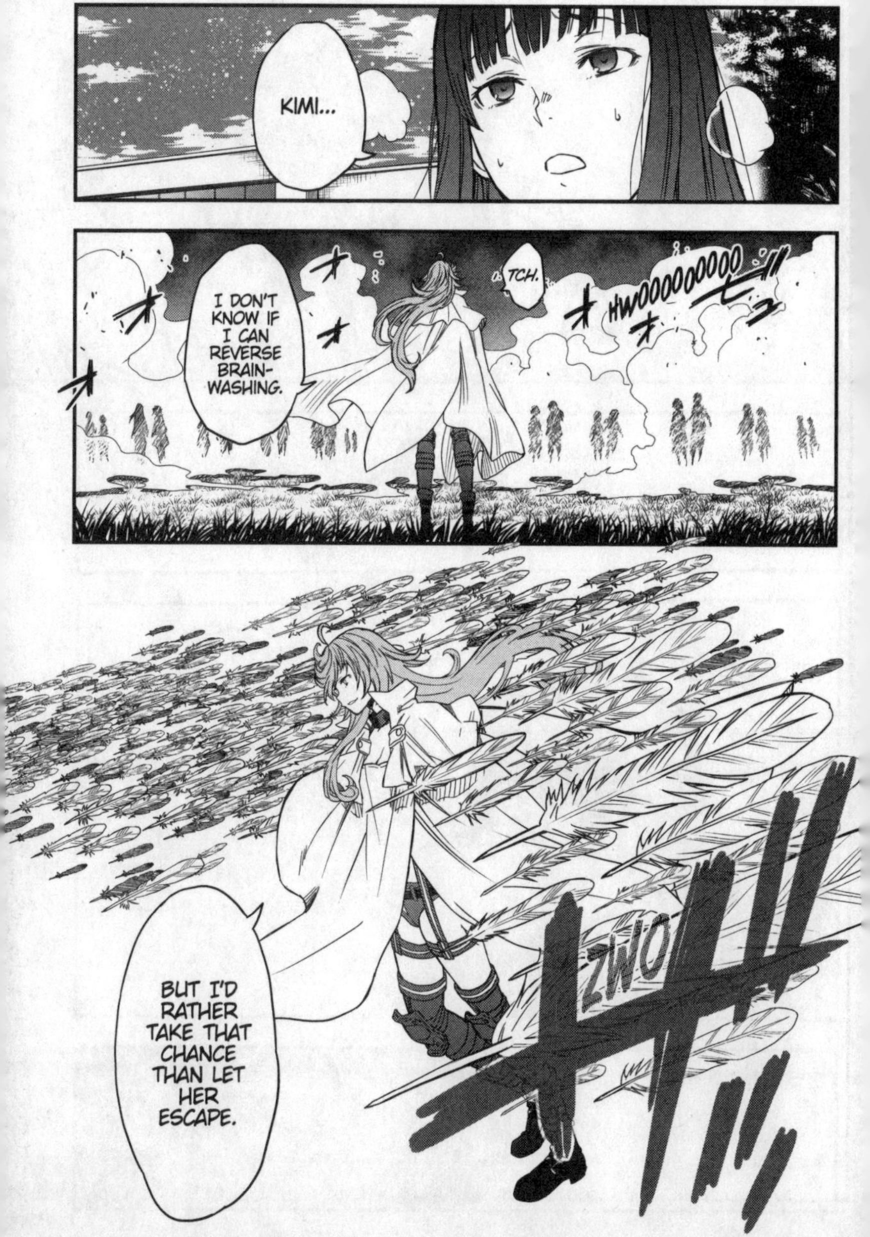
KIMI...
HWOOOOOOOOO
TCH.
I DON'T KNOW IF I CAN REVERSE BRAIN-WASHING.
ZWO
BUT I'D RATHER TAKE THAT CHANCE THAN LET HER ESCAPE.

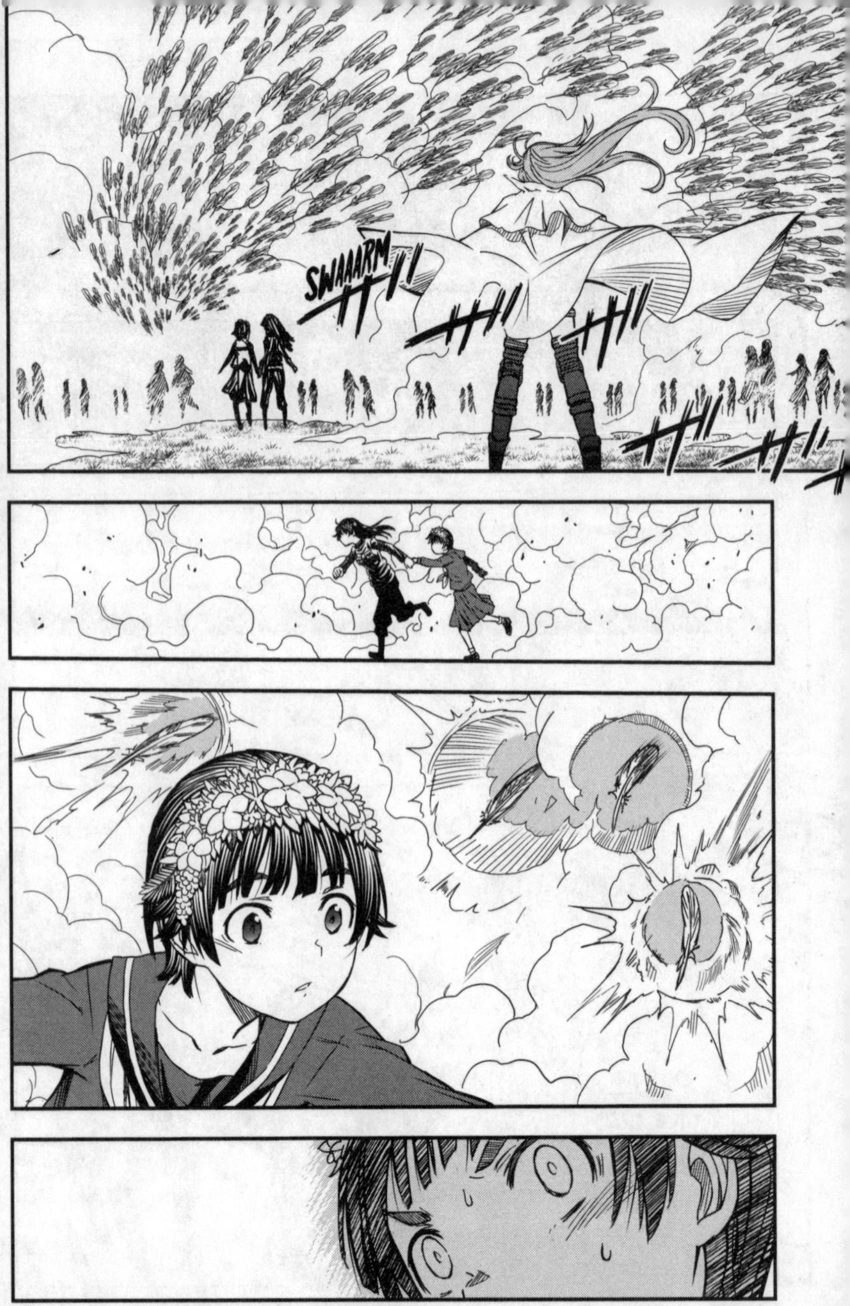
SWAAARM

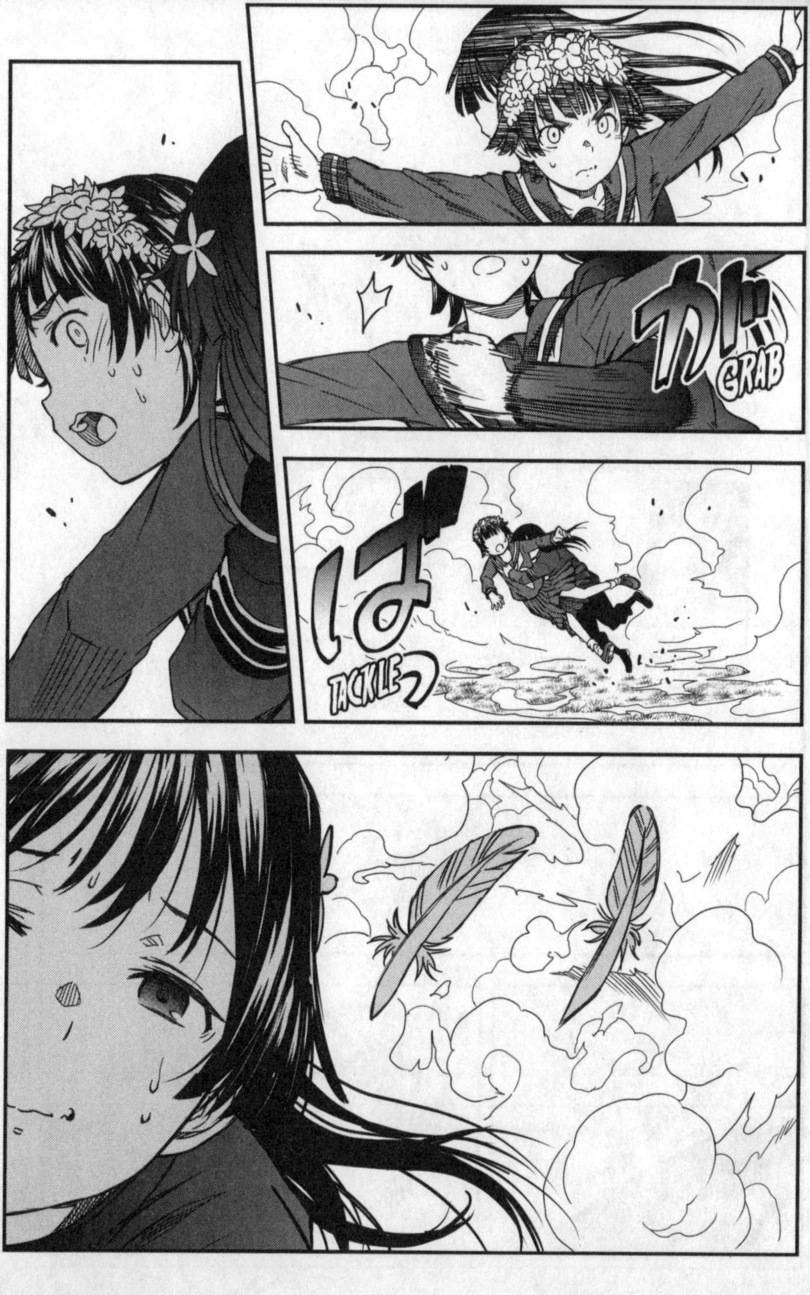
GRAB
TACKLE

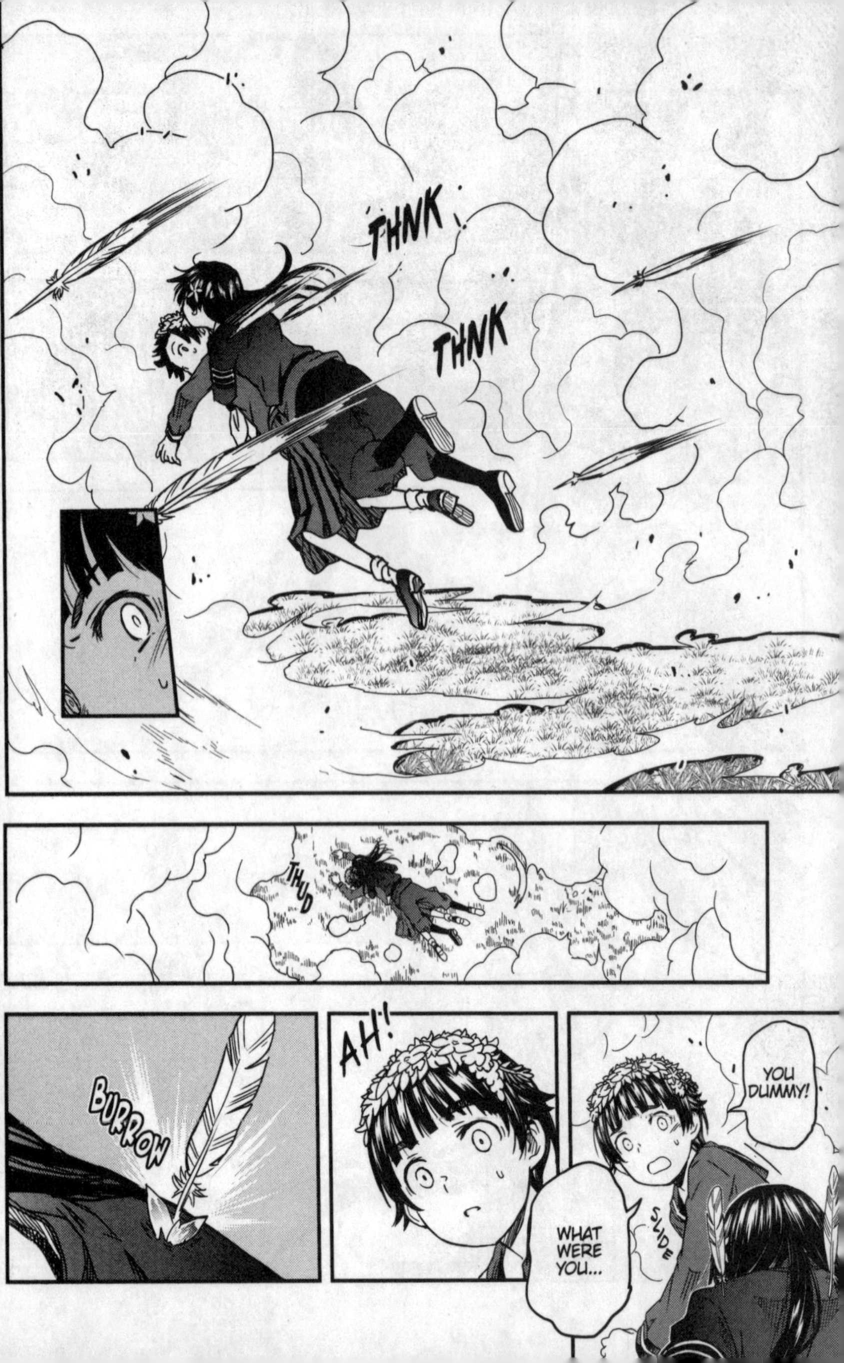
THNK
THNK
THUD
YOU DUMMY!
SLIDE
WHAT WERE YOU...
AH!
BURROW

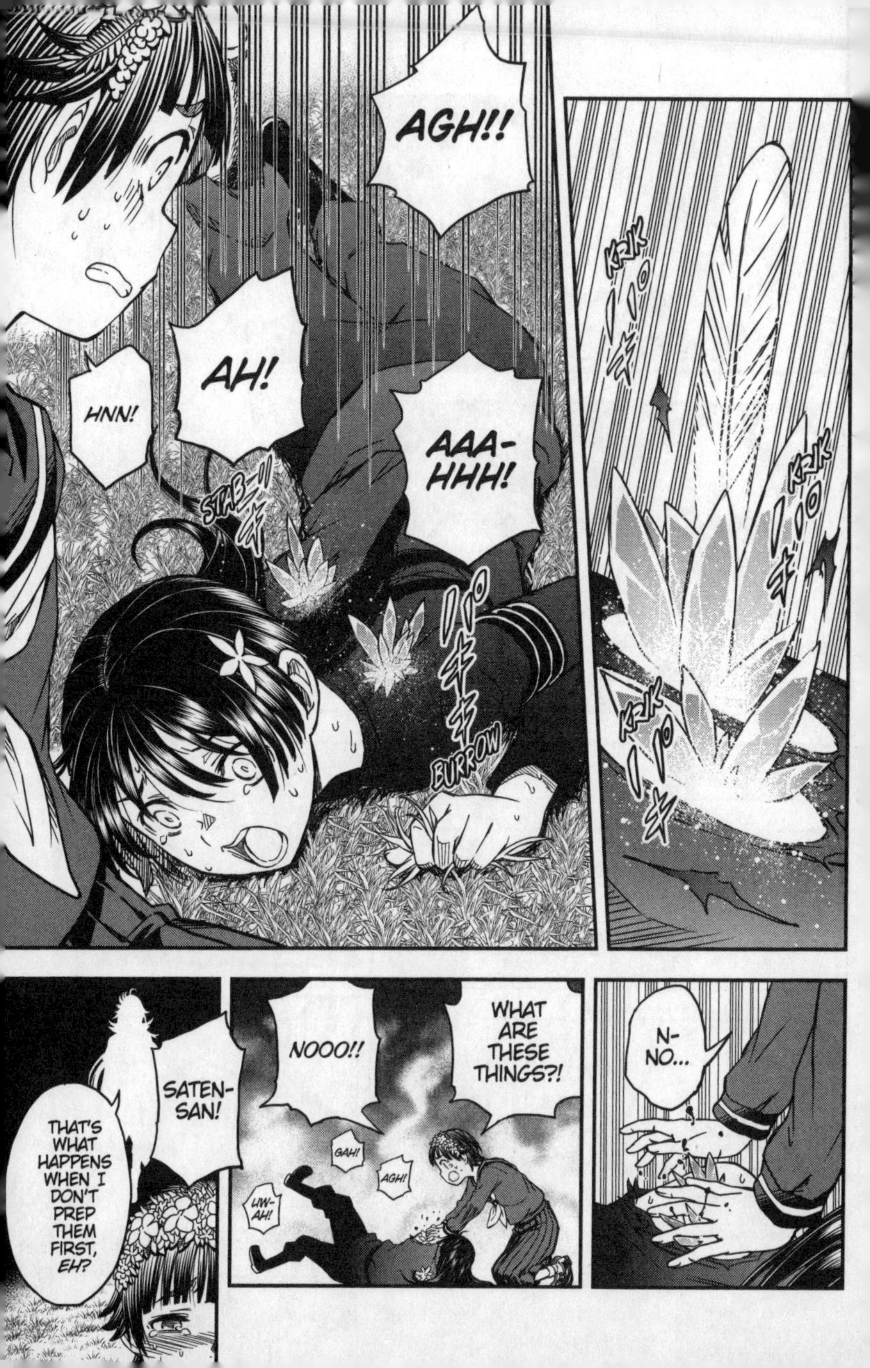
KRIK
KRIK
KRIK
AGH!!
AAA-HHH!
AH!
HNN!
STAB
BURROW
N-NO...
WHAT ARE THESE THINGS?!
NOOO!!
GAH!
AGH!
UWA-AH!
SATEN-SAN!
THAT'S WHAT HAPPENS WHEN I DON'T PREP THEM FIRST, EH?

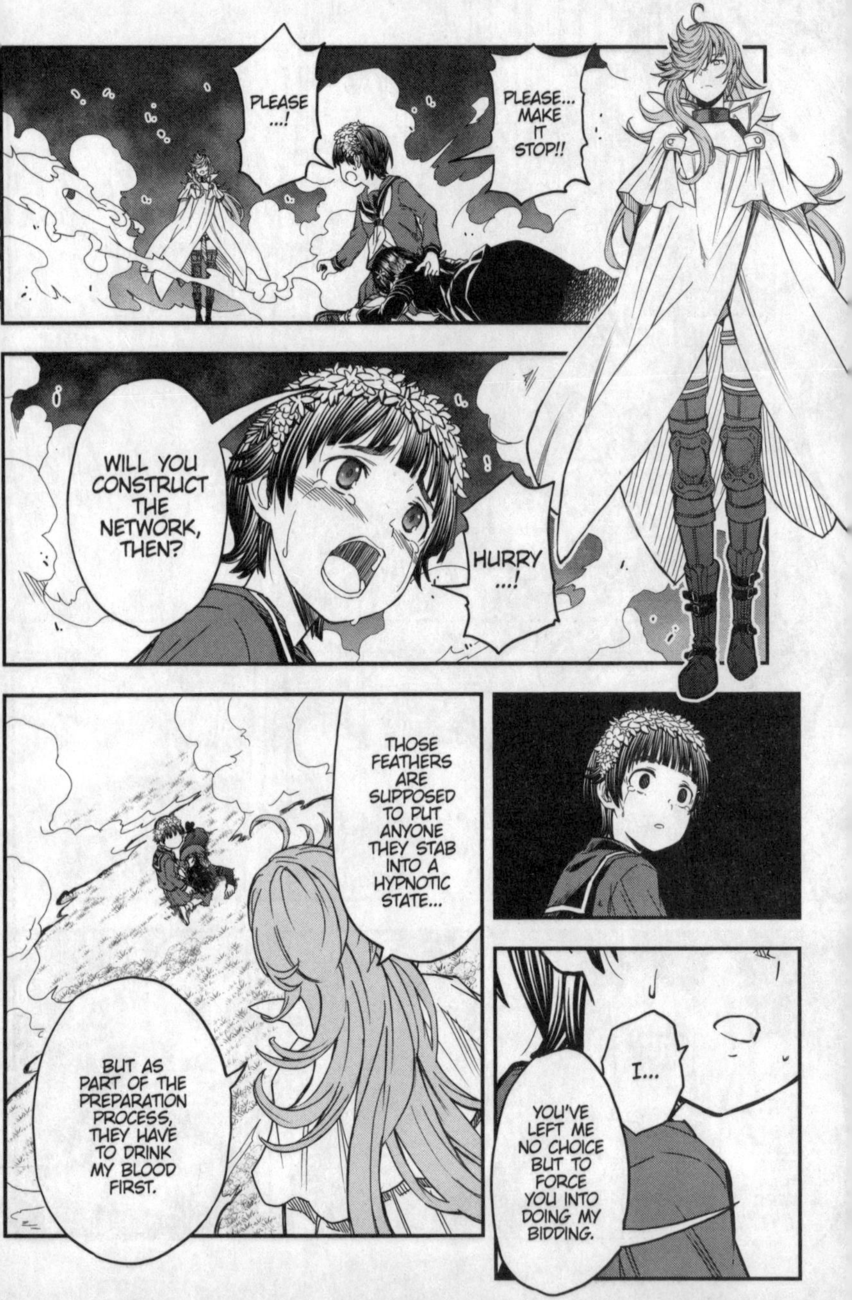
PLEASE... MAKE IT STOP!!
PLEASE ...!
HURRY ...!
WILL YOU CONSTRUCT THE NETWORK, THEN?
I...
YOU'VE LEFT ME NO CHOICE BUT TO FORCE YOU INTO DOING MY BIDDING.
THOSE FEATHERS ARE SUPPOSED TO PUT ANYONE THEY STAB INTO A HYPNOTIC STATE...
BUT AS PART OF THE PREPARATION PROCESS, THEY HAVE TO DRINK MY BLOOD FIRST.

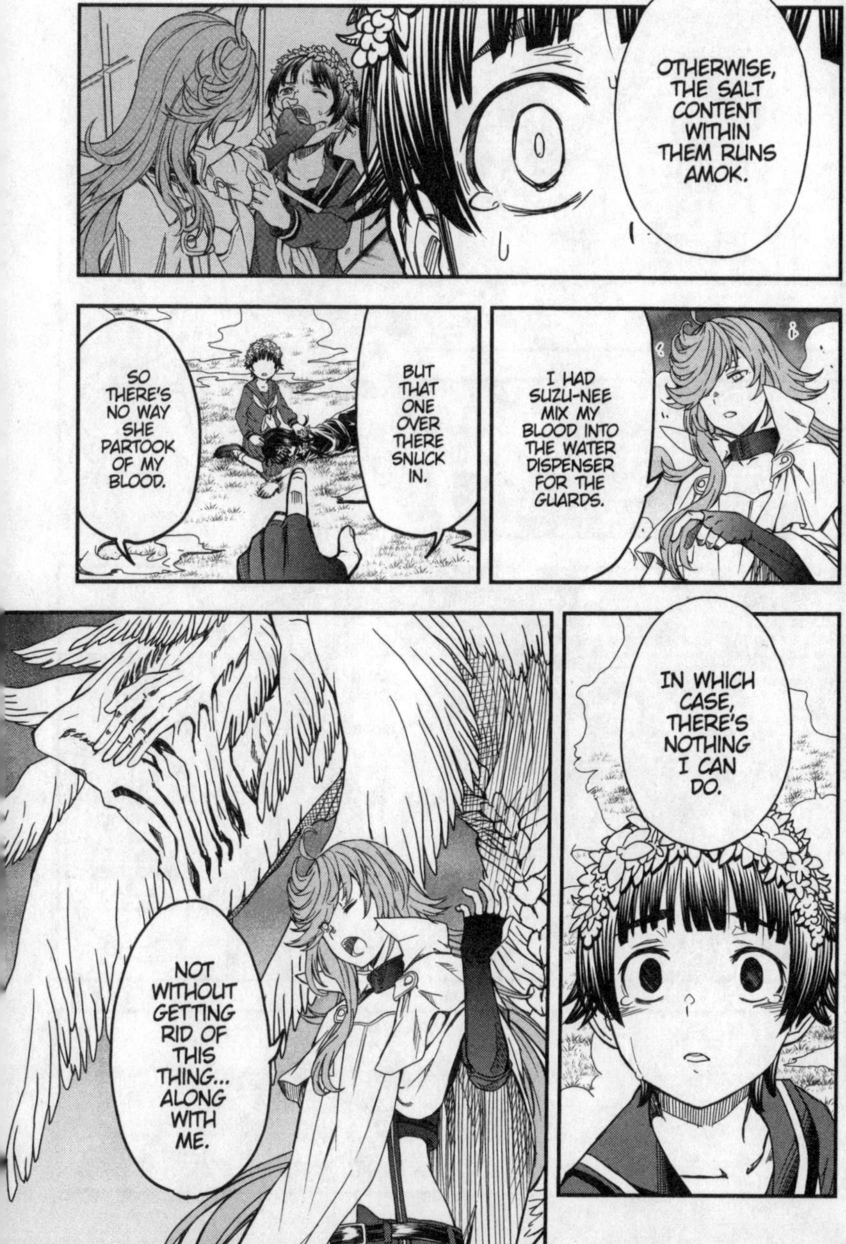
OTHERWISE, THE SALT CONTENT WITHIN THEM RUNS AMOK.
I HAD SUZU-NEE MIX MY BLOOD INTO THE WATER DISPENSER FOR THE GUARDS.
BUT THAT ONE OVER THERE SNUCK IN.
SO THERE'S NO WAY SHE PARTOOK OF MY BLOOD.
IN WHICH CASE, THERE'S NOTHING I CAN DO.
NOT WITHOUT GETTING RID OF THIS THING... ALONG WITH ME.

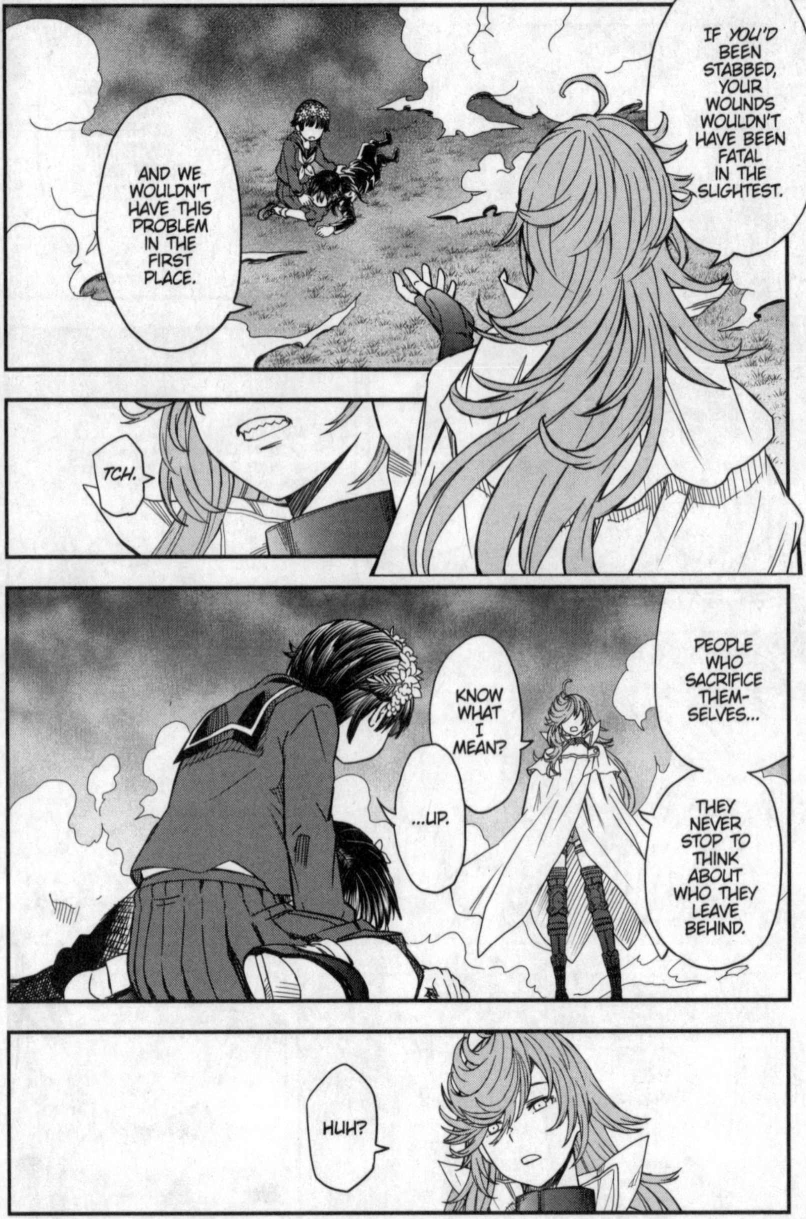
IF YOU'D BEEN STABBED, YOUR WOUNDS WOULDN'T HAVE BEEN FATAL IN THE SLIGHTEST.
AND WE WOULDN'T HAVE THIS PROBLEM IN THE FIRST PLACE.
TCH.
PEOPLE WHO SACRIFICE THEM-SELVES...
THEY NEVER STOP TO THINK ABOUT WHO THEY LEAVE BEHIND.
KNOW WHAT I MEAN?
...UP.
HUH?

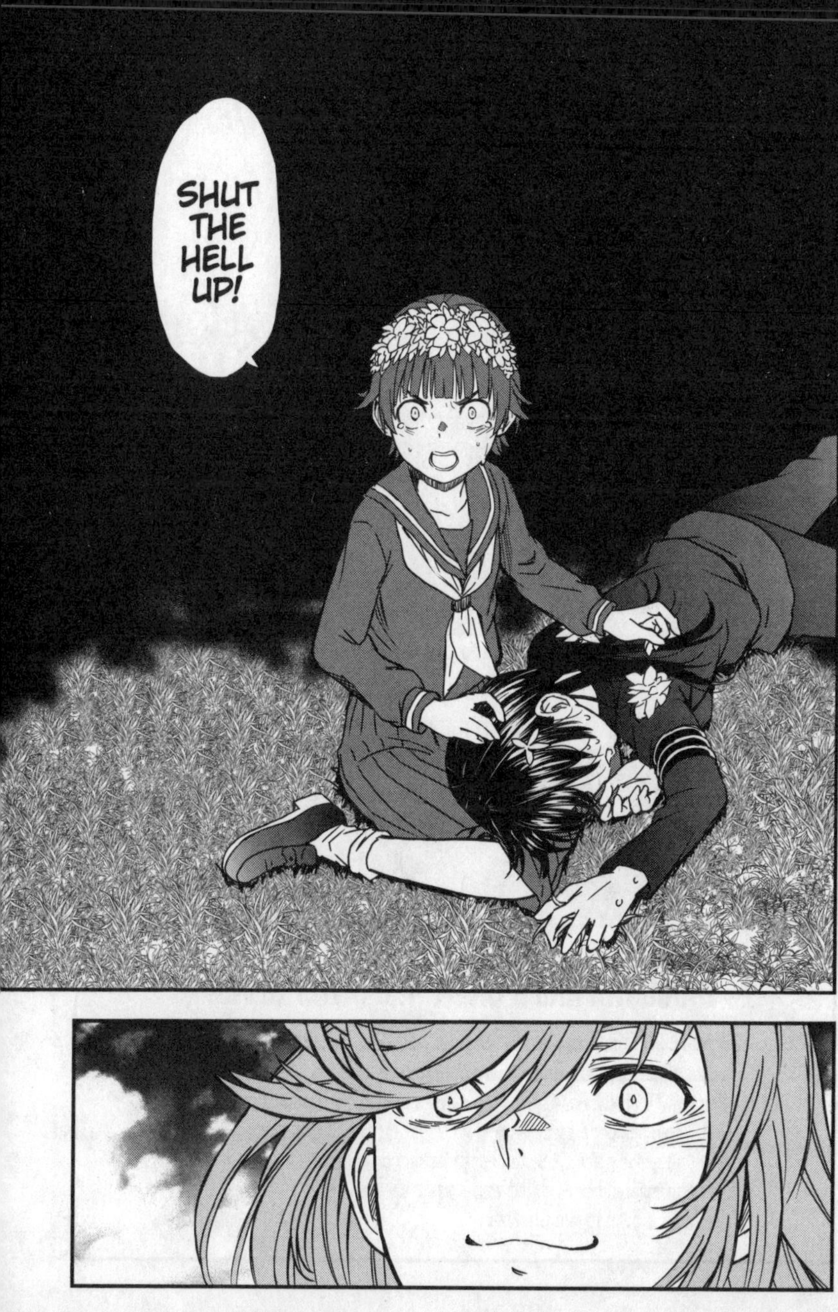
SHUT THE HELL UP!

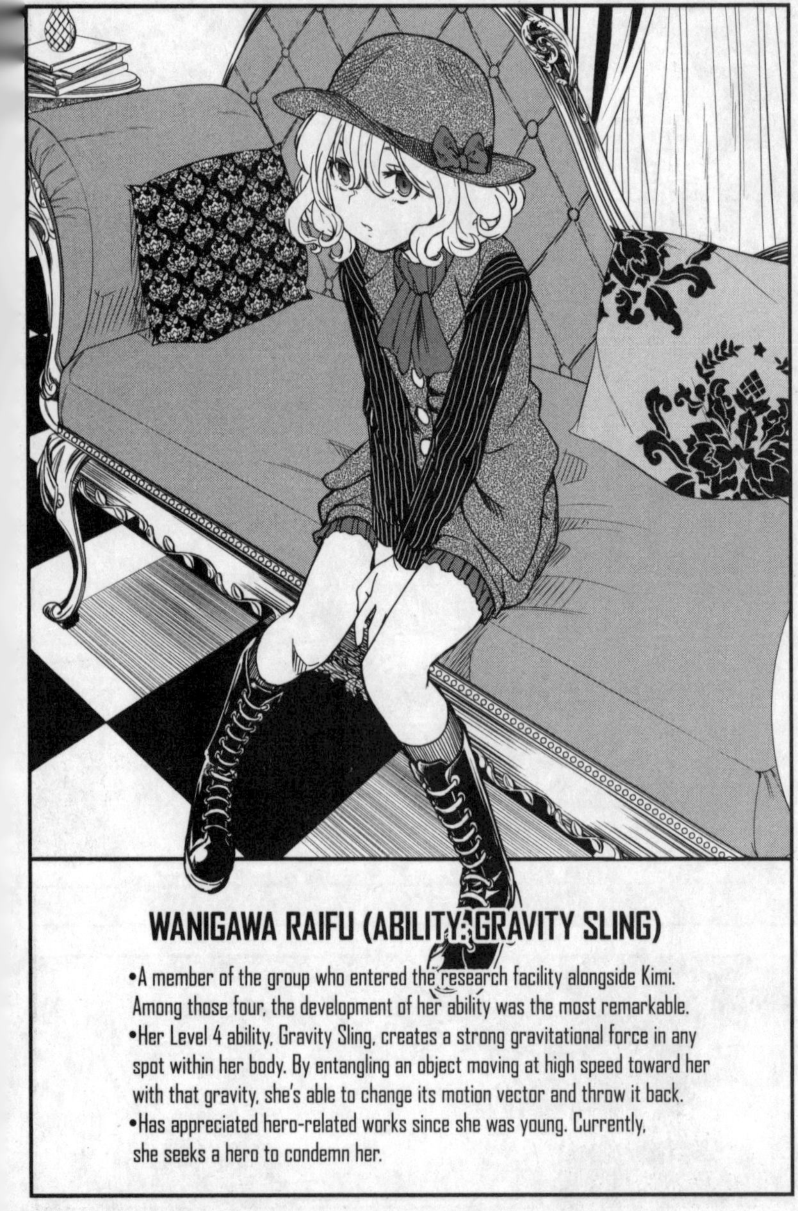

WANIGAWA RAIFU (ABILITY: GRAVITY SLING)

- A member of the group who entered the research facility alongside Kimi. Among those four, the development of her ability was the most remarkable.
- Her Level 4 ability, Gravity Sling, creates a strong gravitational force in any spot within her body. By entangling an object moving at high speed toward her with that gravity, she's able to change its motion vector and throw it back.
- Has appreciated hero-related works since she was young. Currently, she seeks a hero to condemn her.

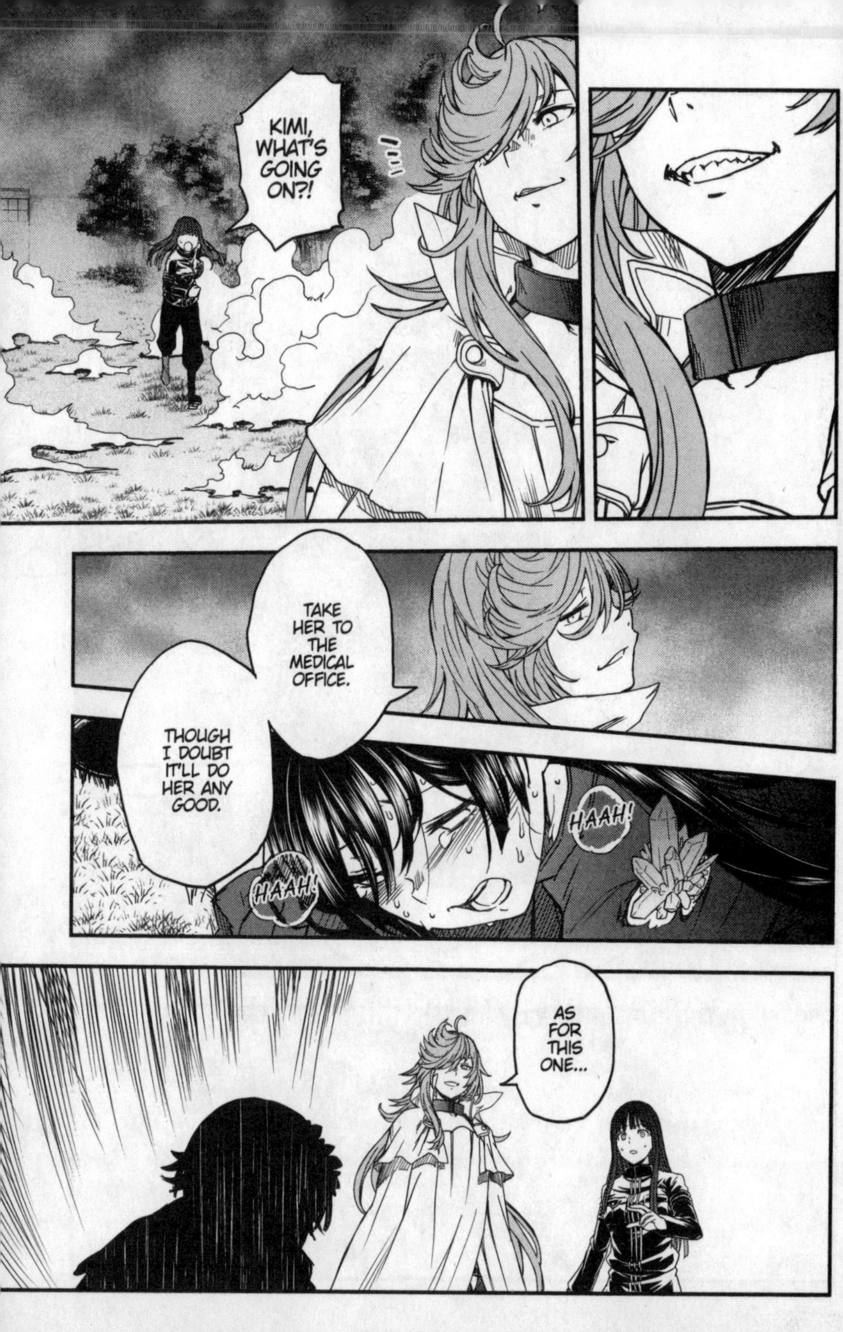
KIMI, WHAT'S GOING ON?!
TAKE HER TO THE MEDICAL OFFICE.
THOUGH I DOUBT IT'LL DO HER ANY GOOD.
HAAH!
HAAH!
AS FOR THIS ONE...

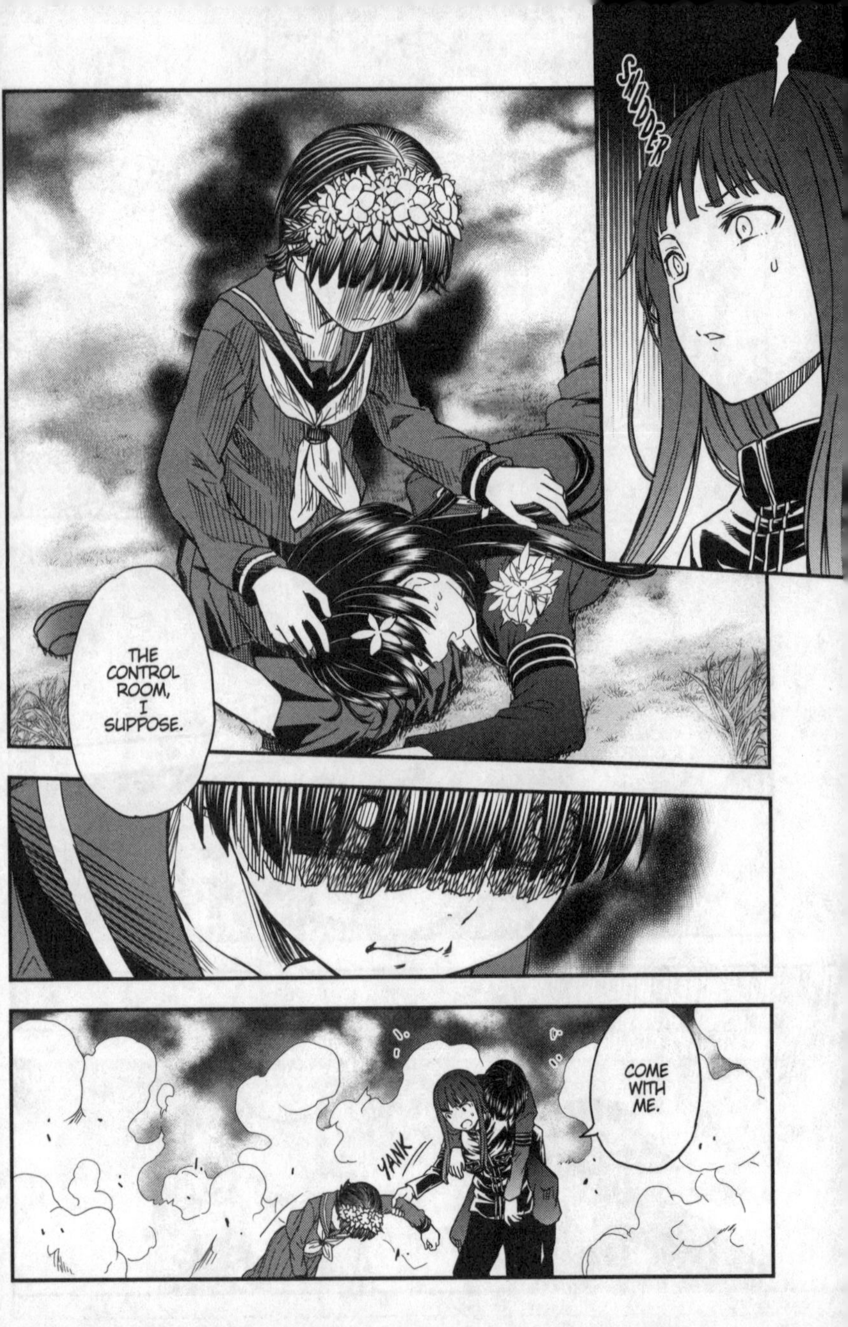
SHUDDER
THE CONTROL ROOM, I SUPPOSE.
COME WITH ME.
YANK

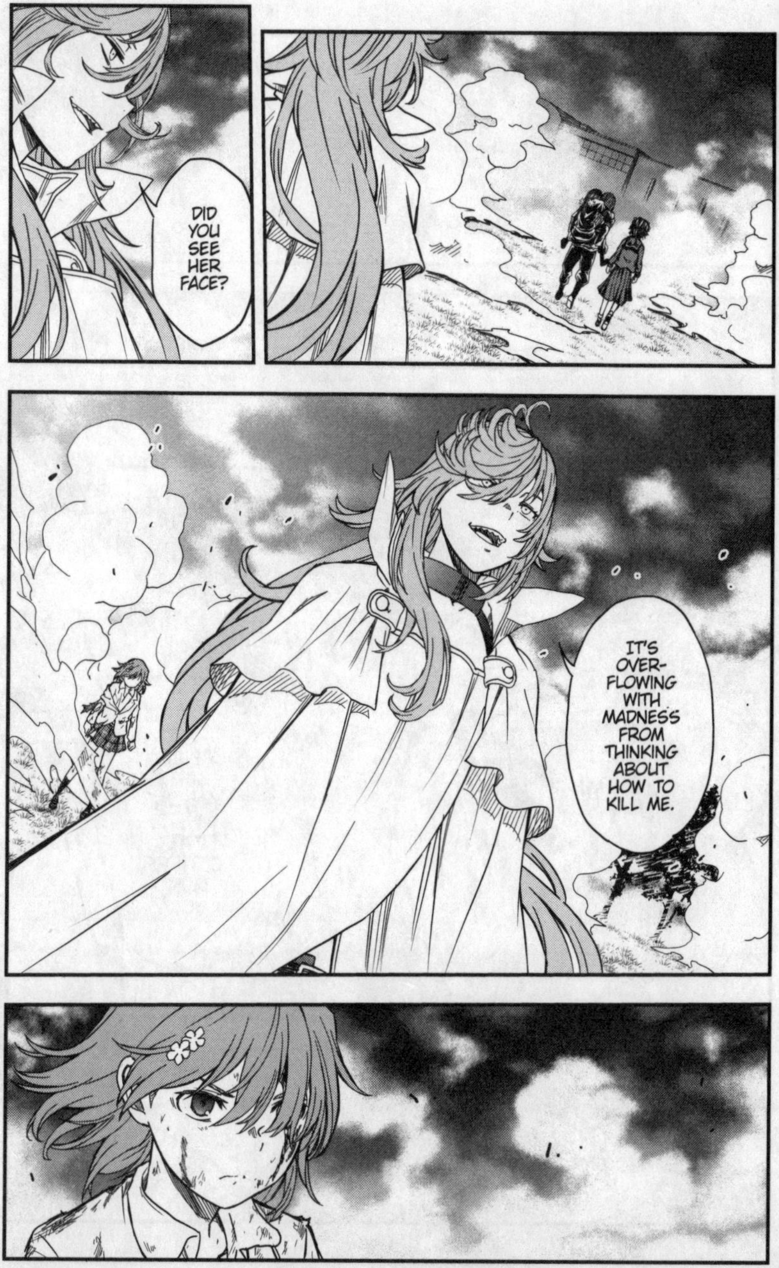
DID YOU SEE HER FACE?
IT'S OVER-FLOWING WITH MADNESS FROM THINKING ABOUT HOW TO KILL ME.

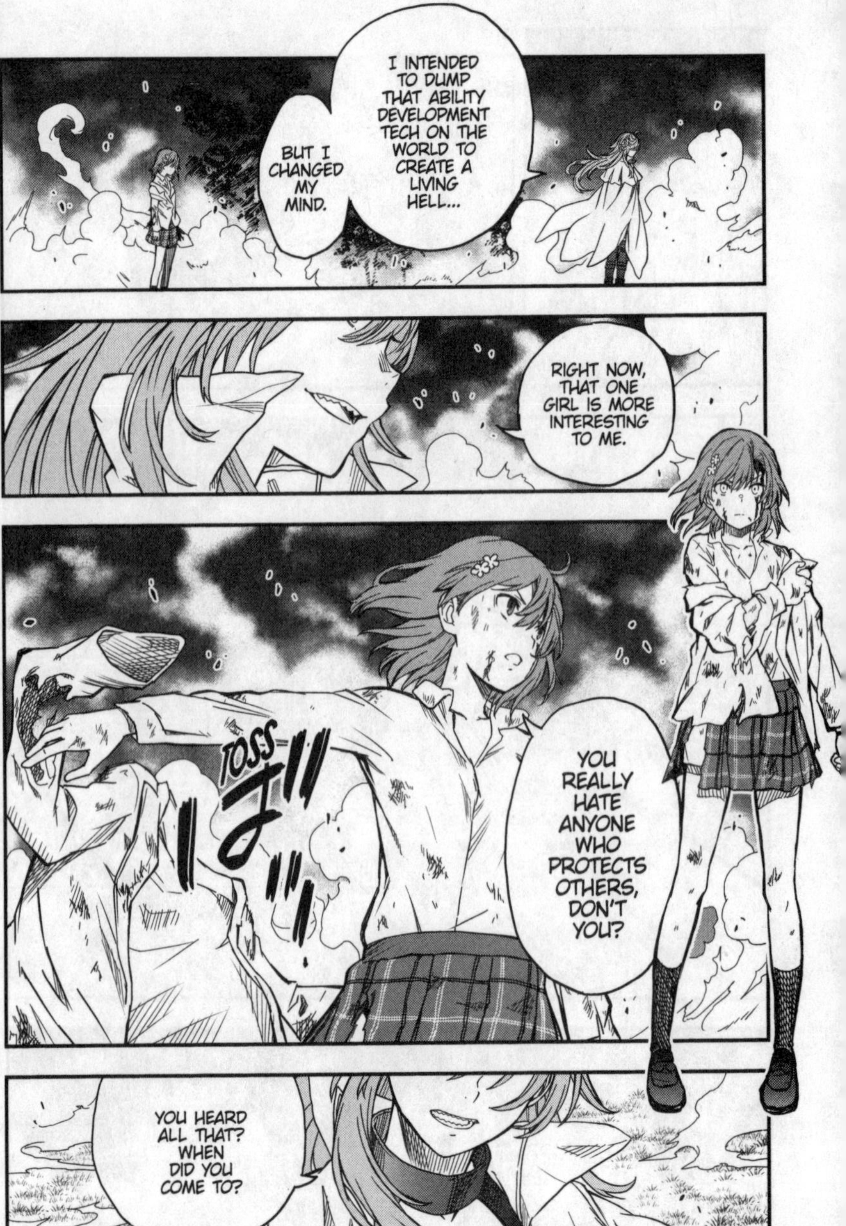
I INTENDED TO DUMP THAT ABILITY DEVELOPMENT TECH ON THE WORLD TO CREATE A LIVING HELL...
BUT I CHANGED MY MIND.
RIGHT NOW, THAT ONE GIRL IS MORE INTERESTING TO ME.
YOU REALLY HATE ANYONE WHO PROTECTS OTHERS, DON'T YOU?
TOSS
YOU HEARD ALL THAT? WHEN DID YOU COME TO?

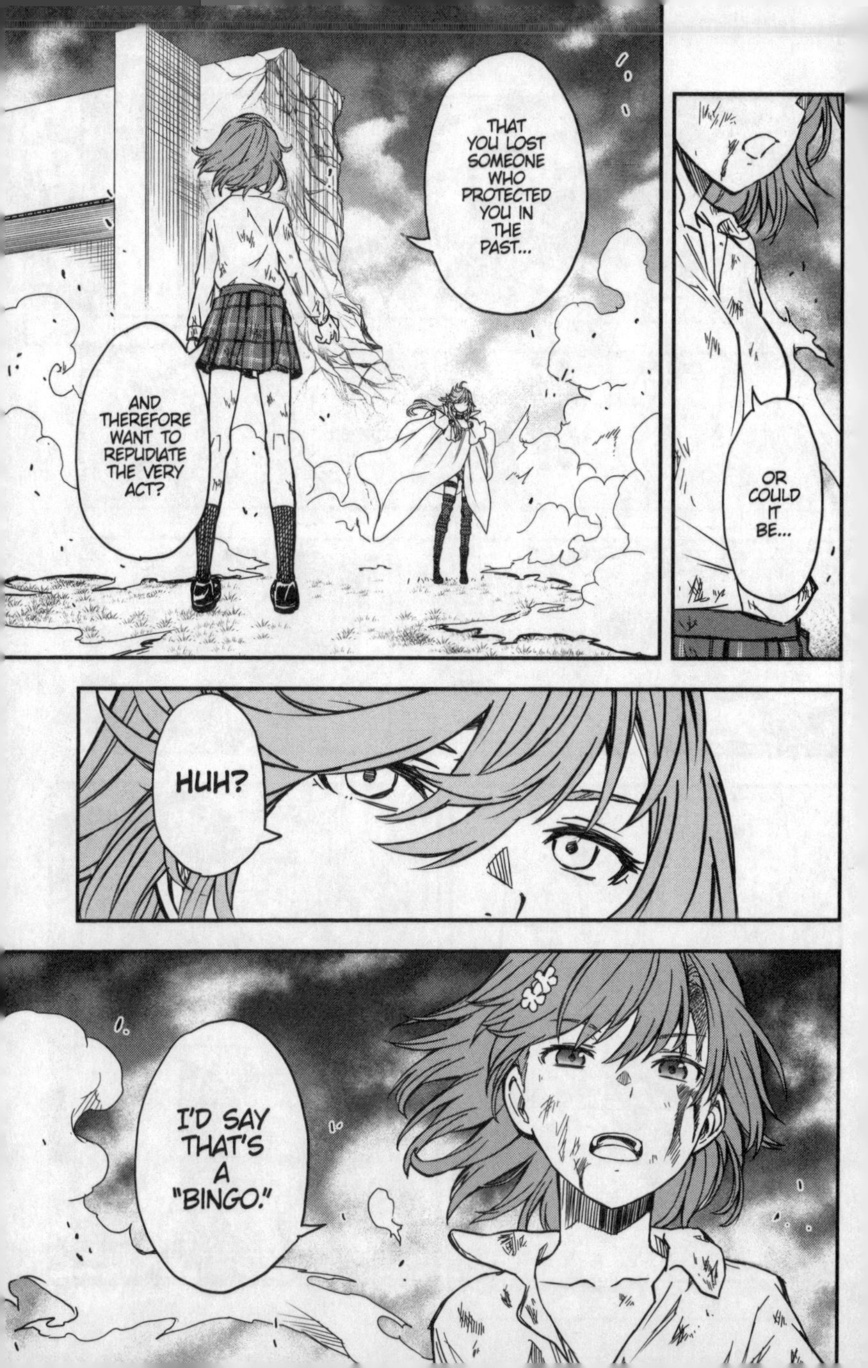
OR COULD IT BE...
THAT YOU LOST SOMEONE WHO PROTECTED YOU IN THE PAST...
AND THEREFORE WANT TO REPUDIATE THE VERY ACT?
HUH?
I'D SAY THAT'S A "BINGO."

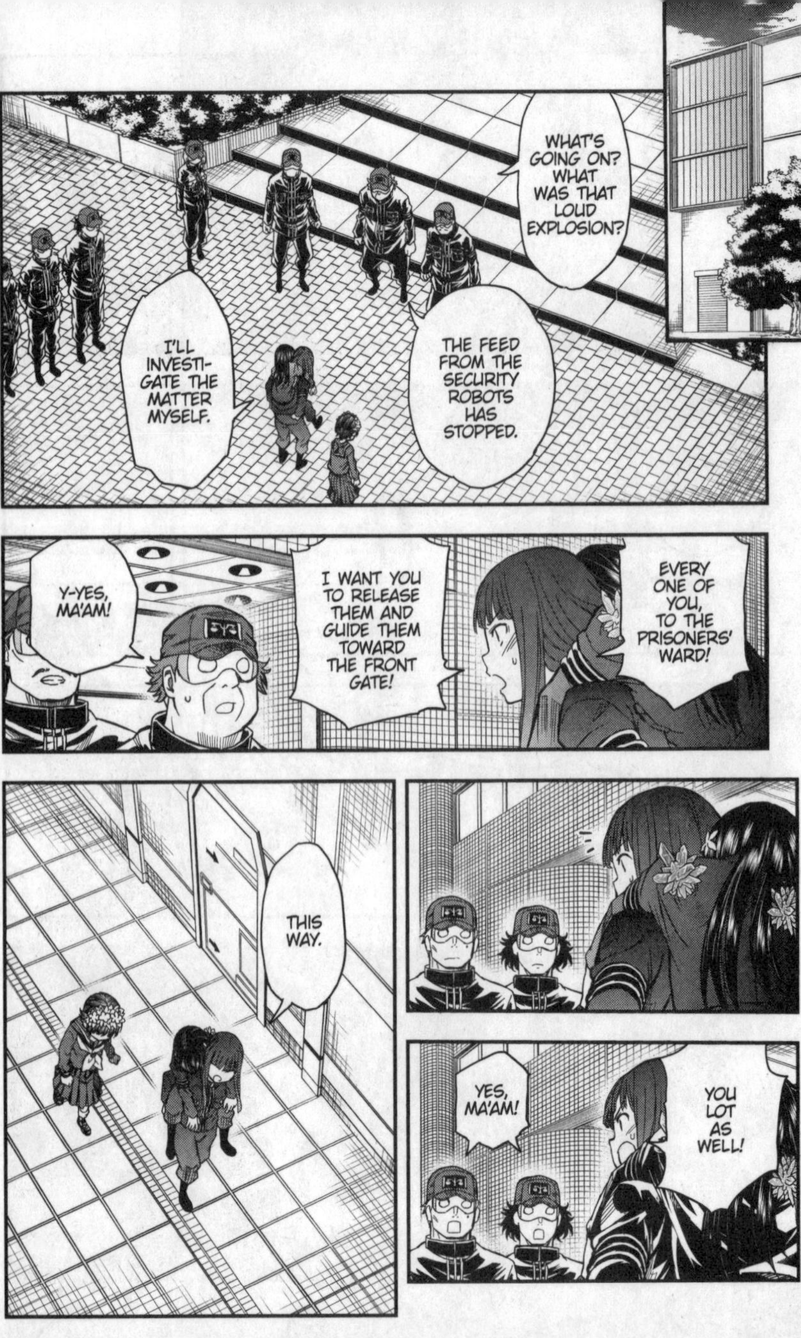
WHAT'S GOING ON? WHAT WAS THAT LOUD EXPLOSION?
THE FEED FROM THE SECURITY ROBOTS HAS STOPPED.
I'LL INVESTI-GATE THE MATTER MYSELF.
EVERY ONE OF YOU, TO THE PRISONERS' WARD!
I WANT YOU TO RELEASE THEM AND GUIDE THEM TOWARD THE FRONT GATE!
Y-YES, MA'AM!
YOU LOT AS WELL!
YES, MA'AM!
THIS WAY.

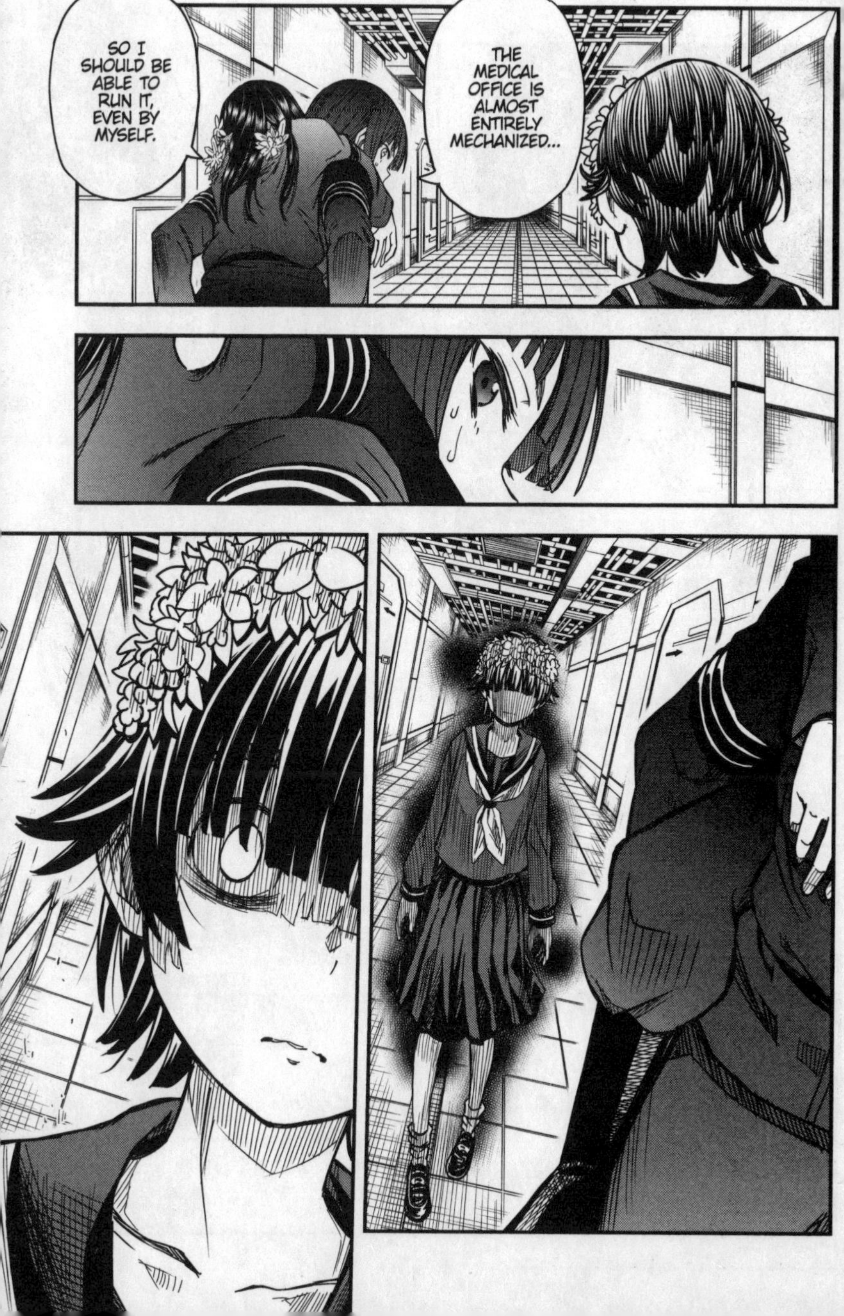
THE MEDICAL OFFICE IS ALMOST ENTIRELY MECHANIZED...
SO I SHOULD BE ABLE TO RUN IT, EVEN BY MYSELF.

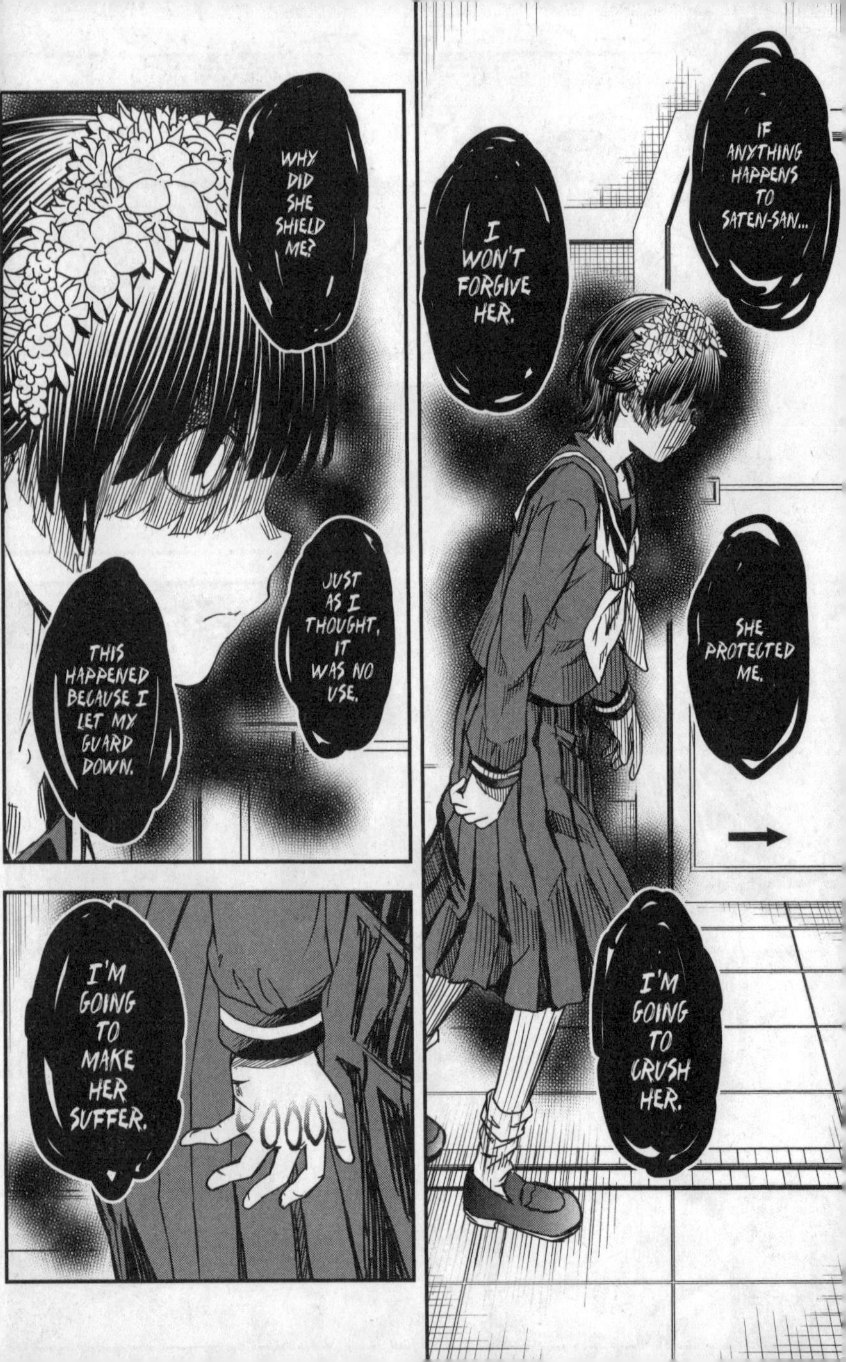
IF ANYTHING HAPPENS TO SATEN-SAN...
I WON'T FORGIVE HER.
SHE PROTECTED ME.
I'M GOING TO CRUSH HER.
WHY DID SHE SHIELD ME?
JUST AS I THOUGHT, IT WAS NO USE.
THIS HAPPENED BECAUSE I LET MY GUARD DOWN.
I'M GOING TO MAKE HER SUFFER.

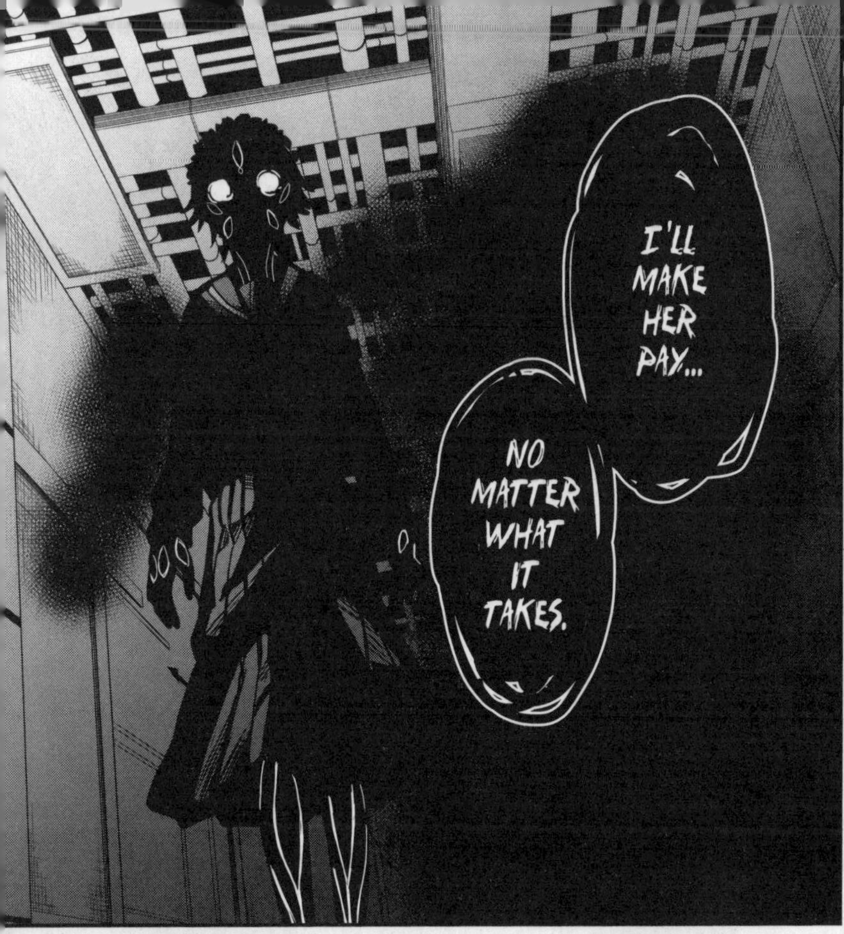
I'LL MAKE HER PAY...
NO MATTER WHAT IT TAKES.
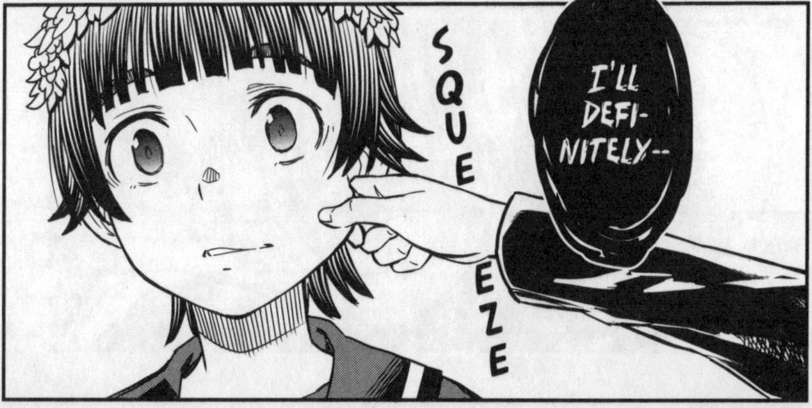
I'LL DEFI-NITELY--
SQUEEZE

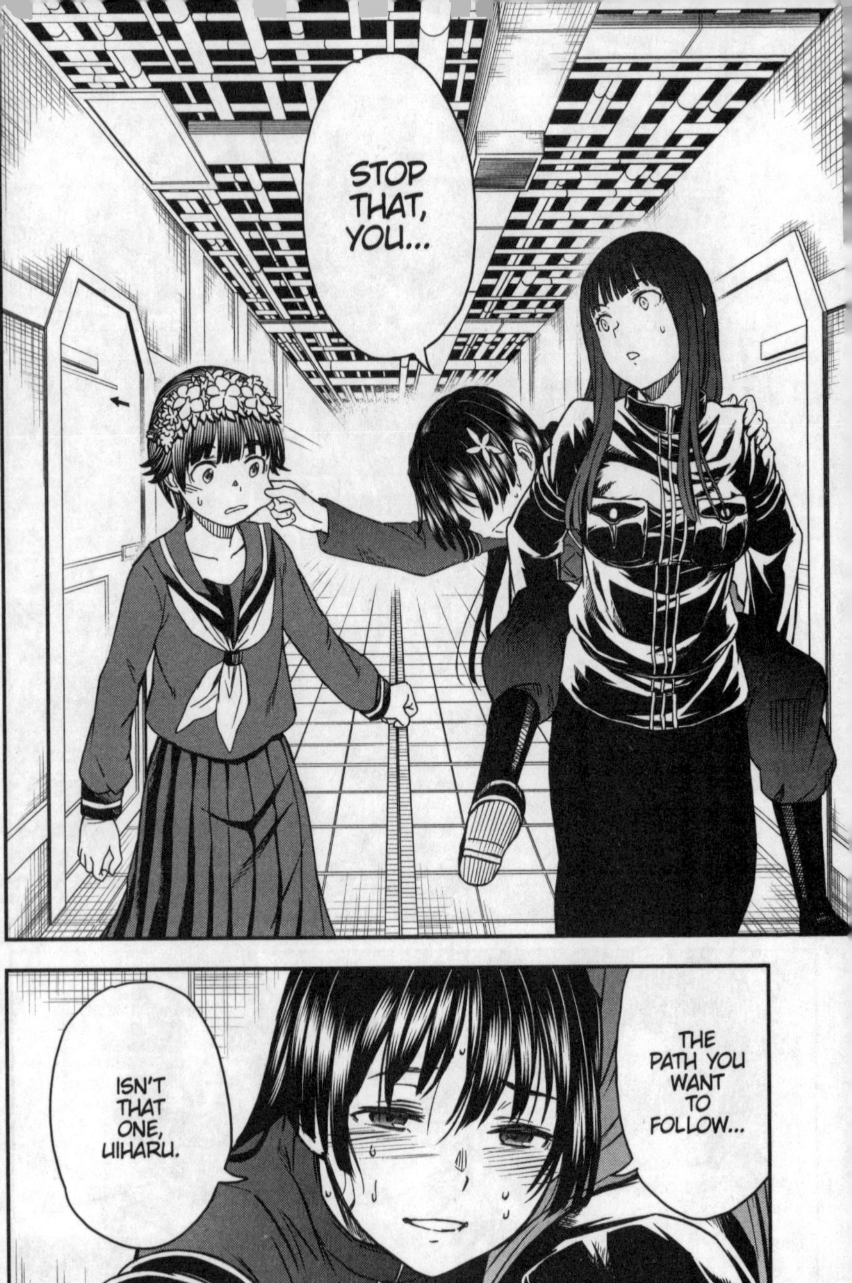
STOP THAT, YOU...
THE PATH YOU WANT TO FOLLOW...
ISN'T THAT ONE, UIHARU.

CHAPTER 125: PRIDE

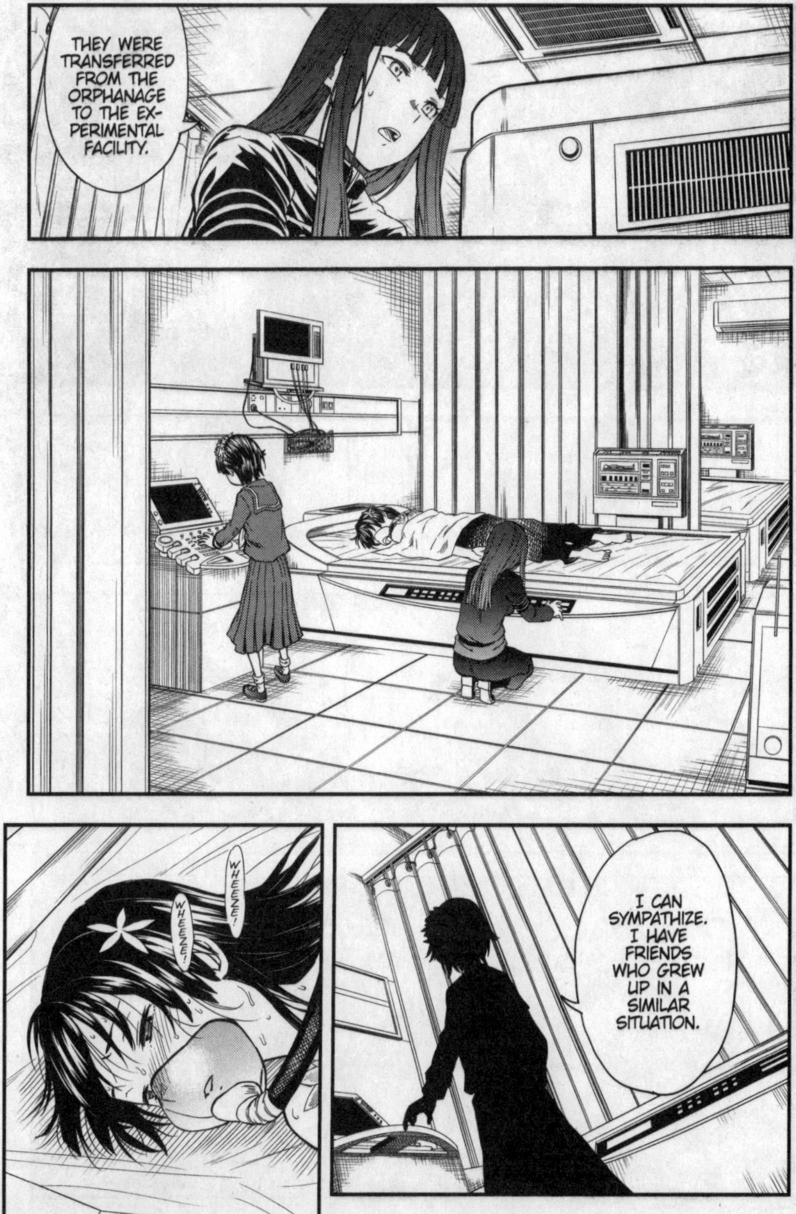
THEY WERE TRANSFERRED FROM THE ORPHANAGE TO THE EX-PERIMENTAL FACILITY.
I CAN SYMPATHIZE. I HAVE FRIENDS WHO GREW UP IN A SIMILAR SITUATION.
WHEEZE!
WHEEZE!

THAT SAID, I CAN'T FORGIVE THAT PERSON.

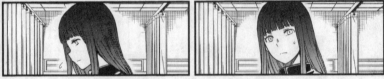

SO...

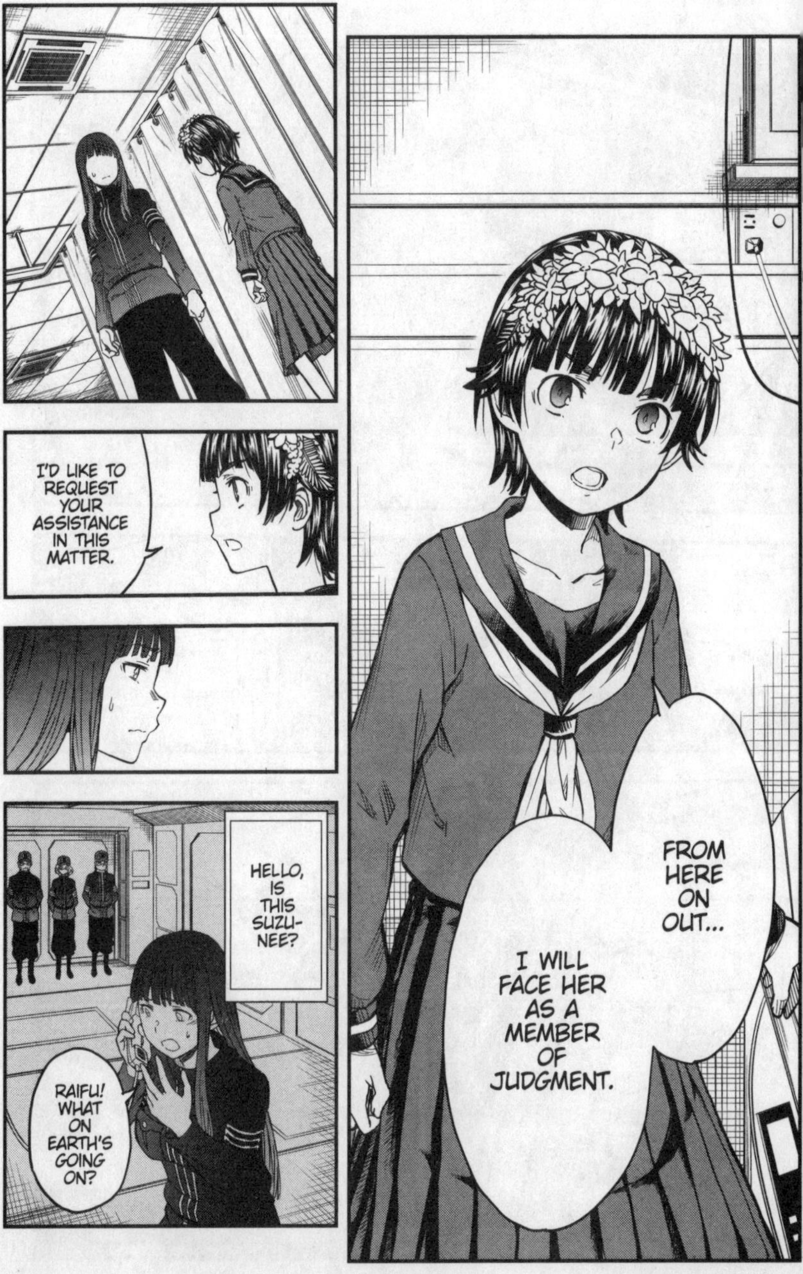
FROM HERE ON OUT...
I WILL FACE HER AS A MEMBER OF JUDGMENT.
I'D LIKE TO REQUEST YOUR ASSISTANCE IN THIS MATTER.
HELLO, IS THIS SUZU-NEE?
RAIFU! WHAT ON EARTH'S GOING ON?

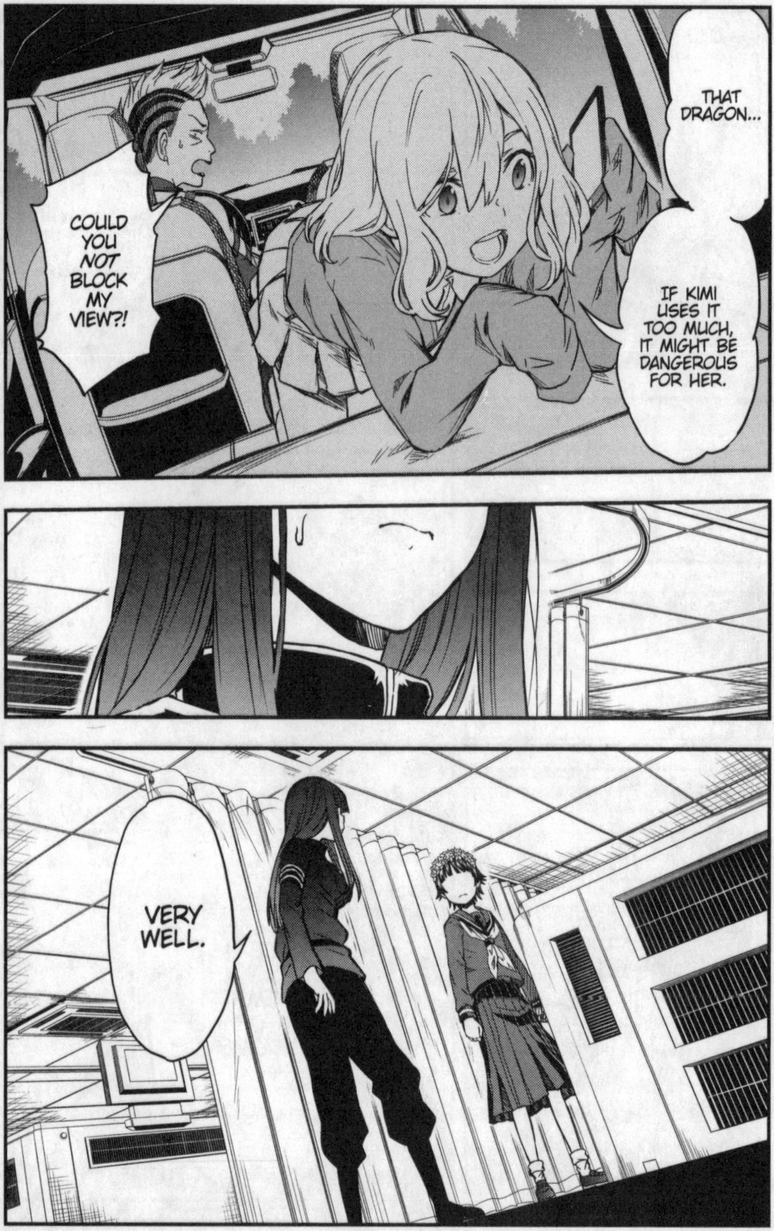
THAT DRAGON...
IF KIMI USES IT TOO MUCH, IT MIGHT BE DANGEROUS FOR HER.
COULD YOU NOT BLOCK MY VIEW?!
VERY WELL.

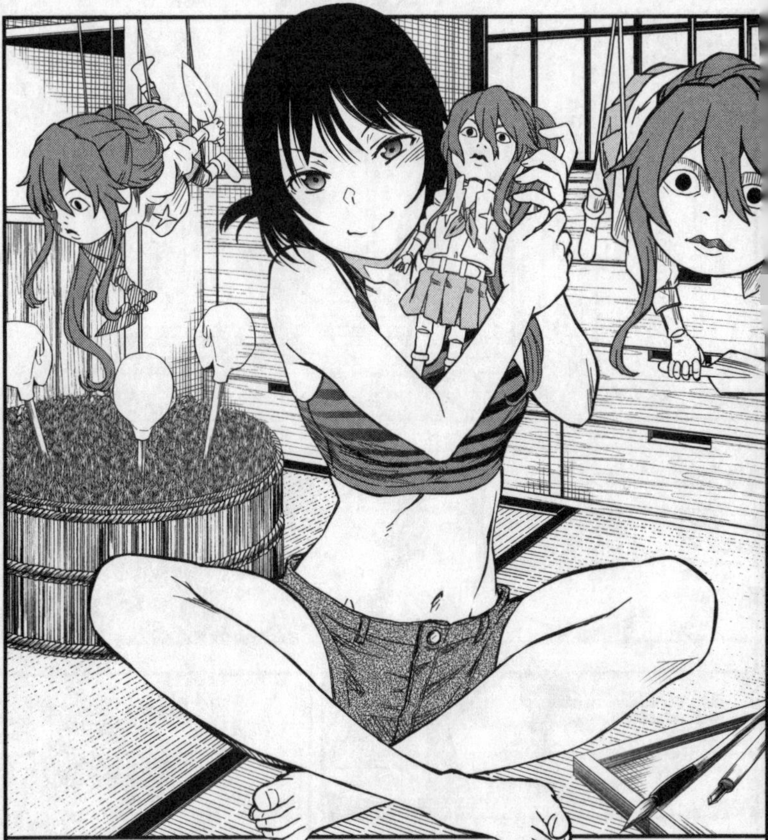

TSURIGANE SARYOU (ABILITY: AIM WATCHER)

- A kunoichi from the Kouga Clan who disguised herself as a Child Error in order to infiltrate Academy City.
- During a camping trip, she and her family were attacked by wild dogs. She was the sole survivor, and was saved by Oumi Shuri, who brought her to the nearest city. Despite being only four years old, she managed to track Oumi to the village of the Kouga in the mountains, where she was adopted.
- While she possesses extraordinary physical abilities, as a ninja, she isn't even second-rate.
- Her Level 3 Ability, AIM Watcher, allows her to visually perceive AIM Diffusion Fields. Additionally, by observing fluctuations in the field, she is able to predict how an opponent's ability may manifest.
- Although generally boyish, she displays a girlish side as well, and enjoys doll-making.

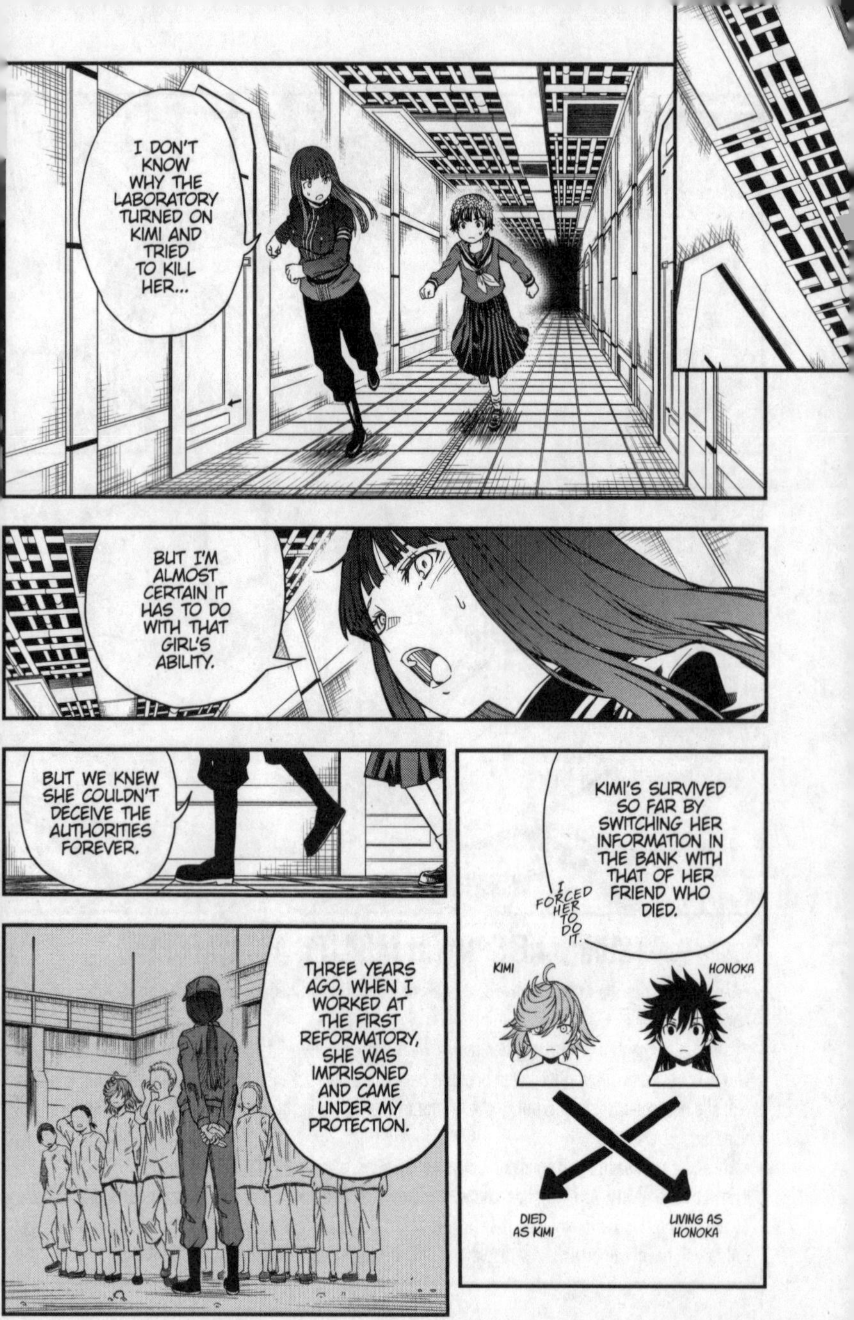
I DON'T KNOW WHY THE LABORATORY TURNED ON KIMI AND TRIED TO KILL HER...
BUT I'M ALMOST CERTAIN IT HAS TO DO WITH THAT GIRL'S ABILITY.
KIMI'S SURVIVED SO FAR BY SWITCHING HER INFORMATION IN THE BANK WITH THAT OF HER FRIEND WHO DIED.
I FORCED HER TO DO IT.
KIMI
HONOKA
DIED AS KIMI
LIVING AS HONOKA
BUT WE KNEW SHE COULDN'T DECEIVE THE AUTHORITIES FOREVER.
THREE YEARS AGO, WHEN I WORKED AT THE FIRST REFORMATORY, SHE WAS IMPRISONED AND CAME UNDER MY PROTECTION.

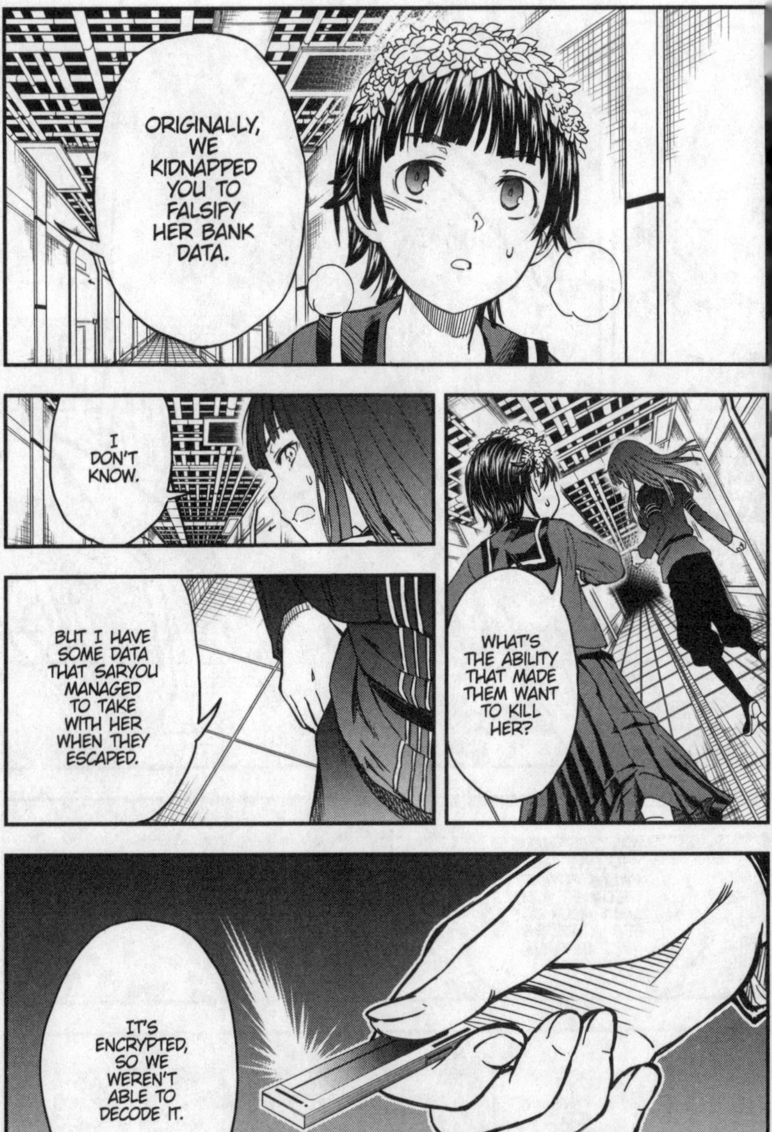
ORIGINALLY, WE KIDNAPPED YOU TO FALSIFY HER BANK DATA.
WHAT'S THE ABILITY THAT MADE THEM WANT TO KILL HER?
I DON'T KNOW.
BUT I HAVE SOME DATA THAT SARYOU MANAGED TO TAKE WITH HER WHEN THEY ESCAPED.
IT'S ENCRYPTED, SO WE WEREN'T ABLE TO DECODE IT.

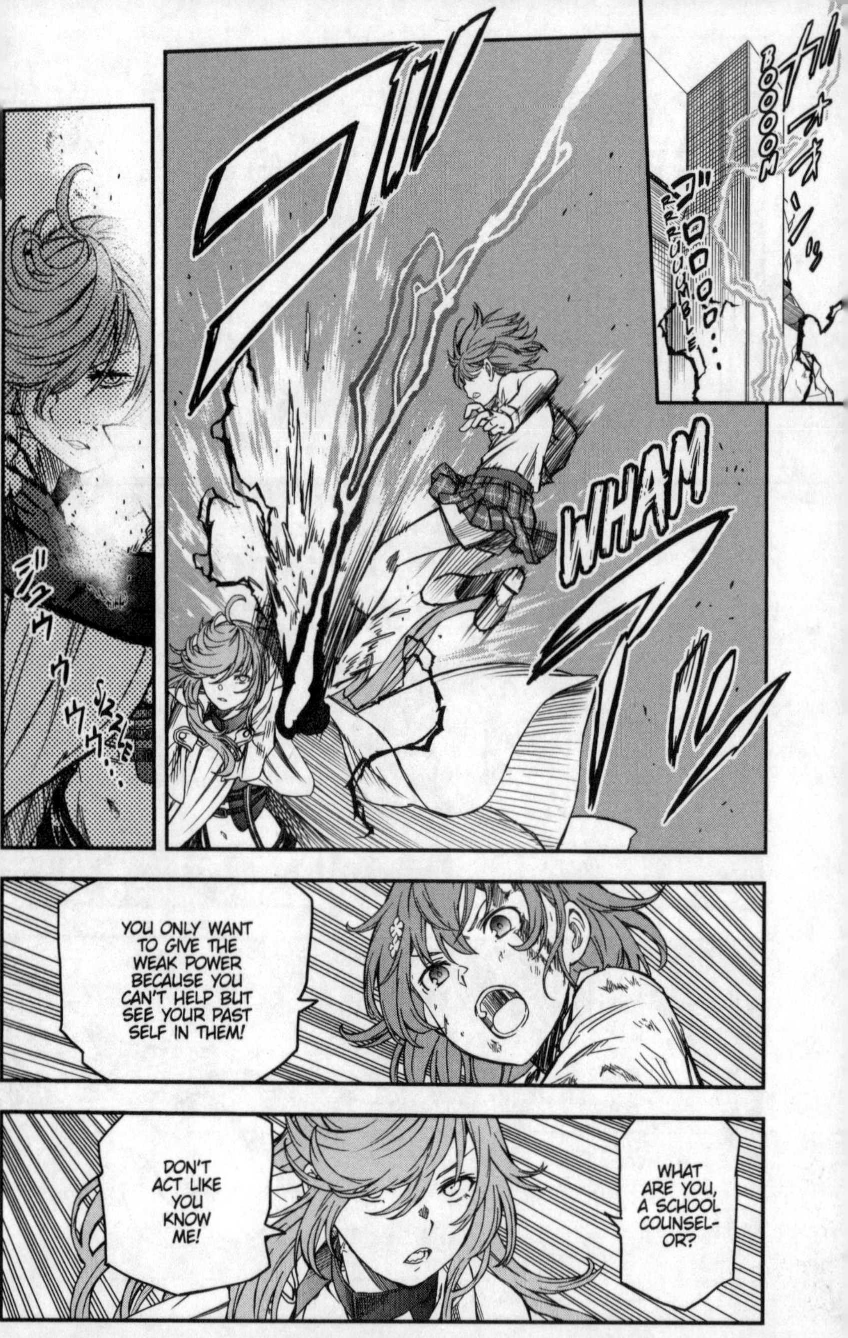
BOOOOM
RRRUUMBLE...
WHAM
SIZZLE...
YOU ONLY WANT TO GIVE THE WEAK POWER BECAUSE YOU CAN'T HELP BUT SEE YOUR PAST SELF IN THEM!
WHAT ARE YOU, A SCHOOL COUNSEL-OR?
DON'T ACT LIKE YOU KNOW ME!

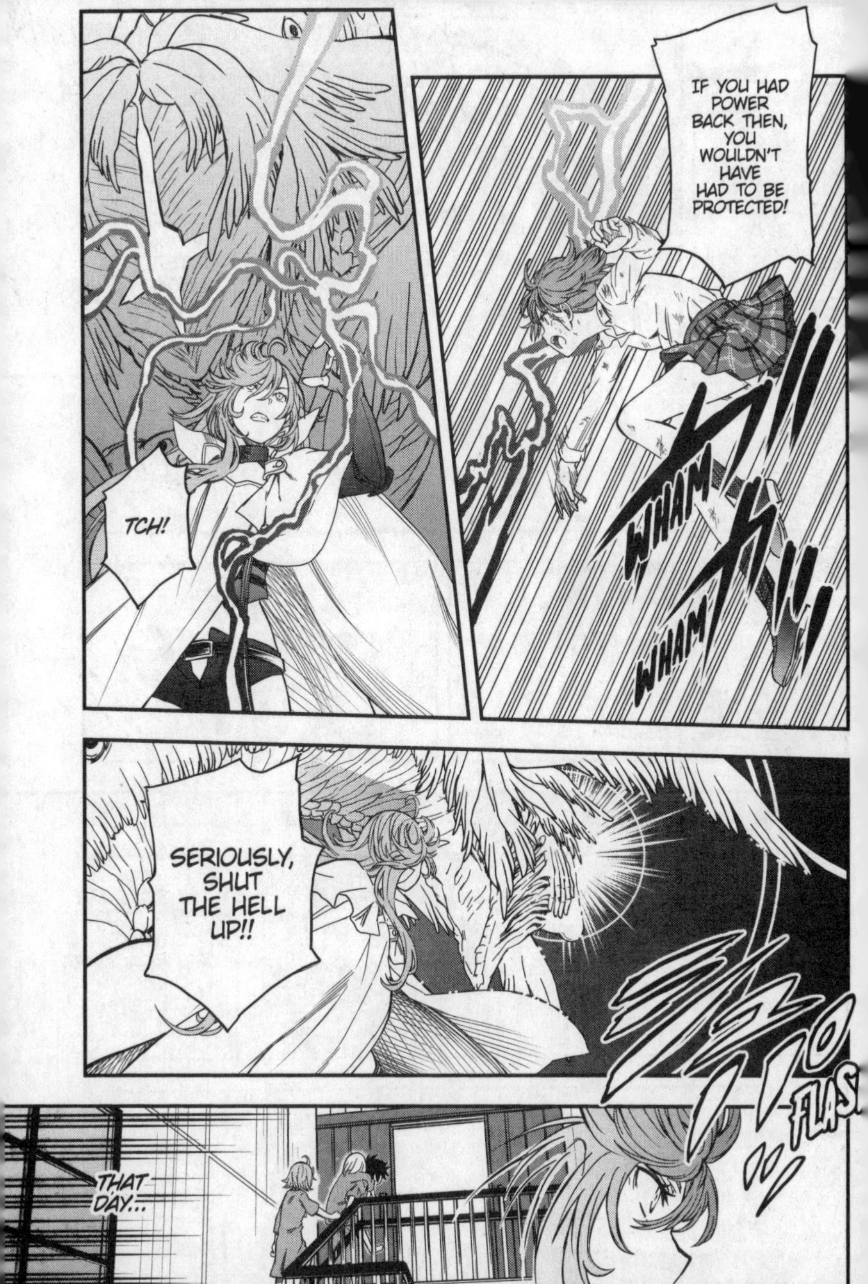
IF YOU HAD POWER BACK THEN, YOU WOULDN'T HAVE HAD TO BE PROTECTED!
WHAM
WHAM
WHAM
TCH!
SERIOUSLY, SHUT THE HELL UP!!
FLAS
THAT DAY...

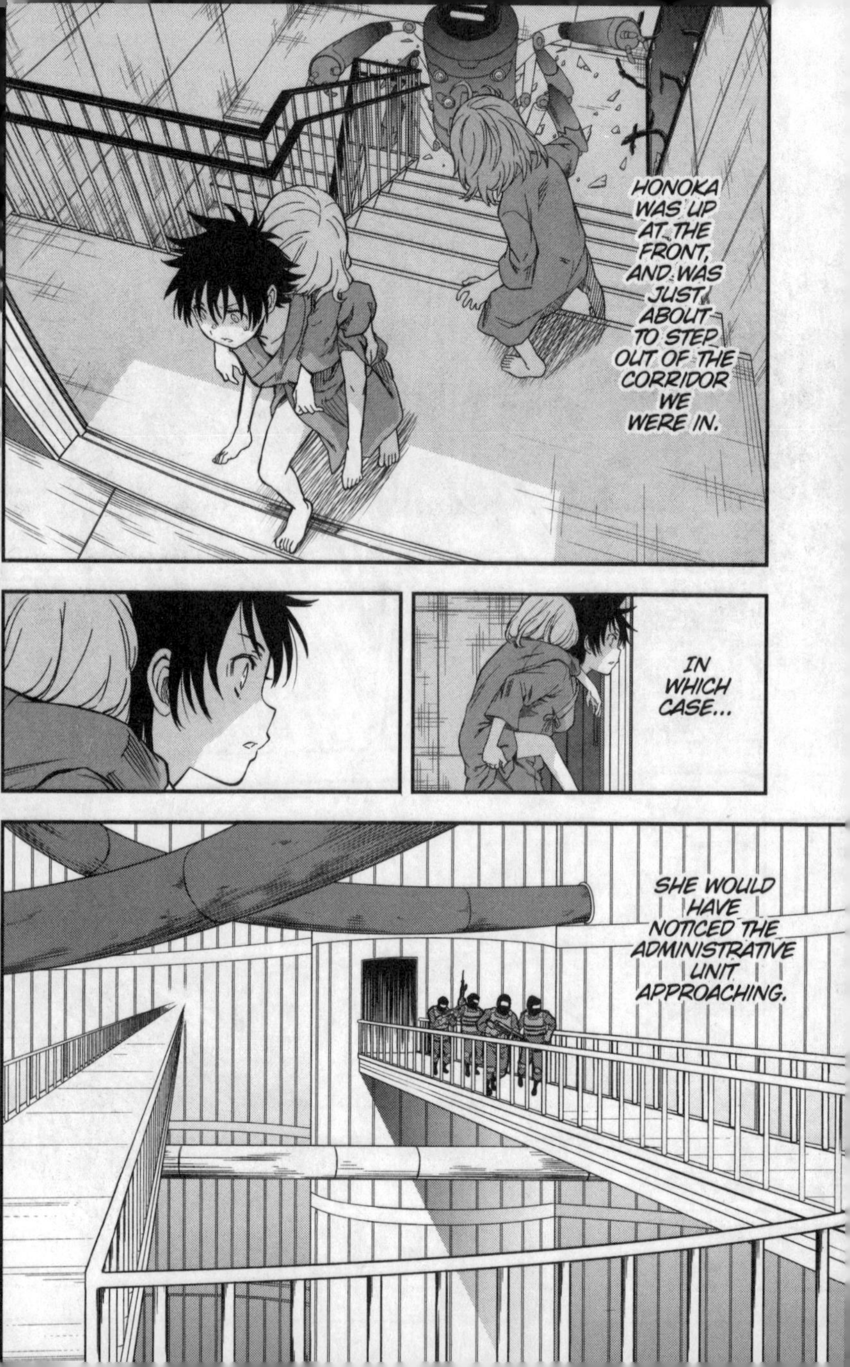
HONOKA WAS UP AT THE FRONT, AND WAS JUST ABOUT TO STEP OUT OF THE CORRIDOR WE WERE IN.
IN WHICH CASE...
SHE WOULD HAVE NOTICED THE ADMINISTRATIVE UNIT APPROACHING.

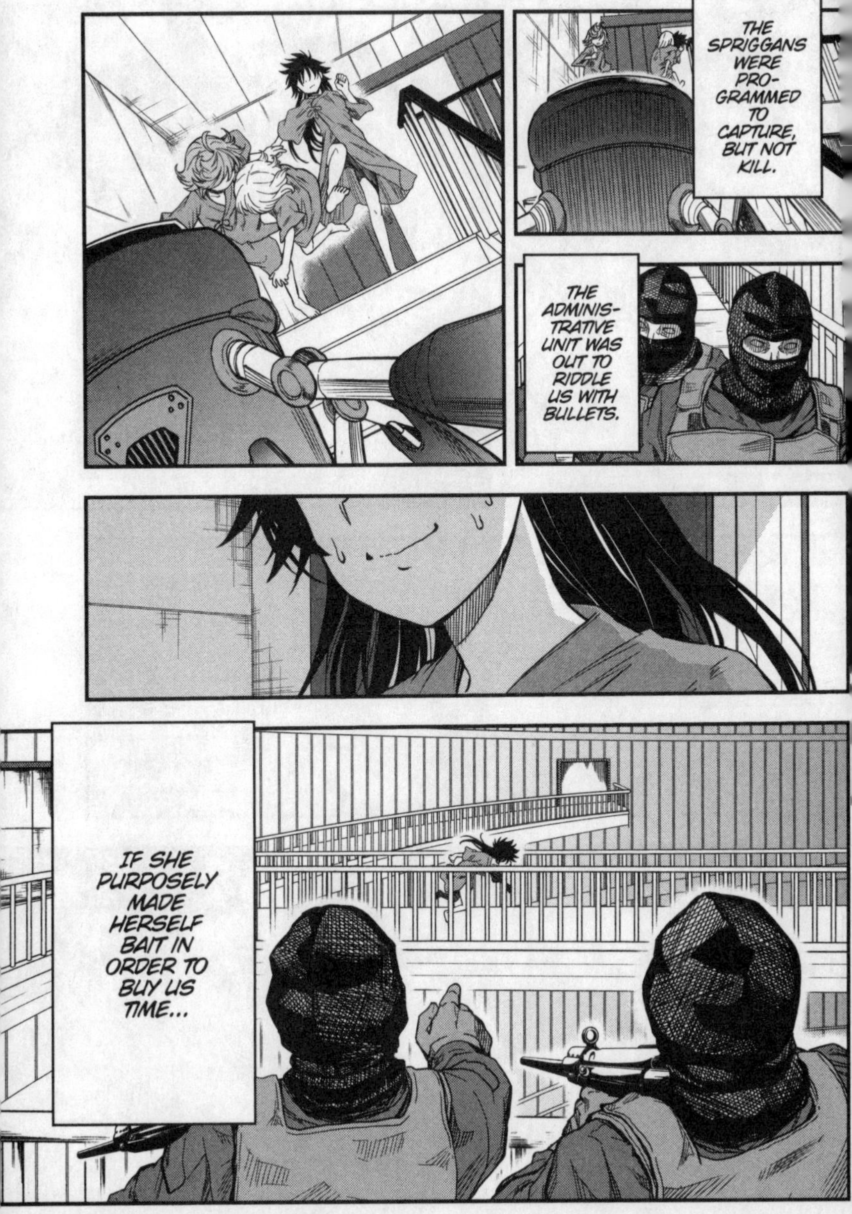
THE SPRIGGANS WERE PRO-GRAMMED TO CAPTURE, BUT NOT KILL.
THE ADMINIS-TRATIVE UNIT WAS OUT TO RIDDLE US WITH BULLETS.
IF SHE PURPOSELY MADE HERSELF BAIT IN ORDER TO BUY US TIME...

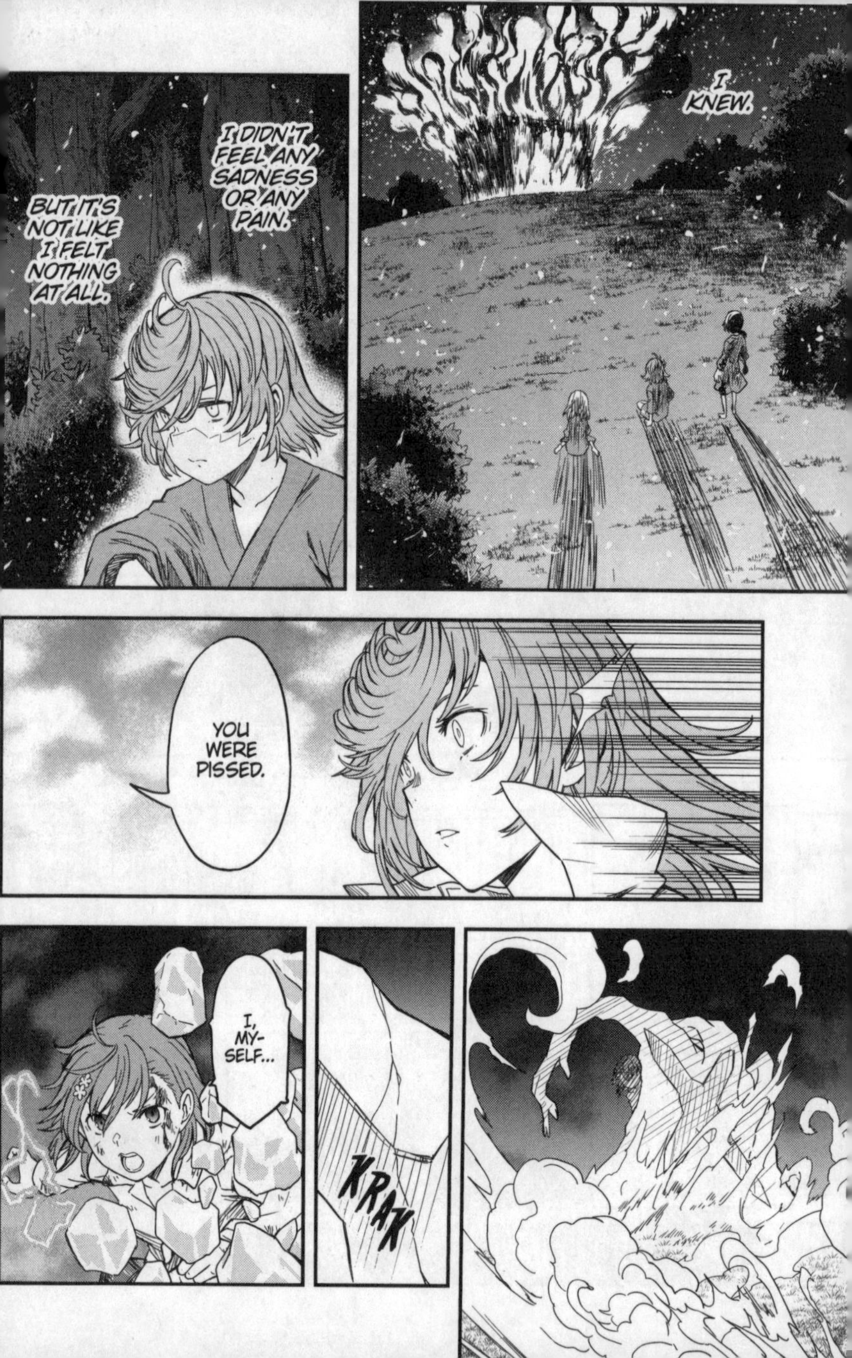
I KNEW.
I DIDN'T FEEL ANY SADNESS OR ANY PAIN.
BUT IT'S NOT LIKE I FELT NOTHING AT ALL.
YOU WERE PISSED.
KRAK
I, MY-SELF...

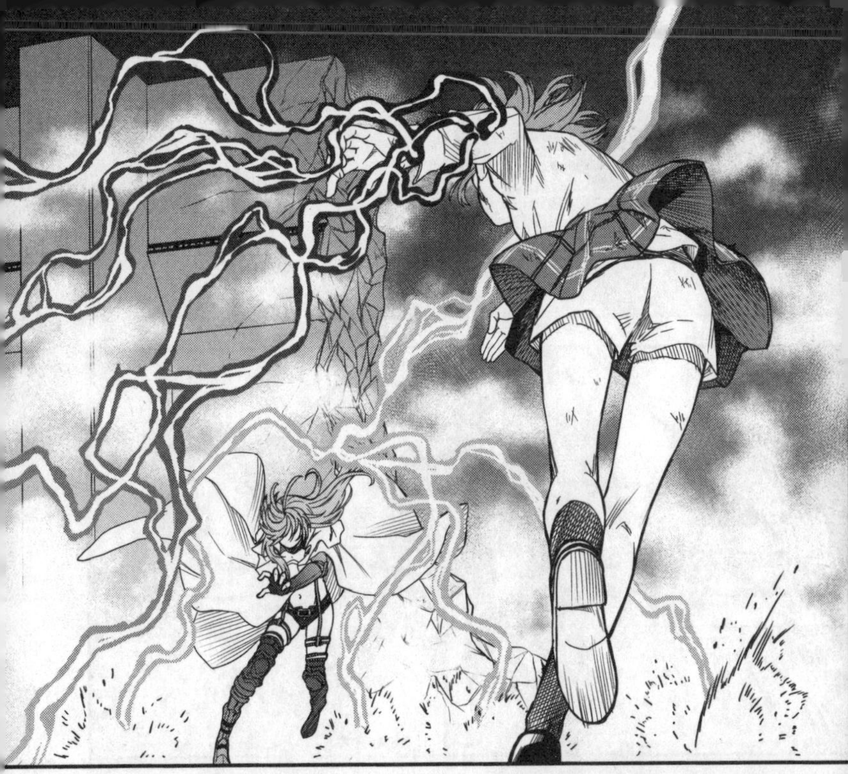

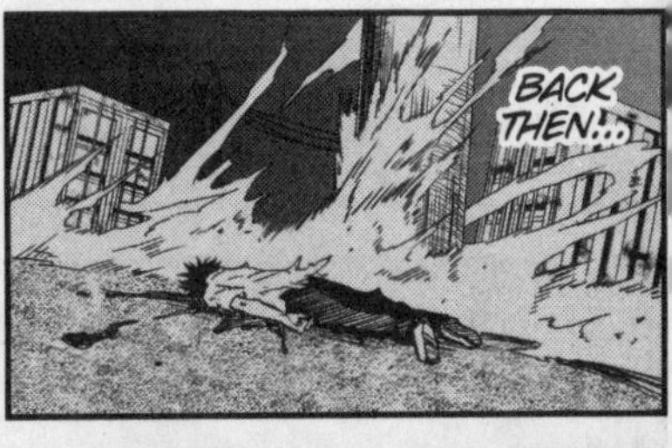
BACK THEN...

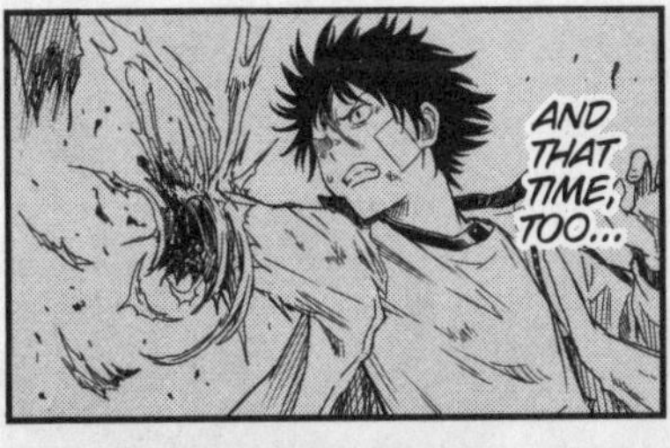
AND THAT TIME, TOO...

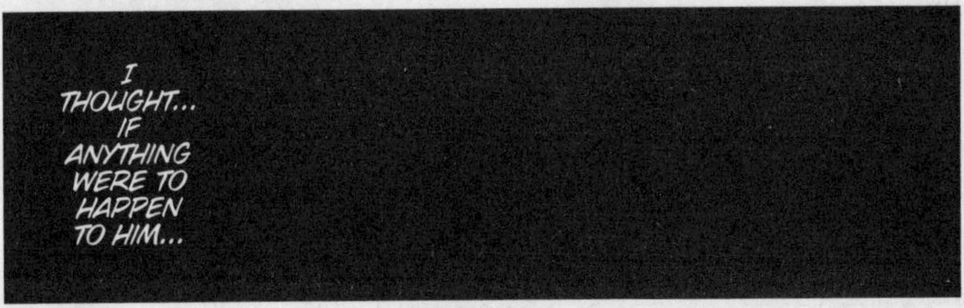
I THOUGHT... IF ANYTHING WERE TO HAPPEN TO HIM...

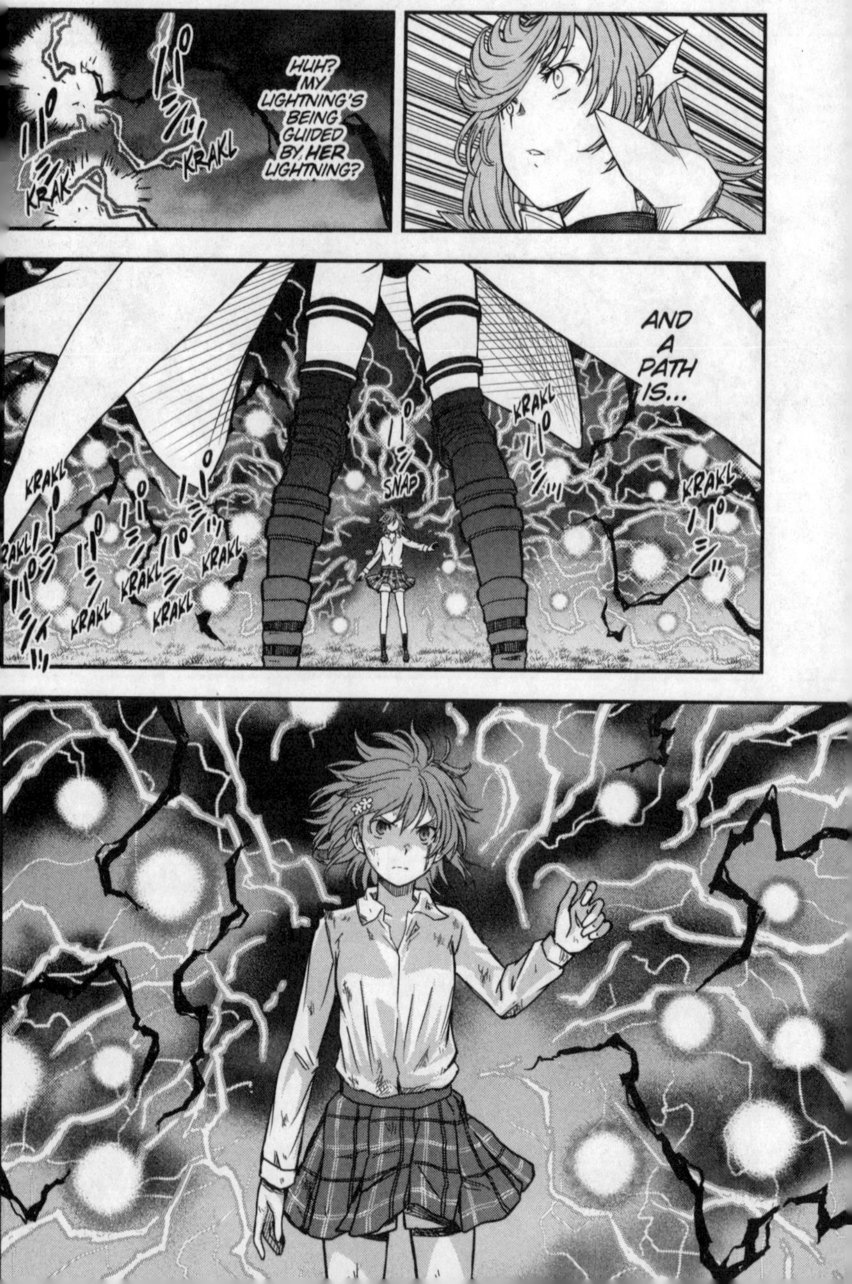
HUH? MY LIGHTNING'S BEING GUIDED BY HER LIGHTNING?
KRAKL
KRAK
AND A PATH IS...
KRAKL
SNAP
KRAKL
KRAKL
KRAKL
KRAKL
KRAKL
KRAKL
KRAKL

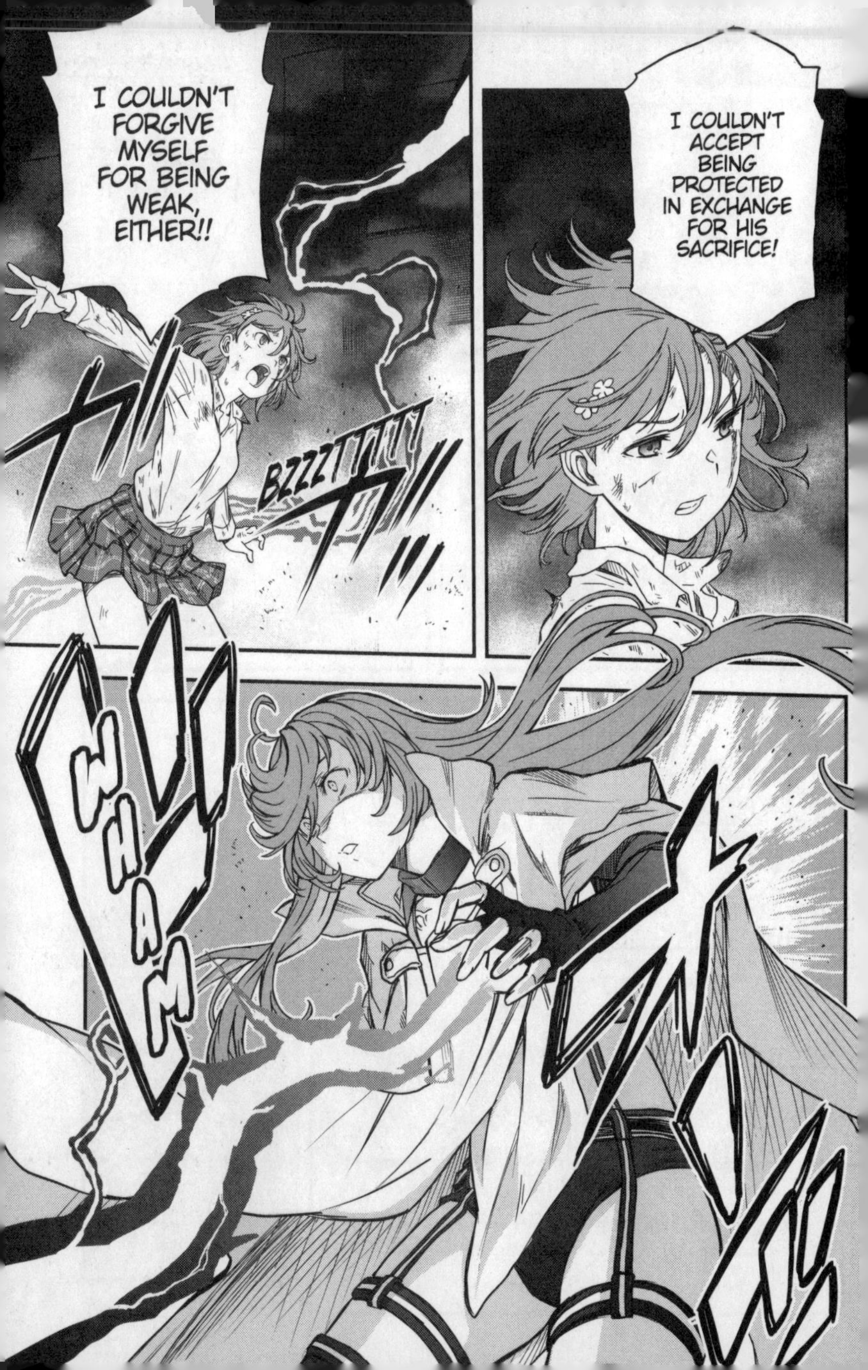
I COULDN'T ACCEPT BEING PROTECTED IN EXCHANGE FOR HIS SACRIFICE!
I COULDN'T FORGIVE MYSELF FOR BEING WEAK, EITHER!!
BZZZTTTTT
WHAM

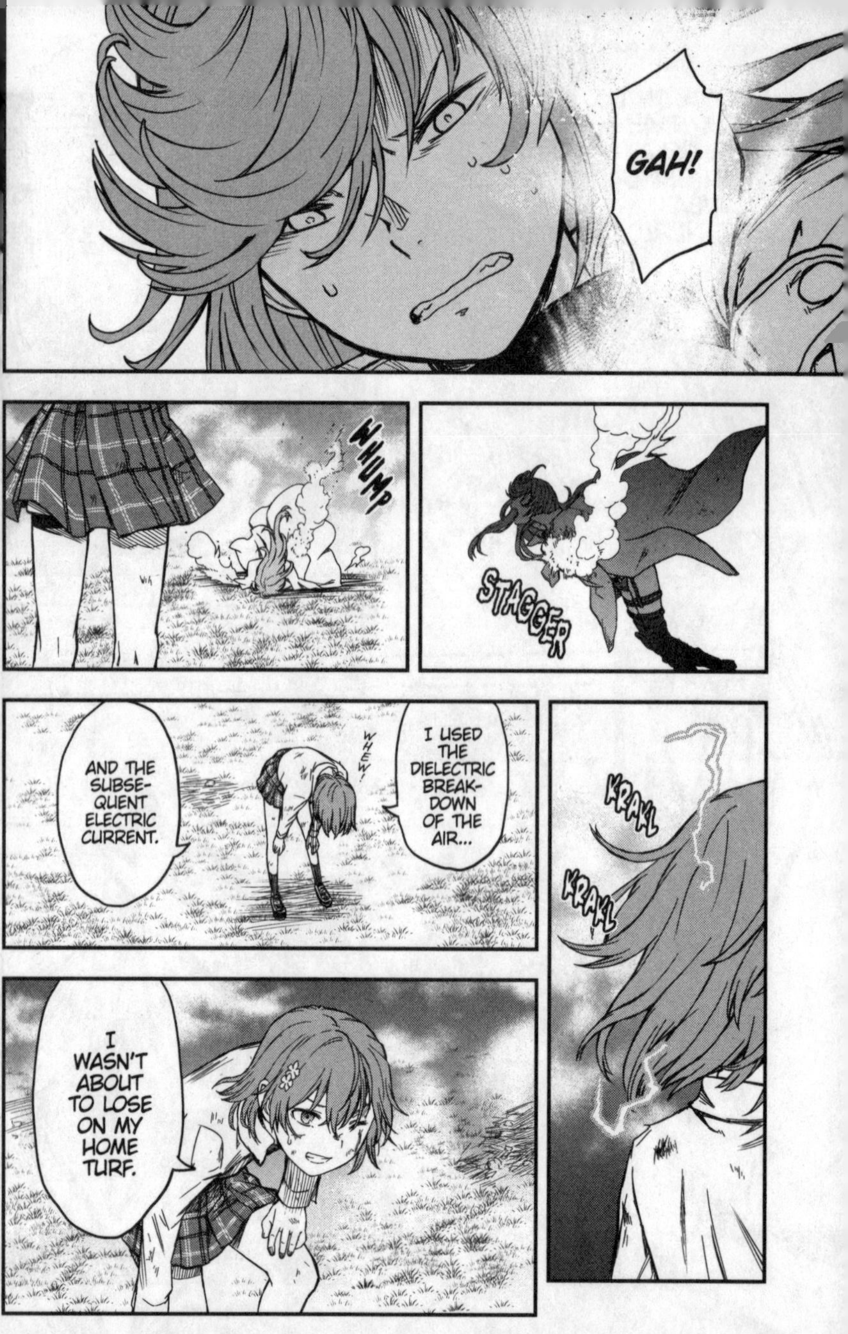
GAH!
STAGGER
WHUMP
KRAKL
KRAKL
I USED THE DIELECTRIC BREAK-DOWN OF THE AIR...
WHEW
AND THE SUBSE-QUENT ELECTRIC CURRENT.
I WASN'T ABOUT TO LOSE ON MY HOME TURF.

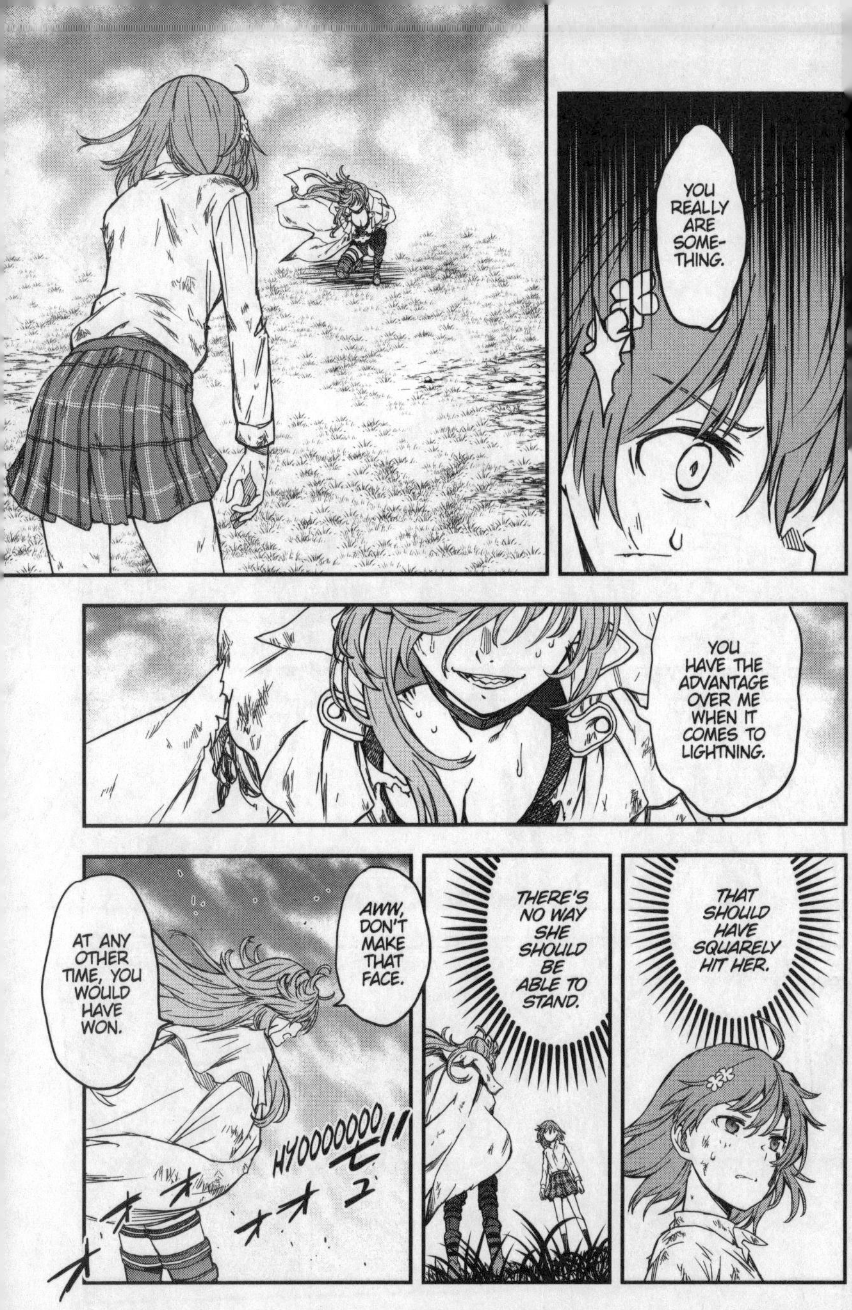
YOU REALLY ARE SOME-THING.
YOU HAVE THE ADVANTAGE OVER ME WHEN IT COMES TO LIGHTNING.
THAT SHOULD HAVE SQUARELY HIT HER.
THERE'S NO WAY SHE SHOULD BE ABLE TO STAND.
AWW, DON'T MAKE THAT FACE.
AT ANY OTHER TIME, YOU WOULD HAVE WON.
HYOOOOOOO!!

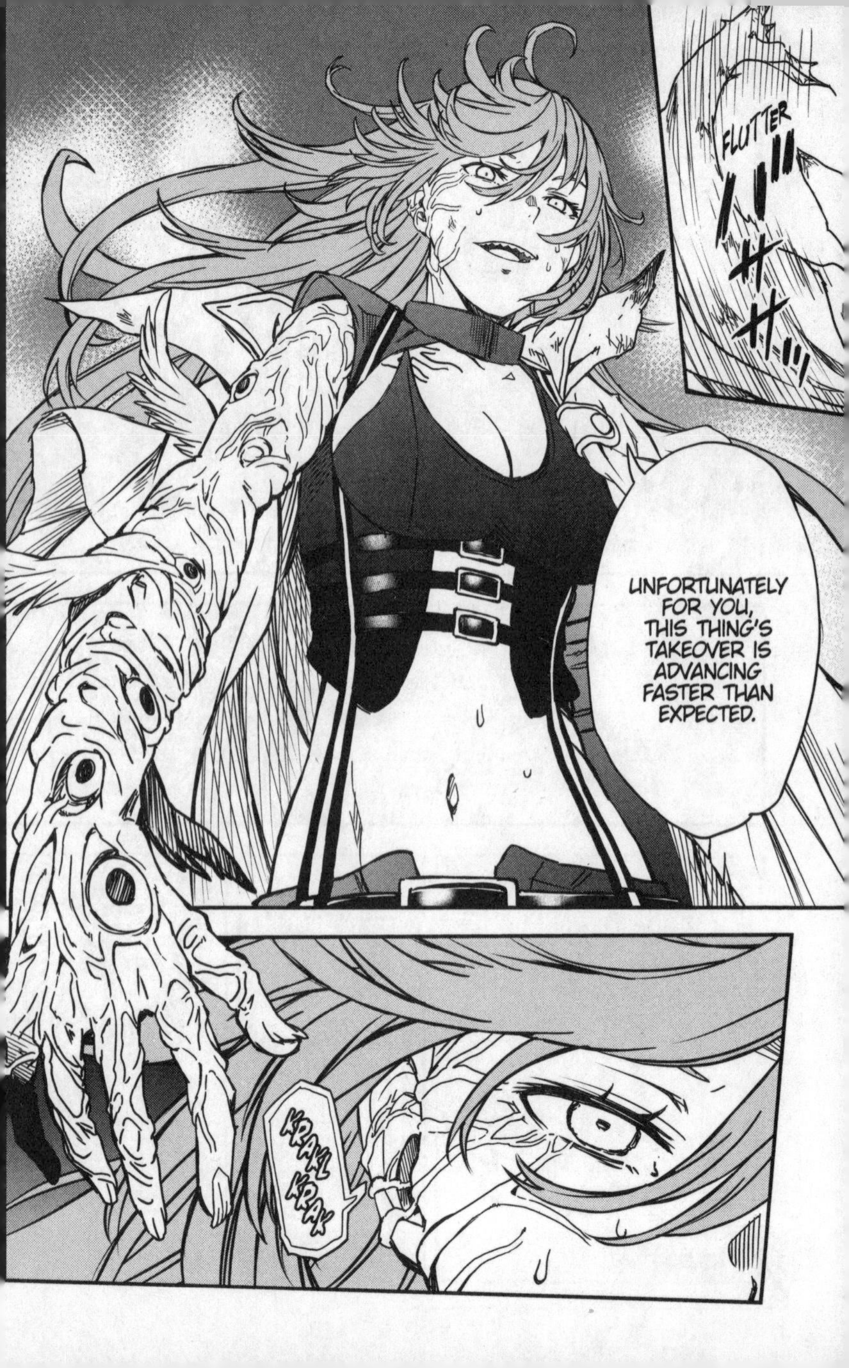
FLUTTER
UNFORTUNATELY FOR YOU, THIS THING'S TAKEOVER IS ADVANCING FASTER THAN EXPECTED.
KRAKL KRAK

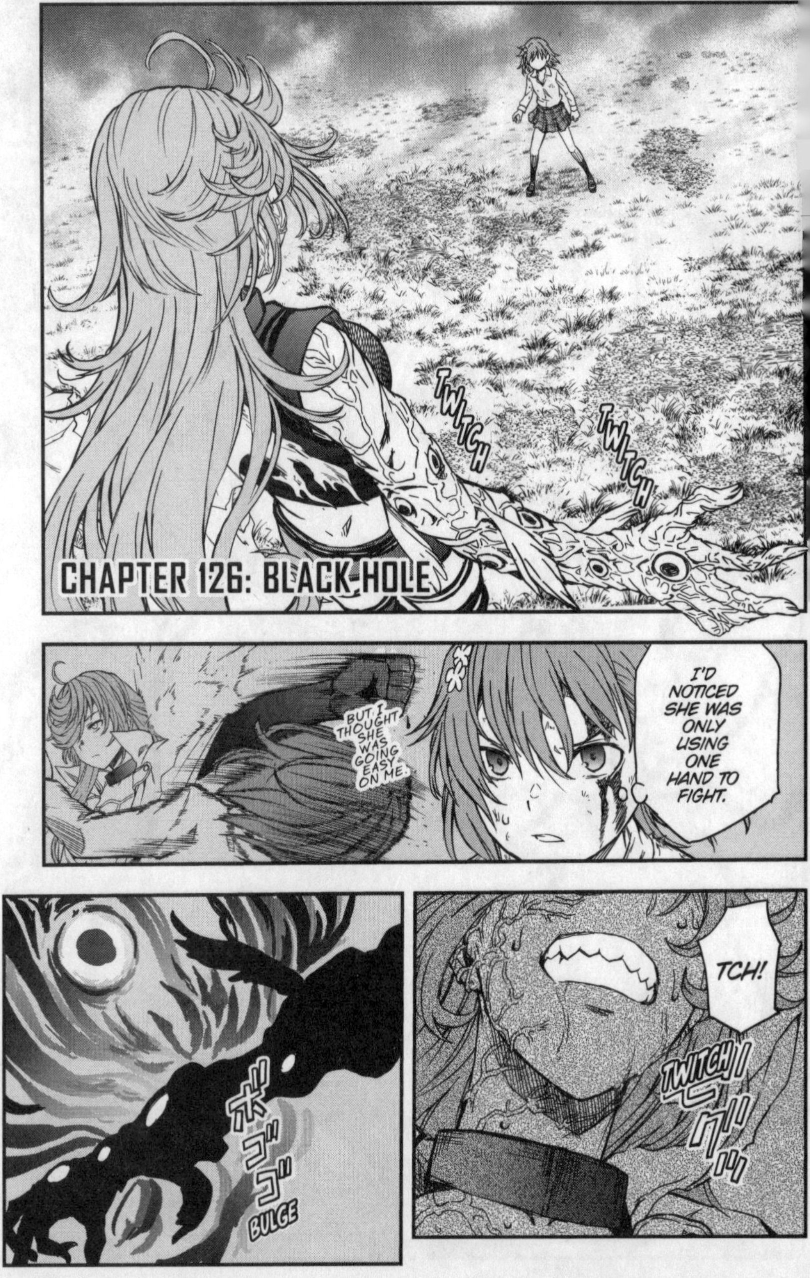
TWITCH
TWITCH
CHAPTER 126: BLACK HOLE
I'D NOTICED SHE WAS ONLY USING ONE HAND TO FIGHT.
BUT I THOUGHT SHE WAS GOING EASY ON ME.
TCH!
TWITCH
BULGE

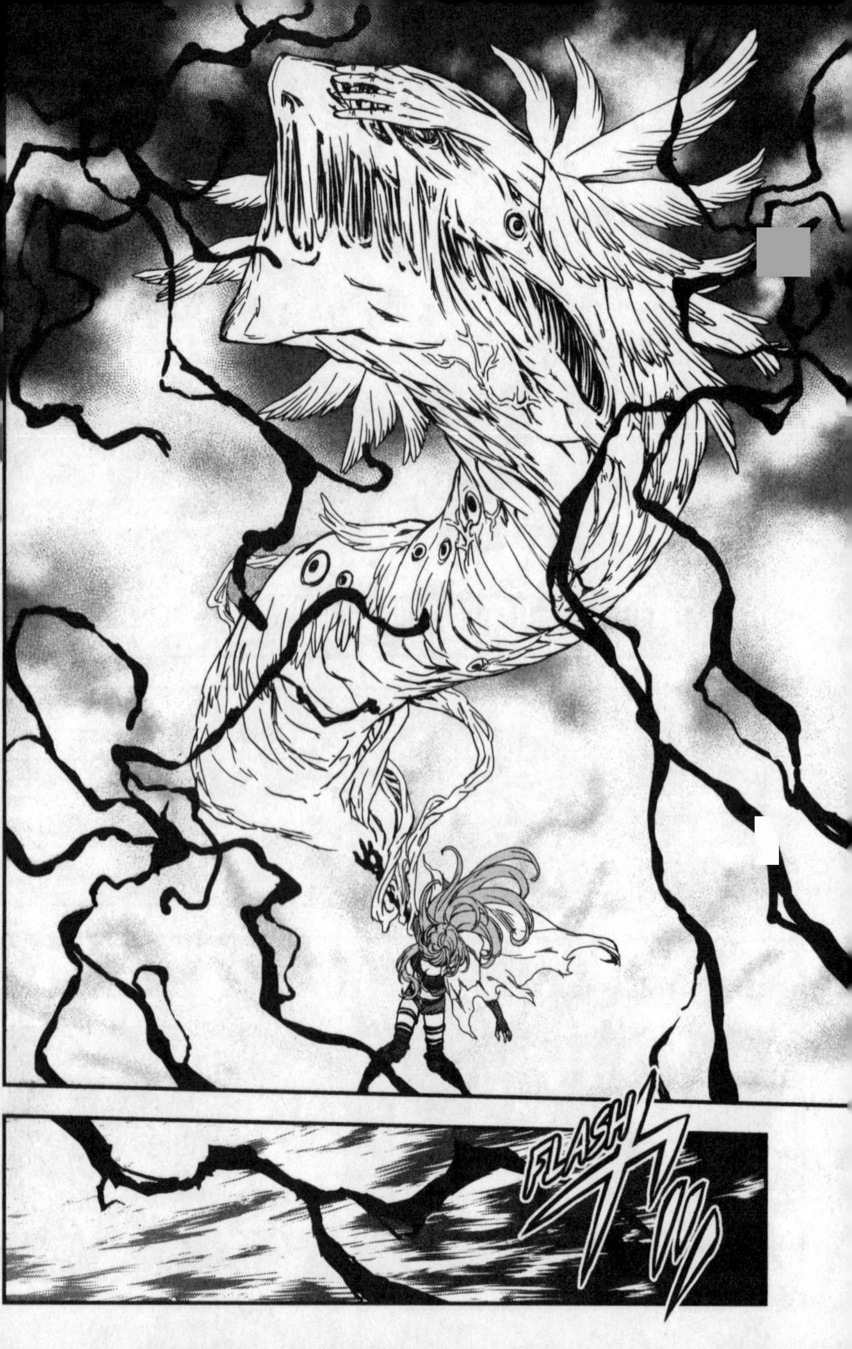
FLASH

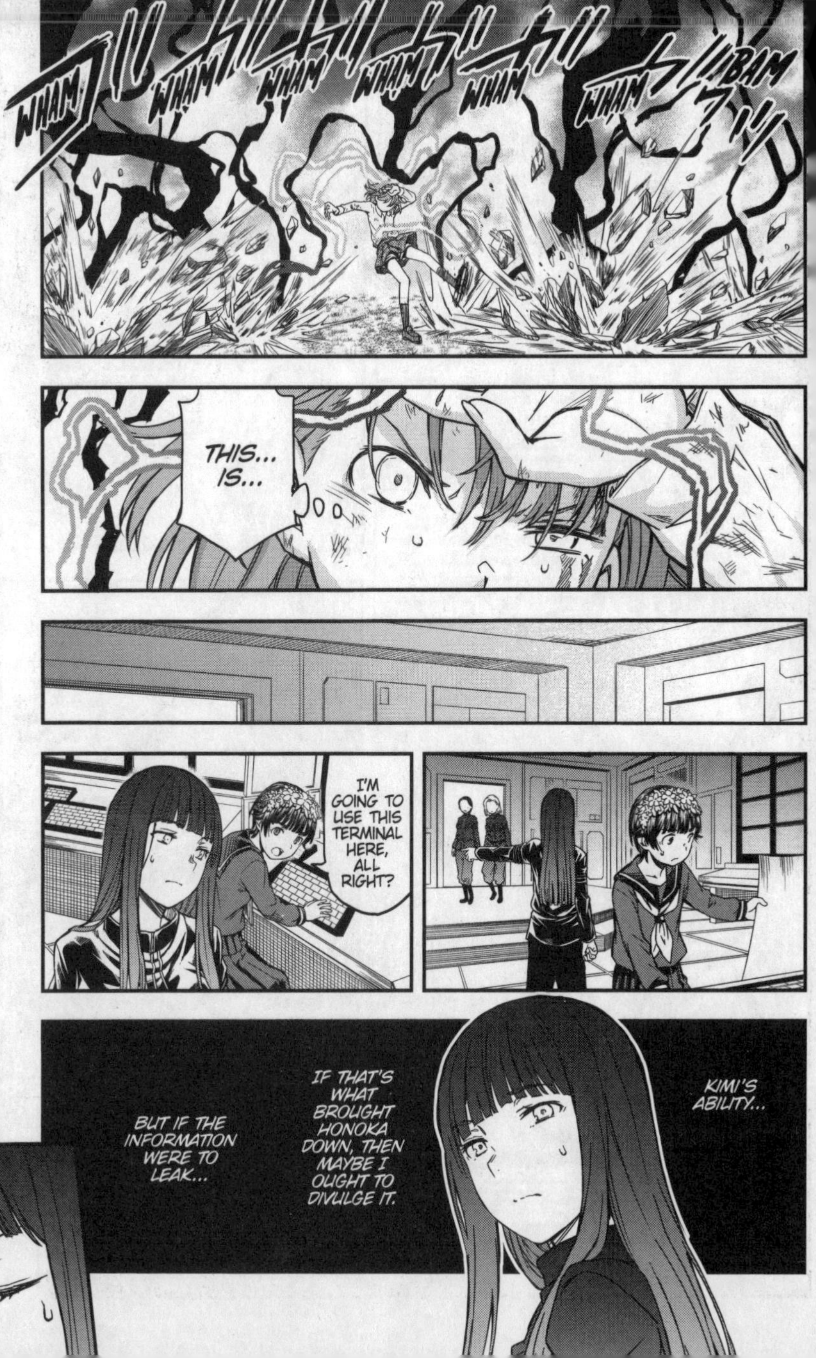
BAM
WHAM
WHAM
WHAM
WHAM
WHAM
WHAM
THIS... IS...
I'M GOING TO USE THIS TERMINAL HERE, ALL RIGHT?
KIMI'S ABILITY...
IF THAT'S WHAT BROUGHT HONOKA DOWN, THEN MAYBE I OUGHT TO DIVULGE IT.
BUT IF THE INFORMATION WERE TO LEAK...

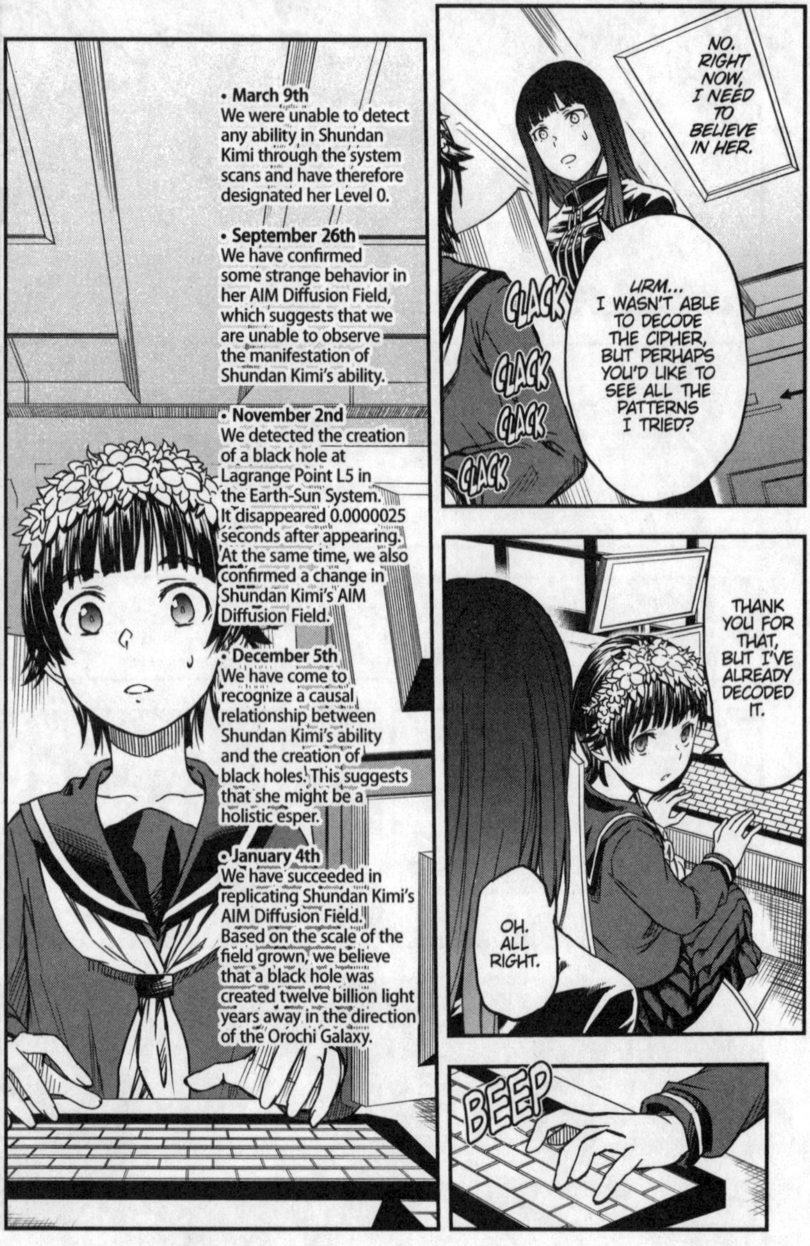
NO. RIGHT NOW, I NEED TO BELIEVE IN HER.
URM... I WASN'T ABLE TO DECODE THE CIPHER, BUT PERHAPS YOU'D LIKE TO SEE ALL THE PATTERNS I TRIED?
CLACK CLACK CLACK CLACK
THANK YOU FOR THAT, BUT I'VE ALREADY DECODED IT.
OH. ALL RIGHT.
BEEP
• March 9th
We were unable to detect any ability in Shundan Kimi through the system scans and have therefore designated her Level 0.
• September 26th
We have confirmed some strange behavior in her AIM Diffusion Field, which suggests that we are unable to observe the manifestation of Shundan Kimi's ability.
• November 2nd
We detected the creation of a black hole at Lagrange Point L5 in the Earth-Sun System. It disappeared 0.0000025 seconds after appearing. At the same time, we also confirmed a change in Shundan Kimi's AIM Diffusion Field.
• December 5th
We have come to recognize a causal relationship between Shundan Kimi's ability and the creation of black holes. This suggests that she might be a holistic esper.
• January 4th
We have succeeded in replicating Shundan Kimi's AIM Diffusion Field. Based on the scale of the field grown, we believe that a black hole was created twelve billion light years away in the direction of the Orochi Galaxy.

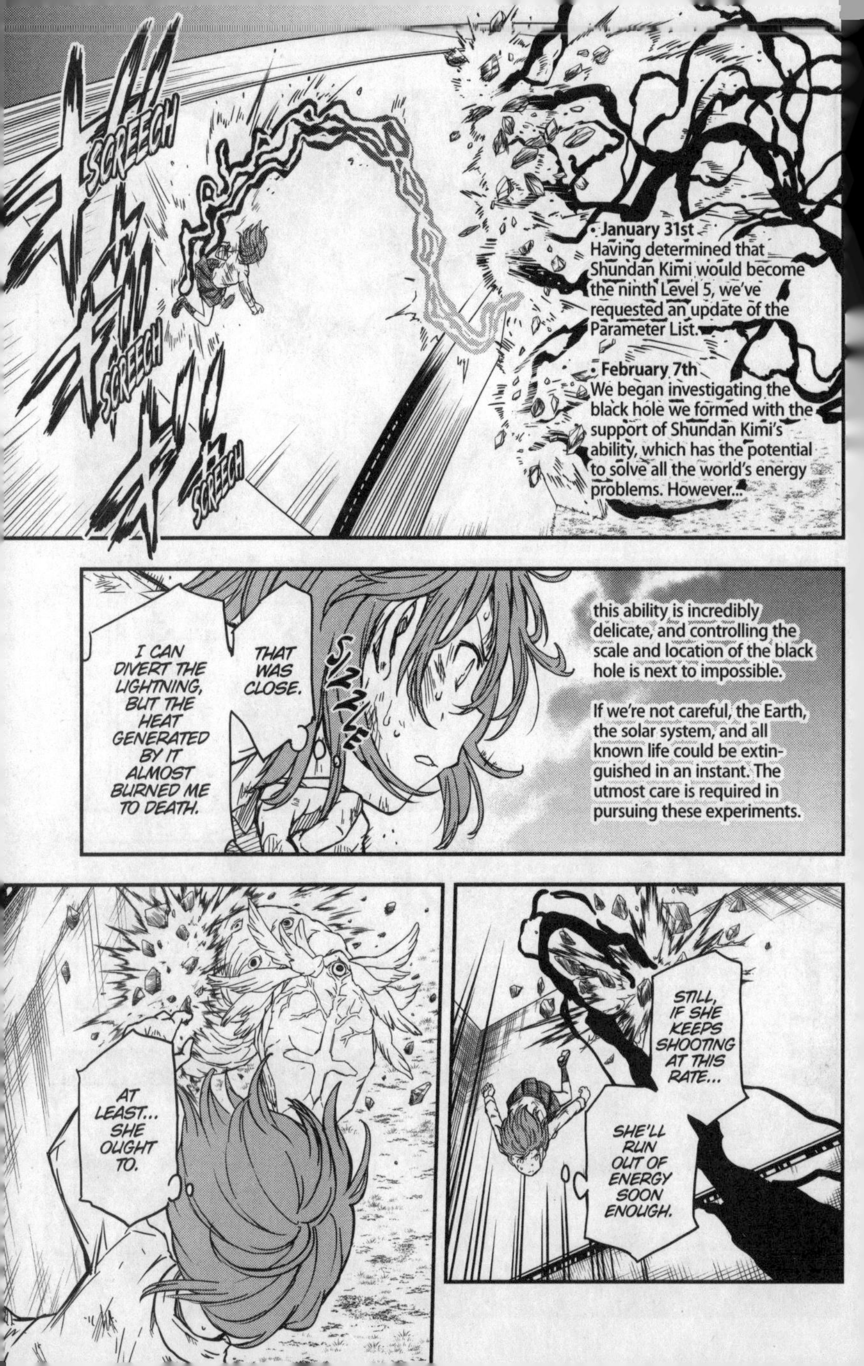
• January 31st
Having determined that Shundan Kimi would become the ninth Level 5, we've requested an update of the Parameter List.
• February 7th
We began investigating the black hole we formed with the support of Shundan Kimi's ability, which has the potential to solve all the world's energy problems. However...
SCREECH
SCREECH
SCREECH
this ability is incredibly delicate, and controlling the scale and location of the black hole is next to impossible.
If we're not careful, the Earth, the solar system, and all known life could be extinguished in an instant. The utmost care is required in pursuing these experiments.
SIZZLE
THAT WAS CLOSE.
I CAN DIVERT THE LIGHTNING, BUT THE HEAT GENERATED BY IT ALMOST BURNED ME TO DEATH.
STILL, IF SHE KEEPS SHOOTING AT THIS RATE...
SHE'LL RUN OUT OF ENERGY SOON ENOUGH.
AT LEAST... SHE OUGHT TO.

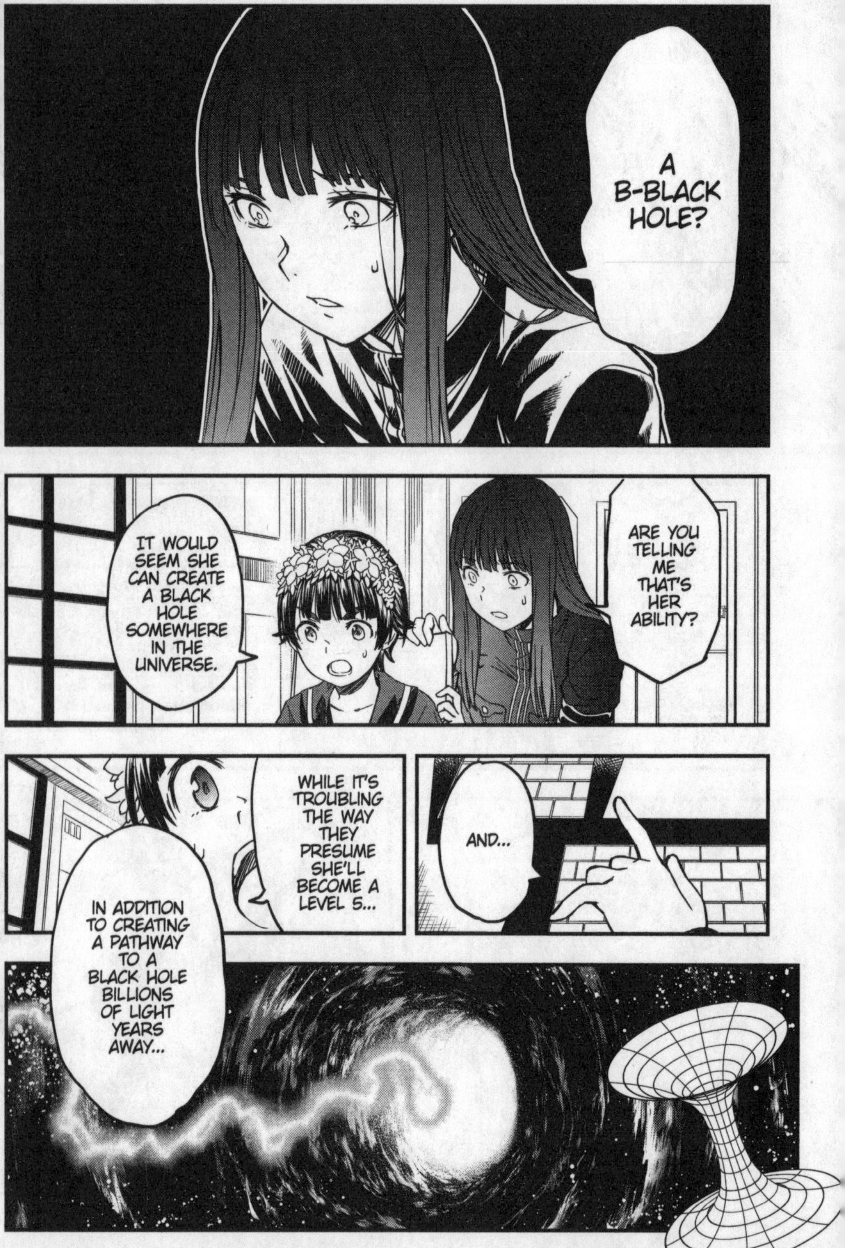
A B-BLACK HOLE?
ARE YOU TELLING ME THAT'S HER ABILITY?
IT WOULD SEEM SHE CAN CREATE A BLACK HOLE SOMEWHERE IN THE UNIVERSE.
AND...
WHILE IT'S TROUBLING THE WAY THEY PRESUME SHE'LL BECOME A LEVEL 5...
IN ADDITION TO CREATING A PATHWAY TO A BLACK HOLE BILLIONS OF LIGHT YEARS AWAY...

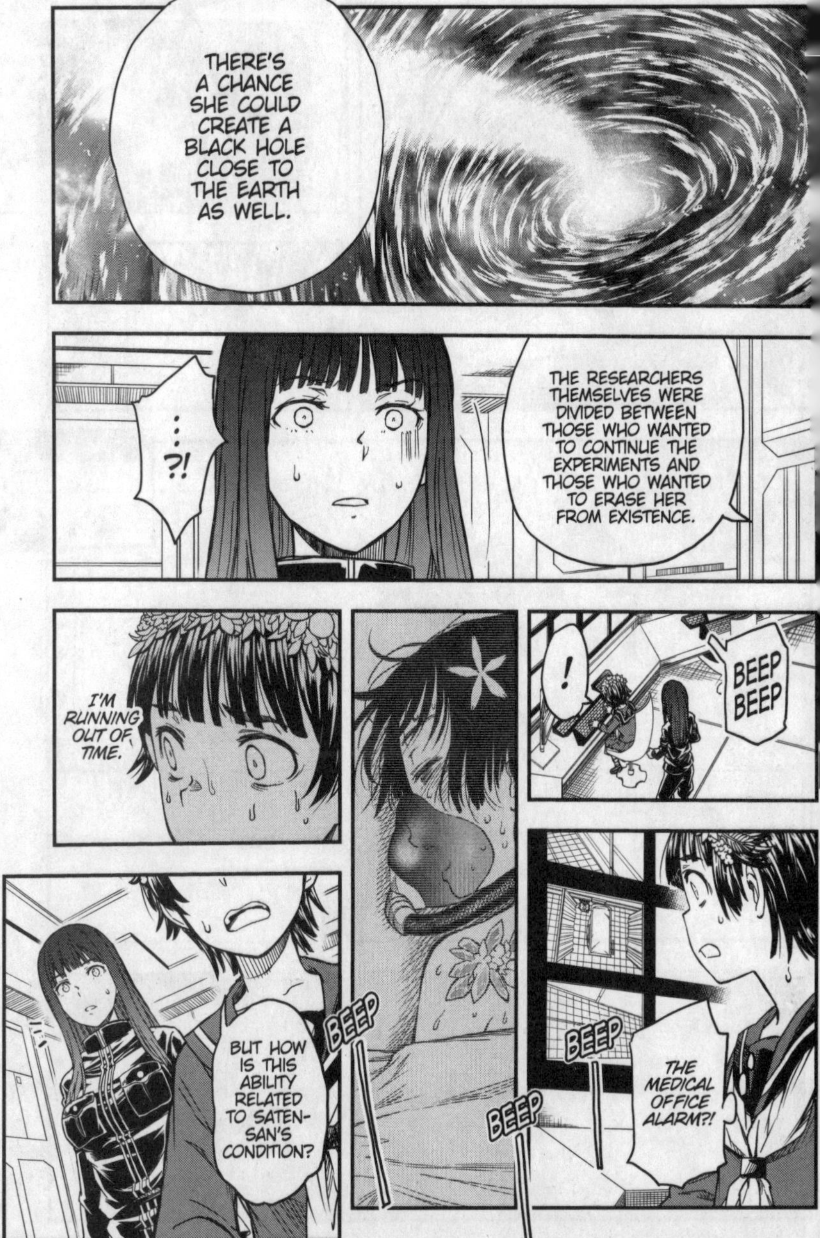
THERE'S A CHANCE SHE COULD CREATE A BLACK HOLE CLOSE TO THE EARTH AS WELL.
THE RESEARCHERS THEMSELVES WERE DIVIDED BETWEEN THOSE WHO WANTED TO CONTINUE THE EXPERIMENTS AND THOSE WHO WANTED TO ERASE HER FROM EXISTENCE.
...?!
BEEP BEEP
!
BEEP
BEEP
THE MEDICAL OFFICE ALARM?!
BEEP
I'M RUNNING OUT OF TIME.
BUT HOW IS THIS ABILITY RELATED TO SATEN-SAN'S CONDITION?

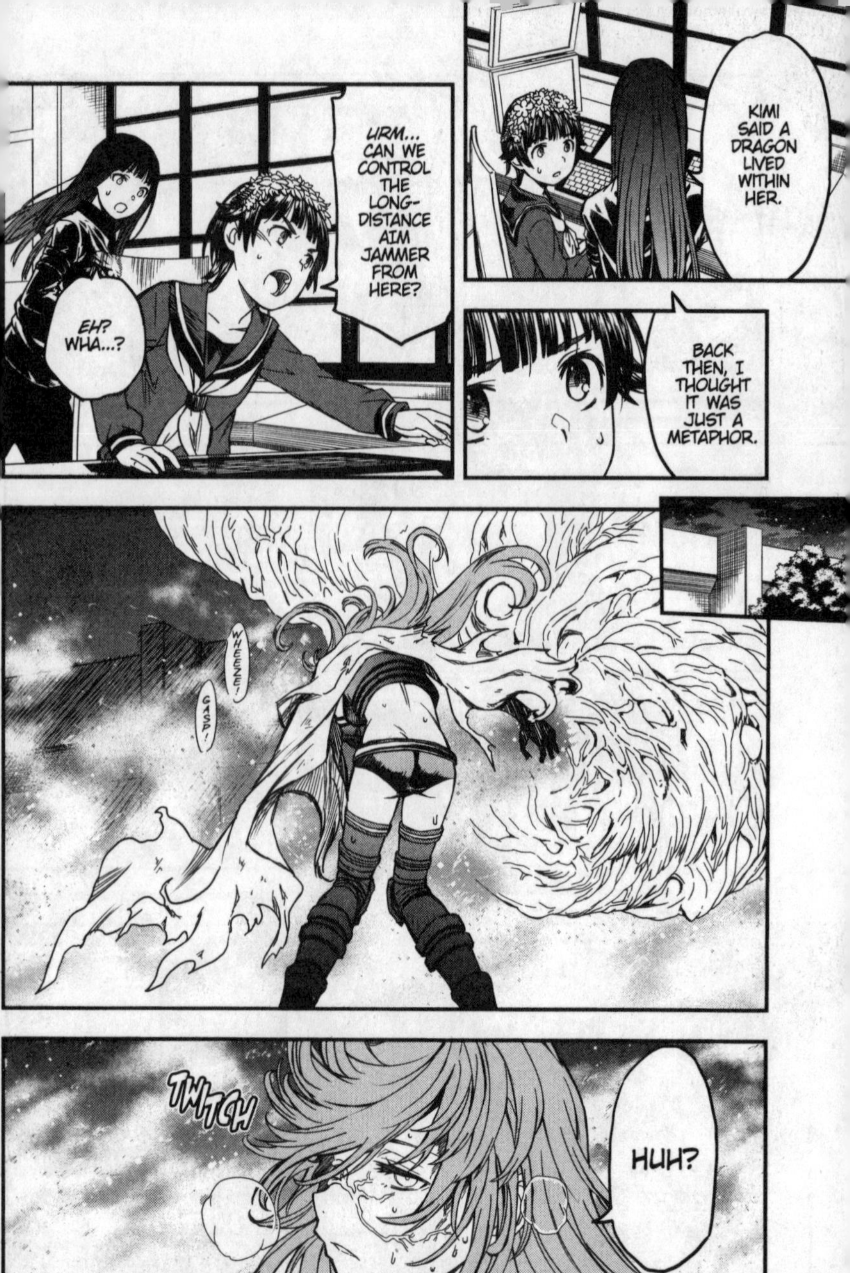
KIMI SAID A DRAGON LIVED WITHIN HER.
BACK THEN, I THOUGHT IT WAS JUST A METAPHOR.
URM... CAN WE CONTROL THE LONG-DISTANCE AIM JAMMER FROM HERE?
EH? WHA...?
WHEEZE!
GASP!
HUH?
TWITCH

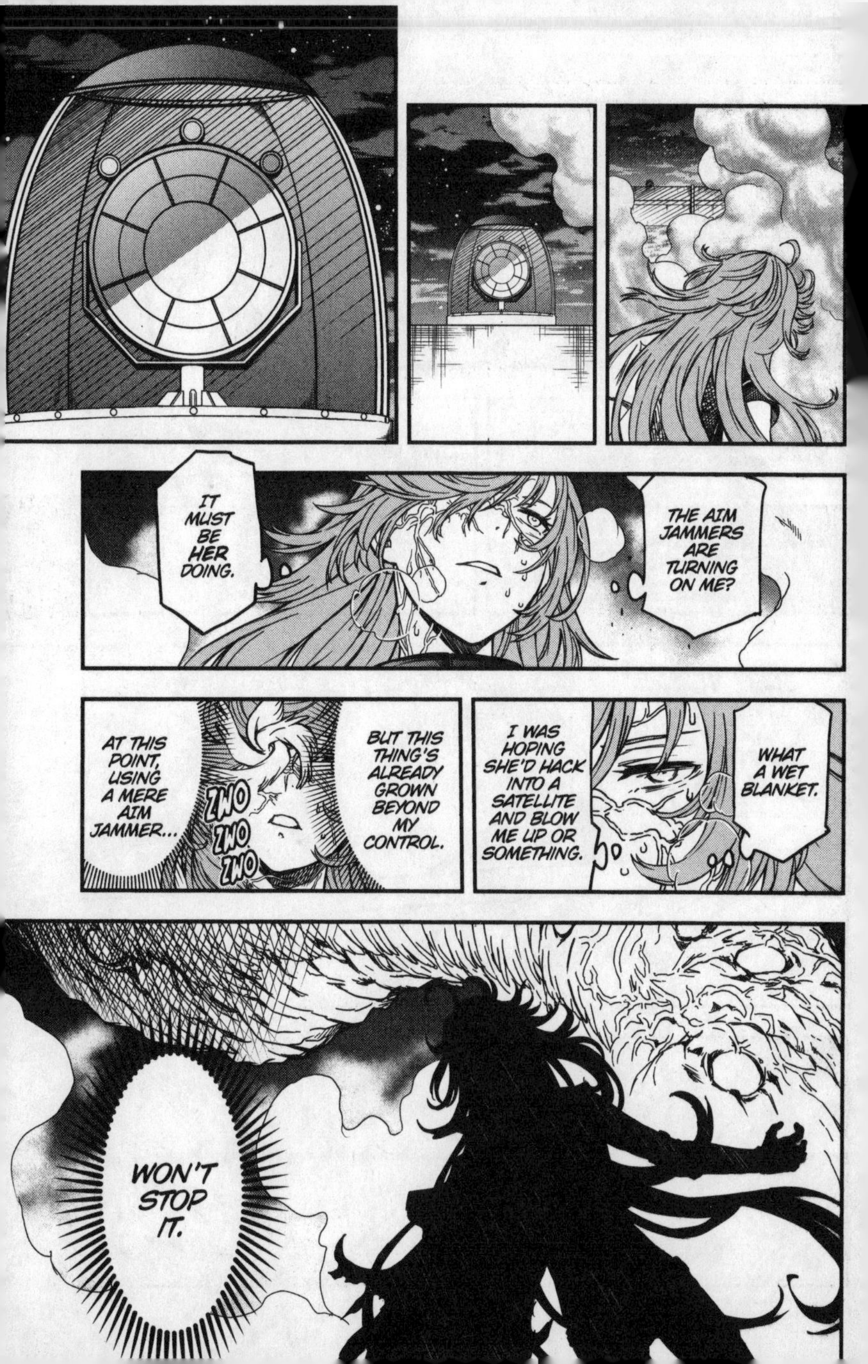
THE AIM JAMMERS ARE TURNING ON ME?
IT MUST BE HER DOING.
WHAT A WET BLANKET.
I WAS HOPING SHE'D HACK INTO A SATELLITE AND BLOW ME UP OR SOMETHING.
BUT THIS THING'S ALREADY GROWN BEYOND MY CONTROL.
ZWO ZWO ZWO
AT THIS POINT, USING A MERE AIM JAMMER...
WON'T STOP IT.

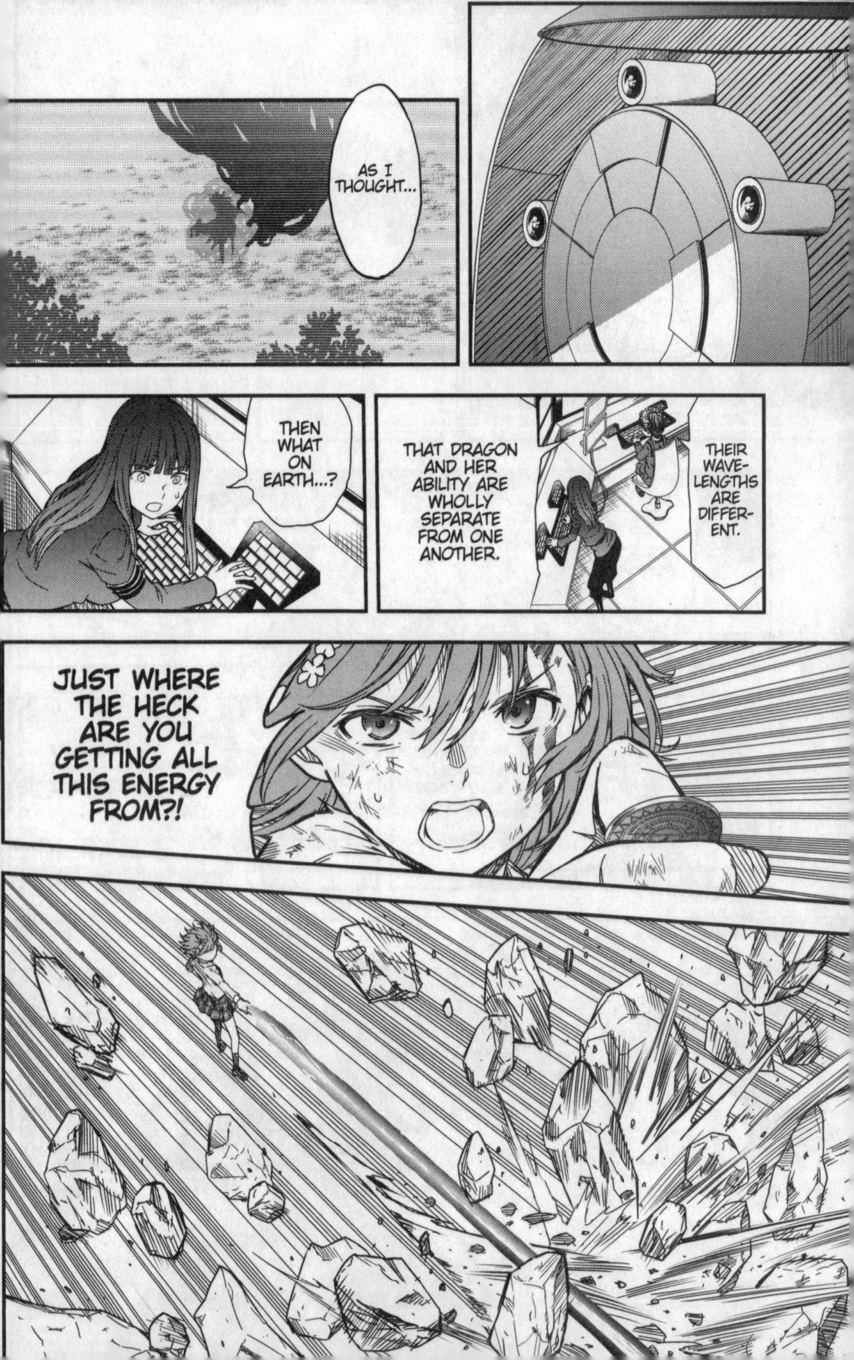
AS I THOUGHT...
THEIR WAVE-LENGTHS ARE DIFFER-ENT.
THAT DRAGON AND HER ABILITY ARE WHOLLY SEPARATE FROM ONE ANOTHER.
THEN WHAT ON EARTH...?
JUST WHERE THE HECK ARE YOU GETTING ALL THIS ENERGY FROM?!

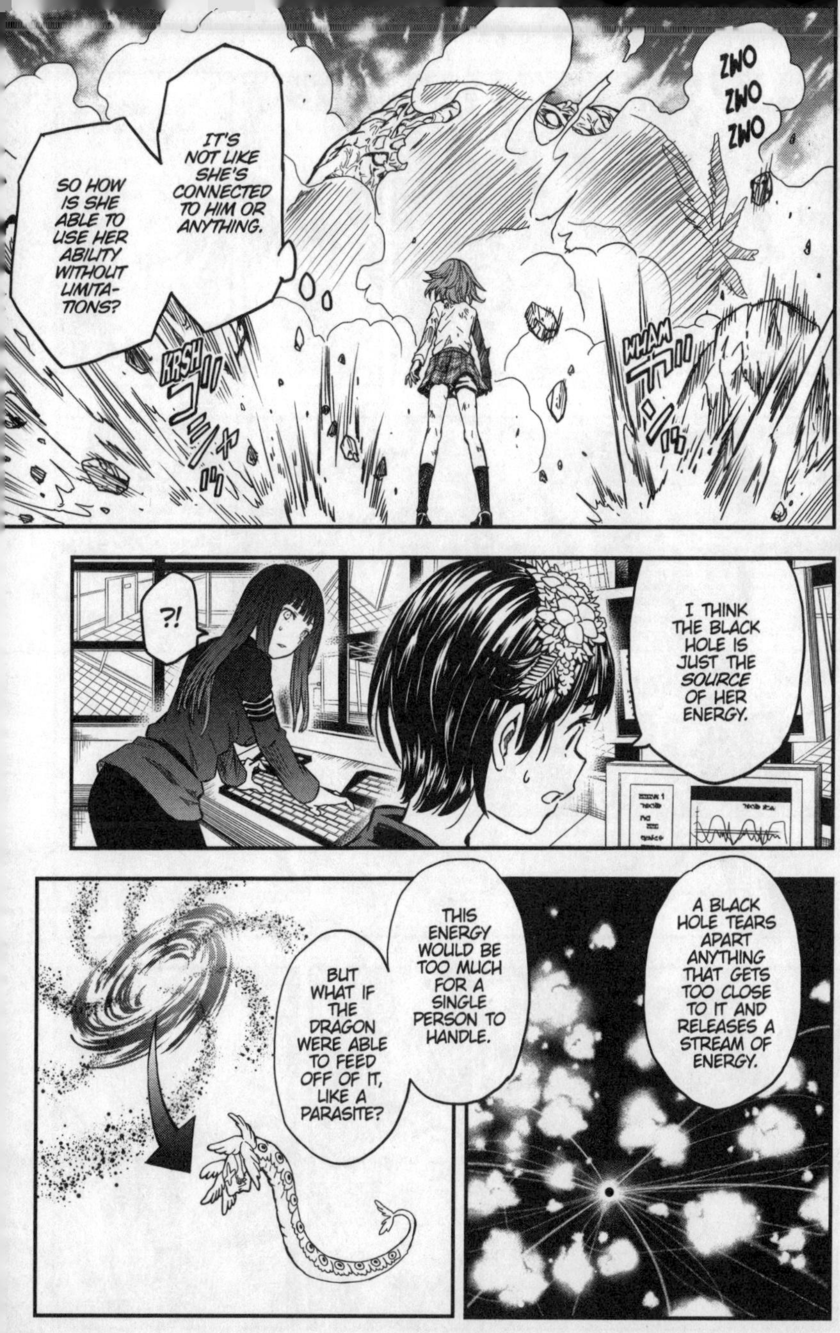
ZWO ZWO ZWO
IT'S NOT LIKE SHE'S CONNECTED TO HIM OR ANYTHING.
SO HOW IS SHE ABLE TO USE HER ABILITY WITHOUT LIMITA-TIONS?
WHAM
KRSH
I THINK THE BLACK HOLE IS JUST THE *SOURCE* OF HER ENERGY.
?!
A BLACK HOLE TEARS APART ANYTHING THAT GETS TOO CLOSE TO IT AND RELEASES A STREAM OF ENERGY.
THIS ENERGY WOULD BE TOO MUCH FOR A SINGLE PERSON TO HANDLE.
BUT WHAT IF THE DRAGON WERE ABLE TO FEED OFF OF IT, LIKE A PARASITE?

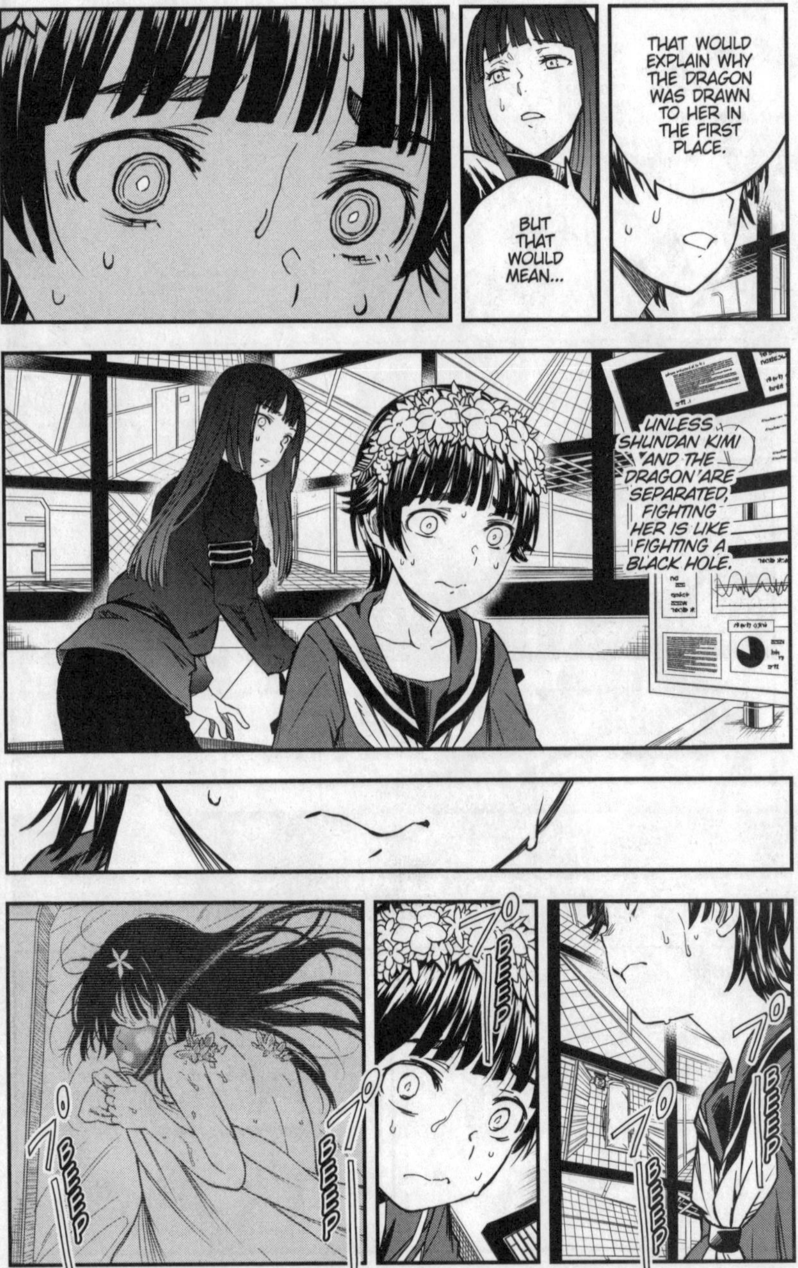
THAT WOULD EXPLAIN WHY THE DRAGON WAS DRAWN TO HER IN THE FIRST PLACE.
BUT THAT WOULD MEAN...
UNLESS SHUNDAN KIMI AND THE DRAGON ARE SEPARATED, FIGHTING HER IS LIKE FIGHTING A BLACK HOLE.
BEEP
BEEP
BEEP
BEEP
BEEP

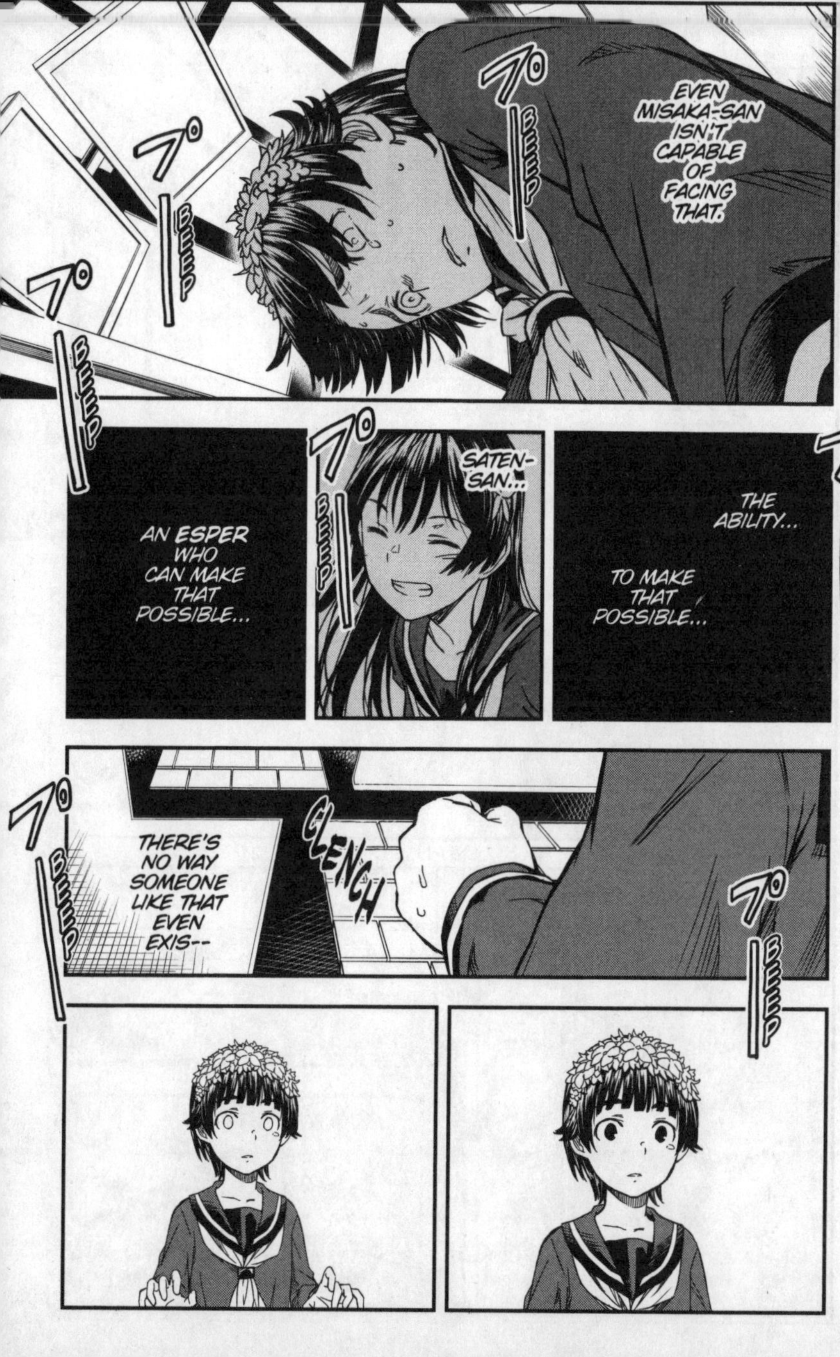
EVEN MISAKA-SAN ISN'T CAPABLE OF FACING THAT.
BEEP
BEEP
BEEP
THE ABILITY...
TO MAKE THAT POSSIBLE...
SATEN-SAN...
BEEP
AN ESPER WHO CAN MAKE THAT POSSIBLE...
BEEP
CLENCH
THERE'S NO WAY SOMEONE LIKE THAT EVEN EXIS--
BEEP

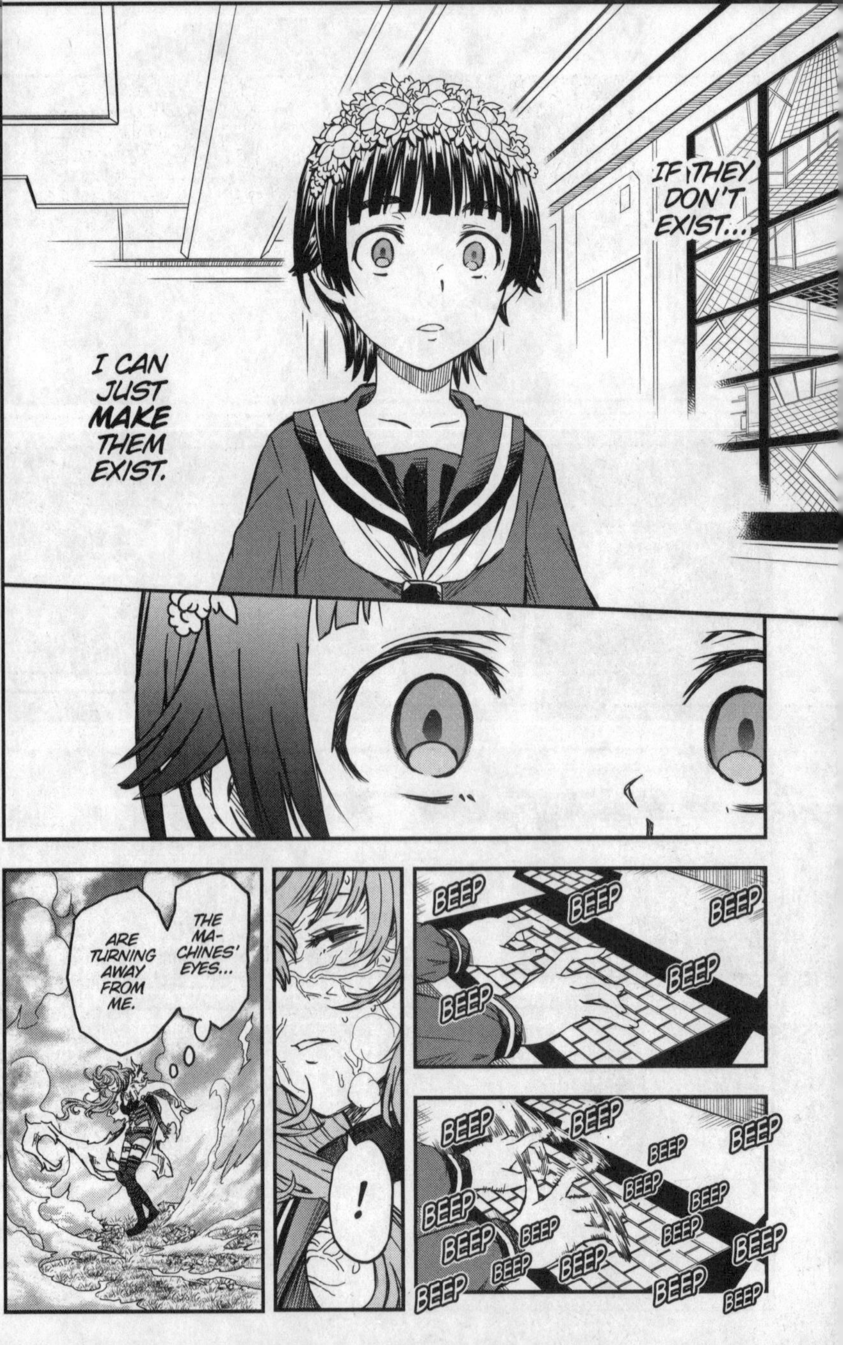
IF THEY DON'T EXIST...
I CAN JUST MAKE THEM EXIST.
BEEP BEEP BEEP BEEP BEEP
BEEP BEEP BEEP BEEP BEEP BEEP BEEP BEEP BEEP BEEP BEEP BEEP BEEP BEEP BEEP BEEP
!
THE MA-CHINES' EYES...
ARE TURNING AWAY FROM ME.

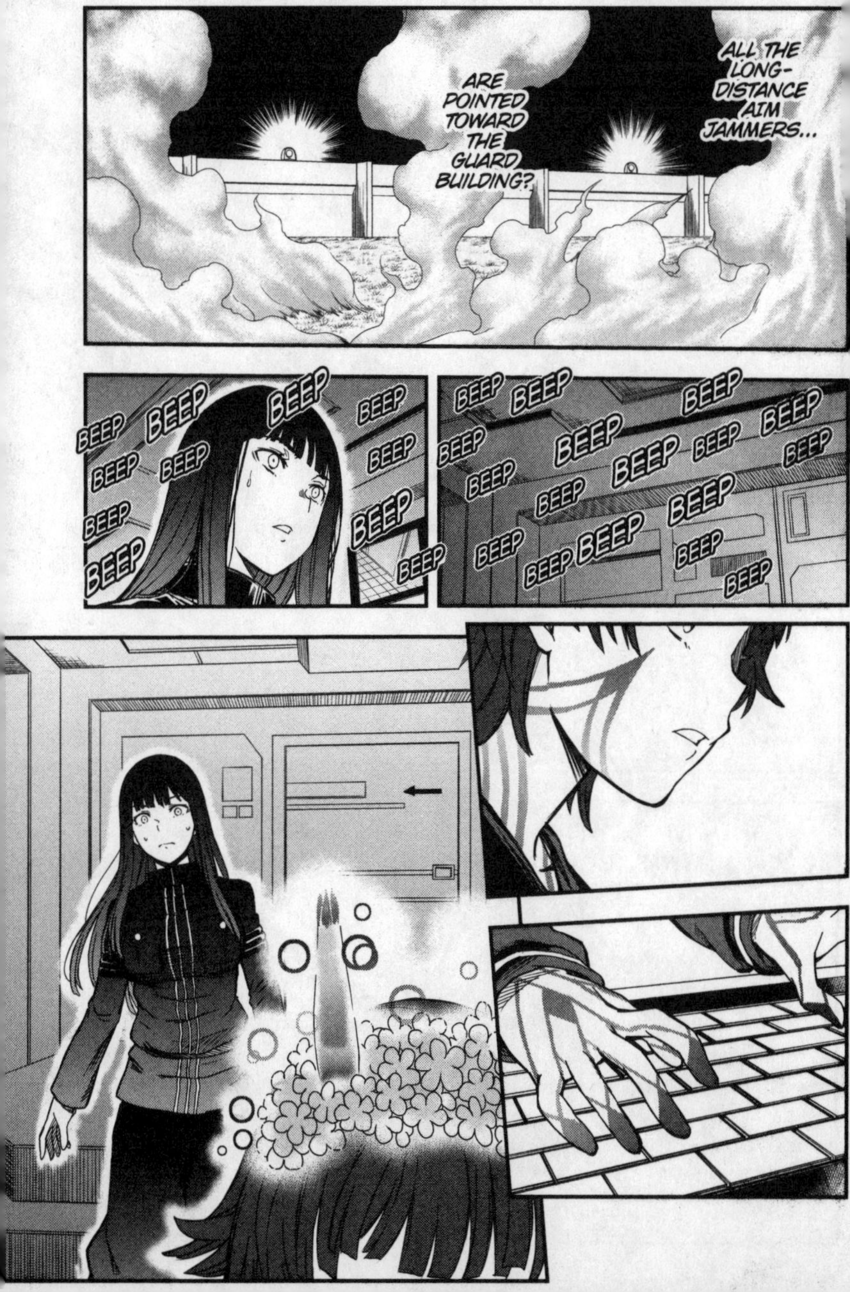
ALL THE LONG-DISTANCE AIM JAMMERS...
ARE POINTED TOWARD THE GUARD BUILDING?
BEEP BEEP BEEP BEEP BEEP BEEP BEEP BEEP BEEP BEEP BEEP BEEP BEEP BEEP BEEP BEEP BEEP
BEEP BEEP BEEP BEEP BEEP BEEP BEEP BEEP BEEP BEEP BEEP

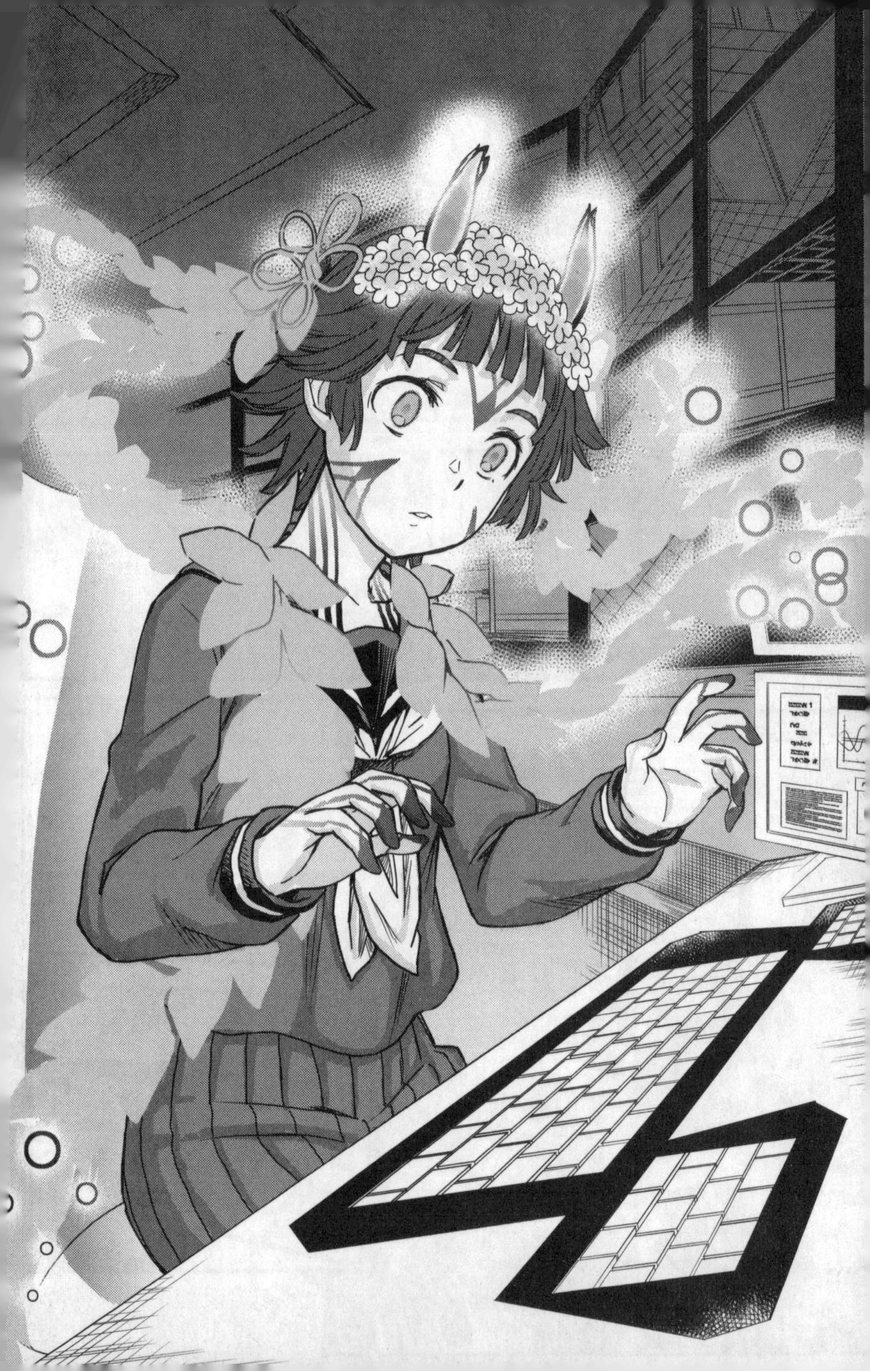

CHAPTER 127: UPSET

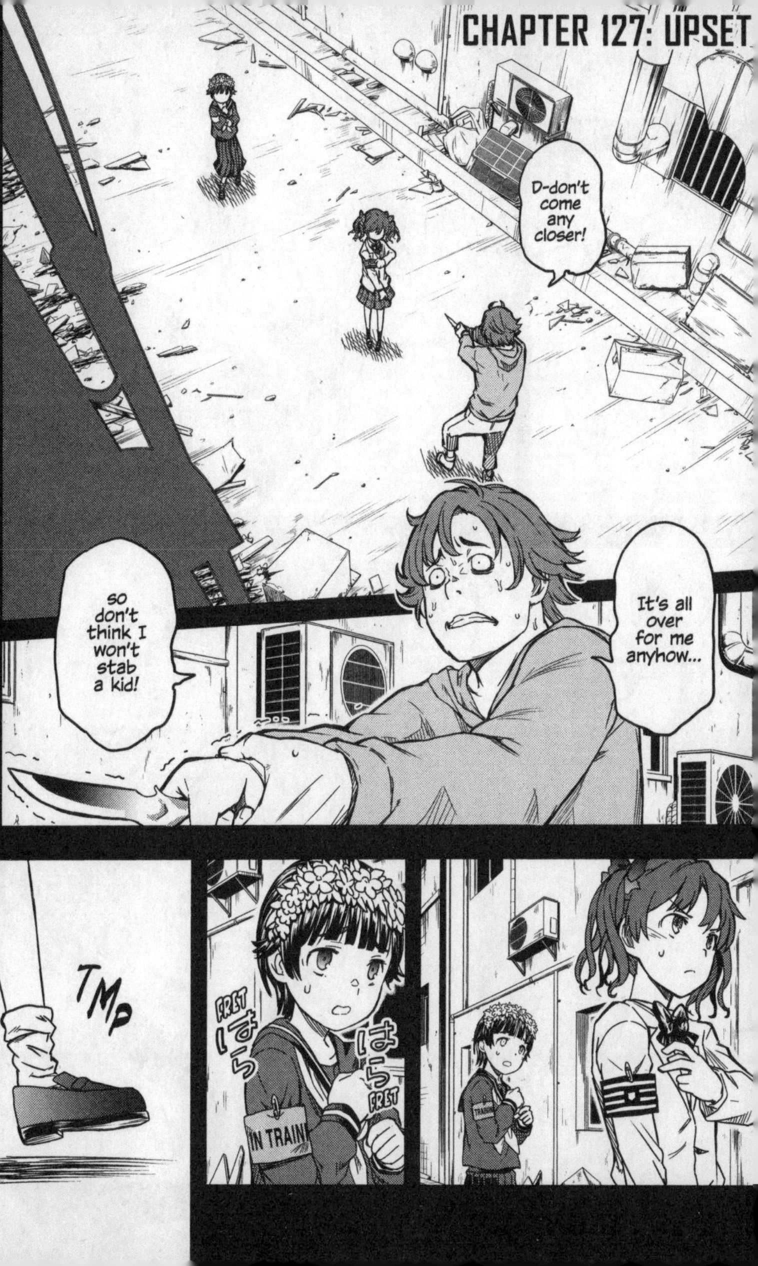
D-don't come any closer!
It's all over for me anyhow...
so don't think I won't stab a kid!
FRET はら
はら FRET
IN TRAIN
TMP

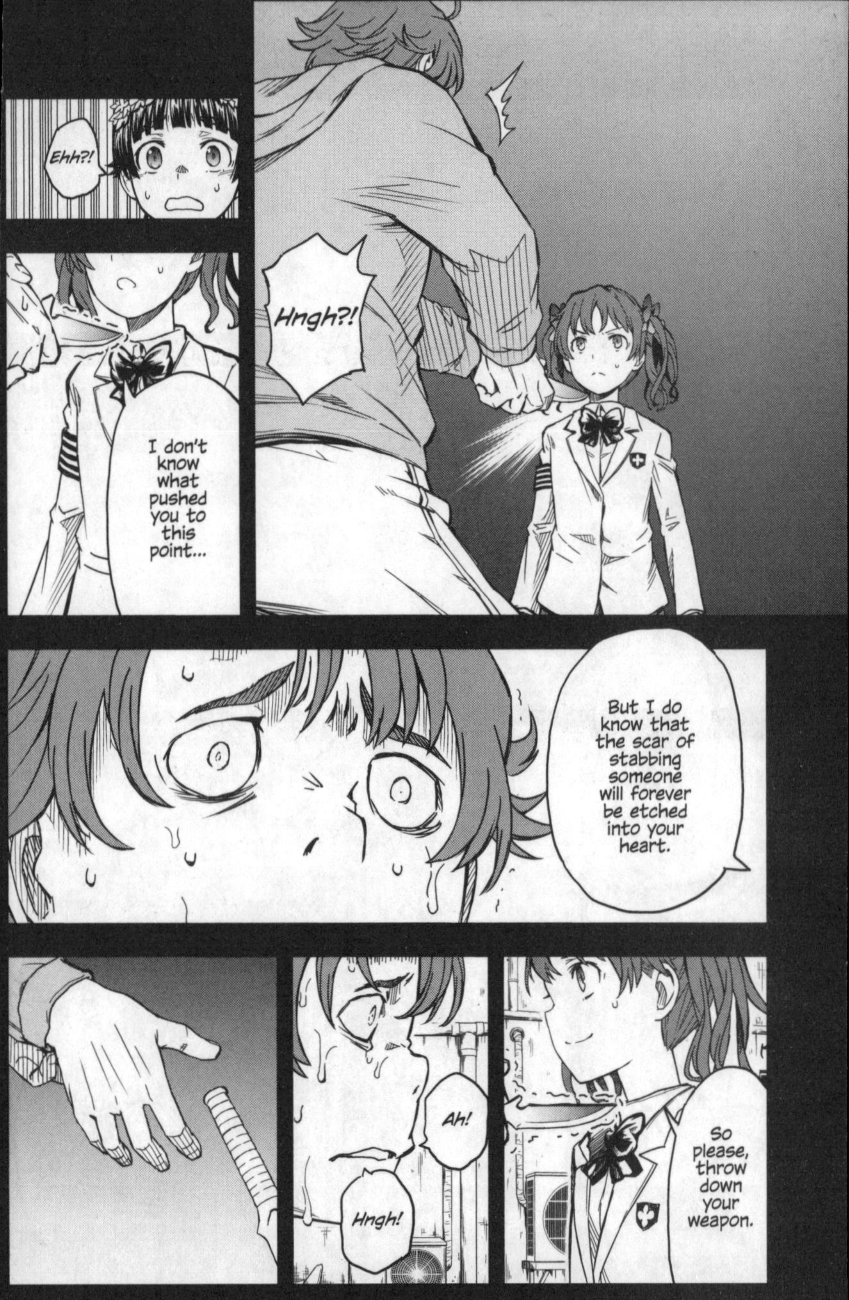
Hngh?!
Ehh?!
I don't know what pushed you to this point...
But I do know that the scar of stabbing someone will forever be etched into your heart.
So please, throw down your weapon.
Ah!
Hngh!

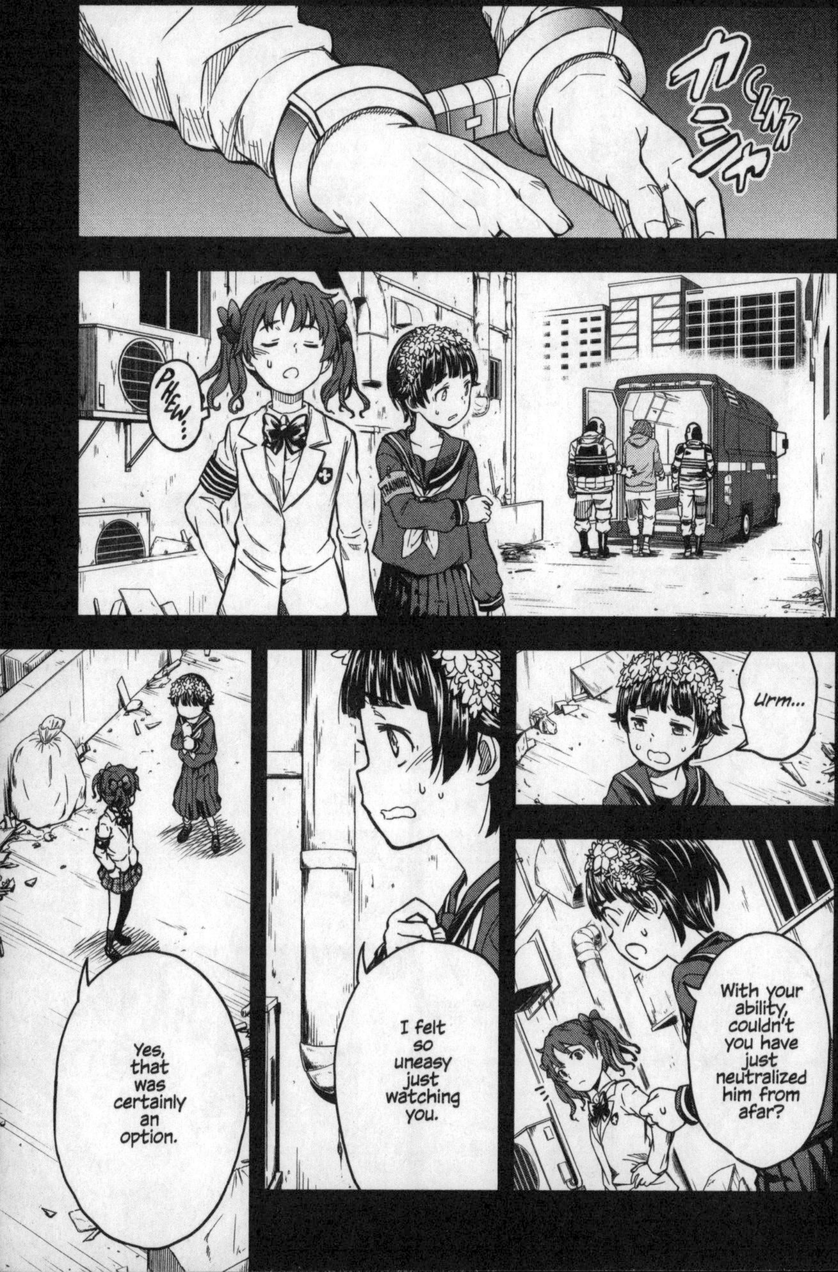
カシャ
CLINK
PHEW...
Urm...
With your ability, couldn't you have just neutralized him from afar?
I felt so uneasy just watching you.
Yes, that was certainly an option.

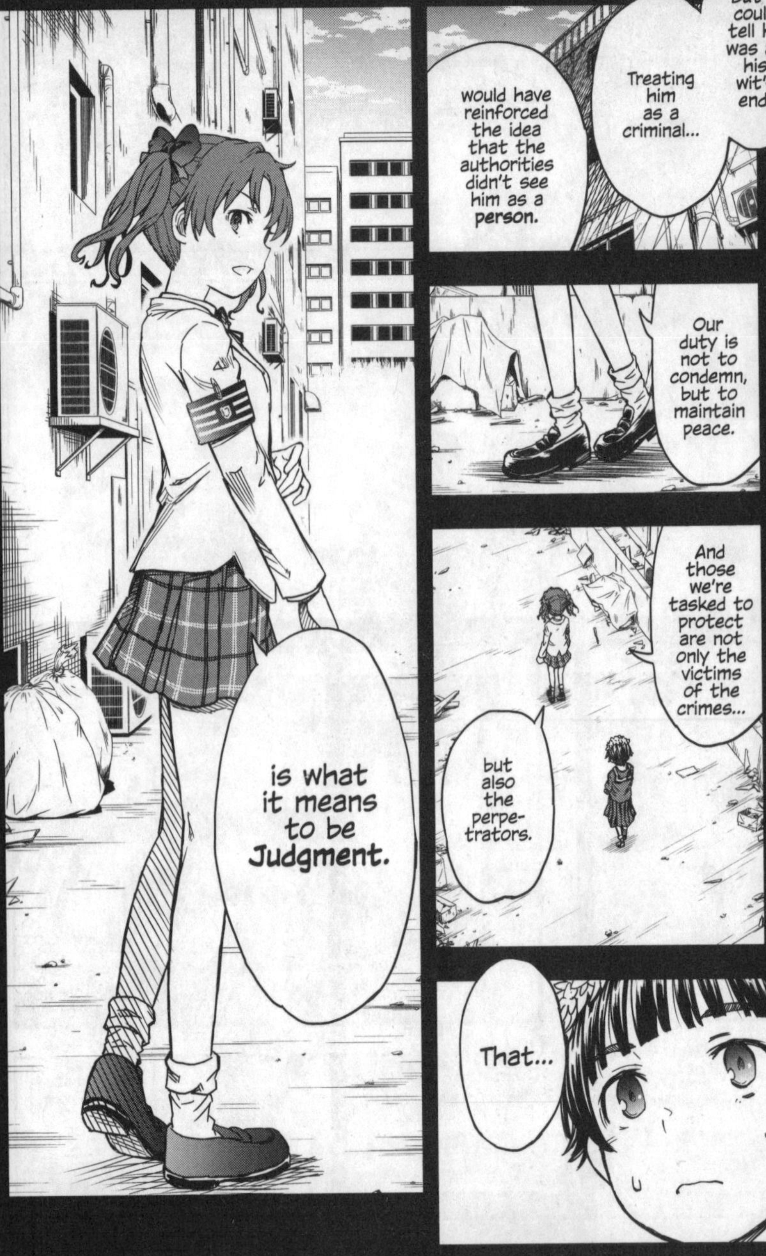
But I could tell he was at his wit's end.
Treating him as a criminal...
would have reinforced the idea that the authorities didn't see him as a person.
Our duty is not to condemn, but to maintain peace.
And those we're tasked to protect are not only the victims of the crimes...
but also the perpetrators.
That...
is what it means to be Judgment.

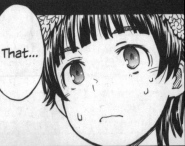

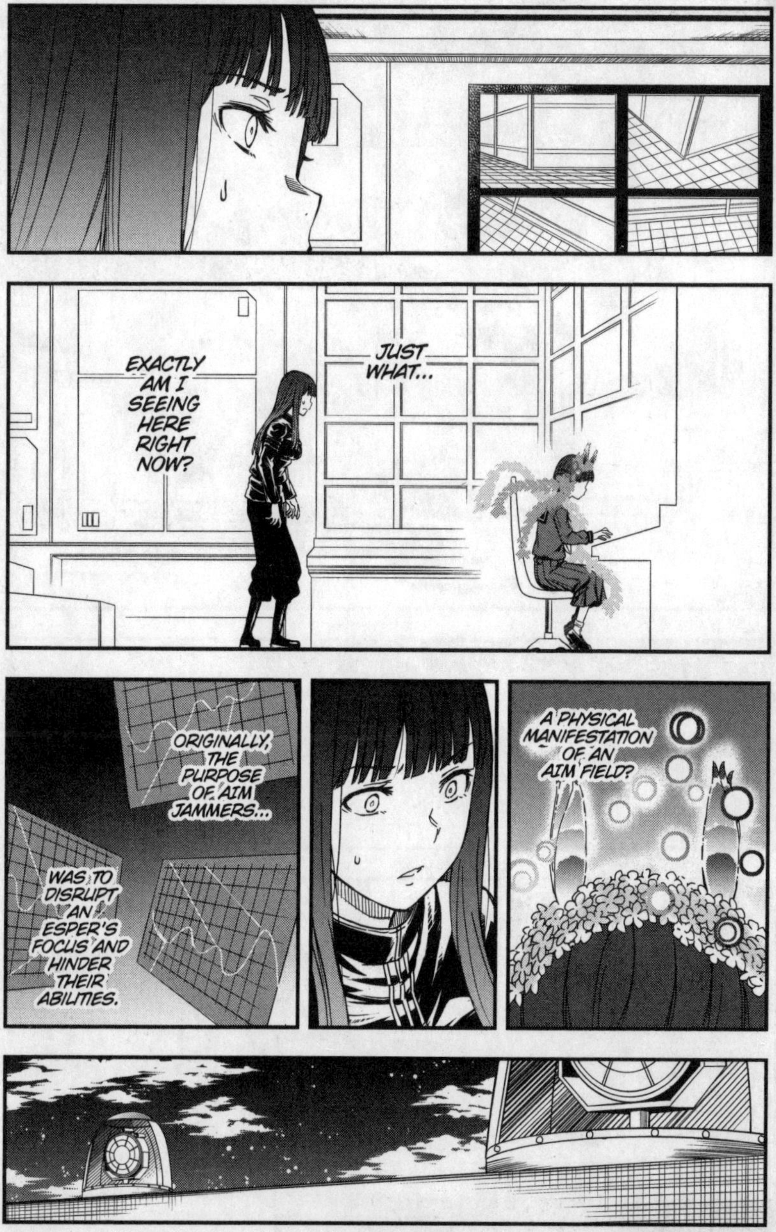
JUST WHAT...
EXACTLY AM I SEEING HERE RIGHT NOW?
A PHYSICAL MANIFESTATION OF AN AIM FIELD?
ORIGINALLY, THE PURPOSE OF AIM JAMMERS...
WAS TO DISRUPT AN ESPER'S FOCUS AND HINDER THEIR ABILITIES.

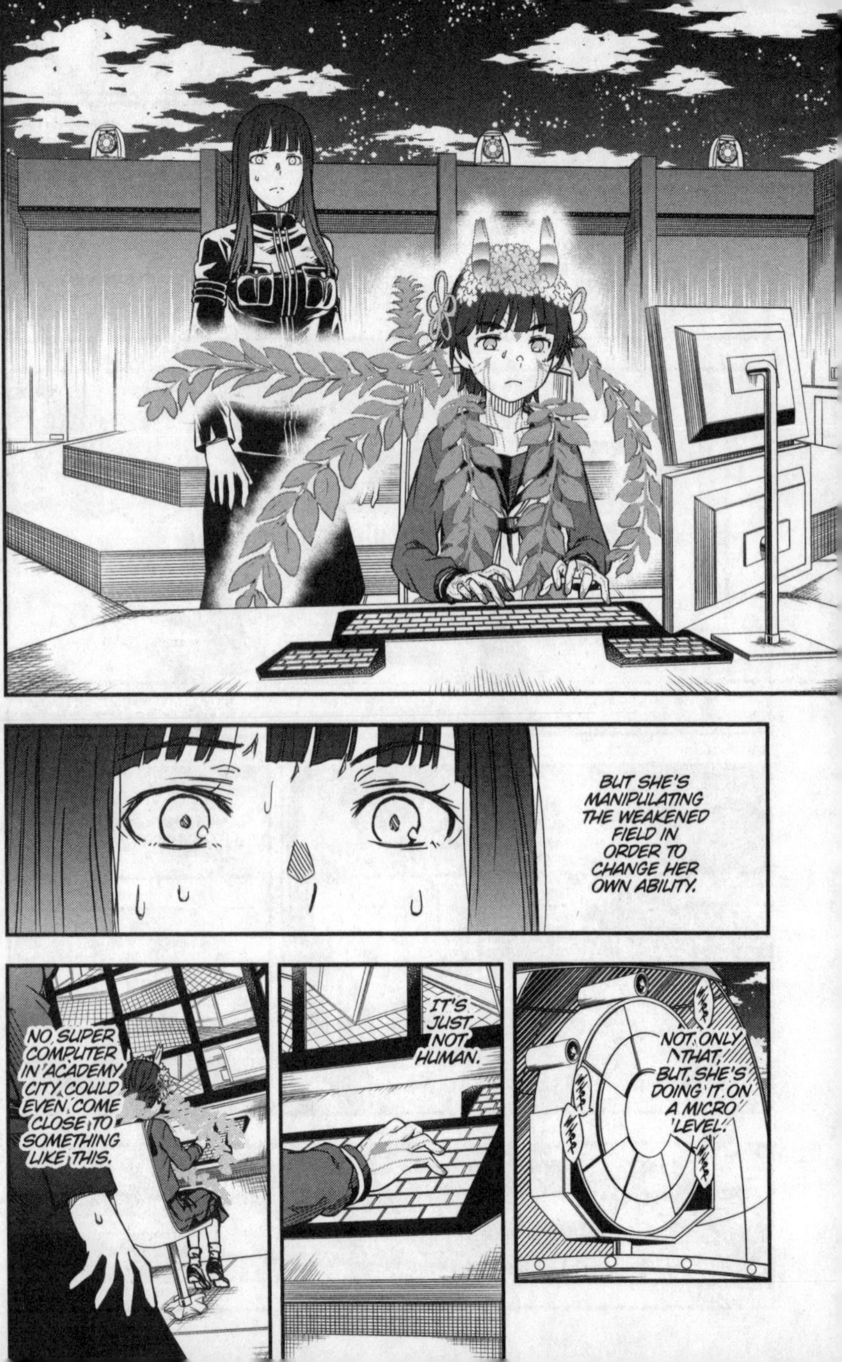
BUT SHE'S MANIPULATING THE WEAKENED FIELD IN ORDER TO CHANGE HER OWN ABILITY.
NOT ONLY THAT, BUT SHE'S DOING IT ON A MICRO LEVEL.
IT'S JUST NOT HUMAN.
NO SUPER COMPUTER IN ACADEMY CITY COULD EVEN COME CLOSE TO SOMETHING LIKE THIS.

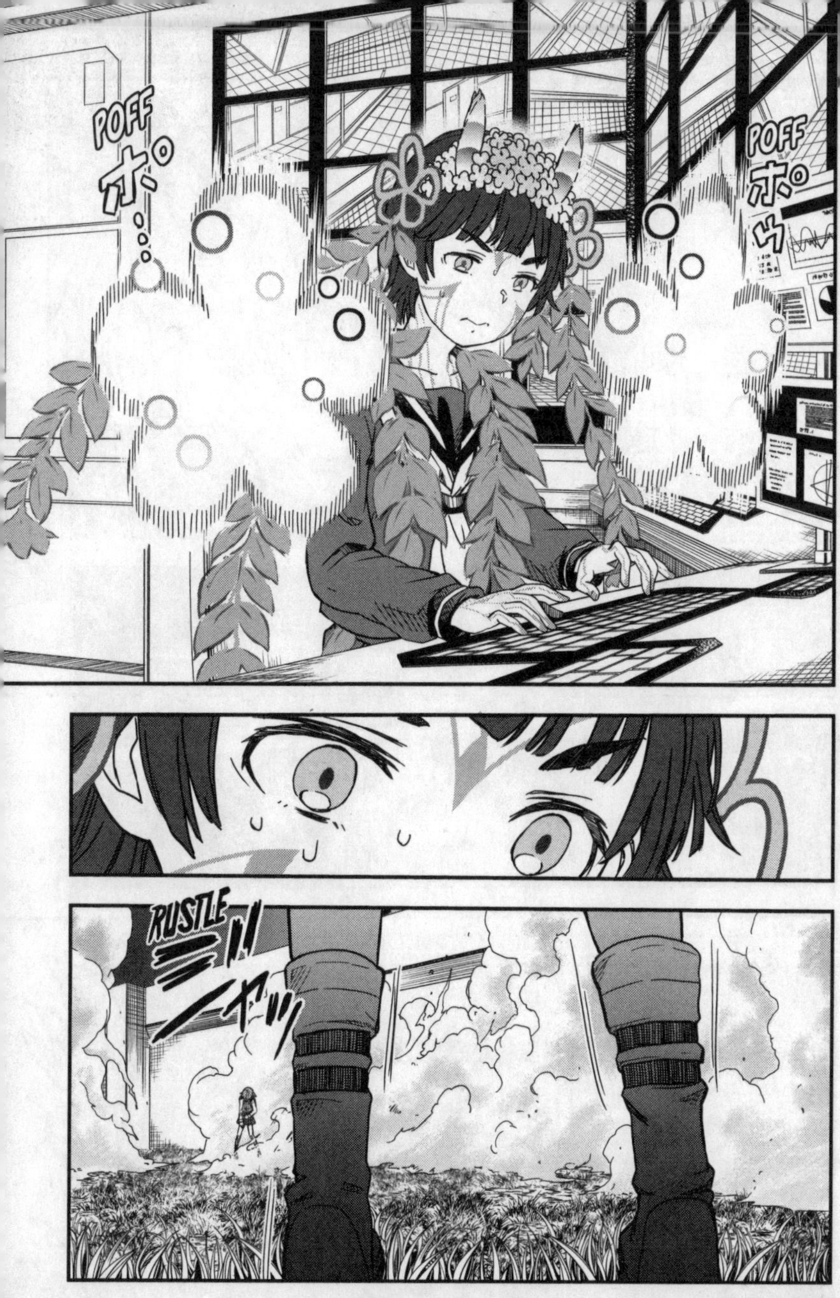
POFF
POFF
RUSTLE

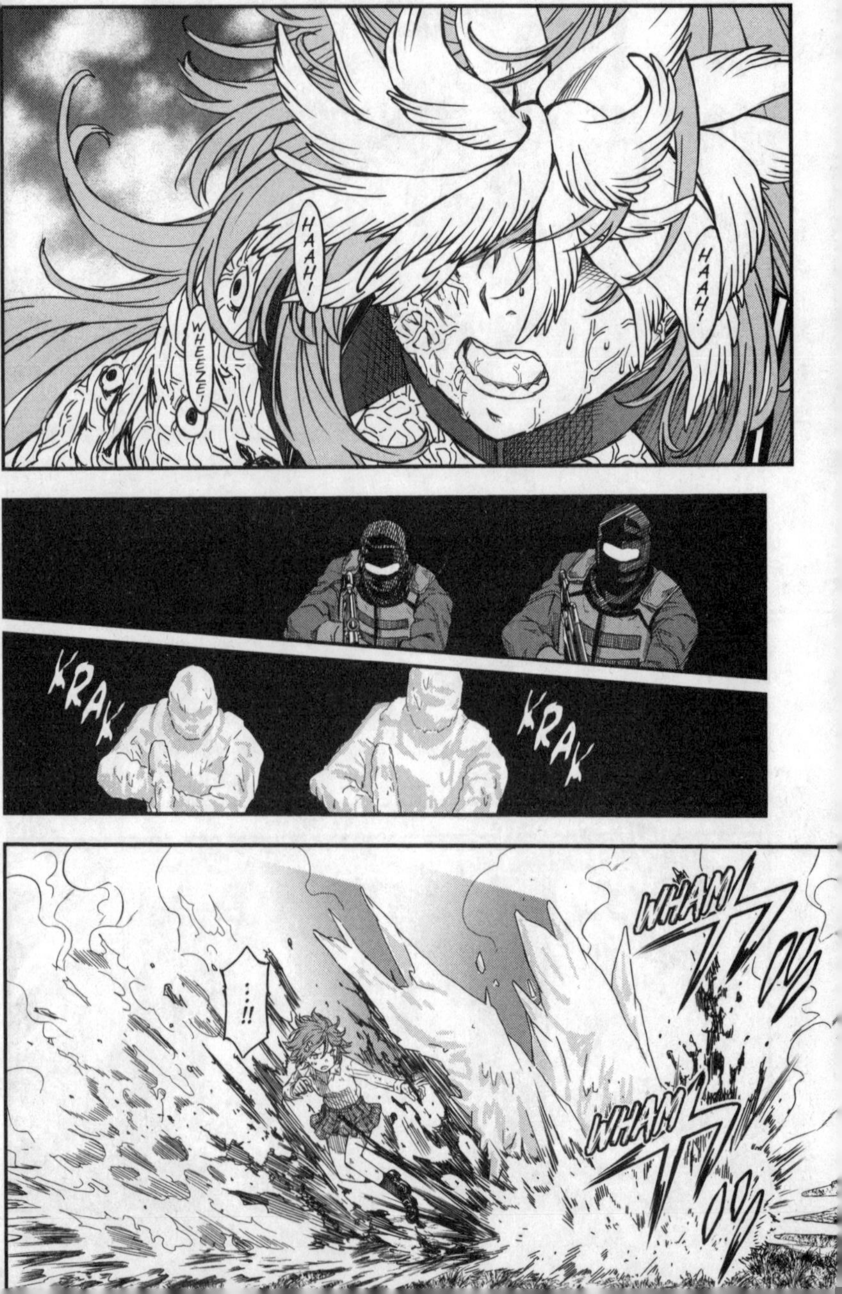
HAAH!
HAAH!
WHEEZE!
KRAK
KRAK
WHAM
WHAM
...!!

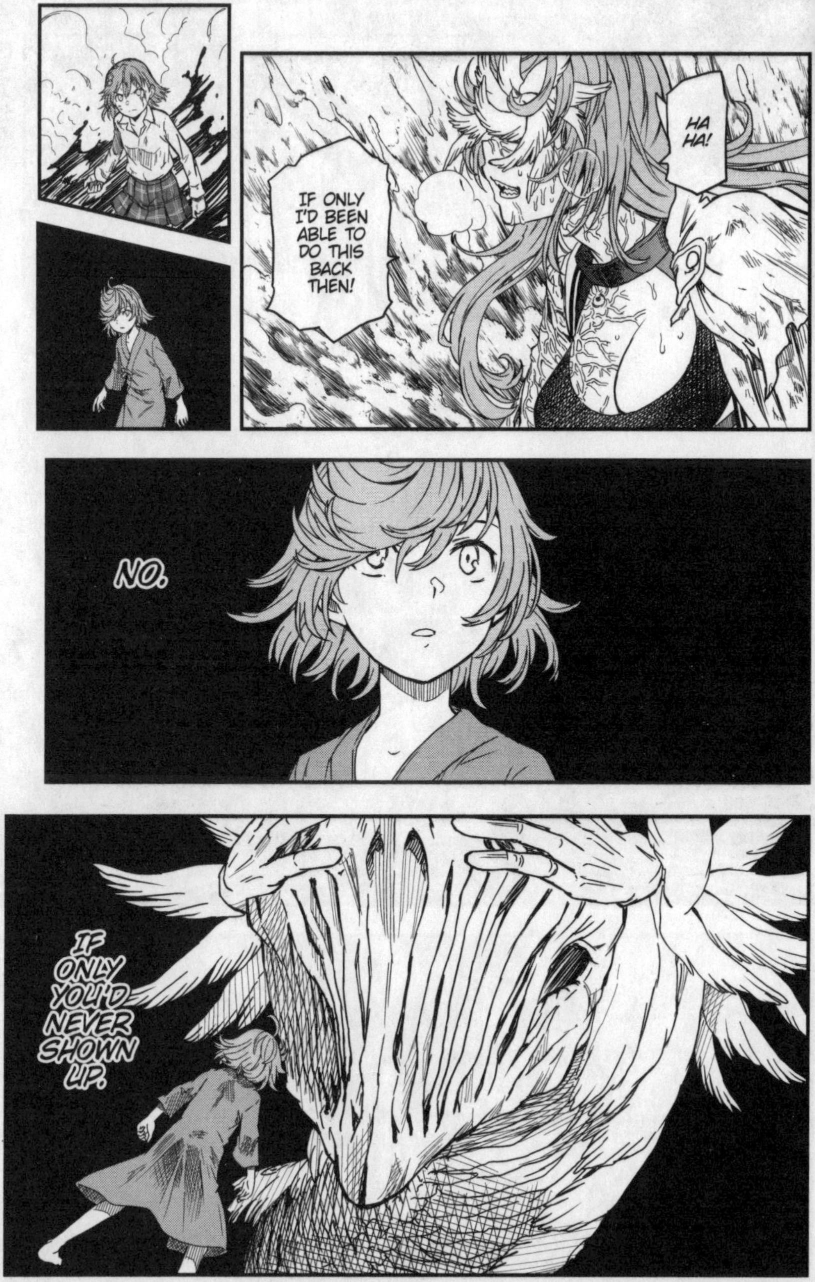
HA HA!
IF ONLY I'D BEEN ABLE TO DO THIS BACK THEN!
NO.
IF ONLY YOU'D NEVER SHOWN UP.

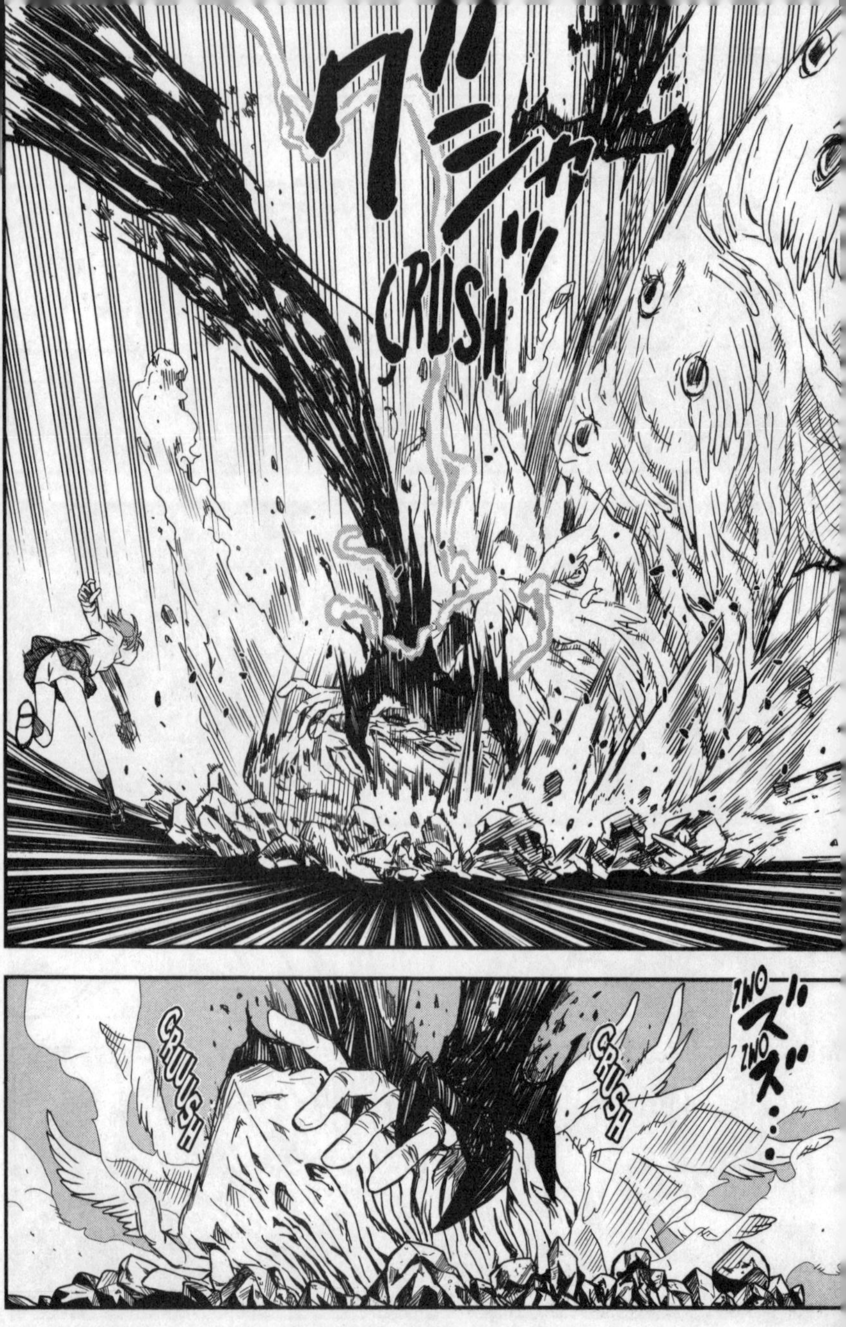
グシャッ
CRUSH
ZWO
ZWO
CRUSH
CRUUSH

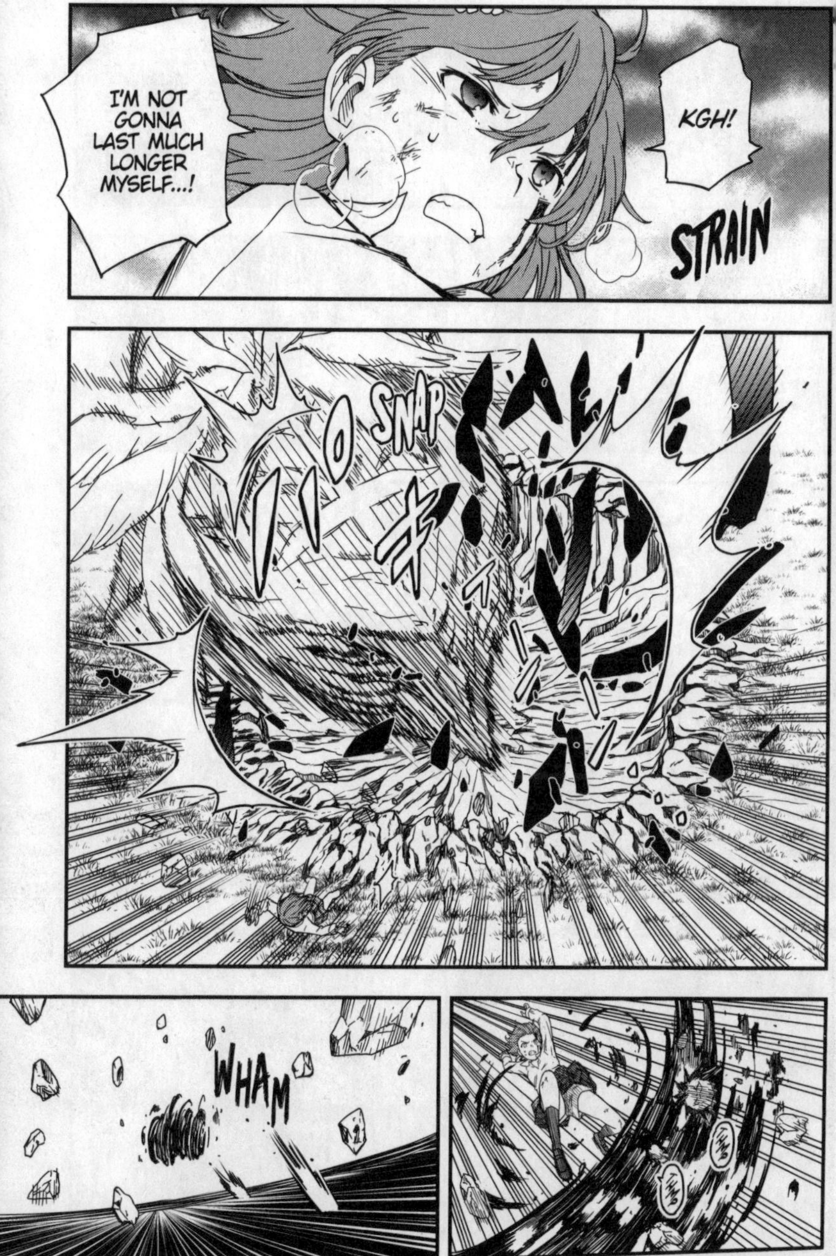
KGH!
I'M NOT GONNA LAST MUCH LONGER MYSELF...!
STRAIN
SNAP
WHAM

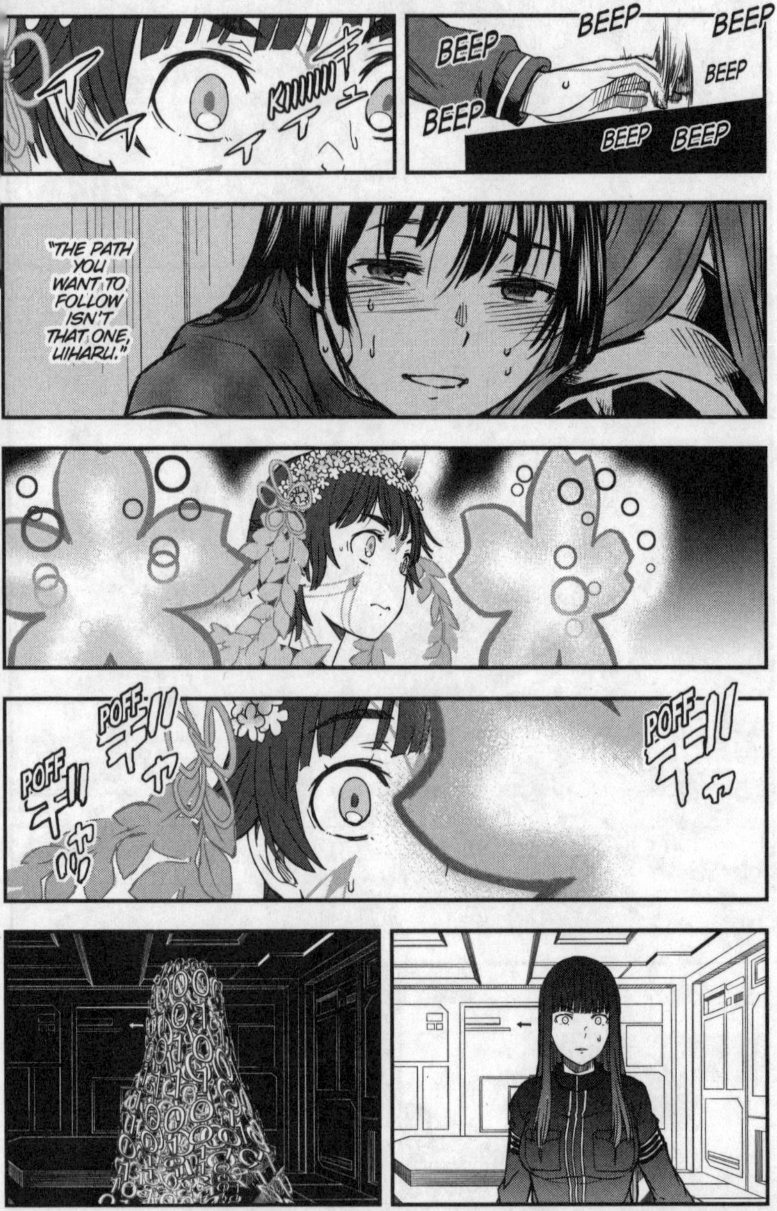
BEEP BEEP BEEP BEEP BEEP BEEP BEEP
KIIIIIII
"THE PATH YOU WANT TO FOLLOW ISN'T THAT ONE, UIHARU."
POFF
POFF
POFF

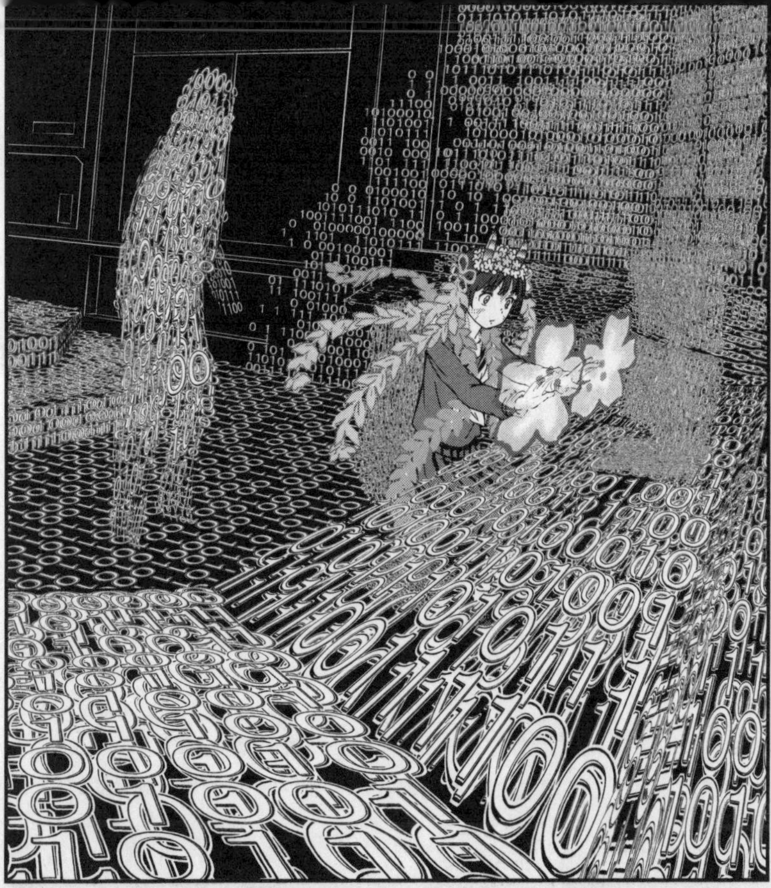

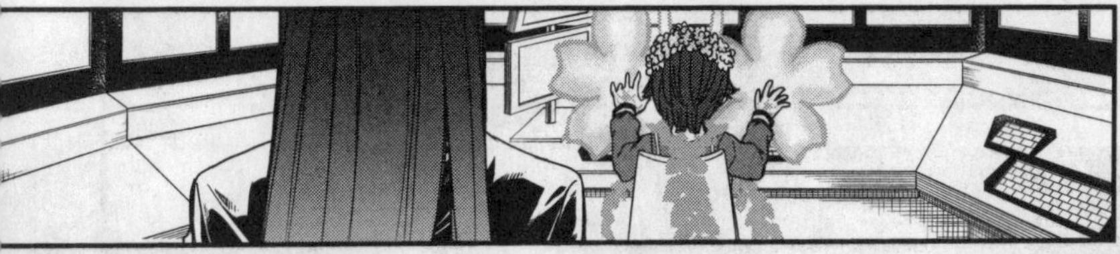

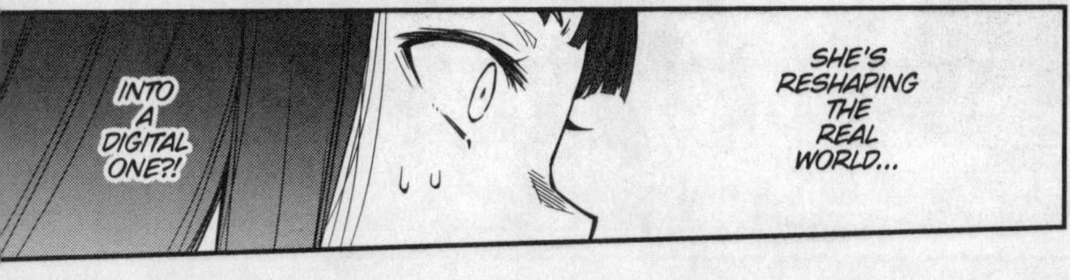
SHE'S RESHAPING THE REAL WORLD...
INTO A DIGITAL ONE?!

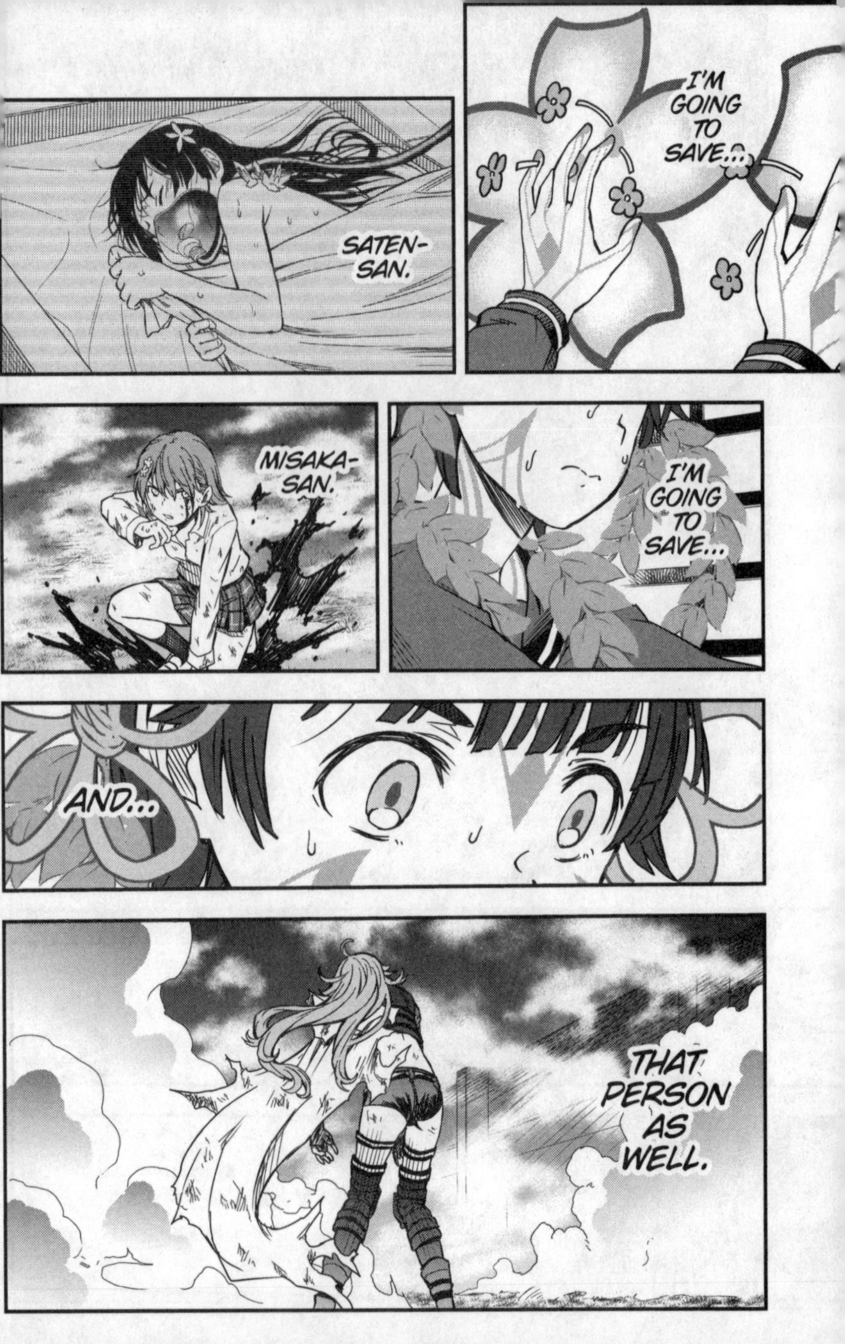
I'M GOING TO SAVE...
SATEN-SAN.
I'M GOING TO SAVE...
MISAKA-SAN.
AND...
THAT PERSON AS WELL.

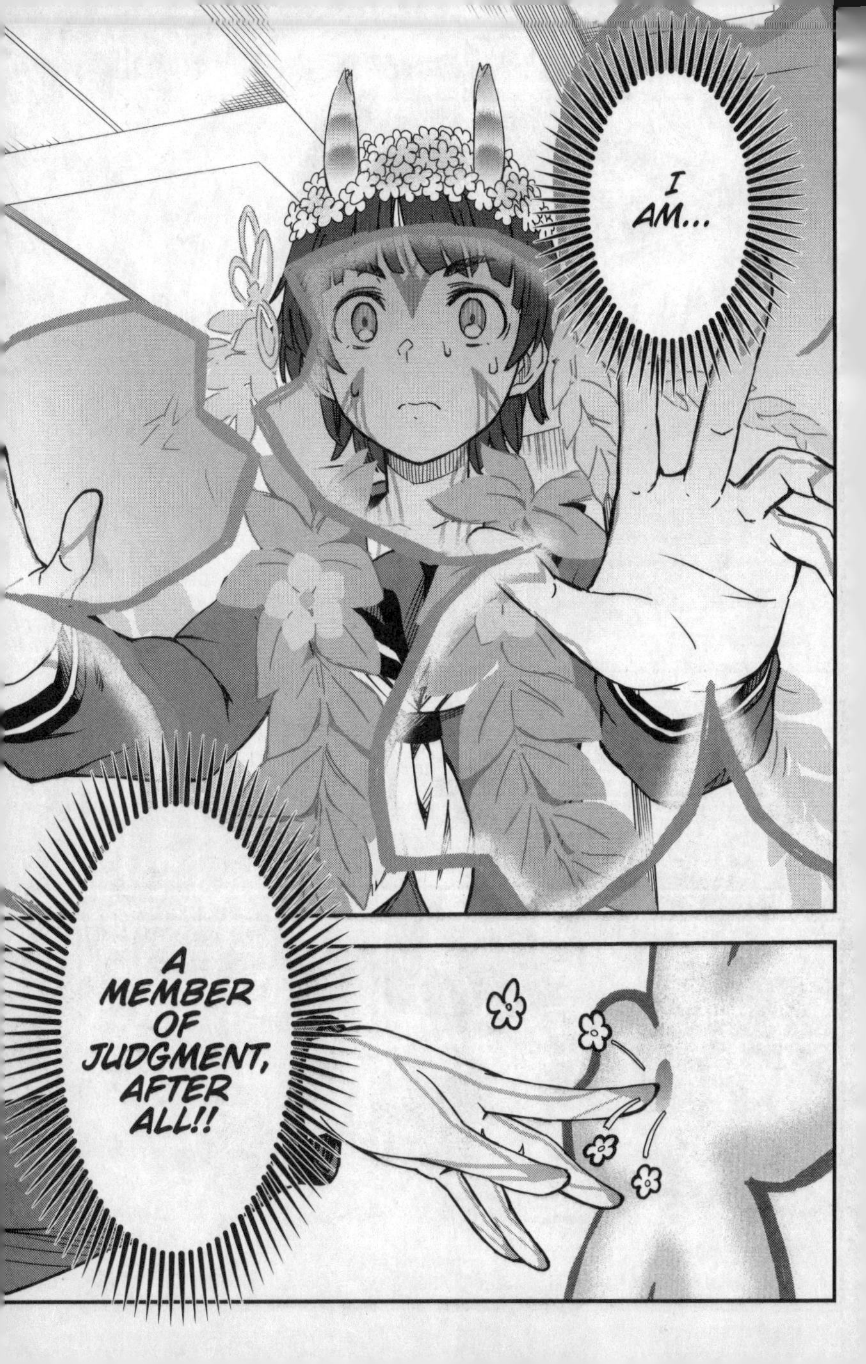
I AM...
A MEMBER OF JUDGMENT, AFTER ALL!!

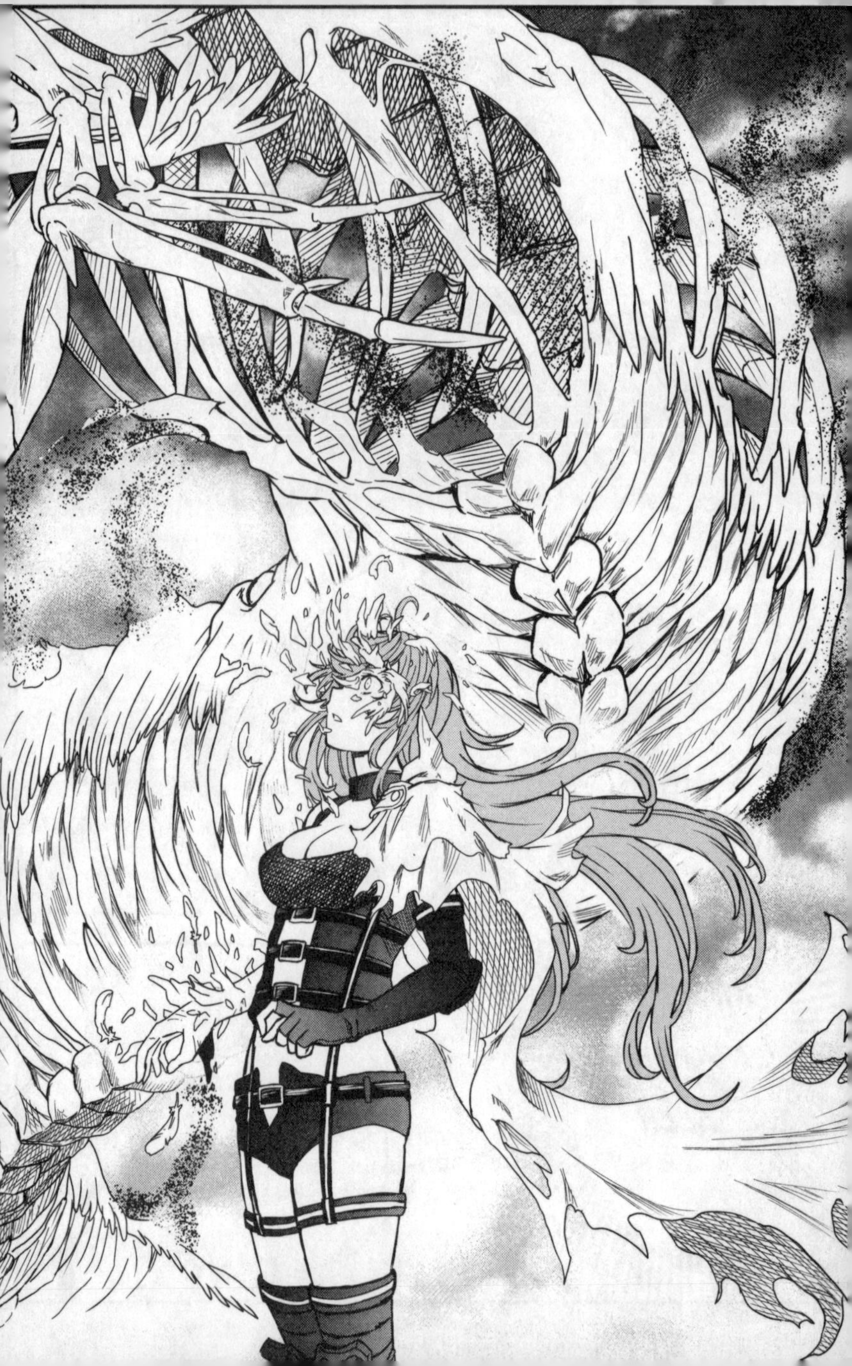

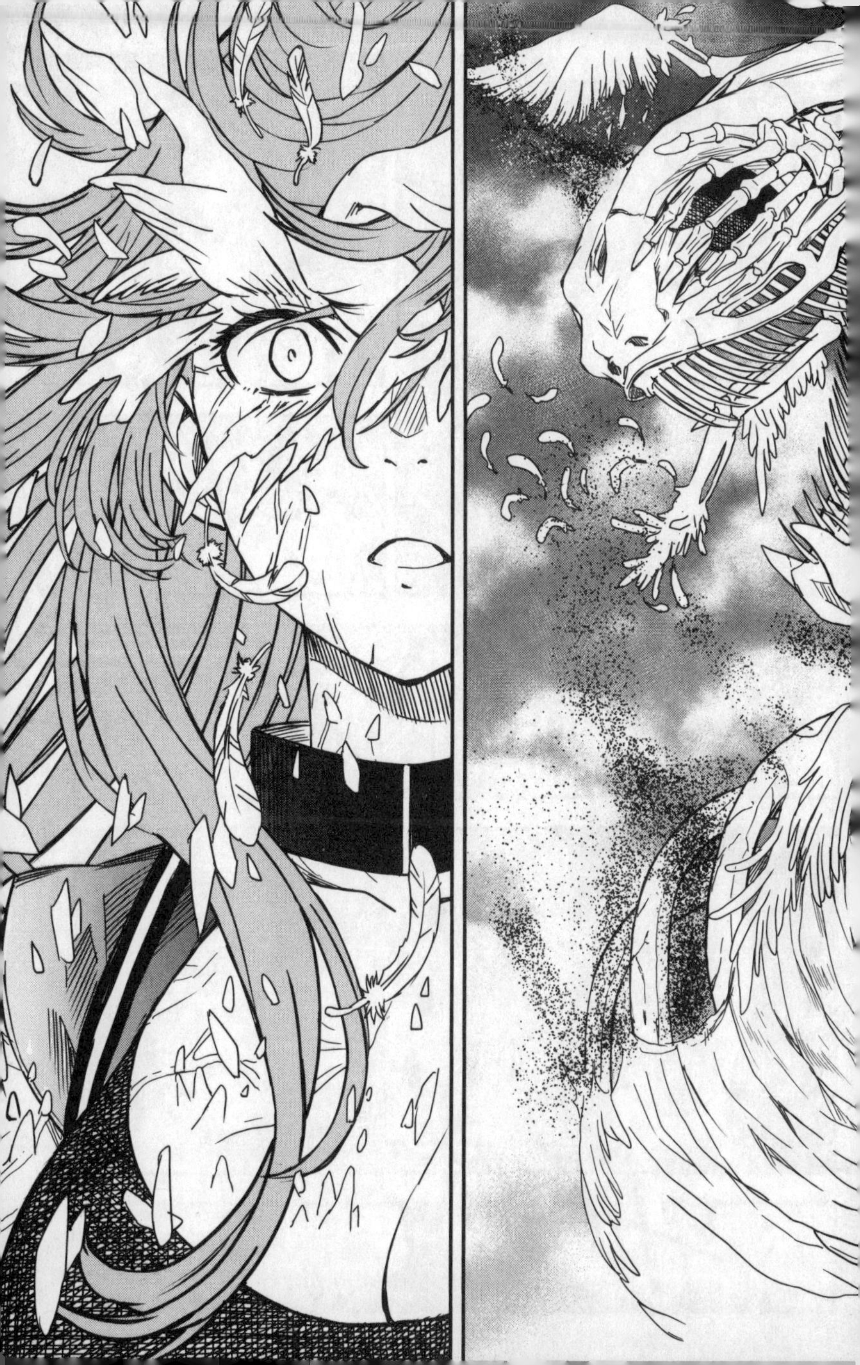

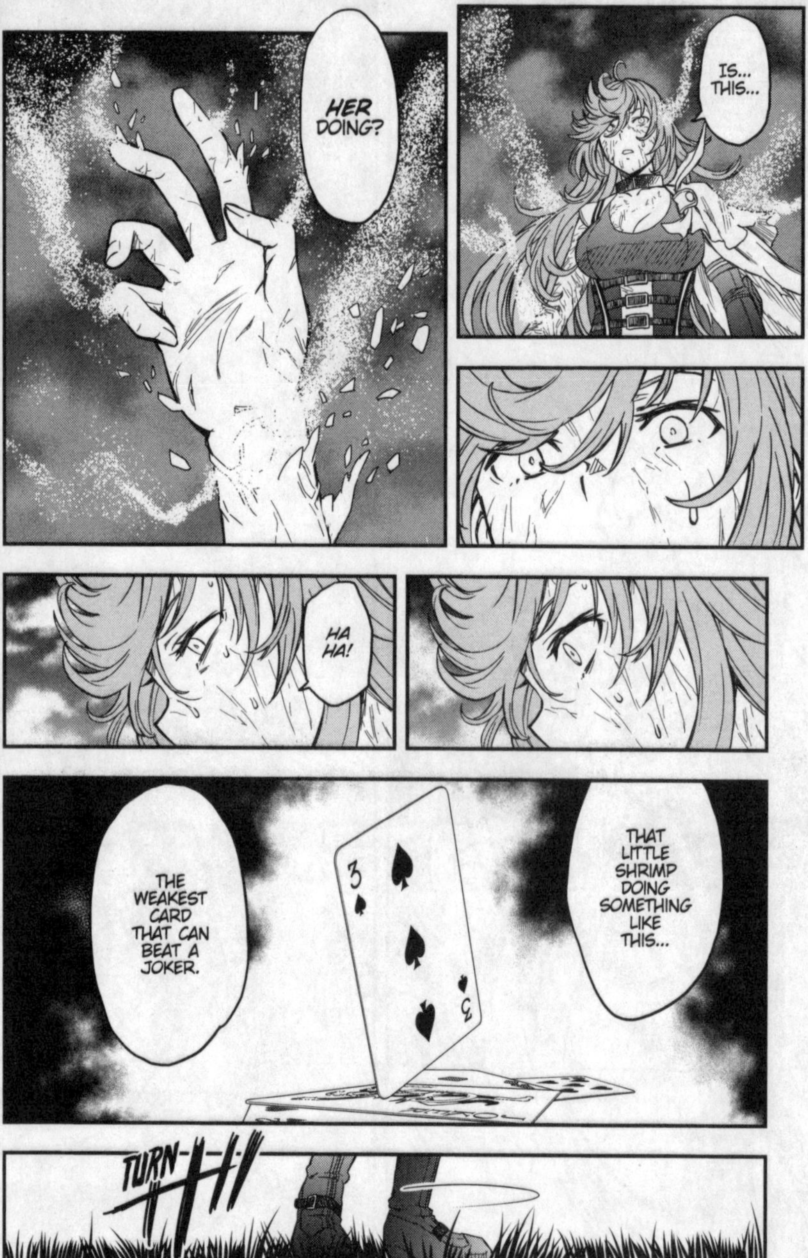
IS... THIS...
HER DOING?
HA HA!
THAT LITTLE SHRIMP DOING SOMETHING LIKE THIS...
THE WEAKEST CARD THAT CAN BEAT A JOKER.
TURN-

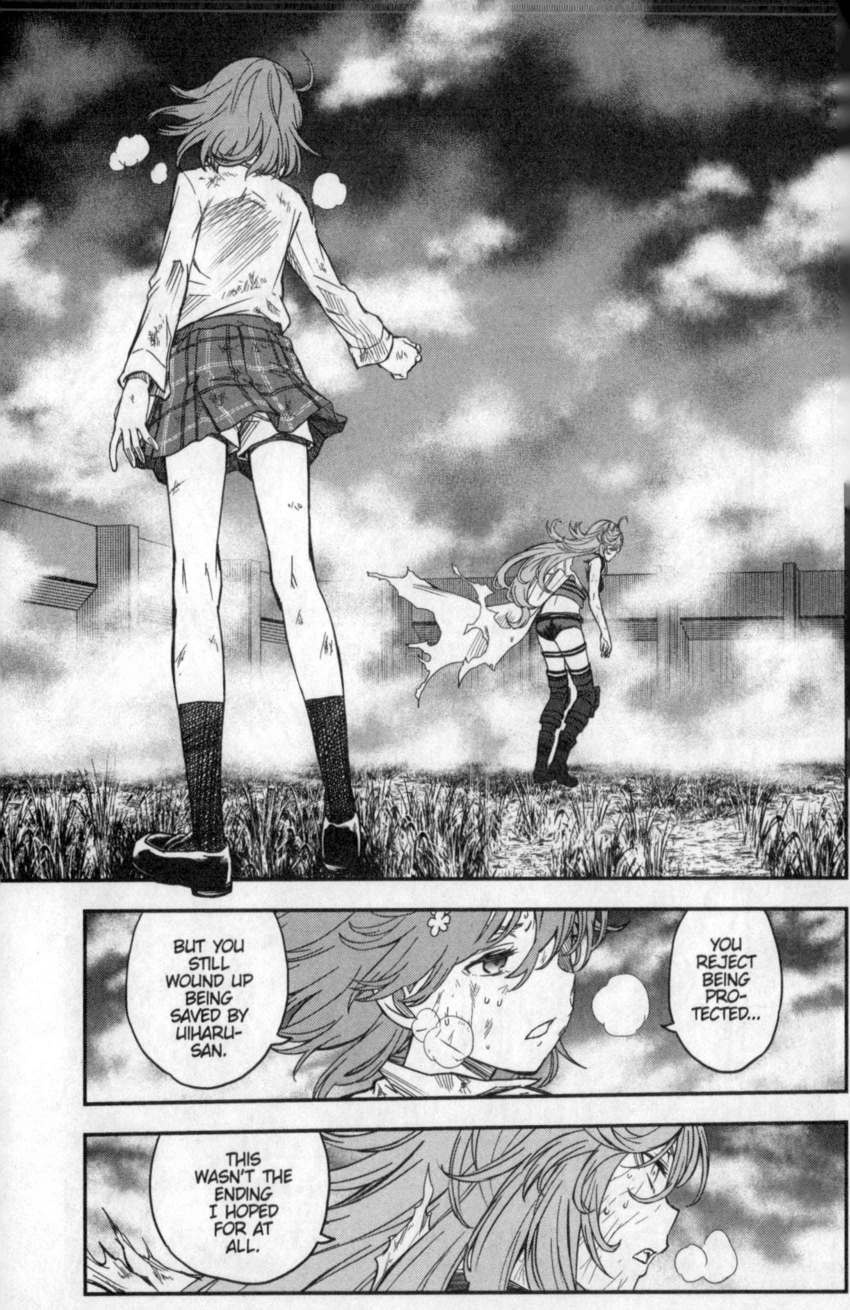
YOU REJECT BEING PRO-TECTED...
BUT YOU STILL WOUND UP BEING SAVED BY UIHARU-SAN.
THIS WASN'T THE ENDING I HOPED FOR AT ALL.

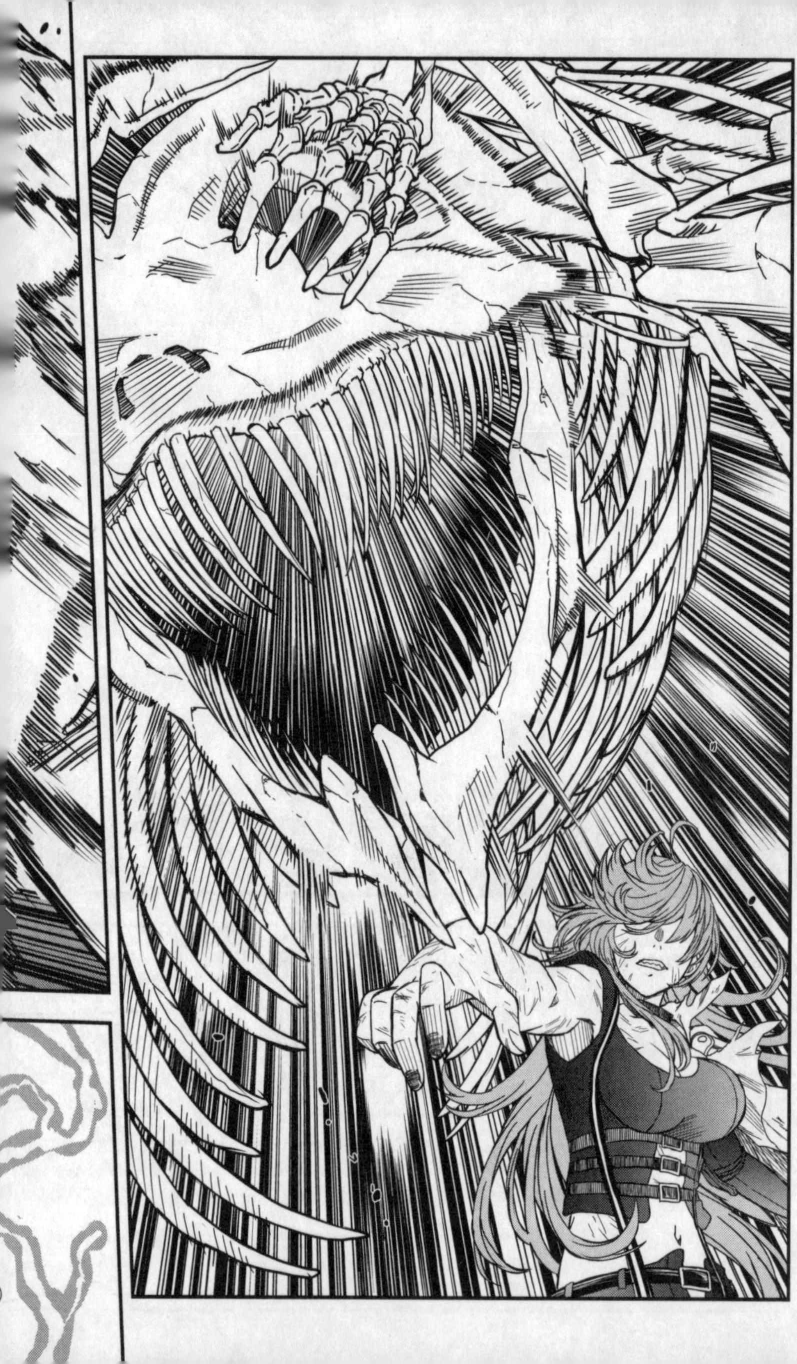

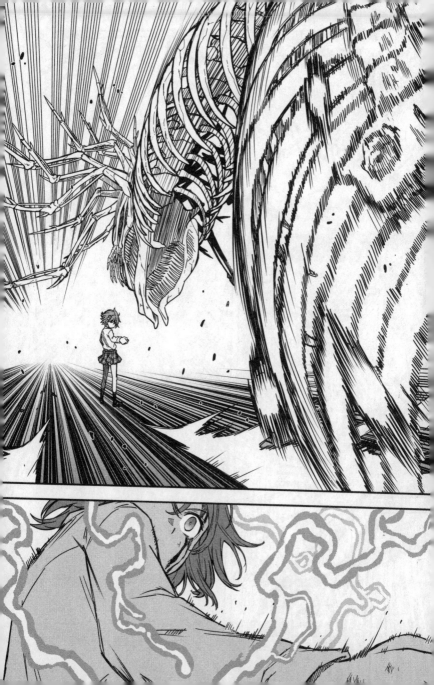

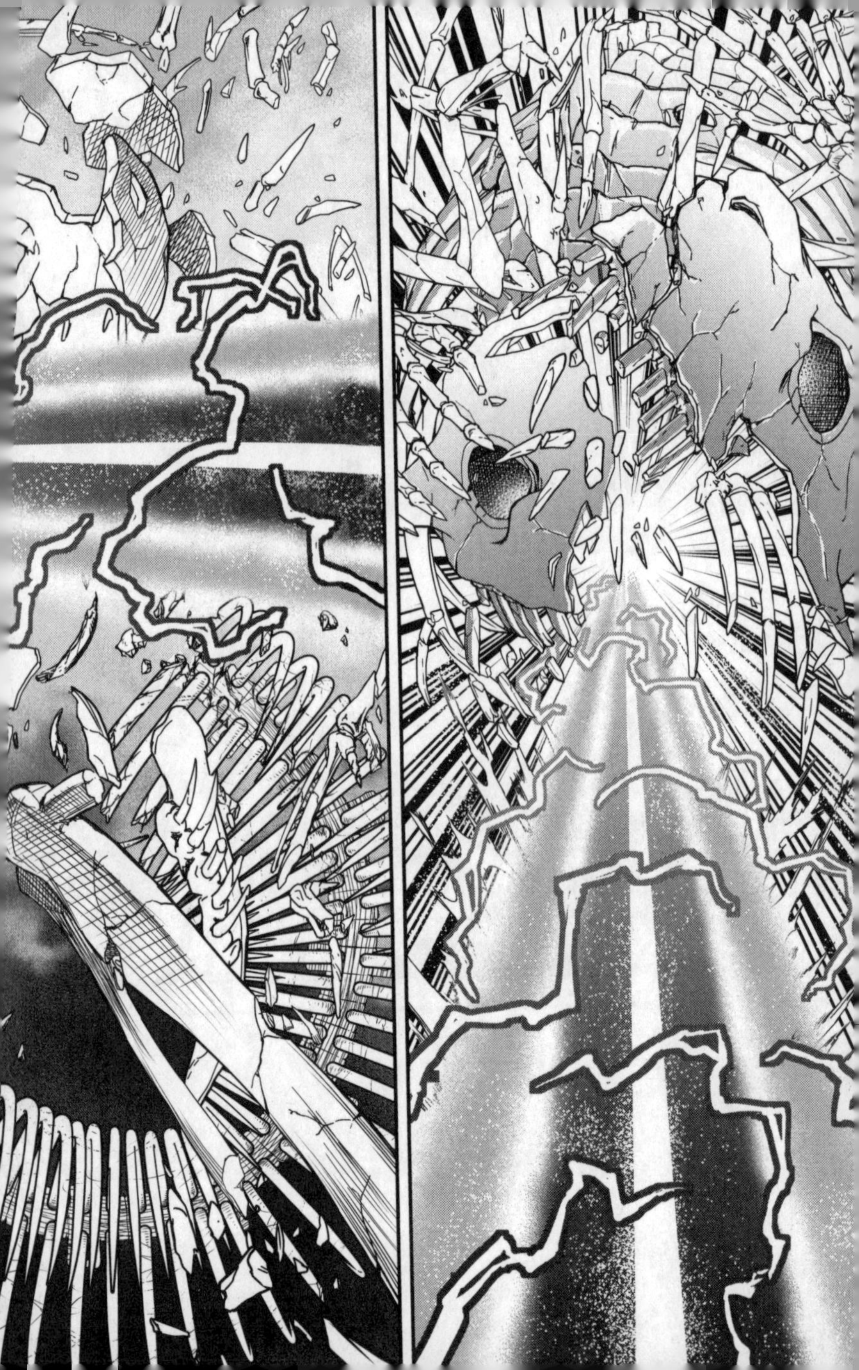

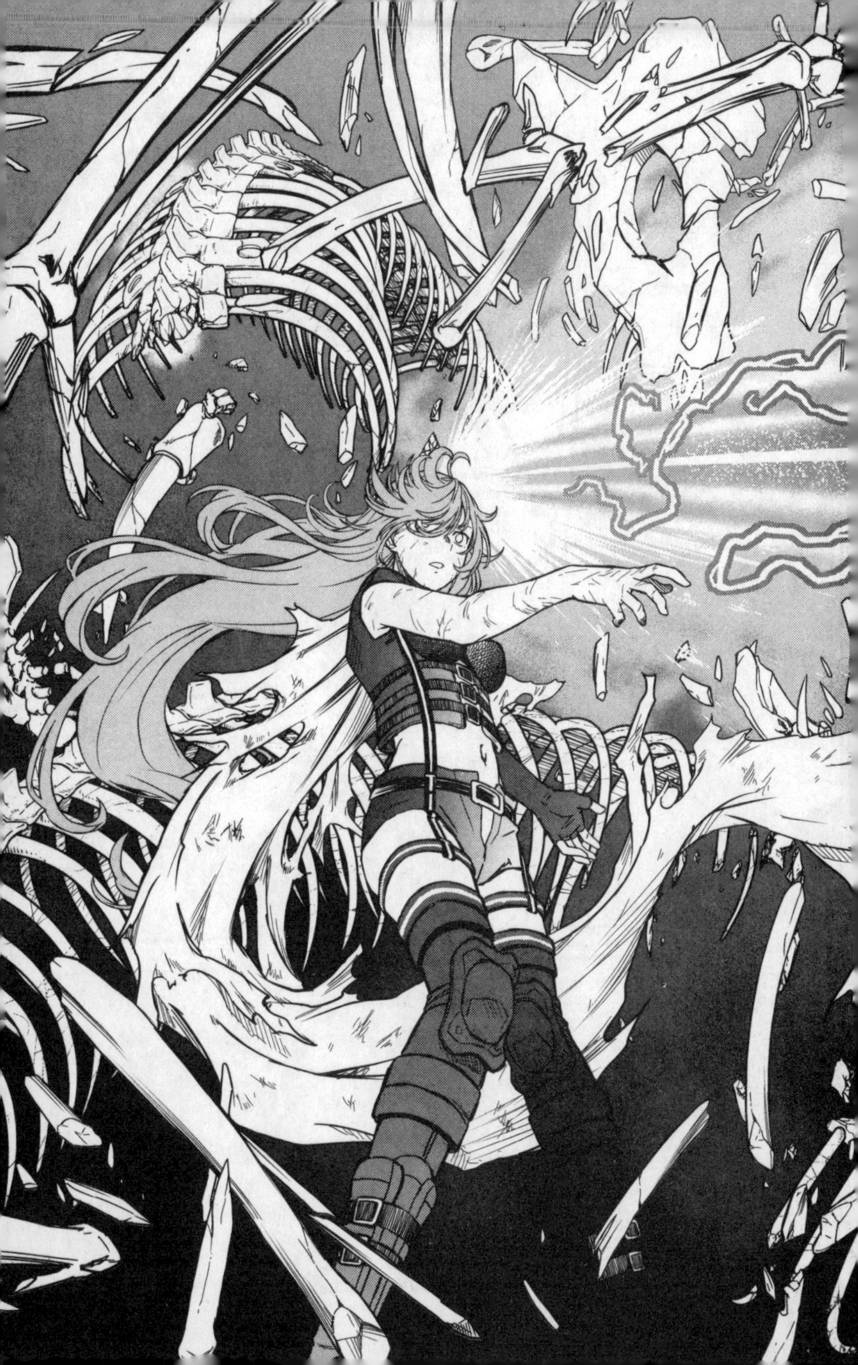

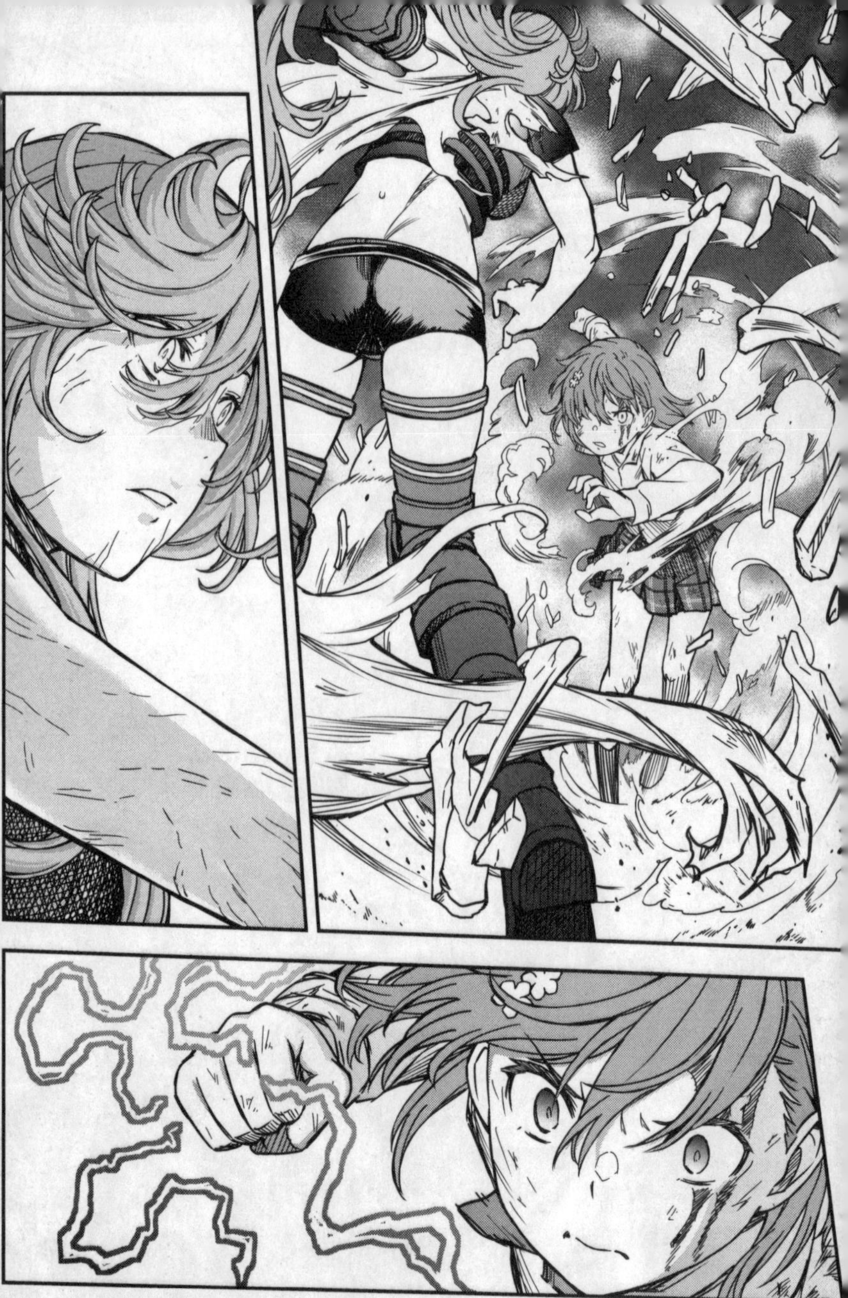

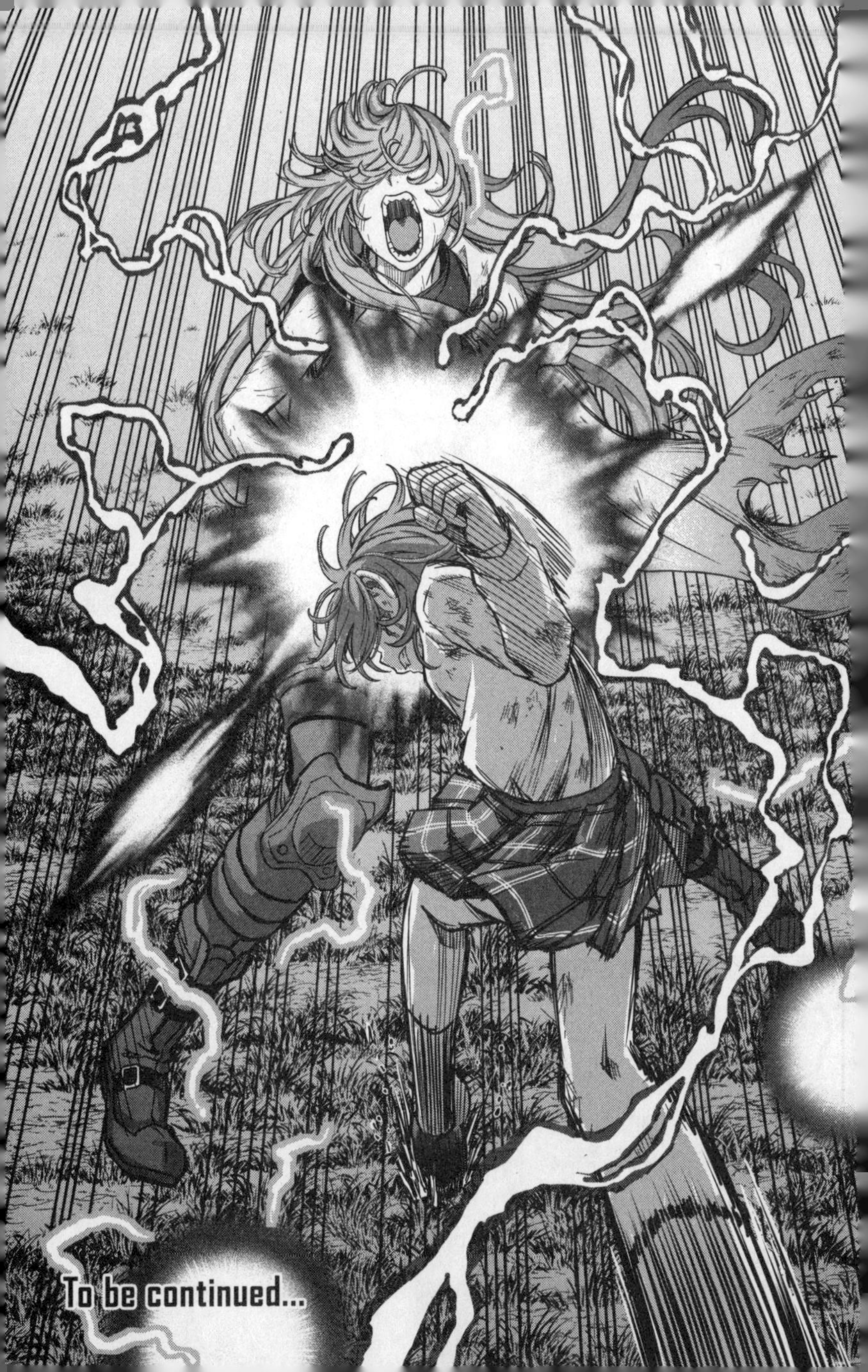
To be continued...

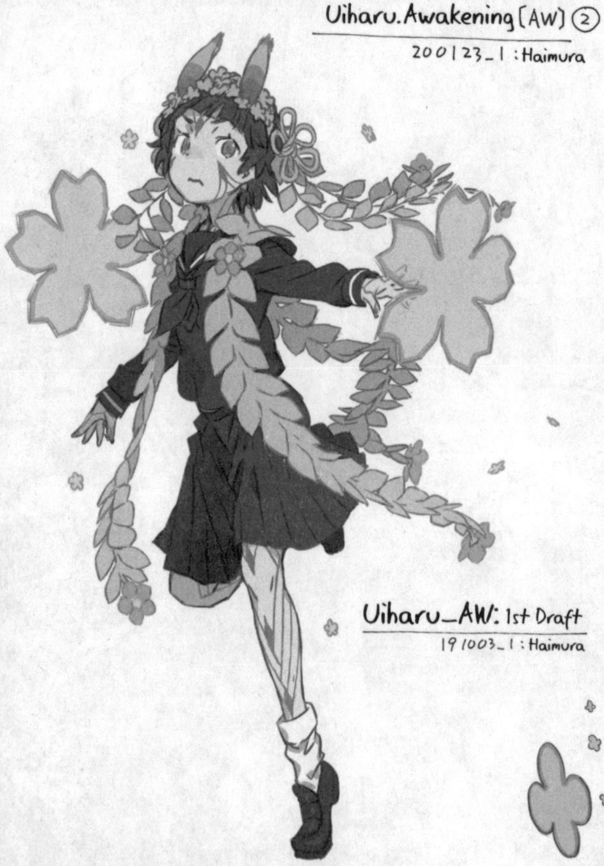
Uiharu.Awakening [AW] ②
200123_1 : Haimura

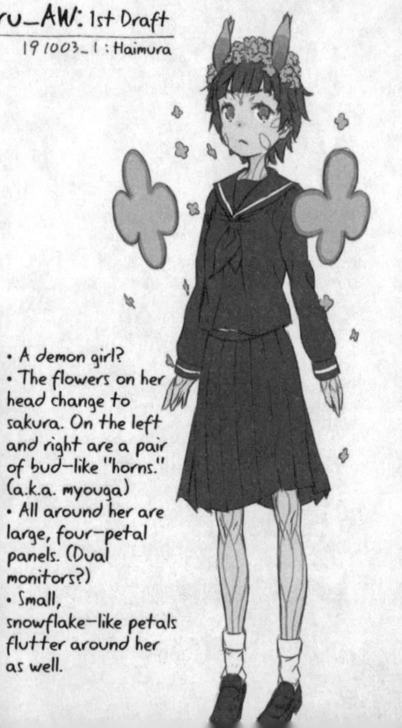
Uiharu_AW: 1st Draft
191003_1 : Haimura
• A demon girl?
• The flowers on her head change to sakura. On the left and right are a pair of bud-like "horns." (a.k.a. myouga)
• All around her are large, four-petal panels. (Dual monitors?)
• Small, snowflake-like petals flutter around her as well.

Awakened Uiharu
Design/Kiyotaka Haimura

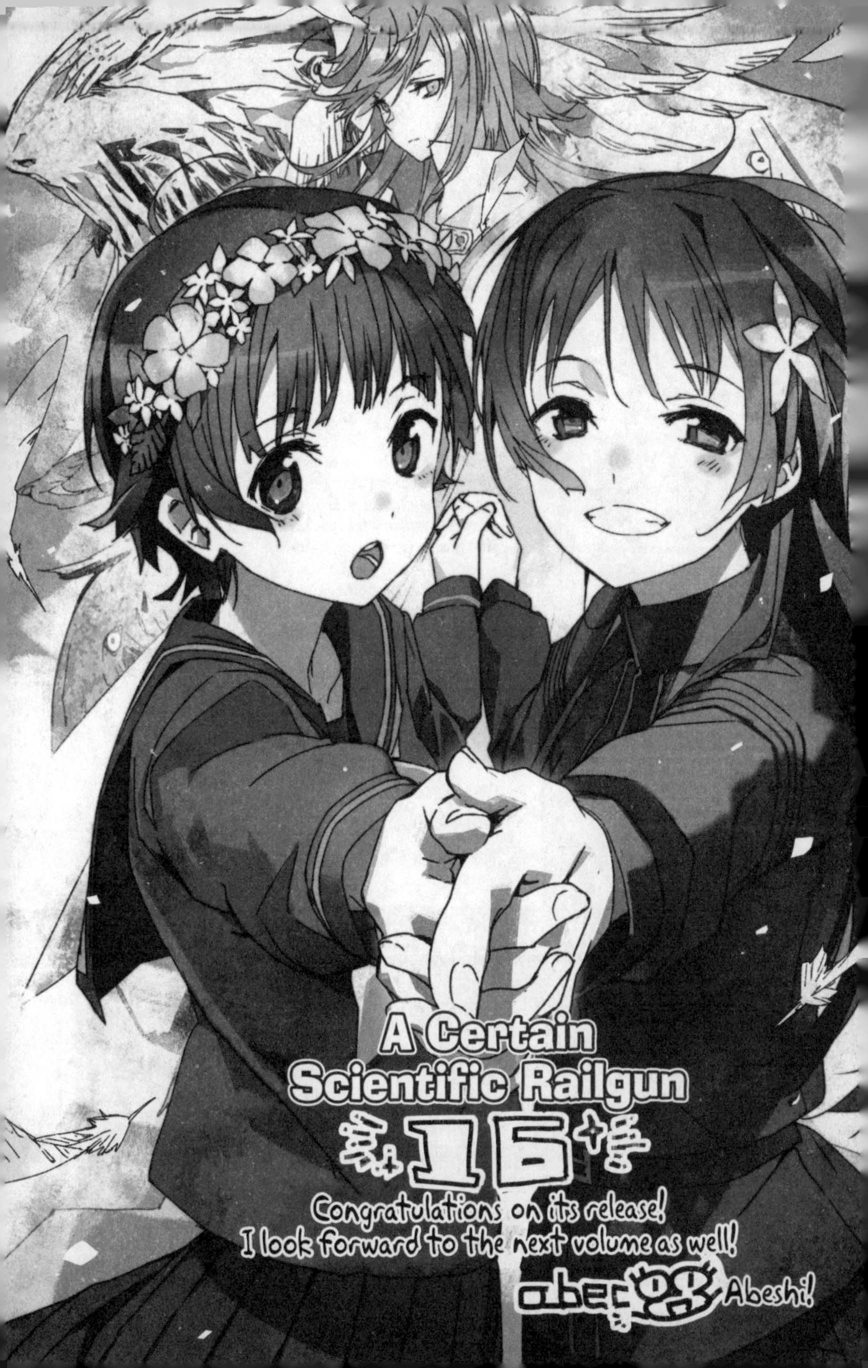
A Certain
Scientific Railgun
16
Congratulations on its release!
I look forward to the next volume as well!
Abeshi!

SEVEN SEAS ENTERTAINMENT PRESENTS

A Certain SCIENTIFIC Railgun

SEP 0 7 2021

story by **KAZUMA KAMACHI** / art by **MOTOI FUYUKAWA**   VOLUME **16**

TRANSLATION
Nan Rymer

LETTERING AND RETOUCH
Roland Amago
Bambi Eloriaga-Amago

COVER DESIGN
Nicky Lim

PROOFREADER
Janet Houck

EDITOR
Peter Adrian Behravesh

PREPRESS TECHNICIAN
Rhiannon Rasmussen-Silverstein

PRODUCTION MANAGER
Lissa Pattillo

MANAGING EDITOR
Julie Davis

ASSOCIATE PUBLISHER
Adam Arnold

PUBLISHER
Jason DeAngelis

A CERTAIN SCIENTIFIC RAILGUN Vol.16
TOARU MAJUTSU NO INDEX GAIDEN TOARU KAGAKU NO RAILGUN Vol.16
©Kazuma Kamachi / Motoi Fuyukawa 2020
First published in Japan in 2020 by KADOKAWA CORPORATION, Tokyo.
English translation rights arranged with KADOKAWA CORPORATION, Tokyo.

Seven Seas press and purchase enquiries can be sent to Marketing Manager Lianne Sentar at press@gomanga.com. Information regarding the distribution and purchase of digital editions is available from Digital Manager CK Russell at digital@gomanga.com.

Seven Seas and the Seven Seas logo are trademarks of Seven Seas Entertainment. All rights reserved.

ISBN: 978-1-64505-987-5

Printed in Canada

First Printing: June 2021

10 9 8 7 6 5 4 3 2 1

FOLLOW US ONLINE: *www.sevenseasentertainment.com*

READING DIRECTIONS

This book reads from *right to left*, Japanese style. If this is your first time reading manga, you start reading from the top right panel on each page and take it from there. If you get lost, just follow the numbered diagram here. It may seem backwards at first, but you'll get the hang of it! Have fun!!

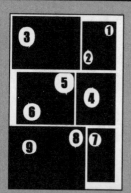